DOWN THE YEARS

DOWN THE YEARS

BY

THE RT. HON.
SIR AUSTEN CHAMBERLAIN
K.G., P.C., M.P.

CASSELL AND COMPANY LIMITED
LONDON, TORONTO, MELBOURNE
AND SYDNEY

First Edition . . . September 1935
Second Edition . . . . October 1935
Third Edition . . . . October 1935
Fourth Edition . . . . October 1935
Fifth Edition . . . . October 1935

PRINTED IN GREAT BRITAIN BY THE EDINBURGH PRESS, EDINBURGH AND LONDON
20.1035

PREFACE

As GOOD wine needs no bush, so a readable book should require no preface, but Publisher's law has decided otherwise and like a good citizen—may I say of the world of letters?—I obey the law.

If I had ever kept a diary, or if my memory were less faulty, I ought certainly to be able to write an interesting book of memoirs, for my life has been passed among interesting people, and I have assisted at great events. As it is, the pages which follow are no more than random recollections of men and events, among which I have moved, based upon an occasional memorandum made at the time, or on letters written to relations, and more especially to my father when he and I were separated. To these I have added slight sketches of some of the men with whom I have worked. If these pages have any merit, they owe it in the former case to the fact that they were written in the midst of, or immediately after the events chronicled and are uncoloured by subsequent results or later judgments and, in the latter case, to the fact that they are written with the sympathy and understanding which are bred of admiration for the man's qualities, and esteem for the man himself. They are not history, but perhaps I may claim that they are sidelights on history and, as such, may have some little permanent value as well as their immediate interest for those who knew the men or can recall the events.

Some of these have already appeared in the *Daily Telegraph* or *Sunday Times* in England, *The Figaro* and *Journal* in

France, *The Christian Science Monitor* in America, and *Co-operation Press-Service for International Understanding* on the Continent.

I have added two or three essays, written for my own amusement in "Idle Hours." The essay on "How great Speeches are prepared," appeared many years ago in the *Empire Review*, where my letters from Berlin also first saw the light, though without much of what is now included. "My Cottage Garden" was written for *The Countryman*. It is endeared to me not only by the memories it evokes, but by a singular act of kindness from a fellow-member of the House of Commons who rejects my politics but shares my love of flowers. On reading the article when it first appeared, he wrote that he could not bear to think of me without a garden and should send me flowers from time to time on condition only that I did not write to thank him. Nearly every week during each succeeding Session these gifts have been renewed. Truly the House of Commons is a place of much kindness.

To the Editors of these Papers and Reviews my thanks are due for the permission to re-publish the articles.

CONTENTS

PART I

MEN AND MEMORIES

7

CONTENTS

PART II

IDLE HOURS

LIST OF ILLUSTRATIONS

PART I
MEN AND MEMORIES

I

A STUDENT IN PARIS

I took my degree at Cambridge in the summer of 1885 and in the following September began a nine months' residence in France. The Aumaitre family with which I was to stay in Paris were at the moment taking their holiday at Dinard-St. Enogat, where I joined them in plain but comfortable lodgings over a baker's shop at the farthest end of what was then scarcely more than the village of St. Enogat. My room looked straight on to the open country and just below us lay the little bay of St. Enogat, from which we could look across the larger bay of Dinard to St. Malo and a semi-circle of rocky islets. I was at once enchanted by the place and thought I had never seen anything more lovely than the red rocks, golden sands and vivid blues and greens of the sea. The family consisted of Monsieur Aumaitre, a Répétiteur-en-Droit who coached pupils for the law examinations, his wife and three children, two boys and a girl whose ages ranged from fourteen to eleven, and Madame Aumaitre's widowed mother, as is so often the case in French households. They were a delightful family, and the children's constant chatter was a great aid to me in my first efforts to speak the French language. With them or other members of the family, I bathed, roamed the countryside and made excursions to places of interest in the neighbourhood, such as the Mont St. Michel and the charming and then unspoiled old town of Dinan. Many of the houses dated from the sixteenth century or earlier and the occupations of their inhabitants seemed as ancient. There were old crones at their spinning-wheels, an old man working at a hand-loom and a group of men at a forge with a dog to work the bellows—like a prisoner on the treadmill, always climbing and never advancing. It was all very new and fascinating to me and, to add to my delight, when we moved to Paris at the end of the month, the elder boy and I broke the journey at Chartres, where I saw for the first time the grandest of all the French cathedrals and the splendour of its marvellous stained glass.

Hardly any of the people to whom I had letters of introduction had yet returned to Paris, nor had the École Libre des Sciences Politiques opened its winter session; so I spent my days walking the streets and visiting the museums and many of my evenings at the theatre. There is no better school in which to learn a spoken language, and no more delightful method. And what incomparable actors they were. Sarah Bernhardt had already left the Théâtre Français and was playing at the Porte St. Martin— not, it was thought, without some loss to her art, but Coquelin was still faithful to the House of Molière. I think he was at his best in *Tartuffe* and *Les Précieuses Ridicules*; but whatever he did, his acting was perfect and Coquelin cadet was only second to himself in these or similar rôles. Coquelin's son had not then begun to act, but though Coquelin declared in later years that his son was a greater actor than himself, this appreciation was inspired by his paternal pride rather than his critical faculty.

Then there was Mounet-Sully in classical tragedy, and for comedy Got, who played magnificently the parts of old men, Delaunay who must, I think, have been already well past the age of fifty but still played the *jeune premier* with incomparable grace and vivacity to the *ingénue* of

Mademoiselle Reichemberg, at whose age at the time it would have been an impertinence to guess, but behind the footlights she was still the perfect representative of the parts which she had taken for so long. I can still see them as I saw them then, playing together in Alfred de Musset's *Proverbes*—"*On ne badine pas avec l'amour*" and "*Il faut qu'une porte soit ouverte ou fermée.*" Nor can I forget the charm and perfect acting of Marie Brohan, who now took such rôles as that of the Duchess in "*Le monde où l'on s'ennuie*" and was the perfect great lady, or Jeanne Samary who played the soubrettes—her lovely rippling laughter was itself sufficient for an evening's entertainment—and Madame Bartet, whom I met again long years afterwards in London. All these one might see at the Français. There were others like Jeanne Grannier and Rèjane not unworthy to rank with them at less historic houses, and Madame Sorel, unless my memory is at fault, was winning her first success at a theatre on the Boulevards.

Meanwhile I was taking a daily lesson from M. Aumaitre in French law and administration and presently, when the École des Sciences Politiques reopened its doors, my mornings and some part of my afternoons were spent there. The School had been founded some ten years earlier by Émile Boutmy, who was still its Director. He and those associated with him attributed a part of France's misfortunes in 1871 to the rigid control exercised over education by the governments of the Second Empire, and they resolved to create a school for the study of history, politics, law and administration where the truth could be told fearlessly, uncontrolled by the wishes or necessities of the Government of the day. It was therefore a private venture; it accepted no subsidy and admitted no interference from the State. It was in this sense that it was The Free

School and not as we speak of Free Education in England. So successful had it been that its diploma was already recognized by the State and most aspirants to a diplomatic career, as well as many others, pursued their studies there. I was the only Englishman among its pupils at the time, but the School already had a European reputation and apart from the French friends whom I made, I got to know a certain number of foreigners, especially from the Balkan States.

As my stay in Paris was limited, I could not take the full course, but, on the advice of M. Boutmy who, though no great lover of the English, received and treated me with great kindness, I attended lectures by some of the most distinguished teachers of the day. Albert Sorel, author of *L'Europe et la Révolution Française*, delivered a course of lectures on the Diplomatic History of Europe from 1832. In the History Tripos at Cambridge my studies had ended with the Peace of Amiens, so this was new ground for me. The wide sweep of his survey, the clarity of his style, the vigour and conviction of his delivery enchanted me, and then, as when I had listened to Sir John Seely on "The Expansion of England," I found history rescued from the Dry-as-Dusts and related to the living problems of to-day. What, for example, could be more penetrating and suggestive than such a phrase as this : " On the day when the Turkish question is settled, Europe will be confronted with a new problem—that of the future of the Austro-Hungarian Empire."

Next came Anatole Leroy-Beaulieu, himself a distinguished publicist, and brother of Paul Beaulieu, the well-known economist. He lectured brilliantly on the political history of Europe from 1870, simplifying it perhaps a little too much in his desire to present it as a coherent

whole, but never allowing the trees to obscure the wood.
I still recall my discomfiture when I was presented to him
by our hostess at an evening party. I bowed ceremoniously;
he bowed still lower but said nothing. I waited anxiously
but still he said nothing; then overcome by confusion and
unable to bear the silence, I took my courage in both hands
and plunged. "Monsieur," I said, "it is a very great
pleasure as well as a privilege for me to be presented to
you, for I have the honour to follow your course of lectures
at the École des Sciences Politiques." I confess I thought
I had acquitted myself creditably for a shy Englishman,
struggling with the difficulties of a language which I had
as yet very imperfectly mastered. What then was my
consternation when Leroy-Beaulieu, sweeping a magnificent
gesture with his crush-hat and bowing this time from the
hips, replied, "Then, Monsieur, I have need of all your
indulgence!" It was useless to attempt to vie with French
politeness; I retired abashed.

Léon Say, Senator and ex-Minister of Finance, was
equally polite, though more restrained. He lectured on
"Democracy and Finance" and one lecture was devoted
to my father's Unauthorized Programme, of which he
was a severe critic. After the lecture he called me up,
expressed his hope that what he had felt bound to say had
not given offence to me and excused himself by a graceful
tribute to the outstanding importance of my father's ideas,
which it was impossible to ignore in any survey such as
he had undertaken.

There was another course on the principal types of
constitution, mainly conducted by Jules Dietz, who was
afterwards for so many years editor of the Débats, but to
which Boutmy and Ribot contributed. "Do you know
Monsieur Clemenceau?" I was asked by my hostess,

Madame Clémentel, one evening during the peace negotiations in 1919. " Oh, yes," I replied, " I have known him and Monsieur Ribot for thirty-five years." " It is not possible," she exclaimed. " You must have been a child at that time." " Nay, Madame, to prove it, I will tell you what each of them did for me; Monsieur Ribot lectured me on the French Constitution and Monsieur Clemenceau introduced me to the *première danseuse* of the Opera ! "

I had in fact been first introduced to Clemenceau, whilst still at Cambridge, by Admiral Maxse, and for greater security carried with me a letter of introduction from my father, who, in his Radical days, found a natural affinity between himself and the French Radical, and dreamed, as Morley has recorded, of a practical co-operation between them in the service of European democracy. I visited Clemenceau at the office of *La Justice*, which was then his organ, dined with him both at his apartment and in restaurants, met many of his political friends of the moment and heard much political talk. I noted in my letters home that he, too, was advocating a graduated income-tax and succession tax, state insurance against inability to work or illness and free education. My sympathies were drawn to him by his congenial view of English Radicalism and his desire for a good understanding with England, but nearly all my other French friends looked upon him with undisguised horror, and warned me against the dangers of his political company.

He had at that time just helped to overthrow the government of Jules Ferry, who was beginning in Tonkin the new French colonial empire of Indo-China. Clemenceau, the Republican of 1870, grudged the diversion of any atom of France's strength to distant spheres whilst Alsace-Lorraine lay unredeemed. I can still picture the scene in the Chamber when, stung to interruption by Clemenceau's fierce invective, Ferry interrupted him :

" And the honour of France, Monsieur ? "

" The honour of France! I will show you how you have smirched it," retorted Clemenceau, and the invective continued more fiercely than ever till, roused to fury, the whole Left of the Chamber sprung to their feet, shook their fists at Ferry and shouted to him, " Down on your knees, traitor! Down on your knees! "

Clemenceau, indeed, at that time was the *enfant terrible* of French politics, the destroyer of Ministries. No one then dreamed that he would live to be unanimously acclaimed as having " *bien merité de la Patrie.*"

It was by Clemenceau and in the lobbies of the Chamber that I was introduced to Blowitz, the Paris correspondent of *The Times.* " Monsieur de Blowitz," said Gambetta, " has all the vices. He is Slav, Jew, Baron and decorated " ; but he was a power in his time, courted by governments and Ministers from Bismarck downwards, and he remains legendary to this day. He, in turn, introduced me to Jules Ferry, but of my interview with him I have to confess that I remember nothing but my amazement at his long Dundreary whiskers.

Ribot and his wife, an American lady, were among the earliest and kindest of my Paris friends. He was in every way a perfect contrast to Clemenceau. If Clemenceau resembled an English Radical, Ribot was the Goschen of French politics, a moderate, like him, with a mind more critical than constructive and a tendency to rest content when he had made a great speech, as if he had already accomplished a great act. In face and figure they were equally contrasted. Clemenceau, when I first knew him, was not unlike in appearance to the Clemenceau whose portrait became familiar to everyone during the war, but he was slight, wiry, talkative and as lively as quicksilver. Ribot was tall, reserved in manner, gentle of speech and moderate in the expression of his views, with a fine head that recalled a portrait of a nobleman by Van Dyck or Rubens. The walls of the Minister's Cabinet at the Quai d'Orsay are decorated with Gobelin tapestries reproducing scenes from the great series of pictures painted by Rubens to celebrate the marriage of Henri IV and Marie de Medici. One of them represents Jupiter carrying Marie to the arms of Henri. Briand, between whom and Ribot not much sympathy existed, told me in later days how on the fall of some government in which he had held the portfolio of Foreign Affairs, he was succeeded by Ribot. The outgoing Minister, as is customary, introduced his successor to the principal officers of the Department and then prepared to take his leave. With his hand already on the door, Briand turned back : " Just a word of advice, my friend, if you permit it. Get rid of that tapestry ! "

" What ! Remove that tapestry ? But it is magnificent."

" Yes, but you know what they call it in the Bureaux ? No ? Ribot carrying off a naked woman." And with that Briand closed the door behind him. " But I didn't have the last word," he added in relating the tale. " Before I could cross the antechamber, the door opened again and Ribot put his head out. " My dear friend, a thought has just occurred to me which may have some interest for you. It has just struck me that it is ten years since I was last Minister of Foreign Affairs. It has taken me all that time to get back."

At the Ribots, I met mainly moderate Republicans,

members of the Academy and men of letters. At another house—-that of M. Rothan, a diplomat of distinction who had been French Minister at Frankfort under the Second Empire, I met at dinner or at evening parties in his fine picture gallery most of those who then wrote for the *Revue des Deux Mondes*, to which he himself contributed reminiscences of his diplomatic career. The modest house of the Darmsteters, Arsène and James, themselves wells of learning, in the Place de Vaugirard, was the meeting place of men of letters and of professors from the Sorbonne. Here I met Renan. Madame Gaston-Paris opened to me her famous salon in the rue du Bac, where on Sunday afternoons I met a host of literary celebrities, amongst others Taine, whom I described as a little, rather dry-looking man who brightened up wonderfully as he talked. The talk was mostly of literary subjects. My letters record an afternoon when the conversation turned first on George Sand and her quarrel with Alfred de Musset and, later, on Victor Hugo. Taine defended George Sand against all attacks, spoke of her wonderful generosity and kindness and said that she was the only communist he had ever known who lived up to her principle that the people had as much right to what she earned as she had herself. Then the talk passed to the Romantic School and the forthcoming publication of the first posthumous volume of the works of Victor Hugo, who had died a few months earlier. " They must make haste," said Taine, " or they will find no readers. The men of thirty don't read him now." He singled out *Les Châtiments* as of all Hugo's work the most likely to endure. The letter concludes with the wish that I could get hold of a copy of Sorel's parodies of his poems—" so full of wit and such fine verse at the same time." I wonder whether they have ever been published. I certainly have never met with them and suppose I must have heard some of them recited in Madame Gaston-Paris' salon.

Another early friend was Cherbuliez, a publicist of distinction, a frequent contributor to the *Revue des Deux Mondes* and the author of several very readable novels, of which the most striking was, I think, *Ladislas Bolski*, a study of a Polish conspirator who betrayed his companions. Cherbuliez was by birth a Genevese who lived and wrote in Paris and, as Henry James did in England during the Great War, naturalized himself in his adopted country as a mark of sympathy with France during the war of 1870. He lived with his wife and daughter close to the Luxembourg. I wrote home in December:

"Last week I was as busy as ever amusing myself. In particular I dined with Monsieur Cherbuliez who sent messages to Father. The party comprised amongst others Jules Simon, and a lady whose name I cannot remember, but who has written *La Jeunesse de Mme. d'Épinay*.

"The conversation was not of a serious character, but these two were very amusing. Jules Simon occupied all dinner-time in telling anecdotes of Victor Cousin, not altogether to his credit. Everyone else listened deferentially and certainly the stories were well told. After dinner the nameless lady (she was in fact Mdlle. Herpin) had her turn and related a series of amusing mishaps which had occurred to her, especially an interview with a M. Scherer, the representative of an Insurance Office, who called on her just when she was expecting M. Edmond Scherer, the eminent critic and whom in her excitement she mistook for the latter. This story and another recounting her interview with 'an expert in disagreeable noises' who called upon her in connection with an action she was threatening against a neighbour were very wittily told and amused us much. We all agreed that they would make into splendid farces."

It is amusing to find recorded my first impression and impudent comment on another Frenchman, who was afterwards so well known and well liked among us and rendered such great service to this country as well as to his own. My letter continued:

"Monsieur Cambon, Governor-General of Tunis, with not much to say for himself, though got up with great care and very good to look at, and Monsieur Rothan were also there."

The Mdlle. Herpin here mentioned was a handsome white-haired lady of equal charm and wit, who, under the *nom de plume* of Lucien Perey, had just published *La Jeunesse de Mme. d'Épinay* in collaboration with her cousin Gaston Maugras. For a time they continued to work together, but later dissolved their partnership and continued their delightful series of eighteenth-century studies separately. She occupied a small but charming apartment in which she had made herself an eighteenth-century salon so that, as she said, she might be in a proper frame of mind for these studies, and here she gave delightful little dinner parties of six or eight people every Thursday and received a few friends afterwards. I was bidden to dine the following week, and afterwards invited to come on any Thursday evening after dinner. On this occasion the Rothans and Cherbuliez, Gaston Maugras and myself were the guests, and as we sat in the little salon after dinner the talk turned on Mme. d'Épinay and her circle. Mdlle. Herpin and Maugras were passionate partisans of that charming if not impeccable lady and sworn foes of all her enemies. On a little table in the centre of the room, among other bibelots, were minute busts of Voltaire and Rousseau, which Mdlle. Herpin had just acquired. While she was denouncing Rousseau's infamy, Maugras picked up his bust and prepared to hang the villain with a strand of wool drawn from the hostess's work-basket. At the critical moment the wool broke and I can still hear Maugras's cry of disappointment: "*Ah, le coquin! A-t-il de la chance?*" (What luck the beggar has!) I think it was Cherbuliez who took up Rousseau's defence, but I thought Maugras's answer conclusive: "No, if Rousseau were right, too many honest folk would be in the wrong."

There were other salons that I frequented. Mme. Menard-Dorian had a fine hotel, full of objects of art from China. This was a salon of the Left, where I met Clemenceau at a ball and Alphonse Daudet, creator of the immortal Tartarin; Mme Schlumberger of an Alsatian family had a lovely hotel *entre cour et jardin* in the Faubourg St. Honoré. She was a Protestant, but lived much in Catholic circles and perished finally in the disastrous fire at the Charity Bazaar [1] which threw all the Faubourg into mourning. She had a son then working in the Foreign Office and a nephew who afterwards became a Member of the Institute. My first meeting with them was at Versailles, where Mme Schlumberger was spending the autumn months. After luncheon they took me over the Château. The elder of the two had taken part in the war of 1870; I have never forgotten the bitterness with which, as we entered the Hall of Mirrors, he suddenly hissed into my ear: "And it was here that that scoundrel the King of Prussia was crowned German Emperor." His talk gave me some idea of the horrors of war and the bitterness it leaves behind in the minds of the vanquished. He himself had just finished his medical studies and was taking a holiday in Italy when war had broken out, but on the news of the first reverses he had returned at once to Paris and volunteered his services. His first

[1] 1897.

experience had been a hasty summons in the middle of the night to some small station near which he was in bivouac. Two troop-trains had collided. Many of the men, closely packed and weary, had fallen asleep as they sat with their heads resting on their rifles for support and when the collision happened scores of them had been impaled.

I owed much during my Paris visit to the kindness of Madame Schlumberger and her son, who was nearer my own age. Years later, I tried to repay a little of my debt when he and his charming wife came to London during the festivities attendant on King Edward's coronation. I was then Financial Secretary of the Treasury, and I invited them to my room which overlooked the Horse Guards Parade, to witness the review of the military contingents which represented the armed forces of all His Majesty's dominions over seas. The first day's parade was confined to the contingents coming from what we should now call The Dominions; he was delighted with the pageant, but it was on the second day devoted to the contingents of India, the Crown Colonies and the Protectorates that he became really enthusiastic. The spectacle of these men of so many different races, creeds and civilizations, each with one white officer and all united in their loyalty to the King-Emperor, profoundly impressed him. "Now," he said, "I understand your English pride. You have a *right* to be proud!"

The names and faces of many others besides those I have mentioned, to whom I was not less indebted for their first cordial welcome and constantly renewed hospitality, recur to my mind as I recall those happy months.

I lived, in fact, wholly among French people—the only exception being certain American ladies, like Mme Ribot, who had married French husbands. In whatever circle I found myself I met nothing but kindness; those to whom

I had taken letters of introduction passed me on to their friends and so my circle of acquaintance widened. The Darmsteters, for instance, took me to call on Ernest Renan, then an immensely fat old man who sat half-buried in a great arm-chair and poured out for my benefit a stream of platitudes couched in the most mellifluous French. Another day I was taken to Pasteur's laboratory and presented to that great Frenchman, but my memories of him are dim, for I regret to say I nearly fainted and was obliged to hurry out into the fresh air. At the Ribots I met Paul Bourget, whom, I am sorry to find, I described as the writer of clever but detestable novels and disappointing in conversation. He was, I think, then and later a good deal of a poseur.

T. B. Potter, then Chairman of the Cobden Club, on a visit to Paris, introduced me to Wilson, President Grèvy's scapegrace son-in-law, and by him in turn I was taken to lunch with the President himself, who had just entered on his second term of office and was shortly to be forced into resignation by the scandals in which his son-in-law involved him.

Of that meeting I have no recollection, but I still recall the scenes at an evening reception at the Elysée, a veritable "bear-garden," as I wrote at the time, where a certain famous beauty of the day was mobbed in a corner of one of the reception-rooms by a crowd of the curious anxious to get a glimpse of her, and an angry crowd of hungry guests besieged the entrance to the supper-room, already crowded to suffocation, and groaned loudly when the doors were closed against them. It was not a distinguished company which was being entertained on that particular evening.

At other times I was taken to the studios of some of the artists of the day. Indeed I saw a little of all worlds except the Faubourg of which I think I caught glimpses only at

Mme. Schlumberger's. Those were the days, in home politics, of the fall of Mr. Gladstone's second Government, of the interim Government of Lord Salisbury (mockingly called by my father "the Government of caretakers") until the redistribution of seats could be effected and elections held on the new franchise; of my father's Unauthorized Programme,[1] and of the general election which placed the balance of power between the English parties in the hands of Parnell, and provoked Mr. Gladstone's final conversion to Home Rule. I suppose my father's name would have been about as popular in the Faubourg as that of Clemenceau himself. Indeed, my father's views created something like consternation even in the moderate Republican circles in which I mostly moved, and excited as much alarm as interest. Only from Clemenceau and, curiously enough, at the opposite extreme of French politics, from the Comte de Mun, did I receive any sympathy for them. Somehow the Count read a note which I had written for the Annales of the École des Sciences Politiques on the once famous "Three Acres and a Cow." He wrote expressing his complete agreement and asked me to call to discuss it more fully with him. He was a devout Catholic, a great orator and at that time still one of the leading figures on the Extreme Right of the Chamber. "His redeeming trait," I wrote, "is a leaning to socialism." It became more than a leaning later. I think it was he who took me one evening to a kind of French Rowton House, but with a definitely evangelizing character. The memory is interesting to me because it was on that occasion that I met Anatole France for the first and last time.

Most of the elder men I knew would have been classed

---

[1] 1885, advocating free education, small holdings, graduated taxation and local government.

27

at home as Whigs and it was with moderate liberal opinion in England that they sympathized, but if they disliked the growth of Radicalism and condemned the tendencies of its domestic policy, they were united in their distrust of Lord Salisbury, whom they thought to be little better than an instrument of Bismarck. "All the party," I wrote after a dinner at the Rothans, "were anxious for Liberal successes in England and dreaded very much the foreign policy of Lord Salisbury. They feel him to be the friend of Germany, and this feeling overcomes in the French Conservatives their sympathy with his domestic policy." Rothan himself crowed "over the check which Bismarck would receive by Salisbury's downfall" and Clemenceau declared a Liberal Government in England to be the necessary counterpoise to Bismarck's Germany.

What a varied and interesting society it was among whom I spent these months; how much was taught me; what new horizons it opened out to my eager eyes; above all, what kindness was showered upon me by all these friends and by others whose names I have not mentioned here. No wonder that, in spite of the exciting changes which were taking place in English politics and of my desire to be with my father at a time of so much anxiety and difficulty for him, I prolonged my stay till the middle of May and left at last with real regret that so happy an interlude was over. I am sure that my words at parting can but faintly have expressed the gratitude that was in my heart.

II

BERLIN IN 1887—THE CLOSE OF AN EPOCH

It was in February 1887 that I started for Berlin as a young man of twenty-three, intent on learning the German language and seeing what I could of German politics and German ways of life. Except for the hot summer months, which were divided between a pleasant stay in the little town of Friederichsroda in Thuringia and a visit to my family at home, I spent the whole year there, returning to England only at the end of the same month in the following year. I have never been back, though my plans for a visit with my wife in 1914 were all made. She had her tickets for the Bayreuth festival; I was to join her as soon as the parliamentary session ended and together we were to ramble through South Germany, finishing up with a week in Berlin. But that visit was never to be made. The war broke out, travel became impossible and there was other work to be done. I never saw the Berlin of William II, nor have I yet seen the Berlin of the Republic. I suppose that I should hardly recognize in it the city that I once knew, so changed must it be, not only in outward aspect but in inward character.

The Berlin of 1887 was, I suppose, not greatly changed in outward appearance or manner of life from what it was while still only the capital of Prussia. It had recovered from the wave of speculation which followed the war of 1870, and from the financial crash which that speculation brought in its train. It had resumed its old simple ways and bore, to the eye of a foreigner accustomed to London and Paris, a slightly provincial air. What is called "society" was narrowly confined almost to the noble families and officers of the army; big business had not made its appearance; *la haute finance* was growing in wealth and importance but was not, I think, as yet recognized at Court except in the person of Bleichroder, the Berlin correspondent of the London house of Rothschild, who owed his position there to the gratitude of Bismarck for the help which he had rendered in fixing, at a higher figure than other authorities thought possible, the indemnity to be paid by France for the war. He was admitted to these exalted circles and I was told that when he and his daughter were invited to Court Balls, it was necessary to command officers to dance with the lady who would otherwise have found no partners. Classes did not mix and only in the circle of the Crown Prince and his English wife did art and letters find recognition. Political divisions were equally sharp. "Do you ever see Dr. Bamberger?" I once asked the British Ambassador. "No," he replied, "for in this country it is useless to know the Opposition since they never become the Government, and besides it is *mal vu* in high quarters." If a foreign representative wanted to find favour in Bismarck's eyes he must not frequent the company of his opponents.

I carried with me a letter of introduction to the Ambassador, Sir Edward Malet, who had married a daughter of the Duke of Bedford of the day. Sir Edward was a remarkable man who had made his reputation as Consul-General in Egypt in the days of Arabi's rebellion, where it was said that, however dangerous the crisis, he was always cool, and however unexpected the summons of foreign representatives to the Palace, he was always the first to appear, and whatever the hour of the day or night at which the summons reached him was always immaculately dressed. He was, in fact, a very able diplomatist who stood deservedly high in the estimation of Bismarck and his fellow ambassadors. It was no light task to fill worthily the position just vacated by Lord Ampthill.

Sir Edward and Lady Ermyntrude received me with much kindness, as indeed did all the members of his staff from Mr. (afterwards Sir Charles) Scott, who was then Councillor of the Embassy and later went as Ambassador to Russia, downwards. It was there that I began my happy friendship with Rennell Rodd (now Lord Rennell of Rodd), then at the beginning of his distinguished career and already clearly marked out for higher things. There, too, I renewed my friendship with my old schoolfellow, Reggie Lister, whose premature death while serving as Minister at Tangiers closed a brilliant career which would surely have led to one of the highest posts in the service. I wonder whether Lord Rennell remembers our parties to the theatres and the suppers afterwards at a small but celebrated oyster bar, where we ate cold partridges and drank Greek wine; or a Sunday at Potsdam with the Scotts, where they had taken a villa by the lake, and we three bathed from a boat instead of from a bathing-shed, and with less clothing than was expected, and were surprised by a boating party of the royal family and the commotion which followed. Mrs. Scott was able to disclaim having seen anybody bathing, but the road in front of her villa was picketed by the police for a fortnight. Simple pleasures, but relished at the time and dear in retrospect. Nor can I forget on the same occasion the delightful reply of her youngest daughter, then I think a child of three or four years old. She had been sitting on my lap for so long that Mrs. Scott feared

31

that I might be tired of her company. " Now I think you might leave Mr. Chamberlain alone. You never want to sit so long on *my* lap. " No," said my charming playfellow, " womens bores me ; mens never does ! "

But to return to Berlin itself. I arrived at a singularly interesting moment, and the year which I spent there was in fact the closing year of an epoch. The three great men who had created the new German Empire still survived, dominating the scene of their triumphs, the last of a race of giants beside whom all other men looked small, all other combinations petty.

The old Emperor's venerable figure, bowed by age but still tall and soldierly, might be seen at the Palace window any morning at the changing of the Guard, and there was always a small crowd of Berliners or visitors from other parts of Germany and abroad waiting to catch a glimpse of the man who by his age and his achievements had become almost legendary in his lifetime. I was there on his ninetieth birthday and stood for hours in the great crowd before the Palace entrance to watch the brilliant succession of German Princes and foreign representatives who came to present their own or their Sovereigns' greetings. It was the year of Queen Victoria's first jubilee, and the homage paid to her was scarcely greater than the respect shown to the aged Emperor.

In winter, when the lake in the Thiergarten was frozen over and we all flocked there to skate, one might see Moltke, taking his daily walk in the park, and the skaters would break off from their figures and cut across the ice from point to point to meet and salute him. But for his uniform, that slight figure, those handsome features, that fine and intelligent face, above all that noble forehead, would have made one guess that he was some great philosopher—a

32

professor perhaps of metaphysics or of the more abstruse mathematical studies—a student at least, wrapt in high thought and undisturbed by the common cares of man. Great student, indeed, he was, but his study was the art of war. Europe was his chessboard and his pawns were armies.

Lastly, there was Bismarck, the Iron Chancellor, the greatest of them all, a veritable colossus in stature as in achievement, tight-buttoned in his general's uniform, still watching from the palace of the Chancellor over the Empire which he had forged by blood and iron. My father had met Count Herbert Bismarck in London and they had become friends. I carried with me a letter of introduction to the Count, which I duly delivered about a month after my arrival. A few days passed and then I received a note from Count Herbert saying that " Prince Bismarck having heard a great deal about your father, and knowing that he is one of your foremost statesmen," had charged him to ask me to dinner. I was to come next day—at six o'clock, I think—" in jacket " which I thought it best to interpret as a frock-coat.

I went, flushed with pride and curiosity, but very shy. As I entered the salon the Prince rose to greet me with a beautiful old-world courtesy, offering me an apology for the absence of the Princess, who was confined to her room by indisposition, as if I had been a guest of consequence, and presenting me to the other guests. As I wrote at the time :

"It was almost a family party—Bismarck, Count Herbert, B.'s daughter and her husband, his secretaries and his doctor, who appears to look sharp after him. I took his daughter in to dinner, and sat between her and the great man, or one of the great man's dogs I should say, whom he kept one on each side of him and stuffed with everything. Bismarck was jolly, talked no politics, either German or foreign, but told stories of his student days, and regretted the degeneracy of the present age. He was particularly shocked at the idea of 'varsity men drinking *coffee*, but complained that the students here were as bad, and so on. Nothing serious but amusing enough. Hamann is in the seventh heaven; my dining with Bismarck casts a reflected glory on his house."

That, alas! is the only record I seem to have made of this memorable evening, but the letter recalls some of the talk that passed at dinner. We were half-way through dinner and I was becoming anxious as I was plied first with one wine and then another, till a formidable row of glasses faced me. I was little accustomed to wine in those days and fearful lest these Bismarckian potations should prove too much for me. Suddenly Herbert Bismarck called out from the other end of the table: " But, of course, you like dry champagne, Mr. Chamberlain." I hastily replied that I had all I could desire, but the Prince checked me, " Don't refuse dry champagne when Herbert offers it," he said, " or you will make an enemy of him for life. He is always seeking an excuse for getting it up." And then Schwenniger, the physician who had discovered how to treat Bismarck's troubles and been rewarded by the professorship of Medicine at Berlin University, to the great indignation of the Faculty, asked, " What do the undergraduates drink at Cambridge? " I confessed with shame that we were a weak generation; wine parties were rare, we mostly asked our friends to come round to coffee. " It's just the same here," exclaimed the Prince. The young men don't know how to drink nowadays." And then he added with a twinkle in his eye, " I can't complain of Herbert and his friends, but the young men of to-day can't drink. When I was a young man, we used to fight and we used to drink—why, we were drunk for weeks together. But the young men of to-day—ah, they'll never be the men we were!" [1]

Nearly forty years later his grandson lunched with me in London. Remembering the stock from which he sprang, I was fearful lest my small cellar should fail to satisfy his wants. Anxiously I consulted my butler and at last said in despair: "Well, you had better get up a bottle of everything there is." To my astonishment, after a single glass of wine, the Prince asked for water. "Prince," I exclaimed, "you a Bismarck and asking for water! What would your father and grandfather have said?" He answered in the Chancellor's own words: "Ah! we shall never be the men they were!" Thus was I revenged.

But to return to the evening with the Chancellor. When we rose from table and returned to the salon, he settled himself on a *chaise longue*, bidding me sit by his side and excusing himself as if I were somebody to whom some explanation were due. "I am like the boa-constrictor; I have only one meal a day and he (pointing to the physician) makes me rest afterwards." A rack of long German pipes stood by his side, and his servant handed him one already charged and lighted it. I remember he made some laughing allusion to the pipe and then talked pleasantly to me, but I feared lest I might outstay my welcome and soon took my leave.

A little later I wrote to my sister:

"All the Secretaries, etc., of the Embassy here are madly jealous of me for having dined with Bismarck. Such a thing

---

[1] Sir Charles Dilke used to declare later that Bismarck had said to him: "A nice boy, that young Chamberlain. Pity that he's such a poor drinker."

has never been known ; not one of them has ever exchanged so much as a good day with him, and even the ambassadors only dine with him once a year on the Emperor's birthday, and hardly ever, if ever, see him on business. So you see how favoured I was, and may imagine how proud it has made me."

After nearly half a century it remains one of the most interesting memories of my life and what stands out most in retrospect is the stately but very gracious courtesy of the greatest figure in Europe to the young man who was his guest.

Another picture of him is given in a letter I wrote a month later :

2/4/87.

" Yesterday morning I spent in the Prussian House of Commons, and was lucky enough to hear some very interesting speeches. The ' House ' is an oblong room, with the President's seat and the tribune in the middle of one of the long sides, whilst the corresponding place on the opposite side is filled by the Ministers' box, partitioned off from the seats of the deputies, and up to which, but *not* inside of it, extends the President's authority, as Bismarck once told him when called to order, thereby producing, as you may imagine, a ' scene.' The House was yesterday discussing a new Government Bill for repealing more of the May Laws against Catholics, another step towards Canossa on Bismarck's part in spite of his ' Never,' spoken ten years or more ago.

" The debate was opened by Dr. Gneist on behalf of the National Liberals. He spoke against the Bill, and I believe his words were words of great wisdom, but like some other professors, who are very distinguished in their way, he is a bad speaker and a bore in the House. Whilst he was speaking, the door from the Ministers' private room into their box slowly opened and Bismarck appeared, dressed in his dark-blue general's uniform with orange collar. All his colleagues got up to greet him and there was what the reporters call a sensation in the galleries.

"Dr. Windthorst, a clever short-sighted little old man, but a very sharp debater, followed with a short speech and read a written declaration on behalf of his section, the Centre or Catholic party. At a first glance he was something like Thiers, whilst the speaker who followed him bore the same sort of resemblance to Gambetta—the stout body, the head stuck upon the shoulders without any neck to speak of, and the rather long black hair brushed away from his forehead. This was Richter, leader of the Freisinnige or Liberal Party, which has come off badly at recent elections. He spoke for about three-quarters of an hour, fiercely attacking Bismarck, assailing him with argument and abuse and laughter.

"Meanwhile, the Chancellor, having run through his notes (written in a large hand on foolscap), was fidgeting uneasily. He is said to be very sensitive to attack, and, though he says sharp things of others, cannot bear them himself. He kept moving in his chair and writing nervously with a great carpenter's pencil. At last Richter finished, and he got up. His speeches read well, but the words do not flow easily as delivered. He always uses the right word, but sometimes it takes him a long time to find it. And his sentences are broken by a short disagreeable cough, which is probably more painful to his hearers than to him. His gestures, too, or rather, I should say his movements (for he uses no gestures) are awkward; he sways from one foot to the other, his hands are always fidgeting, now with his pocket-handkerchief, now with his moustache, and every now and then he gives a sort of jerk that is suggestive of his coat being a bad fit and 'catching' him under the arm.

"But everybody listens with intense interest, for his speeches are full of matter, illustrations from history or contemporary facts in other countries, and sound argument lit up by jokes at the expense of his opponents, apt quotations —more often from Shakespeare than any other writer—or now and again an amusing story. Finally, as the last touch

37

to the speech there comes—if the situation is critical and a majority for the Government uncertain, as is the case in these Church laws—a threat of resignation. ' His honour is engaged. The Pope will never believe that the Bill would not have been carried, if he had really done his best.' So he begs they will spare him the humiliation of this position. Besides *he* says the bill is good and necessary. If they have not confidence in him, he will ask the King to relieve him of his office, which the King, by the by, will *not* do. But the majority is secured, the end is attained in spite of the jeers of the opposition who remember to have heard all this before.

" There is a very faithful account of a more than usually interesting sitting of the Landtag, and I hope it won't have bored you. To make the picture complete I need only add that Bismarck sustains himself during his oratorical exertions by drinking copiously strong brandy and water—a tumbler to every quarter of an hour I counted. None of your nasty water for him."

The correspondent of *The Times* assured me a little later that he had actually seen Bismarck's empty tumbler replaced with a full one seventeen times in the course of a speech in explanation of a new army bill, which had lasted, if I remember rightly, a little over two hours.

I met or dined with Herbert Bismarck, then Secretary of State for Foreign Affairs, on several occasions. One such dinner is recorded in a letter of October 7th, 1887:

" I dined last night at Herbert Bismarck's. Mr. and Mrs. Scott, Graf Bismarck-Bohlen, a Graf Holstein and two people from the Foreign Office, whose names I must find out. It was a very pleasant party. H. B. was in great spirits, talked about father with great admiration, and said I must bring him over here. H. B. said, if only father would come, he would do everything possible to amuse him. In return he promised again to come down to Highbury on one of his visits to England. Father's cigars have left an indelible impression on his mind. He keeps very good ones himself."

It seems strange to find myself writing " a Graf Holstein." I was evidently unaware what a strange and powerful personality was in front of me. Had I realized the part he had already played, still more the part he was destined to play in the future, I should have studied him more closely, for he was none other than the Baron Holstein who had been Bismarck's spy on Arnim, under whom he served in the Paris Embassy, and his tool in bringing about Arnim's fall. He was or appeared at that time to be a great friend of Herbert Bismarck, but it has since been said that he never forgave Prince Bismarck the dirty work he had done for him and he deserted father and son in their fall. For years he was the most powerful figure in the German Foreign Office and did, perhaps, more than any other man to prevent an Anglo-German understanding in the years before the Anglo-French *entente* gave France the only ally whom Germany might have won.

Bismarck had no exaggerated respect for either the Prussian Landtag or the German Reichstag, but on one occasion at least he paid a tribute to the British Parliament. " I rather envy you English statesmen the excitement of the House of Commons," he said to Goschen in the early 'eighties. " You have the pleasure of being able to call a man a damned infernal scoundrel. Now I can't do that in diplomacy." He had perhaps not measured exactly the forms of English parliamentary speech, but with his usual acumen he had seized its substance.

It was on the same occasion that he entertained Goschen and the British Ambassador, Lord Odo Russell, later the first Lord Ampthill, at dinner. A dish of lampreys was served. " Do you know what we call those? " asked Bismarck.

" We call them ' nine-eyes ' (Neun-Augen). I once ate
eighty-one ' eyes ' at a sitting."

" But had you no cause afterwards to regret your
prowess? " asked Lord Odo.

" Ah," said Bismarck, " I have often regretted what I
have eaten but never what I have drunk."

" What? " exclaimed Lord Odo, " have you never been
the worse for your potations? "

" I did not say that I had never been the worse for them,"
Bismarck retorted, " I said that I had never regretted them."

Goschen in later days when I was the junior member of
his Board of Admiralty, loved to tell such stories and told
them extraordinarily well. This one recalls that gallant
sportsman, Henry Chaplin,[1] equally unspoiled by good or
evil fortune. " Is it very bad, old man? " asked a friend
who found him in the throes of a torturing attack of gout.
" It's hell," replied Chaplin, " but thank heaven I have
earned every twinge of it."

After the sitting of the Landtag described in the fore-
going letter, I saw no more of Bismarck either in public
or private. I envied Sir William Richmond who came to
Berlin to paint the Ambassador and Lady Ermyntrude Malet.
Bismarck had a tender spot in his heart for Sir Edward,
whose father he had known and liked and whose appoint-
ment to Berlin he had welcomed. Sir Edward persuaded
Bismarck to sit to Richmond for his portrait and in wel-
coming the artist to Friederichsruh, his country home,
Bismarck had greeted him as Malet's friend and had added :
" There are few things I would not do if Sir Edward asked
me." Richmond stayed a week at Friederichsruh and the
Prince chatted freely with him at sittings and during meals.
Richmond delighted the Chancellery of the Embassy, who

[1] President, Local Government Board, 1895–1900.

had made me, so to speak, a member of their mess, with his stories of the great man. I would have given much to see the Prince thus among his tenants, foresters and retainers. Here he was surrounded by all the formative influences that had determined his outlook on life and given to his genius its particular bent. Great men sometimes give the clearest picture of themselves not in their work but in their recreation. Is any picture of Bismarck complete which does not include that sentence from the *Reminiscences*, which he compiled after his fall, in which he wrote : " I cannot deny that my confidence in the character of my successor (*i.e.* Caprivi appointed Chancellor on Bismarck's dismissal) suffered a shock when I heard that he had cut down the ancient trees in front of his—formerly my—residence. . . . I would pardon Herr von Caprivi many differences rather than the ruthless destruction of ancient trees? " Or again another sentence of reminiscence in some letter to his sister or his wife which I read, I suppose, forty years ago in some published correspondence that I have never in later years been able to trace. I quote it therefore from memory and cannot vouch for the actual words, but of the general sense I am certain. It must, I think, have been written whilst patriotic Prussians still smarted under the humiliation of Olmutz and probably when Bismarck was the Prussian representative in the Bund at Frankfort. It ran as far as I can remember thus : " It was about this time that I reached that confidence in myself out of which a real belief in God's guidance of the world springs." Prodigious! as Dominie Sampson would have said, but the strength of Bismarck's Germany lay in this conviction that God willed the triumph of Prussia and the union of Germany.

The year 1887 was marked by strained relations between Russia and Germany and the air was filled with rumours of war. In March I wrote home that I had seen Moltke out walking alone, saluted with every respect by all who saw him, " And glad," I continued, " they all are to see him out, for if he has time to take a walk, they say, all the preparations for war must be complete, and they may go home with their minds at rest. At rest, however, they are not, for the rumours of a war with Russia in the near future are very disquieting. I was talking to a late member of the Chamber the other day who told me that he thought the best informed people were convinced that it could not be avoided, and if once Russia began, France would certainly follow suit, though she would not lead off alone." My informant was George von Bunsen, son of the old Prussian Ambassador to the Court of St. James's and uncle of Sir Maurice, who was British Ambassador at Vienna when the Great War broke upon the world. I carried with me a letter of introduction to him from my Rugby House-master and to his kindness I owed many happy hours and not a little information about Germany and the Germans of that day.

Bunsen himself was a man steeped in the traditions of the liberal movement of '48. He was a member of the Freisinnige Partei and as such had held for a time a seat in the Reichstag. He and his friends had supported the policy of the Iron Chancellor, reconciled to much that they disliked by his success where the men of '48 had failed, in uniting all the German peoples in the new German Empire ; but he belonged to what we should call the Manchester School of politics, broke with Bismarck when he adopted protection and lost his seat. He was a man of wide culture, liberal views and great charm—in short of those very qualities which endeared the late Sir Maurice de Bunsen to all who knew him.

He amused me on this occasion with stories of Moltke, one of which has a bearing on the passage just quoted from my letter. On the day on which war was declared in 1870 a friend met Moltke taking a similar solitary walk. "What news is there?" he asked the Field-marshal. "Potatoes are up three pfennigs," said Moltke, who was an agriculturist as well as Chief of the General Staff. "How can you think of such trifles at such a moment?" exclaimed his friend. "I should have thought you must be over-whelmed with work." "Ah! my work was done yesterday," replied the Field-marshal; "I shall not be wanted now for ten days." It was, I think, just a fortnight later that the opening battle of the war was fought at Spicheren. Other stories followed to indicate the care with which all the preparations for war had been made and the exact knowledge which the Germans had acquired of all that it behoved the invader of France to know. Though most of them have escaped my memory, they made an impression on my youthful mind to which such ideas were unfamiliar, and the impression deepened as I listened to the talk of the students at the university or the young officers whom I met at dinners and dances.

But the real revelation came from Treitschke, whose lectures on Prussian history at the university I regularly attended. I recorded my impression of his teaching and its effect in a letter dated October 31st, 1887:

"Treitschke," I wrote, "has opened to me a new side of the German character—a narrow-minded, proud, in-tolerant Prussian *chauvinism*. And the worst of it is that he is forming a school. If you continuously preach to the youth of a country that they stand on a higher step of the creation to all other nations, they are only too ready to believe it, and the lecturer who descends to this will be popular and draw big audiences. But it's very dangerous. I fear my generation of Germans, and those a little younger will be far more high-handed and will presume far more on the victories of '66 and '70 than those who won them. There is a school growing up here as bad as the French military school, and if they come to the front, why, *gare aux autres*. They are likely to find a friend in Prince William, who is said to be thirsting for warlike distinction and is the idol of the military party and the youth. . . ."

Again on January 11th next year I wrote:

" V. Treitschke has recommenced his lectures with a field-day against ' faithless Albion,' and, to use his own words, ' cursed the blue from heaven ' over her having got the better of Prussia towards the close of the seventeenth century."

What luckless English Princess had then married some Prince of the House of Hohenzollern, I do not now remember, but I still recall the fierce invective which he hurled against the poor lady's memory. It was, in fact, but a thinly disguised attack upon the Crown Princess Frederick, and as such it was understood and applauded by his class. It was not a comfortable class-room for an Englishman.

Already the Crown Prince's illness was casting its shadow over the future. I had written on November 18th:

" People here are very much saddened by the Crown Prince's illness, which seems quite hopeless. The Liberals, especially, are quite overwhelmed. He was their last hope. As Dr. Bamberger, one of their leaders, said to me the other day, it is the only blow which remained to be struck at them. And now they must look forward to Prince William's accession, a high-tory Prussian officer, caring for nothing but soldiering and anxious above all to win his spurs. Again, as Dr. Bamberger said, ' We must pray that Bismarck may be spared.' Fancy this from a member of the party on whom the Chancellor has so trampled. What irony of fate! But he feels that Bismarck can keep Prince William in order, and perhaps no one else could."

Bismarck himself was reported to have said a little later that for three months the young Emperor would cling to his coat-tails, for another three the old Chancellor would run after him, checking him with difficulty, and that then he would break loose and insist on going his own way.

In November the Emperor Alexander III paid a visit to Berlin and the atmosphere cleared for a moment. "Peace has suddenly broken out," exclaimed some wit, but the clouds gathered again. The arsenals were working overtime; another half-million men were added to the Army and people talked of war between Russia and Austria as almost a certainty and then Germany and Italy would be drawn in. One day in early February Bamberger asked me: "What do they think in your Embassy of the present state of affairs?" I answered that I believed they considered it serious. "And what do you yourself think?" he asked me; to which I replied that I now believed a war near, though till lately I had not joined in the scare, alluding to the scare of a French war last Spring. "Oh, no," he said, "that was all humbug (using the English word) *Aber ich sehe jetzt sehr schwarz.*"[1] He added he thought war with Russia a certainty; as regards France one of three things might happen. It might at once join sides with Russia, or it might wait to see how things went and only take part against Germany if Germany suffered defeat at the beginning; or, on the outbreak of war with Russia, Germany might at once attack France, preferring to anticipate her action rather than to leave her to choose her own time.

---

[1] "But the outlook now seems to me to be very black."

He believed that the last course would probably be the one pursued."

The same evening I reported Bamberger's gloomy views to Sir Edward Malet, the British Ambassador. Sir Edward did not share his fears; there was nothing for the Powers to fight about and the publication of the Austro-German alliance ought to have a quieting effect. I asked what we should do if war came and added that I supposed that we should hold aloof.

"In that case," said Sir Edward, "it's quite certain what the other Powers will do. There will be a short war, quickly patched up, and then they will all turn on us. None of them love us for our *beaux yeux*. If we won't take our part in helping to make or maintain peace, the others will make peace at our expense. They have told me as much here." And then he repeated: "We are the Eldorado of all these Powers; they all would like to plunder us."

This was in the first week of February 1888. I left Berlin at the end of that month. On March 9th the old Emperor died. In June the Emperor Frederick followed him to the grave. Before two more years had passed the old Pilot was dropped and the Emperor William II had fairly begun his disastrous reign.

The old order had passed. Let me close my memories of it by a story told to me by George von Bunsen about the Emperor William I and King Victor Emmanuel which is, I think, honourable to both Sovereigns and characteristic of the men and the times in which they lived.

It is a well-known fact that on the outbreak of the war of 1870 the French Government expected help from both Austria and Italy, and that Grammont led the French Chamber to believe that they had promised it. Victor Emmanuel, not unmindful of the help received from

Napoleon III in the establishment of the kingdom of Italy, desired to go to the assistance of France, but was prevented by the resistance of popular opinion, which made such action impossible as long as French troops occupied Rome and prevented the transfer of the capital of the new kingdom to that city.

Two or three years after the war Victor Emmanuel made his first State visit to Berlin and was met by the Emperor William at the station and conducted by him to the Palace. When the formal presentations at the Palace were completed and the King had been conducted to the rooms which he was to occupy, the Emperor turned to his Staff and said: "I have always admired His Majesty the King of Italy; now I must add that I love him."

One of the Staff asked the Emperor if he would tell them what had happened to make him speak so warmly of the King, and the Emperor William replied:

" At the station and for some little time afterwards there was so much noise and cheering that it was impossible to say anything, but at the moment when it became possible to converse, His Majesty turned to me and said:

" Sire, the late Emperor Napoleon was my oldest friend. I was under infinite obligations to him and, when war unhappily broke out between Your Majesty and him, I did my utmost to go to his assistance, and only desisted when my ministers convinced me that it would cost me my crown. Now that the Emperor is dead, those obligations no longer exist and I hope that Your Majesty will find me as faithful a friend as it was my wish to be to Napoleon III."

Surely a saying not unworthy of *Il Re Galantuomo*.

III

GERMANY AGAIN

1. A Conversation with the German Ambassador in 1908

I WAS at Cambridge in the last days of May 1908 and happened to meet Sir Charles Waldstein [1] and Count Metternich, then German Ambassador to the Court of St. James's, who was passing the week-end with him at King's College. Waldstein asked me to breakfast with him next morning. I was unwilling to desert my wife who had accompanied me, but, Waldstein taking me on one side, pressed his invitation, saying that it was given at the express desire of Metternich, who very much wanted a quiet talk with me. I accordingly yielded. The conversation, even now after the lapse of so many years, seems not without interest. I transcribe the account of it which I sent to my father on my return to London :

" Now I must go back to Waldstein's breakfast and Metternich's conversation. After breakfast, at which we discussed Balzac and Anatole France, socialism, humanitarianism, jingoism and patriotism, Waldstein left to write letters and Metternich began :

M. " You are coming back to power soon—when ? Two years ? Two and a half years ? "

A. " Yes, we are coming back ; but I can fix no date. I hope not too soon."

---

[1] Slade Professor at Cambridge, later known as Sir Charles Walston.

48

M. " And it will be on Tariff Reform? It seems to me that that will be the big question? "

A. " Oh undoubtedly ! "

M. " Well, if your duties are moderate I cannot find that my countrymen think they will do them great harm. They are not much alarmed about them. They think that they will still be able to trade with you unless you put on very high prohibitive duties, and they do not view your proposals with any jealousy. Of course if you put on such high duties throughout the Empire as to forbid foreigners to trade with the Empire at all, I don't think other nations would stand that. There would be a combination of other Powers against you, for the Empire is too large a portion of the world for us to be content to be excluded altogether from its trade."

A. " Well, of course our proposals are for very moderate duties—more moderate for instance than the German. . . ."

M (interrupting). " Oh ! but remember ours are the lowest of any industrial country."

A. " Except Belgium, but . . ."

M. " Yes, except Belgium. If it were not for our desire to maintain an agricultural population and not to become wholly dependent on foreign food, I doubt if we should maintain anything but revenue duties. I don't think our manufacturers much care about them now, but we cannot afford to let our agriculture go."

A. " Exactly, and if you wish to protect agriculture you must give a *quid pro quo* to the industrial classes. You are quite right. I don't blame you. You don't do it to annoy us. You have to look after your own interests. So must we look after ours. I only say that our duties are likely to be lower than yours and they will not exclude trade with you, though they may cause some temporary inconvenience

D   49

and may somewhat alter the character of the trade that is to be done. Your duties have not decreased your foreign trade. They have increased it. You buy more than ever from abroad. So shall we."

M. "Well, but if that is so and we have no need to be enemies, why are you always treating us as an enemy? I confess I am not very sanguine about the situation. Why, for instance, are you so hostile to the Baghdad Railway? What are the trade reasons? What are the strategical reasons which make you so hostile to it? We seek to do trade there, but not to exclude you and others. We do not seek any special trade privileges; and as to strategy, can anyone suppose that we are going to send an army corps down the line to the Persian Gulf? I do not know how they are to get to the line. They would have to go across half Europe and no one explains how. But if they do go and get to the Persian Gulf, what are they to do? Why, there they remain!"

A. "Yes, and a very unpleasant place to remain in too! To tell the truth I do not know that I am a very good person to point out the strategical dangers, as I have never myself seen very clearly wherein they consist. No doubt such a movement would force us to keep extra ships in Indian waters and put us to extra cost; but I admit that I do not see that it would greatly threaten India. But of course if the break-up of the Turkish Empire were to come, I expect that Germany would then claim Asia Minor as her share, basing her claim on the interests she had established there by the railway, etc.; and that would be a very different thing."

M. "Oh! but even if the Turk were driven out of Europe, he would be very strong in Asia Minor. That is his home; that is where all his strength comes from even now. Europe is his weakness. Asia Minor is his strength. That is a very fanciful danger. But now about trade."

A. "Well, as to trade, what Englishmen fear is that without excluding other trade *eo nomine*, all your influence would be used to favour German trade at the expense of British trade. And your influence would be immense and most powerful for this purpose. In any proposals you have made hitherto for French and English co-operation, you will admit that you have always maintained a predominant influence for yourselves. You control absolutely the Anatolian railway and its port. Well, we think that under those circumstances German goods and German traders would fare better than British. Now if you want to meet us, would your Government agree to link up the Smyrna-Aidin line with the new system? That is an English line, it is true, as the Anatolian is German, and it comes to Smyrna, a port where we have no such predominant position as Germany in Anatolia but where England is well represented. Put Smyrna in a position to share on equal terms the trade of the Baghdad Railway and you give us an alternative debouché. That might do something to influence British opinion."

M. "Well, I cannot answer that question, for I do not know what my Government would say."

A. "Well, there is another point. At present you are constructing the railway from the north only. Our people fear that as you get to the Tigris and Euphrates, you will tap and divert the trade which at present goes south to the Gulf. This would not happen if the railway were built simultaneously from both ends. Of course we should expect the same kind of predominating interest at the Gulf that you have at the Anatolian end. I only name these as points for consideration if you really desire English co-operation and wish to remove English distrust. I do not pretend that the moment is very opportune for this kind of discussion and co-operation between the two countries."

Metternich then left the question of the Baghdad Railway and reverted to the general situation, again emphasizing the fact that he had come to view it "very seriously." He spoke very slowly and deliberately, choosing his words carefully and evidently intending me to understand that the position was grave. Of course in his story the German wolf was blameless; the English lamb was troubling the waters. The movement of English opinion was becoming more menacing. The English Press—notably the *National Review*—fanned the flame. "A few years ago it was generally thought in well-informed circles in Germany that England intended to attack Germany. I was the only person, having *voix au chapitre*, who did not take this view. Happily I was right then, but now—well, I am not sure. I do not conceal my opinion that the situation is becoming very grave."

A. "Of course I accept from you the statement that Germans really believed that we were going to attack them. But *you* know England, and you *must* know that no English Government could, if it wished, begin a war unprovoked, merely because it had become convinced that a conflict was inevitable sooner or later and thought the particular moment more favourable to us than a delay. With our politics and people you know that we cannot pursue such a policy as Bismarck's."

M. "But Bismarck did not hate England. He had no wish to quarrel with you."

A. "Oh no! I did not suggest that. What I meant. . . ."

M. "But then why is there this persistent hostility to us? Why is there this constant distrust, this effort to isolate us? Look, for instance, at the President's visit.[1] Nothing could be more natural in itself, but at once your Press begins to talk about a new triple alliance and turns the friendly visit of the French President into a demonstration against Germany. France does not want to be your ally. Your army cannot help her. She has everything to lose and nothing to gain by an alliance and she does not intend to be dragged into a quarrel with Germany by you. She does not wish to be made use of by you. And Russia! Russia is poor and weak. She can do nothing and she does not want to be your ally. Why are you trying to isolate us? Why do you not cultivate an understanding with us?"

A. "Well, Count, before the *Entente* with France was established, before our negotiations with her began, Germany was given her chance. Why did she not take it? You know to what I am alluding—my Father's speech.[2] Of course I know *The Times* d——d it next day and it did not look very easy. But my Father has been d——d by *The Times* more than once and has got over it. He has never been afraid of unpopularity. He was prepared to go on, but the next word rested with Prince Bülow. Why didn't he speak it? Why did he go to the opposite extreme and pour scorn on the idea? You know our proverb : ' He who will not when he may,' can't always be sure of having the opportunity repeated."

M. (throwing up his hands and shaking his head sadly). "Ah! yes, I know. But the times were not propitious. England used to be unpopular in Germany. Germans

[1] M. Faillières' visit to England in the same month.
[2] At Leicester, Nov. 30, 1899, advocating alliance between Great Britain, Germany and the U.S.A.

thought Englishmen cold and haughty. They held aloof so much, and then came our great struggles and England was coldly neutral and we did not like that. Germans thought that England was seeking . . ."

Here M. stumbled and hesitated a good deal about his words. I distinguished "profit" and "risk," but he seemed unable to frame his sentence to his own satisfaction, and so I pleasantly suggested:

A. "You thought England wanted to share the apples without taking any of the risks of robbing the orchard?"

M. "Ye-es. Well, then came the Boer War and all the rest of the world rightly or wrongly sympathized with the smaller Power—perhaps in France more violently than elsewhere—but the feeling was universal. Passions were roused, hot words were spoken, feeling ran high. But the time passed, feelings cooled down and we began to respect you. We saw, as we say in Germany, that the muscles were not swallowed up in fat—*die musceln waren nicht in fett unter-gegangen*. We began to respect and sympathize with you. Look now, all this friendship to France is very artificial. I believe that Englishmen are really more in sympathy with Germans than French. . . ."

A. (interrupting). Oh! do not make a mistake about the *Entente*. It is not artificial. It is very genuine and very widespread and popular."

M. "Just at the moment, yes; but it is not deep rooted."

A. "Well, we are talking frankly—that is the interest of the conversation, and I will continue frankly. Ever since I have known English politics—say since the early 'eighties—there has been a real desire among the masses of our people for a good understanding with France, partly no doubt because they wished to see an end put to the secular rivalry and distrust between these two great nations facing each other across twenty miles of sea; partly because they thought there was a closer communion of ideas between these two great liberal nations than between ourselves and any other."

M. " Oh! but . . ."

A. " Mind, I don't say that the community of ideas is as great as they think. To that extent the basis of the *Entente* may perhaps be artificial—imaginative rather than real; but the feeling is there; and there is nothing artificial about the universal satisfaction felt and expressed at our intimate relations with France."

M. " I believe it is all a false idea. I believe that there is really much more sympathy between us than between you and the French. We do not want to quarrel with you. Why should we? There is trade rivalry, no doubt; but I always find that it is precisely those who are engaged in trade who most dislike the idea of war, however much they fret at the trade competition. And for what else should we fight? For conquest? We do not want conquest—territory. Emigration from Germany has almost ceased. We want markets, but we want to keep our *people* at home. They do not want to emigrate. And what could we conquer? Canada? If the British Empire breaks up, Canada goes to the United States, if to anyone. India? India goes to Russia or to anarchy. Australia? No German is so mad as to dream of conquering Australia. South Africa? Your war has shown that no nation can conquer South Africa if it is united. You could not do it yourself. What remains? A few outlying islands! Great nations do not go to war for such a cause. No one in Germany desires it."

A. " I agree. I do not believe that your people desire

war with us in the abstract—or the Emperor. I don't believe that he desires war at all in his time. What I dread is the growing feeling in your country that a war is inevitable and . . ."

M. " Ah! but that is what your Press is teaching here."

A. " That and the effect of your teaching in Germany on opinion in this country. It is not that either nation desires war in itself, but that all the youth of Germany is being taught that the war must come and that they must prepare for the inevitable conflict."

M. " But I do not know of any such teaching in Germany. I never hear of it."

A. " Well from the days of Treitschke downwards——"

M. " Now listen! Mr. Chamberlain. Till I came to this country I never heard of Treitschke. He was nothing in Germany. He was a firebrand and he insulted everyone. But he had no influence."

A. " That is not my experience. Certainly he was a firebrand. I listened to his lectures and, as you say, he insulted everyone, but especially the Coburgs and the English. But he was a most popular firebrand. With every physical defect a public speaker could have, he was the most popular professor at the University of Berlin. His ' insults ' were received with loud applause at crowded classes. And that is not all. The same thing went on in the public schools. I know it from the stories brought home and the questions asked by the fourteen-year-old son of the man in whose family I boarded. Well, my experience is twenty years old. But my friends who know Germany to-day tell me that the same thing is going on throughout the whole educational system of Germany, from top to bottom. Do you wonder that I agree with you that the situation is grave or that we take note of what is passing? There lies the danger—in the growing belief, deliberately planted in the whole youth of Germany, that a conflict is inevitable. And when such a belief takes hold of the German mind, the whole Bismarckian policy is there to warn us of what may come. I do not criticize Bismarck's action with Austria in '66 or France in '70. I note it. A nation which has thus twice preached the doctrine of ' the inevitable conflict,' which has prepared for it with such patience and endurance, which has even gone to meet the heavy sacrifices which it entailed and has twice provoked the conflict with extraordinary skill at the most favourable moment to itself, whilst leaving to its opponent the odium of appearing at the time the aggressor— such a nation is indeed a formidable opponent when it begins to preach and prepare for a third ' inevitable war.' "

M. " But those are not similar cases. The war with Austria was necessary if Prussia was to have the hegemony in Germany. The war with France was necessary if North and South Germany were to be united. But there is no ' inevitable ' conflict here."

A. " I quite agree; but I dread the state of opinion in Germany—Oh! in both countries, if you will. That is where the danger lies."

We had now been discussing the subject for nearly an hour and a half and I rose to go. But Metternich begged me to wait a little and he again passed the whole situation in review—the survey lasting five or ten minutes, but not revealing anything fresh. He concluded: "I have sometimes been optimistic. I am not optimistic now."

" Nor I," I answered. " We can only wait and see. Let us hope the two Governments will be careful. For my part I think the less we hear of one another the better for the present."

And so we parted. We had talked, as I say, from ten-thirty till past twelve, and though from my summary it looks as if I had done half the talking, that was in fact not so. M. led the conversation and did most of the speaking. Of course my summary is not complete, nor have I always got the order quite right, but I think you will get from my report a good idea of the whole and in some cases the actual words.

There was a good deal more I should have liked to say had time allowed or M. given me the opportunity. But I let him talk on without interrupting him and followed the track he marked without insisting on following out my own thoughts if he interrupted with a new argument. It was in this way that I was prevented from really challenging him for instances and proof of the persistent hostility or aggressiveness of English policy. I wanted to take him to task about the German attitude to the *Entente*, at the Morocco conference and elsewhere, and generally to show him how and why the policy of Germany appeared to us unfriendly. However, perhaps I said enough! and any way the more interesting thing was to hear what he thought or wished to be thought to think!

I told A. J. B. of my conversation with Metternich a couple of days ago. To-day he said that Rothschild had been to him to report a similar conversation. I observed that this looked like the campaign of menacing talk which Germany organized in Paris just before Delcassé fell, " but we won't hound Grey out of office here! "

2. A CONVERSATION IN 1911

I first met Sir Henry Angst during a visit to Switzerland with my father in 1897. He had married many years

earlier an English lady, rather against the wishes of her
parents, who would have preferred that she should choose
an English husband. She had proudly replied that she
would make him an Englishman and he as proudly boasted
that she had been as good as her word. He was at that
time plain Mr. Angst, and had already held the post of
British Consul at Zurich for some years. He was later
promoted Consul-General and his services were recognized
by a Knighthood. He was one of the founders of the
Landes Museum at Zurich, in which are preserved so many
souvenirs of the old life of Switzerland. He loved his
country and its history ; and he loved and admired England
second only, if second at all, to the land of his birth. Whenever he came to London, he visited my father in Prince's
Gardens and his talk was always interesting and well-
informed.

In 1911 my wife and I spent our summer holiday in
Switzerland, travelling direct to Zurich and a couple of
days later Sir Henry Angst carried us off to lunch at his
country house at Regensberg in the hills above the town.
It is (or was at that time, for it may well have changed
since) a quaint little village with less than a hundred houses
perched two thousand feet up on an outlying spur of a
ridge of hills, some fifteen miles to the north of Zurich by
road. Originally it was the castle of the Counts of Regensberg under the Austrian dominion and the central tower,
or keep, which is still standing, dates from the thirteenth
century. Round the castle gathered a few houses and the
whole tiny space was still in Sir Henry's boyhood surrounded
by its old walls and defended by four fortified gates. But
a corrupt mayor, who subsequently absconded with much
of the Commune's money, found it necessary to make
work for the people in order to get their votes and so caused

the larger part of the fortifications and three of the gates
to be pulled down. Even now the view of the village as
you approach it is most picturesque and the panorama
from the village is magnificent—from the Black Forest
and the mountains beyond the Lake of Constance in the
north, round to the mountains at the head of the Lake of
Zurich on the south. In old times the place was of some
importance—the Governors of Zurich lived there—it had
a fair, permission to exercise trades (not usually accorded
to little hamlets of the kind) and the right of low justice.
Angst's people had lived there for several generations.
His mother's people were schoolmasters somewhere on
the Lake for 250 years from father to son. That, he said,
was an old, unchanging Switzerland which already belonged
to the past.

Sir Henry dwelt lovingly on this older Switzerland and
lamented its passing. Industrialism had crept in and was
changing the character of the people in more ways than
one. The country was very prosperous but it was losing
its old spirit. He talked despondently about the future.
Perhaps his pessimism was partly caused by the state of
Lady Angst's health, for she was gravely ill at the time and
died not very long after. He was very pro-English and
very distrustful of German aims.

A letter home recorded the substance of our talk.

He said the Germans had it all their own way in the
German-speaking Cantons. The newspapers were wholly
dependent on them for news and comments on news, largely
copying from the German papers so that their readers saw
nothing but the German point of view. German money
had been flowing into the country and had largely created
its industrial development, but besides this legitimate use
of German capital the " Reptile Press Fund " had also been

used to influence opinion. The people were wholly German in sympathy. He doubted whether if a European war broke out they would make more than a show of resistance. German Switzerland would be swallowed up in the German Empire. A gloomy foreboding indeed, and happily as the result proved quite unfounded.

More interesting was his account of a recent conversation with Bebel, the German Socialist leader. Bebel's daughter was married and living in Zurich and Bebel often visited her. Sir Henry often met him on these occasions and had conceived a great respect for him. He described Bebel as a very fine old man, sober and level-headed, not a wild man at all.

On his last visit, my letter continued:

" Bebel had told him that the German Government was mortally afraid of the progress of the Socialist Party; they expected them to come back 100 strong at the next elections, ' and before that,' said Bebel, ' you mark my words, the Government will try to make some patriotic coup to stimulate the bourgeoisie and rally people to the flag so as to lessen the Socialist gains.' Hence Agadir and the resurrection of the Moroccan question.

" There are many Germans here—some in business and some in disgrace. Angst likes neither class, but he says they talk very freely here, more freely than at home, and their jealousy and bitterness against England is extreme. ' It's useless,' he said, ' to talk of disarmament and peace conferences to Germany. Germany is Prussia—South Germany does not count and has no influence and will have none till a great ruler arises in Bavaria, Saxony, or Wurtemburg, and combines the three in a common policy of resistance to Prussia—but at present Germany is Prussia and Prussia is the Junker. To propose disarmament to him is to rob him of his bread and butter. He has no career save in the army, or under Government. Trade and com-

merce are forbidden to him, and the monarchy is dependent
on him and cannot afford to offend him. How long will
he last? Well, till there is a revolution, or an unsuccessful
war. A revolution will be long in coming. Bebel says,
'We are many, but we can do nothing. There are whole
regiments where every man—Officers, N.C.O.'s and rank
and file—are all Socialists, but we are powerless. We
should be shot down and blown away with grape shot.
We can do nothing but march. But if there were a defeat
at the beginning of the war, there would be a revolt.
Whole regiments would rise.' "

My own comment on this conversation was given at the
end of the letter:

"I confess I doubt the last statement, but Angst feels as
so many of us do, that sooner or later Germany will make
war again and this time England will be the real enemy,
though France may be first struck at."

3. INCREASING TENSION IN EUROPE

Nineteen hundred and eight, the date of my conversation
with Count Metternich, was the year of the annexation of
Bosnia-Herzegovina by Austria under Aehrenthal's leadership and of the revival of the Moroccan question in consequence of incidents at Casablanca arising out of the arrest
by the French authorities of certain German deserters from
the Foreign Legion whom the German Consul had taken
under his protection. Nothing but the weakness of Russia
caused by the disastrous Russo-Japanese war of a few years
previously had preserved peace in the former case, and
though the Casablanca incident was eventually settled by
a reference to the Hague Court, it had for months kept
European nerves on edge.

Nineteen hundred and eleven, the year of the second conversation recorded above was still more disturbed. On July 2nd the world had been startled by the announcement of the sudden despatch of the *Panther* to Agadir, and some three weeks later by the grave warning addressed to Germany by Mr. Lloyd George (then Chancellor of the Exchequer) at the Mansion House. Peace, he had said, was the greatest of British interests, but if Britain was to be treated where her interests were vitally affected as if she were of no account in the Cabinet of Nations, peace at that price would be an intolerable humiliation. Such words coming from the mouth of a Minister who was supposed to belong to the most pacific section of the Cabinet produced a profound impression, which was not lessened when it became known that the King had postponed his visit to Goodwood and that the Atlantic Fleet, which had been on the point of starting for a cruise in Norwegian waters, had been ordered to Portsmouth. A brief statement was made in Parliament on July 27th by the Prime Minister, who appealed to the House to postpone all further discussion. Balfour at once declared that the Opposition would observe the rule that no party differences should prevent national agreement where British interests abroad were at stake, though he added (for it was at the height of the Constitutional crisis and party feeling was running very high) that adherence to it had never been more difficult; and he reinforced the Chancellor's warning by saying that if anyone was counting on their acting differently, he had utterly mistaken the temper of the British people and the patriotism of the Opposition.

It would have been well for Germany if her rulers had remembered this declaration in August 1914 when it is supposed that they reckoned on the violence of the passions aroused by the Home Rule question to paralyse British action and to prevent us from entering the war to defend our own interests or to come to the assistance of France or Belgium.

It was not till towards the end of November that an agreement was reached between the French and German negotiators. Meanwhile the air was full of rumours, some true, some false, of military and naval preparations, and all Europe was kept in a state of strained and dangerous tension. When on the last days of that month the House of Commons was able to proceed to the discussion which it had been promised and the Government made a full statement on the events of the last few months, it was clear for all who had eyes to see and ears to hear how grave the situation had been and how perilously near the nations had stood to the brink of war.

Next year Lord Balfour of Burleigh and I had occasion to visit Petersburg on business. Sir George Buchanan had invited us to stay at the Embassy and it was certain that we should meet the principal Russian Ministers. Before leaving, therefore, I called on Sir A. Nicolson, later Lord Carnock and then holding the post of Permanent Under Secretary of State, at the Foreign Office, to ask if he could give me any guidance as to what it might be wise for me to say or, quite as important, to refrain from saying. He embarrassed me by replying that he would prefer to leave what I should say to my discretion. When, therefore, the Foreign Minister, Sazonov, engaged me in a conversation which must have lasted for nearly two hours, I turned rather anxiously, as soon as we were alone, to the British Ambassador, who had been a listener, to ask if I had been in any way indiscreet. He was good enough to assure me that on the contrary what I had said would be very helpful to him. I carried away from the conversation the impression that neither the Russian Foreign Minister nor the Ambassador had had any very clear impression of the aims and purpose of the British Government and that this uncertainty did not make for peace.

Like other people, I was becoming increasingly anxious as to the future. It seemed to me that the tension in Europe was becoming greater year by year; incident followed incident leaving the nerves of all the parties more strained and inflicting a wound on the pride, first of one nation and then of another, which was neither forgotten nor forgiven. First France had suffered the humiliation of having to dismiss her Foreign Minister at the bidding of Germany; then Russia, still smarting under her defeat by Japan [1] a few years before, had suffered a similar humiliation in the crisis which followed the annexation of Bosnia-Herzegovina, and this time the wound was not in the Far East in an adventure to which her people were indifferent, but in the Near East where Slav pride had always been most sensitive and national feeling was most easily and strongly moved. And now Germany, unsuccessful at Algeciras [2] and dissatisfied with the solution of the Casablanca incident,[3] felt herself equally humiliated by the results of the Agadir crisis.[4] No great nation could suffer patiently a second humiliation such as had now fallen to each of these in turn; any repetition of such an incident would leave the Government no choice but war, for the only alternative to war would be a revolution in which the Government itself would be overthrown.

I did not suspect the German Emperor of desiring war. In spite of his boastful and provocative speeches, I still thought that he in his own person offered the best guarantee

[1] The war of 1904–5.   [2] The Conference of 1906.
[3] 1908.   [4] See p. 63.

that Germany would keep the peace, and I should have been far more alarmed if power had fallen into the hands of the Crown Prince, whom, in my mind, I identified with the military party. What I feared was not that Germany would deliberately provoke war, but that her Government would blunder into it without knowing what they did, for German diplomacy since Bismarck seemed to me the clumsiest in all Europe. Bismarck's successors found it easier to copy his faults than to understand his merits. It was certain that sooner or later the attempt to seek Germany's security by setting all her neighbours by the ears must result in those neighbours perceiving that they only burned their fingers for another's profit and equally certain that sooner or later they would tire of being the dupes of such a policy and prefer to settle among themselves disputes the benefit of which inured only to the advantage of a rival. That was the seed of disaster which lay in Bismarck's post-1870 policy, but Bismarck enjoyed an immense prestige and played his cards with a master hand. The same could not be said of his successors. They failed where he excelled; they had no sense of those *imponderabilia* which Bismarck declared were, in the last resort, always decisive and to which he was himself so amazingly sensitive. No Government so miscalculated the effect of its words and actions on foreign nations as that of Germany under Bülow and his successors.

Peace seemed to me, therefore, to lie at the mercy of an accident which a clumsy hand might provoke at any moment. What would be our position if war broke out? The *Entente*, as I thought, had come to have all the obligations of a formal alliance without its advantages. We had been on the brink of war at the time of the Agadir crisis, yet the public mind was wholly unprepared for it.

If war came, we should be obliged to intervene; it was dangerous to conceal the real position from the country and to attempt to ride a democracy in blinkers. What we needed was something in the nature of a British Monroe doctrine. Many plain American citizens might be puzzled to give a clear definition of the Monroe doctrine, but every American knew that if a foreign nation attacked that doctrine it laid its hand on the very Ark of the Covenant and all Americans would be united to defend it. A formal Alliance, or so I thought, would involve us no more deeply than we already stood committed and would be a beacon to guide the steps of Parliament and the country and to secure a united nation if the struggle came.

But if it had these advantages at home I thought it would be not less useful abroad. It would help to steady the nerves of the French people, and it would give us an influence on French policy which no other method would afford. As it was, we might be dragged into a war fought on some issue which we thought wholly insufficient; but if our support was guaranteed to France on certain conditions, any French Government would make sure that those conditions were fulfilled in the eyes of the British Government before embarking on war.

Lastly, I believed that the knowledge that such an Alliance existed might exercise a sobering effect in Germany, and might prevent the German Government from blundering into a war with us without knowing what they were doing.

I felt so strongly the dangers of our existing situation that at last I sought out Sir Edward Grey and laid my fears and suggestions before him. It is not necessary to repeat his answer here, for he has himself set forth his reasons for not taking the course I urged in the curiously detached and objective account which he has given of his stewardship in the anxious and troubled years during which he presided at the Foreign Office.[1] The plain fact is that even if he had thought it the right policy, he could not have carried it, but it is tempting, though probably futile, to speculate on what might have been. Many continental writers have held that if such a treaty had been known to be in existence, there would have been no war. That was at one time my own view, but in the light of all that we now know, I can no longer sustain it. I now think that it might at most have postponed for a year or two the outbreak of the struggle. If this be true, perhaps it was better that the issue should be fought out then. In the end the invasion of Belgium did for us what I had thought a treaty of Alliance would do: it made our duty plain and brought us into the struggle a United Nation.

[1] See *Twenty-five Years*, by Viscount Grey of Fallodon.

IV

A GREAT SPEAKER
ARTHUR WELLESLEY PEEL

THE first Parliament in which I sat was the one elected in
1886 after the defeat of the first Home Rule Bill in which
the Conservatives and Liberal Unionists together had a
majority of one hundred over the combined forces of
English Home Rulers and Irish Nationalists; but it was
already moribund when I was returned unopposed at a
bye-election in East Worcestershire in 1892, and all thoughts
were already turned to the coming elections. I was
introduced by my father and uncle in the last days of
March. I remember that the strong feeling stirred in me
by the occasion made my hand tremble so violently that
I could scarcely sign my name on the Roll. It is a difficulty
which in my case has often recurred. Growing up in a
circle where political interests held a high place, and looking
forward from boyhood to becoming some day a member
of the House, I early imbibed and have always cherished a
profound respect for its august traditions, and entered it
with an earnest desire to win the good opinion of my
fellow-members. To this day I never rise to address it
without trepidation and that uncomfortable feeling in the
pit of the stomach which in our childhood we used to
call " bath-pain " because we associated it with the first
sudden plunge into cold water. I doubt whether anyone
has ever made a lasting success in the House of Commons
of whom this is not in some measure true, for no man

ever wins the respect of the House unless he himself respects it.

Parliament was dissolved only four months later and my first House of Commons has left only one abiding impression on my mind. It is of the greatness of Mr. Speaker Peel. The House has had many great Speakers, but I doubt whether in its long history it has ever had a greater than Arthur Wellesley Peel. Others have served it faithfully and many of them with great distinction, but Speaker Peel *dominated* it. In the opinion not only of one like myself who was still a young member when he retired, but of older men who had been present at his first election, he stood in a class by himself, over-topping his predecessors, never equalled even by the most successful and respected of his successors. He had a natural dignity and a formal but genuine courtesy which well became the occupant of the Chair, and, besides, a dramatic gift which in great moments raised him so far above his fellow-members that the whole House trembled at his rebuke. At such times his stature seemed to grow before our eyes, his deep resonant voice dominated the tumult and he appeared as the living embodiment of centuries of parliamentary tradition.

One such moment occurred in the closing days of the Parliament of 1892. A Select Committee of the House had been inquiring into the hours of work of Railway Servants, and among the witnesses who had given evidence before it was the stationmaster of some small station on the Cambrian Railway. He had subsequently been called before three of the Directors and the General Manager of the Company and dismissed, nominally for some irregularities in his accounts but really, as was obvious from the questions put to him by the Directors, on account of the evidence which he had given before the Select Committee.

Viscount Peel

From the portrait by Hubert von Herkomer, in Balliol College, Oxford.
By kind permission of the Master and Fellows

The Committee, of which Sir Michael Hicks Beach [1] was chairman, took evidence as to what had passed and made a special Report to the House on the case as a breach of Privilege. Of the three Directors involved one, Sir John Maclure, was an old and much-liked member of the House. A day was fixed for the discussion and an order was made by the House that the honourable member for Stratford should attend in his place and that his co-Directors and the General Manager should appear at the Bar. They were asked if they had anything to say and Sir John Maclure offered an apology with which the others associated themselves. They were then ordered to withdraw while their case was considered, and Hicks Beach moved : " That this House while recognizing that they had expressed their unqualified regret for having unintentionally infringed any of its Rules and Privileges is of opinion that they have committed a breach of Privilege . . . and that they be called in and admonished by Mr. Speaker."

This seemed a rather lame conclusion and there was a good deal of sympathy with the proposal made by T. P. O'Connor to add that the House would not consider that they had purged their contempt till they had reinstated the discharged man. Efforts were made privately to get them to do this, or at least to compensate him, but they remained obdurate. Hicks Beach's resolution was supported by Mr. Gladstone, but his advice was rejected by the great majority of his followers whose zeal for the injured man was perhaps stimulated by the value of the railway vote at the general election which was known to be imminent. A long, wrangling discussion followed and it was not till midnight that a division was taken and Hicks Beach's resolution carried.

[1] Afterwards Viscount St. Aldwyn.

Then the Directors were once more called in. Sir John Maclure evidently felt his position acutely, but the other three appeared at the Bar defiantly and almost jauntily. They had successfully resisted the desire of many members, not confined to one side of the House, that they should compensate the man, and now they were to have what schoolboys call a " pi-jaw " from the Speaker—that was all the House of Commons could do to them.

Mr. Speaker Peel spoke for less than ten minutes. " I would have you to know—each and all of you gentlemen— that though the Privileges of this House are not to be put into operation on any light or trivial occasion . . . yet a Privilege of this House is no unreal, shadowy or un-substantial thing ; it is what the House clings to and what it is determined to maintain." And then after expatiating on the enormity of their particular offence, he declared, " The House in its judgment and, I should add, in its mercy has decided that I should admonish you," and he proceeded to administer the admonition.

The bald words of what he said, recorded in *Hansard*, convey no idea of the devastating effect of that short allocution. The men who had come to the Bar so defiantly a few minutes earlier wilted under his admonition ; beads of perspiration stood out on their foreheads and, when he dismissed them, they crept away like whipped hounds, while the rest of us shook ourselves like dogs coming out of the water and thanked heaven we had not been in the position of poor Maclure.

Peel was not less impressive, though in a different manner, when after his re-election to the Chair in the new Parliament he presented himself before the Lords to receive the royal confirmation of the Commons' choice. The contrast between the dignified humility with which in the time-honoured forms he " submitted himself to Her Majesty's gracious commands " and, when they had been signified, prayed " that if any error should be committed, it may be imputed to me alone and not to Her Majesty's faithful Commons," bowing each time deeply as he spoke, and the lofty tone in which, drawing himself to his full height, he then claimed the Commons' privileges—" freedom of speech, freedom from arrest and freedom of access at all times to Her Majesty " seemed to epitomize history. Every movement, every gesture was intensely dramatic. In truth he was a great actor on an historic stage and he succeeded, as other great actors have done, because he did not merely play a part, but for the time being was that part.

Indeed, so high was his sense of the position to which he had been called while he occupied the Chair, that he thought no occasion too trifling, no pains too great to preserve its dignity. Returning from an Easter recess, I once expressed my hope that he had had a pleasant holiday. He replied that it had not been particularly enjoyable. The fact was, he explained, that as Speaker he could do so little for his constituents at Leamington that when they had asked him to open the new golf course which had been provided as an additional attraction for visitors to the Spa, he had felt bound to accede to their request, though he was no golfer. He had therefore felt obliged to spend the whole of his holiday taking lessons from a professional in order that he might drive the first ball in a manner not unbecoming to the holder of his office and the House of which he was the representative.

Peel owed his original nomination to the Chair to Mr. Gladstone, in whose Government he had been a Junior Whip; but not even Mr. Gladstone could successfully dispute his authority when he had once entered the Chair. "During the struggle which occupied the greater part of the session of 1887," the *Annual Register* recorded when he retired in 1895 after eleven years' service, " Mr. Peel's tact and dignity saved a situation which might easily have plunged the House of Commons into a serious crisis. The attitude of Mr. Gladstone and his colleagues throughout the discussions in Committee on the Irish Crimes Bill of 1887 might have ended in wrecking the authority of the Chair had it been occupied by a less firm or a less wise Speaker." " Without the support of the House," he had said on his re-election in 1892, " a Speaker can do nothing ; with that support *there is little he cannot do.*"

He had proved the truth of his own words. His retirement following so closely on the final withdrawal of Mr. Gladstone from political life marked the close of a parliamentary age.

V

MR. GLADSTONE'S LAST PARLIAMENT

I AM often asked how the House of Commons in recent years compares with the House as I first knew it, more than forty years ago. It is not easy to give a satisfactory answer. Each House of Commons differs from its predecessor and has some special characteristics of its own, though the deep-rooted traditions of the Assembly persist, in spite of even the most violent changes in its composition, and its power of assimilation overcomes in time even the most refractory material. I am inclined to say that in some respects the present House is superior and that the average of ability and knowledge is greater. Certainly the questions which its members are called upon to decide are more intricate and call for more exacting study, but its debates excite less interest among its members and have less influence on the country than in earlier days. More than one factor has combined to produce this result; some are external to the House and beyond its control; others lie in the character of the debates themselves. If the general level of competence is higher, there are fewer outstanding figures. Members take less pains about the form of their speeches and parliamentary oratory is almost a lost art. Above all, the debates have lost that dramatic quality to which they formerly owed so much of their interest, and a vicious habit of reading " speeches " has crept in, largely owing to the fault of the two Front Benches, with the consequence that debates have ceased to be debates and degenerated into the lifeless delivery

75

of written essays. Hartington once yawned in the middle of one of his own speeches. To-day the speaker is often the only member in the House who is not yawning as the steady drone goes on.

Of all the Parliaments in which I have sat—and I am now, I think, in my thirteenth—that of 1892-95 was by far the most exciting. Passion was at fever heat from the very first, parties were very evenly divided, the Government majority was small and the Opposition was determined to use its rights to the uttermost and to give no quarter. When the House met for business in January 1893, the debate on the Address was only concluded by the unusual expedient of a Saturday sitting; that on the introduction (now a purely formal stage) of the Home Rule Bill took five days, and the debate on the Second Reading lasted no fewer than twelve. The later proceedings were in proportion, and the Session itself lasted till within a day or two of the Easter of the following year. " Time," said Lord Randolph Churchill, " is the life-blood of a Government," and the Opposition had decided to bleed the Government to death.

I was appointed junior Whip of our small Liberal Unionist Party, with Harry Anstruther as my chief. The first question that arose was where we were to sit. In the last Parliament our leaders had sat on the front Opposition bench, much to their own discomfort and to the annoyance of the Gladstonian leaders at whom their speeches were constantly directed. My father, who had succeeded Hartington in the leadership on the latter's accession to the peerage a few months earlier, arranged with Harcourt that we should take our places below the gangway on the Opposition side if the Irish would move across the House, but, though they intended to support the Government, they declared that to sit among its supporters would be too compromising and that they must retain their old seats. The Liberal Unionists were, therefore, obliged to seek seats on the Government side, but it was rumoured that the less responsible Gladstonian Liberals meant to refuse the usual courtesy to our leaders and if possible to leave them and us without seats at all. Several members of our Party, therefore, assembled on the first morning, at what was then thought the extraordinarily early hour of six, and effectively occupied the greater part of the third and fourth benches below the gangway on the Government side with our hats—so effectively in fact, that the report spread that I had come down to the House in a four-wheel cab filled with band-boxes, and I was so pictured in caricature! The Government were thus exposed to a crossfire of criticism—from Liberal and Radical Unionists behind them and from the Conservatives in front. It added much to the liveliness of the debates, perhaps also to their bitterness, but it had from our point of view the disadvantage that the leaders of the two wings could not consult in any sudden emergency. It was a lesson in parliamentary art to see how, in spite of this difficulty, Balfour and my father played into one another's hands.

Exactly ten years earlier Mr. Gladstone, complimenting my father on the skill with which he had piloted a complicated Bankruptcy Bill through all its stages, had declared that for himself he might still be of some use in set debate but that he could never conduct a great measure through Committee again. Now, in his eighty-third year, he was triumphantly to refute this self-depreciation. He expounded the provisions of the Home Rule Bill in a speech lasting two and a half hours with scarcely a sign of fatigue; he defended it on second reading at almost equal length and throughout the Committee and Report stages he was always in the forefront of the battle and ever the most skilful of dialecticians. He had at command every resource of the orator except wit. He was occasionally grimly humorous, but if he raised a laugh it was seldom a kindly one. He was pleading and minatory by turns; at one moment he cajoled his hearers, at another he overwhelmed them, and whatever his purpose, he had at his service every resource which art can place at the disposal of native genius. The tones of his voice were rich and varied, his figure full-chested and erect, his gestures free and copious, and nature had given him a magnificent head and "an eye like Mars to threaten or command." " Mr. Gladstone," my father said to me at this time, " is the only man I am afraid to have follow me," and this confession was made when, in the opinion of so experienced a judge as Speaker Peel, my father was " the best speaker in the house with one exception, and the best debater without exception."

It is, I suppose, impossible for anyone now reading his speeches to recapture or even to understand the effect which they produced upon his audiences at the time. Divorced from the personality of the orator and from the moral fervour which he exhaled, those long and involved sentences defy the arts of the printer and exhaust the patience of the student. Yet as they rolled from his lips, each phrase and sub-phrase, each condition and proviso fell easily into place and his followers not only felt that they were listening to the pure milk of the word, but were convinced that they understood him.

Disraeli's speeches live not only by the brilliance of his phrases and the power of his invective, but also by those flashes of insight into the heart of a problem which are as illuminating for us in our difficulties to-day as they were

at the time when they were spoken. In Gladstone's case
there are no such depths of thought and no such prophetic
vision. It might be said of him as Landor makes Romilly
say of Pitt—he, "who could speak fluently three hours
together, . . . came about us like the tide along the
Lancashire sands, always shallow, but always just high
enough to drown us!" He excelled above all in persuading
each man that he had heard what he wanted to hear and
had received the assurance which he sought. "If Mr.
Gladstone had only taken as much trouble that his hearers
should understand exactly what it was that he meant, as
he took trouble afterwards to show that his meaning had
been grossly misunderstood, all might have been well.
As it was, he seemed to be completely satisfied if he could
only show that two propositions, thought by plain men to
be directly contradictory, were all the time capable on
close construction of being presented in perfect harmony."
So wrote his biographer in a phrase which delighted Balfour
as much for what it left unexpressed as for what it said.

Goschen used to relate an experience which illustrates
this trait. As President of the old Poor Law Board in
Gladstone's first administration, he had introduced a local
Government Bill which had shared the fate of so many
ambitious projects and been sacrificed in the "massacre of
the innocents" at the end of the session. Goschen had been
deeply chagrined and had even offered his resignation, but
was persuaded to withdraw it on being promised, as he
thought, the first place for his Bill in the next session.
When the draft of the Queen's speech was submitted to
the Cabinet, he found to his dismay that four or five other
important measures were given precedence. He sought
out the Prime Minister and reproached him. "You can't
do this; you not only promised me first place for my Bill,

but you stated in the House that it would have the first place." Mr. Gladstone demanded to be shown when he had said that. Goschen produced *Hansard* and pointed triumphantly to the words in which Mr. Gladstone had declared that the Bill would be " in the forefront " of the legislative programme of the coming session. " Yes," said Mr. Gladstone, emphasizing his words with outstretched forefinger, " but don't you see that the forefront is *a line, not a point* ! "

Mr. Gladstone had once rather shocked his devotees by describing himself as " an old parliamentary hand." Never did he make a finer display of his parliamentary skill than in this final stage of his public career. In the long and intricate committee discussions on the Home Rule Bill he never missed a point, and it was in vain that ingenious snares were laid to entrap him.

I remember one such incident. Sir Henry James had framed a too ingenious amendment on the supremacy of the Imperial Parliament. If Mr. Gladstone accepted it, the Parnellites would revolt; if he refused it the hollowness of his pretence that that supremacy was maintained would become apparent. The amendment was called at dinner-time. My father, who had been dining every night in the House, believed himself safe for a couple of hours and went off to his Club, telling me that he did not wish to be disturbed. But in less than an hour Akers-Douglas, the Chief Whip, despatched me in a hansom cab to bring him back. Mr. Gladstone had neither refused nor accepted the amendment. He professed his agreement with Sir Henry's purpose, but doubted whether his words were apt to achieve it. He suggested a slight alteration which he thought would better express Sir Henry's meaning. James found himself caught in his own snare. If he accepted

Mr. Gladstone's carefully worded formula there would be no Irish revolt, and he would have admitted that the supreme authority of the Imperial Parliament was now adequately safeguarded. Mr. Gladstone would have scored a triumph. James struggled, but from being the angler he had become the fish and was being slowly but surely brought to the bank. My father hurried back, watched the sport for a few moments and then, following Gladstone's lead, countered with a further amendment just to make the meaning quite plain. And so the merry game went on till the House rose at midnight.

A similar instance of Gladstone's quickness of apprehension occurred in the select committee on the Grants for the Prince of Wales' children. My father had made some proposal which Morley at once vehemently denounced. "Morley is all wrong," said my father to Harcourt, next whom he was seated. "I was trying to help you out of a difficulty." "That's what Mr. G. has just said to me," replied Harcourt.

The duel between my father and Gladstone was constantly renewed. It was indeed a battle of Titans. Each could admire the other's skill; each regarded the other as his most dangerous adversary. We may apply to them the words which F. S. Oliver wrote of Alexander Hamilton: "They never dealt in trivial annoyance. If they wounded, it was not because they desired to hurt, but because their intention was to destroy." "He is the only man except my father whom I always addressed as ' Sir,' " so said my father to me in later years.

But if some measure of restraint was kept in the duels between Gladstone and my father, it was a fight with the gloves off between my father and the Irish. Colonel Saunderson, the witty leader of the Ulster Orangemen, might announce in his richest brogue that "County Cark, Sir, is remarkable for the production of two very marketable commodities—butter and Home-Rule members," and the Nationalists would join in the general laughter and Tim Healy would be content to reply that he would not attempt to "paint the Orange lily." Such a jibe from the member for West Birmingham would not have been so easily forgiven. Tim Healy, not yet mellowed by age and disillusionment, T. P. O'Connor, "the genial ruffian," as a fellow-member described him at the time, Dillon, always a sour spirit, more moved, as it seemed, by hatred of England than love of his own country—these and many lesser men thirsted for his blood. No quarter was asked or given on either side.

Three incidents among many, stand out in my memory. On one occasion my father quoted a violent incitement to outrage from one of Dillon's speeches. Dillon challenged its accuracy and for that once my father had not provided himself with the reference. "I will send the honourable gentleman the reference," he said. "I will reply when the Right Honourable gentleman can produce it," retorted Dillon, and the Liberal and Irish ranks cheered delightedly, believing that this time they had their enemy at their mercy. Some days later in another debate my father recalled the incident. He had sent the reference to Dillon. It was contained in the report of his speech in the *Freeman's Journal*. Dillon had promised to reply: he had not done so. My father now read it again and challenged him directly. Dillon rose in a hushed and expectant House. He now admitted the correctness of the report, but said that the words were spoken in circumstances which might excuse them. He had gone to that meeting fresh from witnessing the massacre at Mitchelstown, where he had seen a peaceful meeting broken

up and blood shed by the police. It was not very
generous of the member for Birmingham to taunt him
with a few rash words—and so forth, amidst the sympathetic murmurs of Liberal Home Rulers. "Austen,"
whispered my father, "get me the date of Mitchelstown.
I know he's lying."

I hurried to the library and searched in feverish haste,
for at any moment Dillon might sit down. Presently a
member found me still searching vainly. "Don't worry,"
he said, "T. W. Russell has given your father the date."
So I returned to the House. A moment afterwards Dillon
resumed his seat and my father rose again. He recalled
how Gladstone had bidden his followers "Remember
Mitchelstown." Dillon had learned the lesson; he had
"remembered Mitchelstown," but he had remembered it
before it had happened! His speech had preceded the riot
at Mitchelstown by nine months. The House rang with
cheers; Dillon's face, always pale, went white; for once
the Irish were silenced. "I ought to have sat down at once.
I was a fool to add another word," my father said to me
afterwards. When he did finish, the debate ended; members
trooped into the lobbies for the division, still buzzing with
excitement. As we moved to the Bar, Gerald Balfour asked
me: "Have you ever seen a man caught cheating at cards
have his hand pinned to the table with a knife?"

"No," said I. "Have you?"

"No, but now I know what he looks like."

In the second incident Healy played the principal part
with a very different result. The House was in Committee
on Morley's Evicted Tenants Bill. "We have heard a
great deal of absentee landlords," said my father, "but this
is a bill to create absentee tenants—men who left Ireland
years ago or their descendants who have never seen Ireland."

Healy rose to reply. He began badly. "Talk about absentee tenants," he exclaimed, "what about absentee landlords. When did a Duke of Devonshire last visit his Irish estates?" "At Easter," interjected Russell. "And before that, how long was it since he had seen them?" "Not since you killed his brother," shouted Russell. It was true. When Lord Frederick Cavendish was murdered in the Phœnix Park the old Duke had extracted a promise from Hartington that he would forgo his annual visit to Lismore. He had lost one son in Ireland; he did not wish to lose another.

Most men, met with such knock-out blows at the opening of a speech, would have stumbled through a few sentences, and sat down in confusion. Not so Healy. He shook himself like a spaniel coming out of the water. In a few moments he was somehow back at the siege of Limerick, describing it with a burning passion that silenced the cheers and counter cheers, and held the House breathless. It was as if the events he was narrating had happened yesterday, and he had come hotfoot from the scene. As he resumed his seat, Balfour rose and, pointing at Morley an accusing finger, exclaimed, "And now, at last, perhaps the Right Honourable gentleman begins to have some glimmering of the depth of the passions he has stirred." Healy had turned disaster into triumph and won a success that perhaps no other man could have secured.

In the third episode my father was again the central figure. It was the incident which led to the fight on the floor of the House. It was the night when the Guillotine, then first applied to any Bill, was to end the Committee stage. My father and Balfour had agreed that to mark the novel character of this violent suppression of free speech the debate should be so arranged that an important amendment should be under discussion as the clock pointed to the hour, and a front bench man be speaking to it. Balfour took the first night. As the Speaker rose to put the question and Balfour was forced to break off and resume his seat, there were angry cries of " shame " and " gag, gag," but nothing worse, though the House was excited and members felt that a parliamentary *coup d'état* had been accomplished.

On the last night it was my father's turn to be the victim of the Guillotine. The matter under discussion was a set of new clauses entirely altering the financial provisions of the Bill as it passed its second reading. My father criticized the new clauses and then recalled how Mr. Gladstone had in like manner boxed the compass on the hotly contested question of the retention of the Irish members at Westminster. In his first Home Rule Bill he had decreed their total exclusion : in the present Bill he had at first proposed that they should be retained for Imperial affairs, but excluded when purely English matters were under discussion. This new plan found favour in no quarter and was riddled with hostile criticism. At the last moment and after much secret lobbying, Mr. G. abandoned it and proposed that the Irish members should be retained for all purposes, but in diminished numbers. What happened is well described by Mr. Garvin :

"July 27th was to be the last of forty-seven sittings in Committee. At ten o'clock the beheading-machine was to begin its final exercises. At a quarter to ten Chamberlain rose from his coign of advantage on the third bench below the gangway. His accents had his peculiarly ominous intonation—the underswell of anger made more contagious by sardonic modulations of voice. Real and pent-up were the passions of that night. Though the Guillotine was

about to descend on masses of undiscussed clauses the dense
tiers of Unionist benches believed to a man that the country
was with them. This view Chamberlain meant to drive
home with blistering mockery. His opponents felt that
his sentences sprayed vitriol.

" We may follow him as far as he got. He gibed—that
the Government by the guillotine procedure had reduced
to a discreditable farce the forms of the Mother of Parliaments. He jeered—that the Ministerialists regarded their
Bill as perfect and unimprovable.

" At this, Roby, an excellent Gladstonian, was misled to
throw in the banal phrase, ' under the circumstances.'
It was notoriously unsafe to interrupt Chamberlain. No
one approached him in seizing upon an interjection to
improvise a satire. Quick as a flash he caught up the word
and sported with it :

" They think that—' under the circumstances ' the proposals cannot be improved. Yes, but they thought the
last scheme was perfect and could not be improved. They
think every scheme as it successively proceeds from the
fertile brain of the Prime Minister is perfect and cannot be
improved—' under the circumstances.' That has been
their attitude with regard to the whole, notwithstanding
the fact that the measure has been changed again and again
in the course of the last few weeks. . . .

" I say this Bill has been changed in its most vital features
and yet it has always been found perfect by the honourable
members behind the Treasury Bench.

" The Prime Minister calls ' black ' and they say ' it is
good '; the Prime Minister calls ' white ' and they say
' it is better.' It is always the voice of a god. Never since
the time of Herod . . .

" It is admitted that his tone and air, as he watched the

clock so as to be sure of putting in as much as possible in a quarter of an hour, were quizzical, not savage; but at the last word—'Herod'—a furious cry broke, not for the first time that summer, from the Irish camp—'Judas!' One more audible sentence, and only one, Chamberlain got in—'Never since the time of Herod has there been such slavish adulation.' Whether he tried to add another syllable never can be known. Typhoon swooped on the House."

A member moved that the words be taken down. The Chairman did not hear the motion or hoped to escape trouble by ignoring it. The hands of the clock pointed to ten. He put the question but his words were unheeded and inaudible amidst the din. Again the member moved, this time seated and with his hat on, that the words of the honourable member for the Scotland division be taken down. Three-quarters of the House remained seated; those who had passed into the division lobbies returned. Logan, the Liberal member for the Harborough division, was seen gesticulating in the middle of the floor and was assailed with shouts of "order! order!" from those nearest to him. "I'll put myself in order," he cried, and forthwith flung himself on the front Opposition bench, falling rather than sitting on the top of Carson. Hayes-Fisher, sitting immediately behind, seized him by the scruff of his neck and propelled him on to the floor. Logan was a big man of the build of the late Colonel John Ward. He fell

> "As falls on Mount Avernus
> A thunder-smitten oak."

One of the Irish, rushing to his support, tripped and fell, knocking off Colonel Saunderson's hat and hitting him a severe blow on the back of his head in his fall. The fight had begun. As Mr. Garvin says, it was more a scuffle than a fight and most of the members involved in it were trying to part the combatants. But it looked worse than it was to the strangers watching this unprecedented violence. " The dread rebuke of hissing from the Gallery helped to recall the House to its senses." Far more potent was the news that the Chairman had done at last what he ought to have done at first—sent for the Speaker. The House awaited his coming in uneasy consciousness of its guilt. He asked the Chairman to tell him what had occurred; the Chairman's account was disputed; the Speaker called angrily on Mr. Gladstone and Balfour to give him the facts. He required and received an apology from T. P. O'Connor. I shall never forget the spectacle of Mr. Gladstone sitting with bowed head and face half hidden by his hands as we once again moved into the division lobbies.

The incident was at an end, but two stories are worth recalling. Mr. Speaker Peel had been unwell. When his doctor called early the next morning, without having opened his daily paper, he found his patient's condition much improved. " I am glad to find you so much better this morning," he said. " That new tonic has given you a fillip." Only later did he discover that it was not his tonic but the row in the House which had restored the Speaker's nerves.

The other story came from Lord Darling, then Mr. Darling, Q.C., the member for Deptford, with whom I was comparing accounts of what we had seen and heard. " Did you hear the hissing in the gallery? " I asked him. " Yes," he said. " It's rather curious. I had two con-stituents up there. I went up afterwards and asked them what they thought of it all. They happened to be two prize-fighters. " We was fair disgusted," they said. "When we saw that fellow let out right and left and no one went down, we was that disgusted that we hissed, we did." Such was the true explanation of the public indignation which loomed so large in the Press next day and finds its echo in Mr. Garvin's pages.

The Parliament maintained its reputation for dramatic surprises to the last. After Mr. Gladstone's retirement in the spring of 1894, the process variously known as " ploughing the sands " or " filling up the cup," continued with diminishing government majorities and little credit to Ministers. The Opposition moved several Votes of Censure, but these only served to rally the divided ranks of the Government's supporters, for no Liberal could afford to absent himself on a day which in advance was marked as critical. The Government, however, were taking Supply on every Friday, then a full parliamentary day. At last my father told me that he had proposed to Balfour that the Unionists should make a special effort to secure the presence of all their supporters, unless they had provided themselves with a " live pair," on these Supply days. " I told him," my father said to me, " that if we could keep our men for a month of Fridays, I would undertake that we should beat the Government. He has agreed and will speak to Akers-Douglas. So now it's up to you and Harry Anstruther to see that our men attend."

The first Friday came.

Campbell-Bannerman, who had with difficulty secured the resignation by the Duke of Cambridge of the post of Commander-in-Chief which he had so long held, was expecting congratulations rather than censure ; but Brodrick (now Lord Midleton) had given notice that he would call attention to the shortage of small-arm ammunition and move a reduction of the vote. The debate proceeded in a comparatively thin House. It was obvious that many of the Liberals were absent. Anstruther and I had succeeded in whipping up all our small party, but the Conservative Whips, with their much larger numbers, had been less successful. Akers-Douglas thought that they had nearly as many absentees as the Government, and I reported to my father during the Division that we had failed.

When, however, the clerk at the table received the numbers from the tellers, he handed the paper with the figures to Akers-Douglas, a sure sign that the Opposition had the majority. The tellers, who were already taking their accustomed places at the table with the Opposition on the Speaker's right and the Government Whips on his left, changed places and a roar of cheering went up from our benches. But the result was so unexpected by Akers-Douglas, that he, generally the coolest and most phlegmatic of men, lost his head. He glanced at the figures, misunderstood them and handed the paper to Tom Ellis, the Government Whip. The tellers again changed places.

The Unionists sat in dismayed silence, whilst the Liberals and Nationalists cheered themselves hoarse. Even as they did so, Ellis, after looking again at the paper, returned it to Douglas, and the tellers changed places once again. By this time everyone was in a state of breathless excitement, and when Douglas read out the figures :

for the reduction . . . 132
against 125

showing a majority of seven against the Government, our pent-up emotions burst forth in a roar of cheering, with difficulty suppressed as the Speaker repeated the figures from the Chair.

The Government, whose majority a few days earlier had dropped to the same figure, when Sir William Harcourt had boldly declared that they would continue as long as they had a majority of one, was too weak to resist even so slight a blow. The Parliament was at an end: ten years of Unionist administration were shortly to begin.

VI

WHEN WAR CAME

THE Great War has been followed by the opening of the archives of all the principal Governments and the publication of their secrets as well as by a mass of biographical material unexampled in any other epoch.

A recent contribution to these revelations is contained in Lord Newton's *Life of Lord Lansdowne*.[1] But Lord Newton has felt it necessary to compress his story within the limits of a single volume, and dismisses the events of the early days of August 1914, in a couple of pages. Lord Newton calls attention to the inadequacy of the late Lord Oxford's reference in his *Memoirs* to the action of the Unionist leaders, and comments on the discrepancy between Lord Lansdowne's note of his conversation with Lord Haldane as to the despatch of the Expeditionary Force and Lord Haldane's subsequent account of his attitude.

But Lord Newton himself has fallen into an error on a matter of historical importance. He writes:

" The acute period of the crisis arrived (as had often been predicted) during a week-end when the various political chiefs were scattered in the country, but, thanks to the energy of the present Lord Lloyd, of General Sir Henry Wilson, and Mr. Maxse, the Unionist leaders were brought hurriedly back to London and at a little meeting late on the Sunday night at Lansdowne House, which was of infinitely greater importance than other gatherings at the same place which have made much more noise in the

---

[1] Macmillan & Co. Ltd.

world, it was decided to offer full support to the Government in the event of war. It was rightly considered that it would be inadvisable to mark as ' Private ' the historic note to the Prime Minister, which was taken by Lord Lansdowne's car to Downing Street on the Monday morning."

There is here confusion between two meetings—one held at Lansdowne House late on the evening of Saturday, August 1st, and another held at Bonar Law's residence early on the following morning, and the delivery of the famous letter to Mr. Asquith is post-dated twenty-four hours at a moment when every hour counted.

In these circumstances it can now do no injury to anyone, and may be useful to the student, that I should publish the record of events which I made at the time. I do not pretend that it is in itself complete—doubtless, much took place of which I was unaware, and some portions of it do not profess to be more than a record of the reports which reached us ; but as far as it relates to facts which were within my own knowledge, it is a contemporary record dictated as to the first part on either the Monday or Tuesday, and continued from day to day. The Memorandum deals with the action of the leaders of Opposition from Saturday, August 1st to Wednesday, August 5th. I copy it textually except where otherwise indicated.

MEMORANDUM

Friday, July 31st, 1914.

I went to Westgate on Friday, July 31st, to join the children, in the confident belief from all that I had heard, publicly or privately, that the Government had made up their minds to support France and Russia in the present troubles.

Saturday, August 1st.

On Saturday, about three o'clock, I received a telegram from Amery saying that owing to serious developments he was coming down to see me and would arrive about five. Owing to a breakdown of his train he only reached Westgate a little before eight. In consequence of what he told me I returned by the next train at 9.37, reaching London about one o'clock a.m. We were met on the platform by George Lloyd, and proceeded to my house. Briefly what they had to tell me was as follows :

George Lloyd had been in communication with Monsieur Cambon.[1] From him he learned that the Government were not supporting France, and were taking no steps in that direction. Monsieur Cambon spoke of the situation as most critical and with great bitterness of the inaction of the British Government. He said : " It is true that you are under no written obligation and there is not a scrap of paper. But there is more. All our plans have been arranged in common. Our General Staffs have consulted. You have seen all our schemes and preparations. Look at our fleet ! Our whole fleet is in the Mediterranean in consequence of our arrangements with you, and our coasts are open to the enemy. *Vous nous avez livré.*" Cambon went on to say that if France and Russia were victorious in this contest, while we stood aside, they would never forgive us. He did not suggest that France would ever join against us, but she would look on at our ruin without a movement of sympathy. Whilst, if France and Russia were beaten, " Well, your condition will be even worse." Then, with a bitter cry, he exclaimed, " Honour ! Does England know what honour is ? "

[1] The French Ambassador.

George Lloyd continued that he had fetched Bonar Law back to town from Wargrave, where he had been staying with Goulding. He had come to the station straight from a meeting at Lansdowne House at which Lansdowne, Bonar Law and Balfour were present. General Henry Wilson had gone with him. The last-named was in despair. Mobilization orders ought already to have been issued, but he could not get any permission to take the most preliminary steps. Wilson and Lloyd had been distressed by their conversation with the leaders at Lansdowne House. Lloyd said Balfour, of course, understands the position, but Bonar Law does not know what it means, and Lansdowne does not seem to understand. I at once said that Lansdowne would obviously appreciate its full meaning—he must have misunderstood him. In any case they had parted without taking any steps, and George Lloyd put it to me that I was the only person who could persuade them to move.

It was now past two o'clock. We parted to go to bed.

Sunday, August 2nd.

Next morning, as a result of telephone communications with Law and Lansdowne, I was at Lansdowne House at 9.15, a quarter of an hour in advance of the time I had fixed, and Lansdowne was not yet down. While waiting for him I hastily wrote a draft letter for despatch by the Unionist leaders to the Prime Minister. The draft (A) was as follows :

" We feel it our duty to declare that, in our opinion, any hesitation in now supporting France and Russia, our intimate friends (with one of whom at least we have for years past concerted naval and military measures affecting gravely her own military and naval dispositions at this moment), would be fatal to the future security of the

United Kingdom; and we offer His Majesty's Government the assurance of the united support of the Opposition in all measures required by England's intervention in the war."

Lansdowne came down at 9.30. I found him as much alive as I was to the perils of the situation, and convinced, like myself, that for England to hang back now was for her to incur indelible disgrace and lasting danger and insecurity. I at once put my proposal (A) before him. He told me that at the close of their meeting last night the Unionist leaders had offered to see Asquith if he desired. They had no answer as yet, and he was reluctant to take any further steps. I argued the matter further with him, urging that it was not a time to wait for the Government, but that he and Law should go down to Downing Street and demand to see the Prime Minister and make him a declaration to the effect of my written statement.

Lansdowne then went to get his breakfast, and while he was at breakfast I drafted (B) as a basis of a further communication to be made verbally to the Prime Minister by the Unionist leaders if in an interview they found that the Government had irrevocably decided not at once to intervene. This was founded on a suggestion made by Henry Wilson to George Lloyd.

B.

" If the Government are found to have definitely decided against the immediate declaration of war, urge (1) that mobilization be at once ordered; and (2) that the Government require from Germany within twenty-four hours a categorical undertaking to respect *in all contingencies* the neutrality of Belgium (or the Low Countries)."

By ten o'clock Lansdowne and I were at Bonar Law's. I repeated my proposal to him, and found him agreed as to the proper policy for this country to pursue, but reluctant, like Lansdowne, to take any further steps unless Asquith invited them to see him. It appeared that on Saturday F. E. Smith[1] had been in communication with Winston Churchill. From him it was learned that the Cabinet was divided, but how much divided could not be exactly stated. Winston and Grey were certainly for fulfilling our national obligations. Asquith was thought also to be in favour, but large numbers of the Cabinet, and probably the majority, were against any action. Winston had invited Bonar Law and F. E. Smith to dine with him and Grey on Sunday night, but Bonar Law had thought that it was undesirable for him to accept this invitation lest he should appear to be intriguing with a section of the Cabinet behind the Prime Minister's back.

I continued to urge my proposal that the leaders should either go down and demand an audience of Asquith or should send him a letter. The Cabinet was to meet at eleven. The matter was urgent. If the communication was made privately to the Prime Minister it could give no excuse to anyone to complain. If the Cabinet were agreed to take the right steps it could be no embarrassment to them, and if there were differences among them it might be proper for those who were ready to act to know the attitude of the Opposition; and here I mentioned that Cambon had told George Lloyd that Grey was pleading the attitude of the Opposition as an excuse for inaction.

It then appeared that Balfour had met Nicolson[2] at

[1] Afterwards Lord Birkenhead.
[2] Sir Arthur Nicolson (afterwards Lord Carnock), Permanent Under-Secretary of State at the Foreign Office.

dinner on Wednesday night; that Nicolson had spoken as if it were a matter of course that we should join in at once with France and Russia, and that thereupon Balfour had very characteristically put the other side of the case, though in fact entirely agreeing with Nicolson: that Nicolson had apparently misunderstood Balfour and reported to Grey Balfour's objections as if they expressed his real mind: that Balfour had become aware of this (on Saturday, I think) and had at once sought an interview with Grey, and, failing to obtain that, had sent a message to Grey's private secretary to explain that he was entirely misunderstood. It also appeared from a telephone message while we were talking that Bob Cecil,[1] having found that Hugh Cecil had written to Winston urging our complete neutrality, had himself written expressing the opposite view and warning Winston that Hugh spoke for no one but himself. Lansdowne and Law seemed to conclude from this that there was no need to do more. I drew the opposite inference, and urged that these were additional reasons for the course which I proposed.

It then appeared that on Saturday Winston had been asked whether there was anything the Opposition could do, and had at that time replied in the negative, and Law put it to me that it would be unwise to do as I proposed if Winston did not wish it. I maintained my opinion; and Law then said that he would try to get into touch with Winston through F. E. Smith on the telephone.

I am not quite clear what exactly followed, as there were two or three interruptions, and I left the room to take a telephone message, but rather suddenly, to my surprise, Law said, "I am not sure that after all Austen is not right. I think we ought to write to the Prime Minister"; and

[1] Lord Robert Cecil.

we there and then agreed on a draft which ran, I think, almost verbally, as follows : [1]

" DEAR MR. ASQUITH,

" Lord Lansdowne and I feel it our duty to inform you that, in our opinion, as well as that of all the colleagues whom we have been able to consult, any hesitation in now supporting France and Russia would be fatal to the honour and to the future security of the United Kingdom, and we offer H.M. Government the assurance of the united support of the Opposition in all measures required by England's intervention in the war."

This was despatched by special messenger to Mr. Asquith, and must have reached him before eleven.

Returning to Egerton Place, I rang up Lloyd and found that he and Amery were together at his house, where I joined them. Lloyd handed to me paper C, information just received by him from the French Embassy.

C.

" Goschen asked Jagow yesterday whether Germany would guarantee not to violate Belgian neutrality. He answered ' No.'

" German Minister in spite of negotiations in Paris at the same time was ' demenaging ' his house preparatory to leaving.

" While Russia and Austria negotiating directly to find satisfactory basis for Serbian difficulty, Germany declares war on Russia. This looks as if it was Germany who was insisting on the war.

" *Private*.—Grey tells Cambon we probably shall not allow an attack on French coasts ; but no assurances as to our attitude if Germany tried to prevent Algerian troops from coming over to France—8000 men will have to come from Algiers."

[1] I have printed the actual text. The version in my memorandum is not exact.

D.

" From George Lloyd at 5.10 that German troops had already crossed the frontier without a declaration of war.

" At 5.45 from Amery:

" ' I have had a message from Wilson that Asquith has allowed him to hold up all the trains that were to have taken Territorials out to camp, except some forty trains which have gone already; having these trains held in readiness means a most important saving of time if mobilization is decided on, and Wilson construes Asquith's consent as a favourable sign as far as it goes.' "

At 9.30 p.m. I joined Lansdowne and Victor Cavendish at Brook's. Having sent a message to Law at the Carlton that we were there he came round with Carson and joined us. Winston had sought and obtained an interview with Balfour in the course of the day, and had talked to him freely about the position. John Burns had resigned, but was holding his resignation over at the Prime Minister's request. The Cabinet were very much divided, and probably a majority of them would go if any action were taken. Meanwhile Winston, acting on his own authority, had mobilized the fleet. As far back as Wednesday all the ships at Portsmouth had proceeded up Channel during the night and had passed through the Channel—" twenty-five miles of ships " was Winston's phrase—without a word having got into the papers on the subject.

At four p.m. Grey had communicated to Cambon that the British Government would not allow the German fleet to act against the French coasts or French shipping in the Channel.

Bonar Law brought with him a communication from Asquith. It was most unsatisfactory. It stated that we were under no obligations to France. He rather inconsistently admitted immediately afterwards that the disposition of the French fleet made it impossible for us to allow the German fleet to attack them in the Channel. It referred us to Mr. Gladstone's declaration, *Hansard* 203, 1887, for the Government's view of the obligations of the Treaty of Guarantee of Belgium. It admitted that it was a British interest not to see France crushed. But the whole document appeared extremely wavering and looked as if the Government were searching for excuses to do nothing. I wrote to Lansdowne that night as follows :

"9, EGERTON PLACE, S.W.,
"*August* 2, 1914,
"11.0 p.m.

" MY DEAR LANSDOWNE,

" With reference to No. 1 of Asquith's memo. to Law (' England is under no obligations express or implied to France '), there recurs to my mind a passage in the account George Lloyd gave to me last night of Cambon's conversation.

" C. said: ' There is no written agreement of any sort or kind. There isn't a scrap of paper. But there is more. Every thing, every act of the last few years gave us the assurance of your support, etc., etc.' And then came a bitter cry: ' Et l'honneur? Est ce que l'Angleterre comprend ce que c'est que l'honneur? '—or some similar words.

" Compare what you said to-night, ' An entente is stronger than an alliance, because it is not defined.'

" Yrs. ever,

"AUSTEN CHAMBERLAIN."

" P.S.—Amery has just been in (11.45), having been at *The Times* and *Morning Post* offices. Both Gwynne and Geoffrey Robinson believe that the Cabinet is stiffening and that the evening meeting was more satisfactory. Harcourt is said to be leading the peace-at-any-price party. Henry Wilson got leave this afternoon or evening to call in all outlying detachments to their regiments. This was refused earlier. Artillery and baggage were moving in Victoria Street as Amery passed through.

" A small crowd was cheering outside the French Embassy as I came home.

" I suggest that you should ask Asquith whether it is true that Germany has refused to pledge itself to observe the neutrality of Belgium.

" I believe German troops are in Luxembourg, but this I think is not new though contrary to the Treaty of 1867 (May 31) article 2 to which we are one of the guarantors."

It was agreed, this time on Law's suggestion, that Lansdowne and he should seek an interview with Asquith, and a message was at once sent to him that night or next morning before the Cabinet. He fixed 10.30 in the morning of Monday, the 3rd.

Monday, August 3rd.

I went to Lansdowne House by appointment at eleven a.m. Arthur Balfour, Lansdowne and Law also present. We were joined a little later by Victor Cavendish and by Salisbury and Bob Cecil, and still later by Walter Long.

Lansdowne and Law had found Asquith very tired and obviously anxious to get rid of them as soon as possible. They had urged upon Asquith that it was inevitable that we should be drawn into the struggle sooner or later, and had pressed him to take part in it with honour and in time instead of waiting till it was too late and we were dishonoured.

It appeared clear that Asquith's memorandum last night

did not represent his real state of mind. He apparently was with Grey and Winston Churchill, but was mainly occupied in trying to preserve as large a portion of his Cabinet as possible.

We heard that Harcourt, Morley, Samuel, Beauchamp, Mackinnon Wood and others were likely to go. Lloyd George's attitude seemed doubtful.

It is noticeable that the *Daily Chronicle* has gone completely round this morning.

Asquith mentioned that Belgium had been offered an *entente* by Germany if she would allow the passage of German troops and had been given till seven o'clock this morning to decide. They asked him, " Is that not a reason for acting at once? " He replied that the Government did not yet know whether the statement was true, but in any case they were agreed that neither on military nor on political grounds ought the Expeditionary Force to be sent at once. When this was reported, Balfour very pertinently asked *when* they had arrived at that decision. It is wholly inconsistent with what we know of their plans at the time of Agadir.

A note from Winston Churchill, handed to Balfour while we were together, explained that Grey had made his announcement about the fleet to the French Ambassador only, and that it had not been communicated to the German Ambassador, who would learn it only from the declaration made this afternoon in the House of Commons. I held up my hands in horror at this slipshod way of conducting affairs, saying : " Suppose the German fleet comes out not knowing of our intentions—is the British Admiral to fire a shot across its bows and order it to go back? "

It appeared the German fleet was already out and its exact whereabouts not known.

I said that Leverton Harris had telephoned to me that Girouard had just been to see him, saying that affairs at the War Office were in some confusion owing to the fact that the Prime Minister had no time for his departmental duties as Secretary of State, and suggesting that Kitchener, who left London at 11.30 this morning, might well be kept and used at the War Office. This idea was taken up, and Balfour sent an immediate note to Winston, then at the Cabinet, asking if it had occurred to the Prime Minister that Kitchener might be more useful in organization at the War Office at this moment than in Egypt. If the Prime Minister approved the idea there would be time to stop Kitchener at Dover.[1]

Tuesday, August 4th.

Milner telephoned me at ten o'clock this morning to ask me if I could join him. I found that he had learned from General Henry Wilson that whilst the Government had at last given the order to mobilize, they had given it in an incomplete form. The full order would be " mobilize and embark." The order actually given was " mobilize." The result of this, according to Wilson, would be that the railway arrangements would be disorganized and that the eventual despatch of an Expeditionary Force would be delayed a further four days. Milner was very anxious that the Opposition should put fresh pressure on the Government. It was not clear what we could do, but he and I proceeded to Lansdowne House, where we discussed the matter with Lansdowne. I left Milner there, joined by Lovat, who had just come from Bonar Law's, and I myself went on to Balfour's. As a result of our

[1] Lord Kitchener was, in fact, stopped at Dover, whither he had motored from Broome Park.

conversation, Balfour agreed to write to Haldane and press the case for the immediate despatch of a 100,000 men, leaving a sufficient nucleus of regular troops in the country.

From Balfour's I went on to Bonar Law's, where I again met Lansdowne. Lansdowne had been convinced by the reasoning of Milner and Lovat and was ready to send a further letter to Asquith. It took some little time to bring Bonar Law to the same conclusion, and it was then too late to convey the letter to Asquith in time to be of any use, as we had been given to understand that the decisive Cabinet would be held at two o'clock.

Wednesday, August 5th.

Yesterday, in the House of Commons, Lloyd George and the Prime Minister asked me to join the Chancellor of the Exchequer in receiving a deputation of traders, bankers and others, to discuss the financial measures which it was necessary to take. We met again at the Treasury this morning and this afternoon, and in the absence of the Chancellor during a portion of the morning's sitting when the Cabinet was meeting, he asked me to take the chair and to continue the business in his absence.

Thursday, August 13th.

We have had some further meetings of the Treasury Committee, notably one to-day, when the Chancellor explained to the representatives of the great accepting houses, to the bankers, and to the traders, his proposals in regard to the purchase of Bills by the Bank of England. He appeared to announce these as a decision already taken by the Treasury in conjunction with the Bank. At a late period of the sitting Lord Mersey protested vehemently against the release of the banks and holders from all liability, but it appeared to me that it was then too late to consider the matter, as the offer had already been made by the Chancellor to the parties concerned and accepted by them. It was undoubtedly more favourable than any of them expected, and I think the Chancellor went too far.

VII

THE FALL OF THE ASQUITH GOVERNMENT
IN DECEMBER 1916

THE future historian of the War years is more likely to complain of a plethora than a dearth of material. The latest additions to the mass which has already accumulated, and continues steadily to grow, is the second volume of Lord Beaverbrook's *Politicians and the Great War*, 1914-1916 and the *Life of Lord Oxford and Asquith*, by Mr. J. A. Spender and Mr. Cyril Asquith. The former book is of extraordinary interest, for Lord Beaverbrook relates events of which he might well exclaim " *pars magna fui* " and he has had at his disposal not only his own contemporary record but all the Bonar Law papers. His intimate relations with Bonar Law, his profound admiration for him, and his desire to win for his memory the high position in the eyes of history and in the hearts of his countrymen, which he believes his due, are the obvious motive of this contribution to the story of the crisis which led to the fall of Asquith's Coalition Government; but he has equally plainly been at pains to try and understand the motives of those from whom he differs, and his judgments of motive at least are generally kindly. He has, however, completely failed to understand the position of the Unionist Ministers with whom I co-operated.

Since I propose here to set out my own account of some of these events, it may be well to begin with a few words

about my personal relations at *that time* with some of the
leading characters in the drama.

For Asquith, as a man, I had warm personal regard and
admiration, and with the foreign policy pursued by Lord
Grey and himself I was in almost complete agreement.
On all the leading questions of domestic policy on the
other hand I had been in sharp conflict with him, and his
handling of the constitutional crisis of 1910 and, more
recently, of the Irish question, had gravely shaken my
confidence in his judgment and power to ride the storm
or even to foresee what lay before him. But at the outbreak of war he had given noble expression to the spirit
and purpose of the nation and contributed powerfully to
its union.

With Bonar Law I had, of course, been much more
intimately associated. I had known him from the moment
that he entered the House of Commons, had admired and
rejoiced at his first successes and growing reputation, and
had looked to him after my father's illness as the most
powerful and convinced advocate of Tariff Reform. This
led me, on Balfour's retirement from the leadership, to
suggest to Walter Long that, as our rival candidatures to
the succession so evenly divided the party at a critical time,
we should both withdraw in Bonar Law's favour. Up to
this time and, indeed, for some time longer, our association
had been particularly close and I think he liked to have,
and placed some reliance, on my advice. But as the Irish
question became more acute and increasingly dominated
the political scene, thrusting Tariff Reform into the background and causing him to drop the fight for the food
taxes, he naturally turned more and more to Sir Edward
Carson, with whose attitude in regard to Ulster he was in
complete and passionate agreement, whilst he probably

thought me lukewarm as I thought him rash and his language dangerous in the mouth of the leader of the Conservative Party, at some stages of the controversy. We thus saw less of one another, and I could not but feel that he had withdrawn some part of his confidence from me; but never, then or thereafter, did such differences of opinion or policy as existed between us weaken our personal friendship or alter what I think I may say was our mutual regard.

With Mr. Lloyd George, on the other hand, I had at that time never been in any closer relations than those which necessarily exist in the lobby or behind the Speaker's Chair between men of opposite parties who are yet obliged to do business together, as he and I had been obliged during the long discussions on his famous budget. I remember saying about that time to some of my colleagues who, by the way, were a good deal shocked by the observation, that if it ever became necessary in some great crisis again to form a " Ministry of all the Talents ", Lloyd George and Winston Churchill were the first two Liberals I should pick; and on being challenged for my reasons, I said that both had courage, imagination and the power to act, and that I had found Lloyd George a good man to do business with, generous in concession where he felt able to concede, and never haggling over details when we had agreed on the main point. This view of him was strengthened when I sat with him on what was known as the Constitutional Conference after King Edward's death in which he showed these qualities in a very high degree. But he had been foremost in the attacks on the honour of my father and other members of my family during the South African War— an offence which I had neither forgotten nor forgiven; there had been both then and later much in his methods of controversy which I intensely disliked and I felt a great distaste for his ways and little confidence in his judgment. I have no doubt that he thought equally poorly of me. It was not till after Bonar Law's retirement in 1921, when I became leader of the Conservative Party in the House of Commons, that any real confidence or regard was established between us. Through the two anxious years which followed, I learned to know him at his best. Whatever mistakes he has made since, I bear witness to his courage and consideration for his Unionist colleagues in the Irish negotiations and his perfect loyalty to me during our two years close association. It is from that time that our friendship dates—a friendship which is independent of all differences of temperament or opinion. But I must repeat that in 1916 when the crisis came I had no reason to like him and did not in fact trust either his judgment or his methods.

At the time of Asquith's fall I was Secretary of State for India, but without a seat on the War Committee, which I attended only when Mesopotamian affairs were under discussion. My record of the events is contained in a private and personal letter which I wrote to the Viceroy of India, Lord Chelmsford, "for your own eye only," and one or two brief letters of comment to my brother. I have tried to confirm my recollections of the attitude taken up by Curzon, Cecil and myself, " the Three C's," as Lord Beaverbrook calls us, and of Walter Long, who acted with us, from other sources, but no reference to these days is to be found in Curzon's or Long's papers, and Lord Cecil was unable to trace two or three letters which he wrote or received.

For some time before the crisis we had all been getting increasingly anxious about the course of the War. The machinery of the large Cabinet of twenty-one members was ill-adapted for effective or rapid decision. The War Committee was hampered by the necessity of obtaining its approval for all large questions of policy whilst the Cabinet itself was saddled with responsibility for decisions which it could not really control. We felt, too, that the Prime Minister failed to direct its discussions or to show the qualities which the Chairman of any Committee, be it the Cabinet or a Board of Guardians, must possess if its discussions are to be business-like. It was not unknown for the Prime Minister to be writing letters while the discussion proceeded, with the result that in a Cabinet so little homogenous and composed of men of different parties so little accustomed to work together, complete confusion prevailed, and when he at last intervened with a statement that, " Now that that is decided, we had better pass on to . . ." there would be a general cry, " But *what* has been decided? " and the discussion would begin all over again. Asquith remained to the last a determined dis-believer in the appointment of a Secretary to the Cabinet and the institution of minutes of Cabinet decisions. After this practice had been introduced by his successor, I re-member that he expressed his surprise at my warm approval of it, declaring that he had never found it necessary and that it was an inroad on established constitutional doctrine and practice. In matters of this kind he was sometimes extremely conservative.

Apart from these general criticisms some of us had felt strongly the delay in enforcing conscription and the sudden announcement of the Derby scheme [1] without previous con-sultation with the Cabinet at the very moment when we believed conscription to have become finally imperative.

[1] For voluntary enlistment by categories.

Some of us, including, I think, Bonar Law, were indeed at that moment meeting Lloyd George in discussion on the steps by which it might be secured and, if we felt that Asquith had been wanting in frankness to his colleagues, it must also be said that we thought that Lloyd George had let us down. So strongly were three of us impressed by the danger of delay that Selborne, Curzon and I only consented to remain in office after an exchange of letters with Asquith in which he definitely pledged himself to propose conscription if the Derby scheme failed to secure all the results expected from it.

Lord Beaverbrook sees in Lord Lansdowne's Memorandum the actual beginning of the crisis which culminated in December, and Lord Crewe, in the Memorandum printed in Asquith's *Memories*, inclines to the same opinion. To Bonar Law and Lloyd George Lansdowne's paper may have appeared as a weakening of the will to victory. It was certainly an accurate and formidable recital of the reports which were pouring into the Cabinet from all their advisers, but the effect on my mind, as on Lord Cecil's who wrote an able rejoinder, was not to persuade me that peace by negotiation was either necessary or possible, but to strengthen my conviction that our methods of conducting war were wholly unsuitable and must be radically revised. It was, indeed, the curse of this war that almost from its outbreak the stakes became so high that no nation could afford to cry forfeit and withdraw from the struggle.

We must then reorganize. When the War Committee was first appointed, I had myself suggested that it should be made the Cabinet and that other Ministers, heads of departments like myself, should work under it, but Asquith would have nothing to do with this proposal, insisting that responsibility must remain with the larger Cabinet, and I do not remember that at that time it received support from any other quarter.

Up to this point there was as far as I know no difference of purpose or attitude between Bonar Law and his Conservative colleagues. The desire to work with Asquith, the idea that the influence which he was supposed to possess with the Liberal, Irish and Labour parties was necessary to national union and the formation of a strong Government, and distrust of Lloyd George and his intentions were common to us all as well as to F. E. Smith, who was not then a member of the Cabinet and formed his views independently. Bonar Law's own attitude is thus summed up by Lord Beaverbrook [November 14th] :

" Bonar Law distrusted Lloyd George and his ambitions. He suspected that Lloyd George's plan of a new executive War Council was not a considered scheme for reorganizing the machinery of war. He suggested it was a scheme for side-stepping Sir William Robertson's authority under the Kitchener-Robertson agreement. In other words, whenever the War Secretary and the C.I.G.S. had a difference about strategy, Lloyd George would carry the matter to his own court of appeal, the War Council, and overrule Robertson there. Finally, the scheme was to exalt Lloyd George at Asquith's expense. This he was quite clearly not prepared to do—at least not without a great deal more thought and argument."

And so said all of us !

But Bonar Law's two most intimate friends and councillors, Carson and Beaverbrook' thought otherwise, and in the end they determined his attitude. Bonar Law had been seriously perturbed by the large following in the Conservative Party which had supported Carson against him a little earlier on some forgotten question about the treatment of German properties in the conquered colonies of West Africa, and he became increasingly restive under Carson's attacks and the response which they called forth from Conservative back-benchers. With all his qualities, Bonar Law had not the power to stand alone, and in the day of battle needed someone to stay up his hands. My first criticism of Lord Beaverbrook's story is that he wholly underrates his own influence with Bonar Law and the part which he himself played in determining Law's action at this and other decisive moments of his career. It is characteristic of Lord Beaverbrook's whole attitude to Bonar Law to represent himself as merely the clarifying medium which enabled Bonar Law to precipitate his own thoughts, and perceive them clearly. No one who ever saw them together, or even reads this book, can accept that account of their relationship.

Beaverbrook, like Carson, was resolved that Asquith must go. During the next few days he was active in the endeavour to bring Carson and Bonar Law into line and to link up Bonar Law with Lloyd George. The result was seen when Bonar Law for the first time summoned a meeting of the Conservative Ministers at his house on Thursday, November 30th.

By this time Bonar Law, Lloyd George and Carson had come to an agreement. Asquith was to retain the Premiership, to preside at the Cabinet and to lead the House of Commons, but all effective power was to be transferred to a War Committee of four, of which Lloyd George was to be chairman, and it was known that the other members were to be Bonar Law himself, Carson and Henderson. Asquith was to have the right to attend when he thought necessary and to refer decisions of the Committee to the Cabinet, but this proviso was plainly a face-saving device, the obvious result of which would be that the Prime

Minister would become a *roi fainéant* with Lloyd George as Mayor of the Palace. And not only would this have been the result, but it was equally plainly the intention of the authors of the scheme.

Bonar Law still [November 30th] desired to keep Asquith as Prime Minister; he still considered the influence which Asquith was supposed to wield indispensable to the creation of a stable government, but he had deeply committed himself to Lloyd George's plan, and his purpose in summoning his colleagues was to win their support for it. All the Unionist members of the Cabinet were present except Balfour, who was confined to his house by illness, and Lansdowne, and all except Bonar Law himself felt the strongest objection to this scheme.

I wrote my letter to the Viceroy on Friday, December 8th, that is three days after Asquith's resignation, which took place on the 5th, and the day before the constitution of the new Government was announced in the Press.

It will be convenient to reproduce that letter at this point of my story.

" *Private and Personal.*

> " INDIA OFFICE,
> " WHITEHALL, S.W.,
> " *8th December* 1916.

" MY DEAR CHELMSFORD,

" In my last letter I undertook to give you some account of the events of the past week or two which resulted in the acute Cabinet crisis and in the resignation of Mr. Asquith's Government. I was unable to accomplish this in time for the last mail and perhaps that is just as well as, subject to the proverbial slip ' twixt the cup and the lip,' I can now carry the story to its end in the formation of a new Government.

" It had been for some time apparent to all of us that the late Government could not continue without some vital reconstruction of that part of the machinery which was specially concerned with the management of the war. Asquith has many virtues. He is a gentleman in the fullest sense of the word. Very pleasant to work with, very loyal to his colleagues, and with a great equanimity in good or evil fortune which is in itself a considerable asset in times like these. He had—or was believed to have—a very considerable influence among that section of the Liberal Party which was most addicted to peace, and in the Labour Party, and this influence has no doubt served throughout the war to keep down pacifist demonstrations and to secure for the Government the support of large bodies of opinion which would have viewed with suspicion, and probably with resentment, any Government which they considered of more naturally bellicose tendency, even though its policy had been exactly the same. On the other hand Asquith lacks the power to drive. Whether he was always deficient in it, or whether the habit of waiting on events and on colleagues has grown upon him in these later years, I cannot say. In any case the result was the same. Any Committee—call it War Council or Cabinet or what you will—is apt to dissolve in talk unless the Chairman keeps them steadily to the point at issue and makes it his business to secure from them a decision on each question as it is raised. Asquith never so understood his duties. He waited on others. He no doubt often averted conflict, but he never contributed a suggestion. He only once in my experience directly helped us to a rapid decision.

" Then, second to Asquith in the Cabinet, we had Lloyd George, a man of great energy and great resolution with quite extraordinary powers of gathering round him men of capacity, but himself uncertain in temper, very emotional, liable to be unduly exalted at one moment and unduly depressed at another; altogether a man in whose judgment I have no great confidence.

116

" Had either of these two been a little different, everything would have been different, and such reconstruction as became necessary, owing to their respective defects and qualities and as grew naturally out of our experience of war conditions, might have been carried out quietly and decently without any cataclysm. But you must take men as they are, and it is no use lamenting that they are not something else.

" About three weeks ago Bonar Law, who, as I think, throughout earnestly sought to keep the peace between them, told the Prime Minister that in his opinion a reconstruction of the Government had become necessary. He made certain proposals with this object in view, to which he had previously obtained the assent of both Carson and Lloyd George; but his Unionist colleagues were not informed of them till later (Thursday, November 30th) and, when so informed, were unanimously of opinion that they were open to grave objection, and made certain alternative proposals. These did not commend themselves to Bonar Law who had, as was evident, committed himself too deeply to Carson and Lloyd George. Lloyd George, towards the middle of last week, presented to Mr. Asquith a proposal which was very much in the nature of an ultimatum; the whole Harmsworth press and the *Morning Post* were mobilized in support of him, and Asquith was bidden to stand and deliver.

" This was the situation on Saturday last (Dec. 2nd). On Sunday (Dec. 3rd) morning the Unionist members of the Cabinet, with the exception of Balfour, who was ill in bed, and Lansdowne, who was in the country, met at Bonar Law's house. The Sunday papers known to be in close relation with Lloyd George announced that he had presented his terms to the Prime Minister; that they had been rejected and that Lloyd George's resignation would appear in Monday's papers. It was obvious that the situation was quite intolerable. Lloyd George was in revolt and the controversy on his side was being carried on in the Press by partial and inaccurate revelations.

Asquith, Grey and Balfour were being openly denounced and told that they must go. No Government could continue to exist on such terms, and since the Prime Minister had failed to assert his authority and to reorganize his administration in time, we thought that the ordinary constitutional practice should be followed and the man who had made the Government impossible should be faced with his responsibilities. If he could form a Government, well and good. If not, he must take his place again as a Member of an Asquith Administration, having learned the limits of his power and deprived thenceforward of the opportunity for intrigue. In any case, power and responsibility must go together and the man who was Prime Minister in name must be also Prime Minister in fact. It seemed to us at that time that the only hope of a stable Government still lay in combining somehow or another in one administration the separate forces represented by both Asquith and Lloyd George. We were all of us of opinion that reconstruction had become necessary. We did not think that with a Parliament constituted like the present, a Unionist Government, or a Government under a Unionist Prime Minister, would have any chance of success. It was not for us to say which of the rival Liberals could secure the greatest amount of support in the Liberal Party and in the Parties which habitually worked with it. But we felt that the continuance of the existing Government had become impossible and that this question must be solved before any stable Government could be formed. Accordingly, we drew up a statement expressing our concurrence with the views expressed by Bonar Law about a fortnight previously, that reconstruction had become inevitable. We added that, in our view, the publicity given to Lloyd George's intentions had rendered internal reconstruction no longer possible, and we advised the Prime Minister that he should tender his own resignation carrying with it that of all his colleagues, and, if he was unable to accept this advice, we requested Bonar Law to hand to him our collective resignation. . . ."

The exact terms of this statement or resolution were:

" We share the view expressed to you by Mr. Bonar Law some time ago that the Government cannot continue as it is.

" It is evident that a change must be made and in our opinion the publicity given to the intentions of Mr. Lloyd George makes reconstruction from within no longer possible.

" We therefore urge the Prime Minister to tender the resignation of the Government.

" If he feels unable to take that step we authorize Mr. Bonar Law to tender our resignations."

My letter continues:

" The Prime Minister, who came up from the country that morning (Sunday), received Bonar Law immediately on his return. What passed at this interview is somewhat obscure. Bonar Law believes that he conveyed our whole mind to the Prime Minister; I have no doubt that he intended to do so, but I doubt if he ever really understood it. In any case it became evident subsequently that the Prime Minister had not at all understood our action which he regarded as a sudden desertion of himself, without warning and without cause, by all his Unionist colleagues. He asked for time to consider his decision and to consult Lloyd George. He invited Bonar Law to see him again after his interview with Lloyd George, and meantime Bonar Law consented not to hand him our resignation. This was comparatively unimportant, but unfortunately he refrained from handing him our resolution, which he had not even read to him. . . ."

This statement is specifically confirmed by Asquith. He says explicitly in his *Memories*: " the resolution (of the Unionist Ministers) was not shown to me." Lord Beaverbrook is wrong in supposing that any one of us then or afterwards charged Bonar Law with bad faith or suspected him of it. We thought that he had blundered. We raised no objection to his holding up the formal presentation of our resignations for the few hours which the Prime Minister asked for consideration, but we felt strongly that the actual words of our resolution should have been communicated to him and a copy informally given to him. The sequel shows that we were right; for lack of this commonplace precaution, misunderstandings followed which could easily have been avoided. Our real complaint was that Bonar Law was acting with Lloyd George and Carson to the exclusion of his Unionist colleagues in the Cabinet, and that we were not properly kept informed of the policy which he was pursuing. On this point we had already become uneasy when he first disclosed to us the direction in which his mind was moving on November 20th, and Long had then (December 2nd, not as printed in *Politicians and the Great War*, " 2.10.16 ") addressed a strong appeal to him in which, after declaring, " I am profoundly anxious about the situation and believe that it must have a very serious effect upon the prosecution of the War," he went on " to implore you to do all you can consistently, of course, with your own convictions, to carry your Unionist colleagues in the Cabinet with you," and concluded, " what I care for is that we should act together, act promptly and use our combined strength to save the country from a grave danger."

My letter to Chelmsford continues :

" In the course of the afternoon Asquith saw Lloyd George, and (I think under the reaction of what he considered our unjustifiable desertion) he accepted Lloyd George's terms—no doubt they were put to him with every consideration, and in as acceptable a form as possible— in regard to the status, functions and number of the War Committee, whilst reserving for further consideration the question of its personnel. Lloyd George had proposed a Committee consisting of Bonar Law, Carson, Henderson and himself. I certainly would not have served under such a Committee nor would Curzon or Cecil. We have little confidence in Bonar Law's judgment and none in his strength of character. Carson was a great disappointment in the three months during which he sat in Asquith's Cabinet. He is an Irish sentimentalist as Lloyd George is a Welsh one. He and Bonar Law would merely have emphasized Lloyd George's failings whilst echoing his views, and these are known to have been at variance more than once with those of the General Staff and Command-in-Chief on questions relating to the larger strategy of the war. It was very proper to include Henderson as a representative of Labour. He is a very good fellow, but on all the larger issues of policy he would have been a cipher. Be that as it may, Asquith hereupon decided not to resign himself but to call for the resignation of all his colleagues and to reconstruct his Ministry, and we were so informed a little before eight (by Bonar Law who had arranged to meet us at F. E. Smith's house) by which time Curzon and Long had left town.

" On Monday (December 4th), however, Asquith changed his mind. This, I think, was due in the main to his finding the substance of Lloyd George's conversation with him in the morning papers and to the fact that it was there universally represented in the Lloyd George press as a complete surrender by the Prime Minister, who was to be left in his position only on condition that the whole conduct of affairs was placed in Lloyd George's hands. Some at least of Asquith's Liberal colleagues, under these circumstances, strongly urged him to reject Lloyd George's terms and to act upon the advice which we Unionists had already given him. By Monday night Asquith had definitely decided to inform Lloyd George that he could not accept his proposals and on Tuesday morning he received Lloyd George's reply [1] which, I need scarcely say, was his resignation, coupled

[1] See *Politicians of the Great War*, p. 262

with a perfunctory promise of support to Asquith's re-constituted Government and a very clear statement that he should proceed to agitate the country against him. Upon this Bonar Law announced that he had definitely decided to throw in his lot with Lloyd George. I have, I think, already said that Bonar Law was acting with Carson and Lloyd George throughout, even to the exclusion of all communication with the Unionist Ministers who were left in complete ignorance of his views till after he had definitely committed himself to these two."

I again interrupt the narrative of the letter to deal with the meeting in my room at the India Office on the morning of the decisive Tuesday. It was composed of Curzon, Cecil, Long and myself, and Lord Beaverbrook gives to the chapter in which he describes it, the title of "The Court Martial." This is simply ludicrous to anyone who knows the facts. I had gone to my office as usual at that time about ten in the morning. A little later, Cecil [1] came in to ask if I had any news; he was followed a few minutes later by Curzon with the same question on his lips, and as the three of us had thus come together accidentally and without premeditation we telephoned to the Local Government Board to ask Long to join us. None of us had heard anything from Bonar Law since Sunday evening. We did not know what he was doing or what the Prime Minister had decided. Our responsibilities were great, and we were profoundly anxious and completely in the dark. The situation was intolerable, and Long agreed to ask Bonar Law to join us, or himself to call a meeting of all his Unionist colleagues at the earliest possible moment that day. Bonar Law fixed four o'clock that afternoon as the time and his room in the Colonial Office as the place for our meeting. I do not think that he conveyed to Long at this interview

[1] Lord Robert Cecil.

at all the impression which Beaverbrook's words suggest. At any rate it was not till three years later, and then by accident, that I learned the unfortunate inferences which Bonar Law had drawn from what was, as I have explained, this unpremeditated meeting in my room. We had no idea of ousting Bonar Law from the leadership; we desired, as Long's letter already quoted shows, to act with him and were only anxious that he should take us into his confidence so that we might speak and act in union.

My letter continues:

" On Tuesday afternoon the Prime Minister sent for Curzon, Bob Cecil and myself."

This is the first and only time the three of us met Asquith during these fateful days. Lord Crewe places this meeting on Monday morning, but Lord Crewe's memorandum was written on December 20th, twelve days farther away from the events than my own; Lord Beaverbrook follows him and states that the Tuesday meeting was our second appointment and that we " simply went over the old ground with reiterated emphasis." I am confident that my letter, written only three days after the meeting, is correct. We only once saw Asquith during these fateful days and that was on this Tuesday afternoon immediately before our four o'clock meeting in Bonar Law's room. The resolution passed at this meeting confirms the fact, for it begins, " Curzon, Cecil and Chamberlain have reported to us the substance of what passed at your meeting with them *this afternoon.* . . ." If the decisive interview had taken place the day before, we could not have failed to mention it. Lord Beaverbrook's mistake about the date invalidates his account of what happened on the Monday.

With this explanation I resume the quotation from my letter:

"On Tuesday afternoon the Prime Minister sent for Curzon, Bob Cecil and myself. He told us the whole story from his point of view, and we explained to him the meaning of our resolution, which he had not previously understood. He put before us the various contingencies in considerable detail, setting forth the pros and cons of the different courses open to us with great fairness. He asked whether we should be prepared to go on with him whilst Lloyd George and Bonar Law resigned. To this we replied that our only object was to secure a Government on such lines and with such a prospect of stability that it might reasonably be expected to be capable of carrying on the war; that in our opinion his Government, weakened by the resignations of Lloyd George and Bonar Law and by all that had gone on during the past weeks, offered no such prospect, and we answered this question therefore with a perfectly definite negative. This was evidently a great blow to him. Had we replied in the affirmative, he would clearly have been prepared to make the attempt and believed that he would have had the support of the great bulk of the Liberal Party and of the Labour and Irish Parties.

"He then asked us what our attitude would be towards Lloyd George if he attempted to form an administration. We replied again that our only object was to get a stable Government capable of conducting the war successfully. We had come under no obligation to Lloyd George, our hands were perfectly free, but we should be prepared to support, to join or to serve under any Government which offered a prospect of fulfilling our conditions. Whether Lloyd George could form such a Government we did not know.

"We told him that in our opinion the co-operation of himself and Lloyd George was really necessary. Bob Cecil had the courage to suggest to him that the finest and biggest thing that he could do would be to offer to serve under Lloyd George; but he would not allow Cecil to develop this idea, which he rejected with indignation and even with scorn.

" On leaving the Prime Minister we joined the rest of our Unionist colleagues in Bonar Law's room whilst the Prime Minister met his Liberal colleagues and Henderson. This time Lansdowne also was with us but Balfour was still confined to his house. After some discussion among ourselves we sent Curzon across to Downing Street with a letter in which we repeated the advice which we had given on Sunday, saying that in our opinion the resignation of the Government had now become absolutely necessary, and that it was imperative that it should take place that day.[1]

" We added that we believed the Prime Minister had come to the same conclusion, but, if this were not the case, we must ask him to act upon our resignations. It appeared that his Liberal colleagues, with some hesitation on the part of Crewe and Henderson, had given him the same advice earlier in the day. He called Curzon into the room where they were assembled, and, after asking a question or two about our attitude and views, informed him and the Liberals that he had decided to tender his resignation. Harcourt tells me that this was the first intimation the Liberal Ministers had of his decision.

" I am told, but I do not know this on trustworthy authority, that either the King did not ask, or Asquith declined to tender advice as to the name of his successor. In any case the King sent for Bonar Law. Feeling that there was a possibility that Asquith might more readily serve under him than under Lloyd George and being still anxious to secure the co-operation of both, Bonar Law did not at once decline. He proceeded forthwith to ascertain that Lloyd George would be willing to serve under him and, having ascertained that, he asked Asquith if he would do the same. He should of course have reversed the order of his visits, gone straight to Asquith from the Palace, asked

[1] The actual terms of this communication were: " C., C. and C. have reported to us the substance of what passed at your meeting with them this afternoon. After full consideration, we are unanimously of opinion that the course which we urged upon you on Sunday is a necessity, and it is imperative that that course should be taken to-day.

" We hope that you have arrived at the same conclusion, but, if this is not so, we are obliged to ask you to accept our resignation."

Asquith if he would serve under Lloyd George, and, on getting a refusal, made an appeal to Asquith to waive all personal considerations and consent to serve under *him*.[1] I think Asquith might have done it. He would have seen that Bonar Law was not a mere tool of Lloyd George and could act independently of him, and it was due to Asquith's position, if he was to be asked to serve under someone else after himself being Prime Minister, that he should be the first person approached by that someone, on receiving the King's Commission. But as Bob says, Bonar Law is an amateur and will always remain one. It is not by any means the only mistake he has made in these negotiations.

"As it was, he appears to have informed Asquith that he had first secured Lloyd George's assent since it would have been useless to invite Asquith if Lloyd George had declined! He was met by Asquith with a resolute refusal. He and Carson, I believe, or he and Lloyd George then proceeded to consult Balfour. I think it was at Balfour's suggestion that a conference was held at the Palace. According to the accounts that I have received of what passed, the proceedings were opened by Balfour who made a strong appeal for unity and offered suggestions for a basis of agreement. Lloyd George expressed his readiness to serve either under Bonar Law or under Balfour if Asquith would do the same, and it was thought by some of those who were present that some impression had been made on Asquith and that he would assent. After consultation, however, with his Liberal colleagues and on their advice, he definitely refused. Bonar Law then resigned his commission and Lloyd George was entrusted with the task of forming a Ministry. He at once asked Balfour, one of the proscribed of the week before, to take the Foreign Office. Balfour replied, 'You are putting a pistol to my head, but in the circumstances I say "Yes."' He had already secured the co-operation of Carson, as I think I told you. Derby was acting with him, but none of the Liberal Cabinet Ministers would give him any support.

---

[1] *i.e.* Bonar Law.

By yesterday afternoon he had secured the support of the Labour Party and he had promises of support from about half the Liberal Party, some eighty of whom, he said would have joined with him in a campaign even against Asquith, whilst another fifty or so—a growing number—who would have supported Asquith if he had attempted to form a Government, were equally prepared to support Lloyd George, if he was the man to whom the task was entrusted.

"At this stage Curzon, Long, Cecil and myself were informed by Bonar Law of the position. We were shortly afterwards invited to see Lloyd George, and having put to him certain questions, and ascertained the position and constitution of the small body to whom the conduct of the war would be entrusted, and received answers to some other pertinent questions, we accepted his invitation to serve in his Government. There was not one of us who would not have been glad to escape from this necessity, but this is not the time when, on grounds of personal convenience, or indeed on any personal grounds whatever, one has a right to refuse such service as one can render to any Government which offers a prospect of the successful conduct of the War, still less to what appears to be the only possible Government of that kind.

"I deeply regret that the relations between Asquith and Lloyd George should have reached a point at which neither could serve under the other. I still more deeply regret, this being so, that Asquith should have definitely refused to serve under anybody. I think that in so doing he lost an opportunity of rendering great service to his country, and showing a magnanimity and public spirit which would have placed him high in public estimation. It was his definite refusal to serve under anyone and his apparent relapse into a state of complacent satisfaction with all the proceedings of the old Government, that definitely decided me—and, I think, my colleagues—that we had no choice but to accept office under Lloyd George. Once this general decision had been taken the two things about which I felt most strongly were, first, that it was necessary to have someone on the War Committee in whose strength and judgment I had sufficient confidence to be satisfied that Military opinion would not be disregarded or overruled in Military questions, and above all in questions of strategy ; and, secondly, that this War Committee, necessarily having all real authority, should itself be in name as well as in fact the Cabinet, and that there should not be a great body of Cabinet Ministers without real influence on the general policy of the war and yet sharing the responsibility for decisions in which they were not consulted and exposed to constant criticism for acts of omission or commission in which they had no part. The former condition was fulfilled by the inclusion of Curzon in the War Committee, and the latter by making the Committee identical with the Cabinet. We pressed Lloyd George to include also Milner, either in addition to or in place of Carson, in this body, but we were told that his addition was impossible because it would necessitate the inclusion of another Liberal —even as it stood there was only one Liberal to three Unionists—and would upset Lloyd George's agreement with the Labour Party, who had been promised one seat in a War Committee of five. As to the substitution of Milner's name for Carson's, Bonar Law who was present at part of our interview, could only say that it was useless to discuss it as Lloyd George was pledged up to the eyes to Carson.

"This long story is for your eye only. I have not, hitherto, given you any similar political gossip, but I expect that at least your curiosity will be gratified by knowing something of the *dessous des cartes*.

"Yrs. very sincerely,

(sd) "AUSTEN CHAMBERLAIN."

"*December* 11*th*.

"P.S.—The list of the new Government is in the papers to-day except for the Under Secretaryships. You will see

that some changes have been made. I am glad to find that
Milner is, after all, a Member of the War Committee whilst
Carson goes to the Admiralty. This new Committee, or
Cabinet, got to work on Saturday, and I hope that we
shall all now settle down to business again. At one stage of
the business, when Lloyd George appeared bent on excluding both Curzon and Milner from the War Committee,
I had clearly made up my mind not to take office. However, *dis aliter visum*. I should have been sorry to leave
unfinished work in which I have been deeply interested.
But I should have been a happier man if I could have
regained my freedom."

A passage from a letter to my brother, written on the
same day as this postscript, supplements it :

"It is amusing to think that part of Lloyd George's
ultimatum to Asquith (the Sunday, or second edition) was
that he must get rid of Balfour, and that he started out
with the intention of turning Curzon off the War Committee
and not putting Milner on!

"I told Curzon on Saturday the 2nd, when I first
learned of Lloyd George's terms and their rejection, that
tho' after the 'Die-hard' business, when I felt his desertion bitterly, I had said that I would not go tiger-
shooting with him again, yet values changed and opinions
had to be reconsidered. I had seen him at work and
learned to appreciate his qualities and I would serve under
the proposed Committee if he were added to it, but not
otherwise.

"I added that I had long held the view that the War
Committee should be the Cabinet, and I would not sit in
a *Cabinet* with *no* power under a War Committee with *all*
the power. I believe I originally stood alone in this view,
which I urged when the old War Committee was formed.
. . . We have got the three things I thought most necessary
for the public service—the inclusion of Curzon and Milner
in the War Committee and the formal constitution of the
War Committee as the Cabinet."

It only remains for me to add, first, that Curzon had no authority from us to tell Asquith that we would not serve under Lloyd George or any man who could form a stable Government, and that the assertion that he did so is not borne out by his letter to Lansdowne recounting the meeting at Bonar Law's on Sunday the 3rd; and, secondly, to repeat my caution that my letter to the Viceroy does not express my final judgment on the men and events of which it treats. There are some phrases and expressions in it which I should revoke to-day, and which may shock some of those who chance to read them. But I have thought it best to print the letter word for word as it was written, while I was still under the immediate influence of the events related, so that there may be no suspicion that I have allowed my account of what I then did or felt to be biased by my subsequent knowledge or feelings.

It is fitting that I should close my story with Asquith's reply to the letter I wrote him when the die was cast. It shows the magnanimity of his mind—never more conspicuous than in the years which followed his resignation.

" 10 DOWNING STREET,
" WHITEHALL, S.W.,
" *Dec.* 6, 1916.

" *Personal.*

" MY DEAR AUSTEN,

" I was much touched by your very kind letter. I have been treated by all my Unionist Colleagues during the last two years with unvarying loyalty, and I owe them a great debt of gratitude for their whole-hearted co-operation in most difficult times.

" None has been more helpful than yourself, and I hope and believe that the relations of real friendship which we have come to form will long outlast the ties of office.

" Yours very sincerely,

" H. H. ASQUITH."

No wonder that men served him gladly.

VIII

CABINET-MAKING AFTER THE WAR

THE small War Cabinet as finally established by Mr. Lloyd George in 1916 was certainly a great improvement on the unmanageable system which it succeeded. It gave a much more energetic direction to the War effort of the nation and its armies, it inspired a new hope and confidence in the country and among its allies. It was, I think, particularly successful where it established something like the dictatorship of one highly competent man, as the present Lord Maclay for Shipping and the late Lord Rhondda for Food, in place of the committees among which the control of these matters had previously been spread.

But the system was not without serious defects of its own. The Cabinet was overwhelmed with work; it was difficult to secure its attention for other aspects of national policy such as the rising problems presented by the Government of India; and though the Cabinet was small and in the last resort the decision rested with half a dozen men, the Cabinet room was often overcrowded with the ministerial representatives of other departments and their officials. In particular, Treasury control of expenditure, always most difficult in war-time, when everything else must be subordinated to the successful conduct of operations, became practically non-existent.

The Chancellor of the Exchequer had no time for anything except the highest problems of finance and was obliged to leave to Lord Chalmers, who was recalled to the Treasury, the duty of defending before the War Cabinet the interests in its charge, whilst in 1917 Lord Buckmaster and I, then both out of office, with Mr. Keynes as representative of the Treasury, were appointed a committee to control the dollar expenditure of all departments, which was causing anxiety both to the British and United States Governments, and to present the British case to an " Inter-allied Commission of Purchases and Finance " which was presided over by Mr. Crosby, ably assisted by Mr. Paul Cravath. It is pleasant to recall that Mr. Crosby asked for a memorandum on the way in which the British case was prepared, as our demands were found to be proportionately much more moderate and our estimates more trustworthy than those of the other Allies. I do not remember that we ever had an indent passed by us rejected, or even reduced, by the Commission, or refused by the United States Government.

It was obvious, in these circumstances, that when peace was made the problems of post-war finance would be among the gravest of those which would confront the Government of the day, and that the task of the Chancellor of the Exchequer would be at least as difficult as that of any of his colleagues, for, apart from the huge debt, internal and external, created during the War, war charges would remain long after war had ceased, the normal control of the Treasury over the expenditure of other departments would not be easy to re-establish, and the Chancellor would be forced to maintain taxation at the War level when in every quarter the taxpayer would be expecting and clamouring for relief. Obviously he would need in a very special degree all the authority with which his office could be invested and, in more than the usual measure, the confidence and support of the Prime Minister.

It was in such circumstances that on the morning of
Friday, January 10th, 1919, I received from the Prime
Minister, then in course of reorganizing his Government
after the General Election, a letter saying that he had
submitted my name to the King for the office of Chancellor
of the Exchequer and that His Majesty had been pleased
to approve the nomination. The letter seemed to me
unnecessarily curt in the form of its announcement that
Bonar Law would continue to occupy the house usually
allotted to the Chancellor of the Exchequer and in the
terms of the offer itself. It requested a very early reply
as Mr. Lloyd George desired to have the matter settled at
once as he was leaving that day for Paris. For the rest it
contained a very sensible proposal that instead of bringing
all Treasury disputes direct to the Cabinet they should be
taken to a small committee consisting of the Prime Minister,
Bonar Law, the Chancellor of the Exchequer and another
colleague, like Lord Milner.

On receipt of this letter I called on Bonar Law. I told
him that, as he was aware, I had no desire to return to the
Treasury and that the stipulation about the house removed
the one amenity which lent any attraction to the office.
He replied, very stiffly, that his occupation of that house
was a *sine qua non* with him—that he could not do his work
as leader of the House unless he had the facility of access
to the Prime Minister, which the occupation of No. 11
gave to him.

We had a rather stormy conversation. In fact we both
lost our tempers for the first and last time in our long
friendship, but the breach was healed by some kindly
words from Bonar Law the same afternoon and left no
scar on our relations.

As I was leaving he asked me what I proposed to do.

I told him that I proposed to consult my wife and that my inclination was, if she was prepared for such a course, to refuse the offer.

He suggested that I should in any case see the Prime Minister; and I replied that that would certainly be necessary if I did not refuse outright.

As I was leaving he overtook me in the passage, and added that perhaps in saying what he was going to say, he was not quite loyal to his Chief, but that he thought that I might fairly insist, if I took office, that it should carry with it a seat in the Cabinet.

"Do you mean," I said, "that the offer does not carry Cabinet rank? In that case I will not look at it for a moment"; and he replied that he did not know what the Prime Minister's intentions were—I must ask him.

After consulting my wife, I decided that in view of the strong reasons which there were for the retention of the Downing Street house by Bonar Law, I could not make that a ground of refusal, that I would see the Prime Minister, and that my answer should depend upon what he might say to me.

I accordingly called upon the Prime Minister by appointment at 2.15. I began by saying that I thought it better to speak plainly, and he asked me to do so. I then said that Bonar Law had probably told him—and in any case it was the fact—that I had never wished to go back to the Chancellorship of the Exchequer.

He said that he was not surprised at it; for though, as I knew, he had expressly stipulated when he went to the Ministry of Munitions that he was to have the right to return to the Chancellorship whenever he wished, he had quickly made up his mind that nothing would ever induce him to go back.

I said, "Then you will not be surprised that the office has no attractions for me. You have offered it to me in what I must consider a very curt manner at the very last moment—very much as you would throw a bone to a dog. I must say that I am not particularly flattered."

He interrupted me to say that he had come to town on Monday intending to see his colleagues personally, but his time had been so occupied on Tuesday and Wednesday with urgent problems of demobilization that he had had no opportunity of seeing any of them; and probably the others felt very much as I did. He was very sorry but it had been unavoidable.

I accepted this explanation and passed on to say that in offering me the office he had informed me that he proposed that Bonar Law should retain the Chancellor of the Exchequer's house. This, I said, was the one amenity of the office which for me had some attractions—owing to its proximity both to the office and to the House of Commons, and still more for the facility which it gave of constant and easy access to the Prime Minister, who was himself First Lord of the Treasury.

The Prime Minister here said that he understood my feelings, but that it really was impossible to carry on the arrangement by which the leadership of the House was held as a separate office on any other terms.

I replied that I appreciated the cogency of this argument—I made no complaint of the arrangement, though I thought it might have been expressed with more courtesy to me. But that brought me to the first condition of my possible acceptance. As I had said, the occupation of No. 11 placed the Chancellor in close proximity to the Prime Minister and afforded him the means of ready access to him at all times. Since I had rejoined Lloyd George's Government I had only once seen him outside Cabinet.

He interrupted me to say how much he regretted that he had not been able to see more of his colleagues, but his day's work had never begun later than seven—often at six—and lasted till ten at night. Even his meals were business meals: that very morning he had had people to breakfast and lunch to discuss business for whom he had been unable to find any other appointment, since his whole morning had been taken up by a deputation through which he hoped he had averted a railway strike.

Again accepting this explanation, I said that the office of Chancellor of the Exchequer was at all times a difficult one—that Bonar Law had told me that morning that he thought the situation at the present moment more difficult than it had been at any time while he had held the office. Even in ordinary circumstances the Chancellor was necessarily often involved in contention (even if it were friendly contention) with the Heads of other great Departments, and his position would be quite intolerable and indeed impossible, if he did not possess the confidence of the Prime Minister and receive his loyal support. Such support was naturally doubly necessary in times of such difficulty as the present.

The Prime Minister entirely agreed with my statement of fact and incidentally observed that Asquith had always given him that kind of support when he was the Chancellor of the Exchequer—" though not," he added, " when I was Minister of Munitions," and he interjected that he thought that that was the fault of McKenna, to whom Asquith's fall was due. As to the support for which I asked, his answer depended upon whether we were agreed about certain lines of policy.

I said at once that I recognized that the old Gladstonian Treasury tradition was quite unsuited to the moment—that we had got to take a much larger view of our responsibility; when I asked for his support I did not mean that he was to pledge himself always to be of my opinion, but that I must be assured that he gave me his confidence and that he intended to help me. I added that I recognized such a pledge could not be put into any tight form—no words of either of us could bind him in the future. The whole value of the assurance would depend upon the spirit in which it was given.

He then said that he agreed that a new tradition would have to be established at the Treasury. He thought that there would have to be considerable changes in the staff. The men at the top were clever men, but they were only the more powerfully obstructive for their cleverness. They were steeped in the Cobden-Gladstone doctrines of the *laisser-faire* school and that was not suited to these days. In his view there were four large policies with which we must proceed. The first was Housing; the second was the development of our Imperial Possessions; the third, Communications; and the fourth, Land Settlement. Did I agree with him as to the necessity for these measures?

I replied that I entirely agreed about Housing, and that unless we could make a really large effective start with it before the close of the new Parliament, we should be confronted with a wave of Bolshevism. I regarded it as a necessary measure for social security. As regards Empire development, that was (as he himself had indeed stated) my father's policy. I had what I might call an hereditary interest in it and I should be glad to do all I could to forward it. As to the other two, I agreed, subject, however, to the character of the financial situation which I might find on taking office and the possibility of obtaining the necessary funds. What the financial situation was, of course, I did not yet know. I could say nothing about it until I had got into the Treasury except to recall Bonar Law's description of its gravity, which I had already quoted.

He accepted this statement as perfectly satisfactory.

After some further conversation about the organization and staffing of the Treasury itself, I put my second condition to him. This was that whatever Cabinet be formed, large or small, the Chancellor of the Exchequer should be a member of it.

At this he pulled a wry face and said that was a difficulty. He had some ideas about an Imperial Cabinet and a Home Cabinet. He believed that Milner had communicated some similar plan to Bonar Law, but he had not had time to see it or to work out his own ideas. If he brought me into the Cabinet, he would have to bring in others—Long, Churchill, other Secretaries of State, etc.

I replied that I was sorry to make trouble and that no doubt he could find others who would take the Chancellorship of the Exchequer without a position in the Cabinet, but in my opinion nobody ought to do so, for he would never have sufficient authority for his very difficult and delicate task. I suggested that perhaps he would like to think the matter over and that I had better leave him to do so. If he decided against my contention, I would ask him to take my answer as a refusal.

He, however, preferred to continue the discussion. He asked how could there be a Cabinet at home when the Prime Minister, Bonar Law and the Foreign Secretary were all in Paris. They must to a large extent be plenipotentiaries—they could not be constantly referring to a Cabinet at home for instructions. His idea had been not to appoint any Cabinet.

I then inquired who would be responsible in his absence—who would be in a position to summon a meeting of Ministers if one was required—or to take decisions?

" Ah there ! " he said, " that is what the King asked. He is very gravely disturbed. I told him that I was prepared to support any decision which Bonar Law took."

" But," said I, " Bonar Law says that he is going to Paris with you as one of the Peace Delegates."

" Yes," said the Prime Minister ; " he insisted that his party would not understand it if he were not included in the Delegation."

I replied that I thought that Bonar Law was quite wrong—that his business was to stay behind to preside over the Cabinet in the Prime Minister's absence and to take urgent decisions on his behalf.

The Prime Minister then sent for Bonar Law and reported to him the purport of our conversation.

Bonar Law replied that he was determined to go to Paris but that he did not expect to stay there more than a few days—very probably he might be recalled on Monday or Tuesday. He had intended to conduct the business by personal conference with individual Ministers or groups of Ministers.

I said that I doubted whether this would be acceptable to any of the Ministers or whether they would stand it. In any case it seemed to me an unworkable and unsound arrangement and I could not be a party to it.

We then went backwards and forwards over the old ground—Bonar Law feebly sympathizing with my claim that the Chancellor ought to be included.

The Prime Minister repeated that he could not do this without including others, and again went through his list; to which Bonar Law retorted, " that means a Cabinet of fifteen—and that is impossible ! "

At this point I again offered to leave them to discuss the matter together, saying that if they decided against me, my answer might be taken as a refusal. Once again we went over very much the same ground. At last I observed that I myself did not believe that the Prime Minister could limit his Cabinet to ten members. I saw no great objection to fifteen, and raised none to the inclusion of the other people whom he had named; but that if he was not prepared for this step, it seemed to me that it would be possible for him to say, without raising difficulties, that the Chancellor of the Exchequer would continue to be a member of the War Cabinet as the holder of that office always had been. In recent times (though I thought it a mistake) the Heads of the fighting services and Foreign Office had not been members of the War Cabinet. He would, therefore, not be bringing in a new official.

He and Bonar Law at once replied that Bonar Law had sat in the War Cabinet not as Chancellor of the Exchequer, but as leader of the party and leader of the House.

I replied that the public would not make that distinction; I thought that, if the Chancellor were not in the Cabinet, it would be considered that the office was being placed in a position of unprecedented inferiority, and I repeated that I could not accept it on those terms.

Bonar Law then made the suggestion that the *personnel* of the old War Cabinet should continue unaltered: that this would mean that I should be a member of the War Cabinet—though I should not be specifically appointed to it as Chancellor of the Exchequer: this arrangement to continue at any rate until the Prime Minister returned from France and was able to make his final dispositions.

"Well," asked the Prime Minister, "will you accept that?"

I said, "Yes—on its being clearly understood between us that if at any time you form a Cabinet—big or small—without including the Chancellor of the Exchequer, I shall resign, and that you will not have any cause of complaint on my doing so."

"Very well," said the Prime Minister, "then we will try that," and thereupon the interview ended.

This arrangement was maintained in theory at least for some ten months. Only in the late autumn was the Cabinet reformed on the pre-war model, but in fact the principal Ministers, whether nominally members of the Cabinet or not, habitually attended its meetings on all important occasions and took part in its discussions, but constitutionally they had no responsibility for them. I do not think the plan had anything to recommend it. It would have been far better to form a representative Cabinet at once.

It is curious, as I re-read the notes which I made at the time of this conversation, to reflect that the project of two Cabinets—one for Imperial and the other for Home Affairs—to which both Bonar Law and the Prime Minister seem to have inclined at this moment, was but a revival in a different form of the project for a War Committee and a Home Affairs Committee put forward by the other Unionist Ministers during the negotiations which preceded the fall of Asquith's Government, and then so vehemently opposed by both Bonar Law and Lloyd George. The whirligig of Time brings its revenges. Looking back, I am clear in my own mind that it was well for the country that it was rejected on both occasions.

But if this inversion of our respective rôles is curious, it is still stranger to find not only Lloyd George who, at that moment, had certainly some excuse for taking an exaggerated view of his position, but also a man generally so sober in judgment and so little inclined to exalt his own position as Bonar Law, actually proposing to govern without a Cabinet and only to summon to their councils as and when they pleased such other Ministers as they thought necessary.

The War had, indeed, come near to upsetting the Constitution when it could be proposed by the Leader of the Tory Party to place England under a Duumvirate.

IX

THE SIGNATURE OF THE IRISH TREATY

THE Irish Treaty is little more than a dozen years old. It was signed on December 5th, 1921. Yet of the men who signed it four have already passed away. Arthur Griffith, leader of the Irish Delegation, died within a few months, worn out by toil and suffering. Michael Collins was murdered during the troubles which followed upon the establishment of the Free State and the withdrawal of the British forces.

Birkenhead and Worthington-Evans lived some years longer, and passed away in peace, but they, too, died midway in their careers, leaving to their friends not only the memory of fine service faithfully performed, but lasting regret for the work they might still have done had their lives been spared to the allotted span.

Birkenhead played a vital part in the negotiation of the agreement, upon which I could never have entered without his aid. I well remember a morning soon after the first opening of communications with Mr. de Valera, when Birkenhead walked into my room in Downing Street just as I was telephoning to say that I must see him.

" You and I," he said, " bear a great load of responsibility. Unless we are agreed, we shall smash the party and destroy any chance of settlement. It is time we each knew exactly where the other stands."

And then he proceed to explain his views with that clarity and brevity which always distinguished him in

144

council. I found that he had come to say to me what I had meant to say to him, and thenceforth we co-operated without a shade of difference throughout the long negotiations, the many conferences, and the parliamentary struggle which followed.

To the public Birkenhead sometimes showed himself cynical, flippant and violent. To his colleagues in any time of difficulty or crisis he was a tower of strength—the most loyal and unselfish of friends, careless for himself but careful for them; gay and light-hearted in moments of ease; serious, cool-headed and with nerves of steel in time of stress and danger. The very fact that life was to him a gallant adventure, to be as gallantly encountered, created a link between him and Michael Collins without which we might never have reached agreement.

Arthur Griffith and Michael Collins were the outstanding figures among the Irish Delegation. United in their passionate love of Ireland, in all else they were as different as two men can be—Griffith, small, quiet, drab, almost insignificant in appearance, with the air of a tired scholar worn out by too much burning of the midnight oil; Collins, tall of stature, with swaggering gait, loud voice and noisy laughter, a figure that seemed to belong to the open spaces and the rough life of frontier settlements or mining camps.

What exact part Collins played in the murderous outrages of those troubled times, I do not know. There had been a price set on his own head, and he would have met with short shrift had he fallen into the hands of those who sought his capture. He bore us no malice for it; to him it was the fortune of war.

He told with humour the story of his narrow escapes,

and at such moments was the spirit of Irish recklessness and fun.

The fighting and its grim accompaniment of murder and arson were to him but incidents in the battle for freedom. He held the lives of his enemies as cheaply as he held his own.

He had his own code of honour, and to it he was true; but it was not mine, and between him and me there could be no real sympathy, and perhaps only partial understanding. It was not the least of Birkenhead's services in the Conference that he did enter into Michael Collins's mind, won his sympathy and secured his confidence.

To Arthur Griffith all this bloodshed was abhorrent. There was nothing of the swashbuckler or corner-boy about him. He had been a student of history and politics, and—if I mistake not—at one time a college lecturer.

He had thought that he could find a model for the future relations of Ireland and Great Britain in some modification of the constitution of the Austro-Hungarian Empire, and had published a thoughtful book in which he examined this possibility. But the Great War had intervened, the union of Austria and Hungary had been dissolved, and he had in the main ceased to regard their former relationship as a suitable model on which to base the future Irish settlement.

Some new solution had to be worked out, and he was ready, and even eager, to consider calmly and dispassionately any scheme which, whilst recognizing the national status of Ireland and securing freedom from British interference in its internal affairs, would continue its association with the British Empire and give peace to its distracted people.

He had, I think, no hatred of England in his heart; he was ready, as so few Irishmen are, to forget and, therefore, to forgive, and though he stood firmly by what he conceived to be the rights of Irish nationhood, he was broadminded enough to understand, and within those limits to endeavour to meet the British point of view.

Differing as the two men did in outward appearance, in their outlook on life, in their previous training and in the methods by which they pursued their ends, they were united in their devotion to their country's cause and in their desire for peace.

Collins, for all his spirit of recklessness and devil-may-care ways, was not without a sense of realities.

In the hard school of experience he had been forced to recognize that, whilst he could continue the fight and inflict infinite trouble and loss on England and her friends, there could be but one end to the struggle if England persisted : and that, even if wearied of so much bloodshed and of so thankless a task, she finally abandoned the struggle, Ireland's ruin would have been accomplished before that end was reached.

In the offer of the British Government, if sincerely meant and loyally pursued, they saw the opportunity to realize all that was essential in their aims and to save their native land from anarchy and destruction. Collins, no less than Griffith, desired peace.

Far different was that dark spirit who accompanied them and their colleagues as secretary of the Irish Delegation. Erskine Childers was the nephew of a Cabinet Minister,[1] who in Mr. Gladstone's Governments had been successively First Lord of the Admiralty, Chancellor of the Exchequer, and Secretary of State for War.

He had become known before the Great War as the author of that brilliant story, *The Riddle of the Sands*, and in the War itself he had fought gallantly in the British Air

---

[1] The Rt. Hon. Hugh Childers.

Force. Thereafter—exactly how or why I will not speculate —he had thrown himself into the Sinn Fein cause, and, as is apt to be the way with converts, his new faith burned with the intensest flame. Here was no will for peace, no desire for conciliation.

Erskine Childers's love for England had turned to inextinguishable hate. Once again the old adage was illustrated in his person; he had become more Irish than the Irish themselves. I see him sitting with his back to the window behind Arthur Griffith's chair, aloof and hostile.

Is it a mere trick of fancy that when I try to conjure up his features, his face is always in shadow—as dark as the thoughts behind it? He, too, met a tragic fate as a rebel against the Free State which issued from the Conference.

This is no place to write the history of the Conference. It dragged on for weeks; more than once it was on the brink of disaster. Its first sitting was held on October 11th; the end did not come till December 5th.

On that day we sat morning and afternoon and late into the night. The Ulster Parliament was to meet the next day, and Mr. Lloyd George, the Prime Minister, had promised Sir James Craig, now Lord Craigavon, that he should know the result of the Conference before the opening of its session.

Yet we seemed as far from agreement as ever; indeed, the prospect of any agreement seemed to have receded since we last met. All the old questions were reopened; the Irish delegates appeared to have gone back on the decisions already reached. The Conference adjourned for lunch.

Once again the chance of settlement seemed likely to be shipwrecked on the position of Ulster.

Time was passing. It was already evident that the messenger to Sir James Craig would be unable to catch the boat train, and special arrangements were made for his journey.

Then Mr. Lloyd George appealed to Arthur Griffith, reminding him that he had undertaken that, if we consented to such a provision for Ulster as we now offered to him, he would not let us down.

Griffith answered, simply, "I said I would not let you down on that, and I won't."

Again the discussion was resumed, and roamed over many points. At last the Prime Minister put the decisive question: Were they prepared to stand by the agreement as now drawn?

Griffith replied that he was, but he still spoke only for himself.

That, said the Prime Minister, was not enough; if we signed, we should sign as a delegation and stake the life of the Government on our signature. Was the Irish Delegation prepared to do the same?

"I have to communicate with Sir James Craig to-night. Here are the alternative letters which I have prepared, one enclosing the Articles of Agreement reached by His Majesty's Government and yourselves, and the other saying that the Sinn Fein representatives refuse the oath of allegiance and refuse to come within the Empire.

"If I send this letter, it is war—and war within three days! Which letter am I to send?"

And he concluded with a passionate appeal to them to think again before they rejected so generous a settlement.

It was now nearly eight o'clock. The Conference adjourned to meet again at ten. It was 11.20 before the Irish delegates returned; what struggles had passed within the Delegation during those hours we could only conjecture, but the atmosphere had changed.

Some explanations were asked and given; the meaning of some passages was made clearer.

The Prime Minister thereupon asked whether, if these changes were accepted by the British Government, the Irish representatives " would sign as a delegation and recommend the agreement with their united strength to the Dail."

This time Griffith replied, in the name of them all, that they would.

" Then," said the Prime Minister, " we accept."

When all had signed and copies of the document had been exchanged between the two parties, we moved down our side of the table as the Irish representatives rose to leave, and shook hands with them for the first time, expressing our hope that we might together have laid the foundation of a permanent understanding and lasting friendship between our two peoples.

A braver man than Arthur Griffith I have never met.

Here is a problem for the psychologist. The day had been one of unrelieved strain. The tension reached its height during the long wait for the return of the Irish delegates in the evening. Peace or war—the issue still hung in the balance.

But there is a limit to human endurance; the reaction came. I recall that as we waited, our talk was of the merriest, and the room rang with laughter.

THE TREATY OF LOCARNO
BRITAIN'S GUARANTEE

THE people of this country are being invited in certain quarters to repudiate the Treaty of Locarno. The invitation is addressed to them in the name of Peace: Locarno, it is said, places the direction of British policy in the hands of France and our army and navy at the service of French policy.

It involves us—so the argument goes—in quarrels in which Britain has no conceivable interest, and exposes us to dangers from which, but for this unhappy entanglement, we should be completely immune.

The integrity of France or Belgium, it is urged, is no concern of ours; we are not interested in the existence of the demilitarized zone; we will not stir a finger to save the Polish Corridor. These are not British interests, yet for each and all of these the Treaty of Locarno would oblige us to fight. Thus our new Mentor in article and speech.

Before examining these assertions, it may be well to recall briefly the circumstances which gave rise to the series of treaties negotiated at Locarno in October 1925, and signed two months later in London, after being submitted to and approved by the Parliaments of all the countries concerned in them.

When the representatives of the Allied and Associated Powers met in Paris at the conclusion of the War to draw up the terms of peace, France, which had been twice invaded within the lifetime of them all, one-third of whose territory had been occupied and devastated by the enemy, and whose manhood had been decimated in the struggle, demanded the left bank of the Rhine as security for the future.

The representatives of Britain and America, determined not to create a new " Alsace-Lorraine," rejected this demand, but after prolonged negotiation offered France a treaty of guarantee as the price of her relinquishing it. The British Parliament approved the guarantee, but made their acceptance of it dependent on the approval of the United States. The American Congress refused its approval, and the guarantee therefore failed.

France, which had abandoned one form of security on promise of another, found herself without either. She was thrown back on such support as she could secure elsewhere.

Her Treaties of Alliance with Poland and Czechoslovakia were the immediate result.

There followed four years of irritating and embittering friction between the Allies and Germany. The Peace Treaties were signed, but peace found no place in the minds and hearts of men or in the policy of States. Some of the conditions imposed by the victors on the vanquished were inexecutable and remained unexecuted.

Knowing that they could not discharge their liabilities in full, and fearing that anything they did would be construed only as evidence that they could do more, the Germans made no real effort to satisfy even the reasonable demands of the Allies. Refusal was followed by sanctions, sanctions by further resistance, and that resistance by still heavier sanctions.

Peace rested, not on good will or assent, but solely on the incapacity of the vanquished to renew the struggle.

Some day the wheel of fotune would turn. It would be possible for Germany to find an ally, and on that day, embittered by suffering, provoked by constant interference, seeing no other hope, however desperate the throw, she would stake all on a new gamble, and Europe would be faced with another and yet more appalling Armageddon.

This was the prospect which faced Mr. Baldwin's second Administration when it took office in 1924, but it is not to be supposed that there had been no previous effort to avert it.

In the endeavour to allay the fears and suspicions which were poisoning international relations and deflecting national policies, Mr. Lloyd George had reverted in 1922 to the idea of a treaty of guarantee, but in the then prevailing relations of France and England the idea was still-born. Next year the Assembly of the League of Nations elaborated a Treaty of Mutual Assistance in the framing of which Lord Cecil took a great part.

Lord Cecil, I think, at that moment represented the Government of the Union of South Africa presided over by General Smuts, but at Geneva he was generally regarded as expressing the mind of Great Britain.

Nevertheless, that Treaty was rejected by the Labour Government, which had succeeded Mr. Baldwin's, on the double ground that it would not, in fact, produce security, and that its acceptance would impose intolerable burdens on this country. The Dominion Governments equally rejected it.

In view of this rejection, the Assembly of 1924 set to work to devise a new scheme which might give the sense of security that was the necessary preliminary to any measure of disarmament by States which felt themselves threatened.

This time the " gaps " in the Covenant were to be filled

up; the aggressor was to be defined; every possible contingency was to be foreseen and provided for in advance and the obligations of the signatories were to be exactly stated. When the emergency arose, a majority of the Council would determine for every country what action it was its duty to take.

> " Theirs not to reason why;
> Theirs but to do or die."

The rest would follow automatically.

These proposals were embodied in a Protocol for the Pacific Settlement of International Disputes, usually referred to as the Protocol of Geneva. It was approved by the Assembly, at which the United Kingdom was represented by Mr. Henderson and Lord Parmoor, but before it could be considered by the Labour Government that Government was defeated and replaced by Mr. Baldwin's second Administration.

It fell, therefore, to Mr. Baldwin and his colleagues to determine the attitude of this country towards it, and in so doing to decide its fate; for it was recognized on all hands that the Protocol could not survive refusal by this country to assume the obligations and undertake the liabilities which it would have imposed upon us. Without the British Navy the Protocol was useless to those who had devised it.

The Protocol met immediately with a very critical reception in the Dominions. It was felt in some that it menaced their Sovereign rights, in all that it imposed excessive liabilities and exposed them to unnecessary dangers.

His Majesty's Government in this country shared these objections, and in the following March gave expression to them in a carefully considered declaration to the Council of the League.

" The Protocol," they said, " purports to be little more than a completion of the work begun, but not perfected, by the authors of the covenant. But surely this is a very inadequate description of its effects. The additions which it makes to the original document do something quite different from merely clarifying obscurities and filling in omissions. They destroy its balance and alter its spirit.

" The fresh emphasis laid upon sanctions, the new occasions discovered for their employment, the elaboration of military procedure, insensibly suggest the idea that the vital business of the League is not so much to promote friendly co-operation and reasoned harmony in the management of international affairs as to preserve peace by organising war, and (it may be) war on the largest scale.

" It certainly seems to His Majesty's Government that anything which fosters the idea that the main business of the League is with war rather than with peace is likely to weaken it in its fundamental task of diminishing the causes of war without making it in every respect a satisfactory instrument for organizing great military operations should the necessity for them be forced upon the world."

For these and other reasons, therefore, the Government of the United Kingdom, in full agreement with the Governments of the Dominions, declared their inability to accept the Protocol. Was no other course open to them? A mere negative, without the suggestion of any alternative, would have been disastrous.

Germany had not complied with the disarmament conditions of the Treaty of Versailles, and France was determined not to evacuate the occupied territory unless some other form of security was assured to her. As soon as it became known that the decision of Great Britain on the Protocol was likely to be unfavourable, a new wave of unrest spread over Europe, and the situation, already threatening enough, became even more menacing.

It appeared to His Majesty's Government, examining the situation, that :

" the brooding fears that keep huge armaments in being have little relation to the ordinary misunderstandings inseparable from international (as from social) life—misunderstandings with which the League is so admirably fitted to deal. They spring from deep-lying causes of hostility which for historic or other reasons divide great and powerful States. . . .

" What is feared is not injustice but war—war deliberately undertaken for conquest and revenge. And if so, can there be a better way of allaying fears like these than by adopting some scheme which should prove to all the world that such a war would fail? "

Rejecting, therefore, the Protocol, with its universal application and its incalculable liabilities on the one hand, and feeling on the other that it was equally impossible after all that had passed, to revert to the ideas of 1919 and 1922 and to revive the project of an alliance with France and Belgium directed against Germany, the British Government determined to try what could be made of a suggestion which had reached them from Germany whilst they were engaged in their consideration of the Protocol. In this they thought they detected the basis of a possible agreement, uniting Britain, France, Germany and Belgium in a common determination to maintain the peace of the West.

Their decision was announced in the following words :

" Since the general provisions of the Covenant cannot be stiffened with advantage, and since the ' extreme cases ' with which the League may have to deal will probably affect certain nations or groups of nations more nearly than others, His Majesty's Government conclude that the best way of dealing with the situation is, with the co-operation of the League, to supplement the Covenant by making special arrangements in order to meet special needs.

"That these arrangements should be purely defensive in character, that they should be framed in the spirit of the Covenant, working in close harmony with the League and under its guidance, is manifest.

"And, in the opinion of His Majesty's Government, these objects can best be attained by knitting together the nations most immediately concerned, and whose differences might lead to a renewal of strife, by means of treaties framed with the sole object of maintaining, as between themselves, an unbroken peace. Within its limits no quicker remedy for our present ills can easily be found nor any surer safeguard against future calamities."

More than once in the years preceding the Locarno Conference the rulers of Germany had suggested the possibility of a mutual pact for the preservation of peace. The first of these suggestions had been made by Dr. Cuno, then Chancellor of the Reich, in December 1922.

To relieve the fears which impeded the evacuation of the occupied territory, Dr. Cuno suggested that "Germany and France, in common with the other Powers interested on the Rhine, should enter into a mutual pledge, of which a Power not interested on the Rhine should be trustee" (the United States was intended), "not to wage any war against one another for a generation" (that is, for twice the length of the period of occupation envisaged in the Treaty of Versailles) "without a plebiscite."

The proposal was obviously inadequate in point of time and security, and, as importing the guarantee of the United States, unrealizable.

A similar, though different, offer was made by the German Government in May 1923, but it was again coupled with conditions unacceptable to the Allies and was refused by them.

Four months later, Dr. Stresemann, who had become Chancellor, made a further suggestion for a bilateral pact between the Great Powers interested on the Rhine, for a mutual guarantee of existing frontiers, but the proposal was curtly rejected by M. Poincaré.

In January 1924, Dr. Stresemann, who in the interval had ceased to be Chancellor but continued to hold the portfolio of Foreign Affairs, determined, in conjunction with the new Chancellor, Dr. Luther, to renew the attempt.

He was moved, as we know from his own papers, by three main considerations:

i. He feared that the new British Government might be contemplating a treaty of alliance with France and Belgium directed against Germany;

ii. He had become convinced, largely by the arguments of Lord D'Abernon, the very able representative of this country in Berlin, that to attempt the reconquest of Alsace-Lorraine would be a hopeless task, and that in the question of security lay the only key to any possible solution of the recurring troubles with France; and

iii. He dreaded a new occupation of the Ruhr and further coercive measures in default of agreement.

His first proposals were made to the British Government, but on their insistence were a few days later communicated to M. Herriot, at that time President of the Council and Foreign Minister.

The communication made by the German Government was to the effect that Germany desired a peaceful understanding with France.

She was prepared to negotiate a comprehensive arbitration

treaty and to enter into a mutual pact of guarantee with the powers interested on the Rhine. Similar arbitration treaties might be concluded with the other States which had common frontiers with Germany.

Further, a pact expressly guaranteeing the existing territorial status on the Rhine would be acceptable to Germany, and this pact might, in addition, guarantee the observance of the articles of the Treaty of Versailles, which established a demilitarized zone on the right bank of the Rhine.

I summarized the effect of these proposals in a passage which, to guard against all possibility of misunderstanding, was immediately communicated to the German Government. These proposals, I said, amount to this:

" That Germany is prepared to guarantee voluntarily what hitherto she has accepted under the compulsion of the Treaty, that is, the *status quo* in the West; that she is prepared to eliminate, not merely from the West, but from the East, war as an engine by which any alteration in the Treaty position is to be obtained.

" Thus not only in the West, but in the East, she is prepared absolutely to abandon any idea of recourse to war for the purpose of changing the Treaty boundaries of Europe, though she may be unwilling, or unable, to make the same renunciation of the hopes and aspirations that some day, by friendly arrangement or mutual agreement, a modification may be introduced into the East, as she is prepared to make in regard to any modification in the West."

It was in these proposals, if properly developed, that the British Government saw the necessary alternative to the Protocol.

The guarantee, which they were not prepared to extend to every country and every frontier, might properly be given in respect of a part of the world close to their own shores, which had been the cause and the scene of all our greatest struggles.

For a purpose so limited and in a sphere so circumscribed, Great Britain might rightly, and as a measure of self-defence, undertake a responsibility which would be intolerable and inexecutable if extended to the whole world. The German proposals went far beyond anything which they had previously suggested. But it was certain that they would be as barren of result as their earlier suggestions unless Great Britain was prepared to give her guarantee for the observance of the pact in the West. His Majesty's Government decided to offer that guarantee.

Could any British Government have taken the responsibility of refusing it? Such a refusal would have plunged Europe into chaos and made war certain sooner or later—and sooner rather than later.

In the months which followed, every effort was made to reach a settlement of the outstanding questions relating to the police and disarmament, and to prepare the way for a meeting of the representatives of the interested Powers. A first draft of the Treaty of Guarantee was prepared in the Foreign Office and, after being discussed with the French and approved by the Cabinet, was communicated to the Germans, so that their representatives might come to the Conference in full knowledge of the proposals which would be made to them.

The Conference itself met at Locarno in October 1925. Thanks to this careful preparation, its object was achieved in a little less than a fortnight. It was attended by the representatives of seven Powers—Germany, Great Britain, France, Belgium and Italy (at first taking part only as an observer, but presently announcing her adhesion to the Guarantee Treaty), and later Poland and Czechoslovakia.

The work of the Conference was embodied in eight Treaties. To only one of them, the Treaty of Locarno *par excellence*, is Great Britain a party.

This is the Treaty of Mutual Guarantee between Germany, Belgium, France, Great Britain and Italy. By it Germany and Belgium and Germany and France respectively covenant never to resort to war against each other, and to settle all disputes between them by peaceful means. Also the five Signatory Powers, collectively and severally, guarantee the maintenance of the territorial *status quo* resulting from the frontiers between Germany and her two Western neighbours as fixed by the Treaty of Versailles, and the observance of the conditions laid down for the demilitarized zone constituted by that Treaty.

In all cases but one, the decision as to whether the *casus fœderis* has arisen is entrusted to the Council of the League of Nations. The only exception to this rule is the case of actual invasion, or a flagrant violation of the stipulations regarding the demilitarized zone, if the guaranteeing Power is itself satisfied that " the violation is an act of unprovoked aggression, and that by reason either of the crossing of the frontier or the outbreak of hostilities, or the assembly of armed forces in the zone, immediate action is necessary."

In this case each party undertakes to come at once to the help of the victim, but even in this case the ultimate decision is left to the Council of the League, which will be immediately convoked, and all parties agree to conform to its judgment.

The subsidiary treaties concluded at the same time comprise the arbitration conventions between Germany and Belgium and Germany and France, which determine the methods for the peaceful settlement of all disputes provided for in the Treaty of Guarantee; and Arbitration Treaties between Germany and Poland and Germany and Czecho-slovakia for the similar regulation of all disputes between them by peaceful methods.

Finally, there are two treaties between France and Poland and France and Czechoslovakia, in which these Powers guarantee to one another the faithful observance of the undertakings reached between Germany and themselves; but the aid which each promises to the other in accordance with Articles XV and XVI of the Covenant is confined to the case of unprovoked attack on either by Germany.

This is a restriction of the obligations involved in the earlier treaties of alliance between these countries, limiting the claim of either for assistance from the other to cases of unprovoked aggression so as to bring them into harmony with the guarantees given in the West and with the spirit of the Covenant.

With the last-named treaties Great Britain has no direct concern. They impose no obligation on us and subject us to no liability. They strengthen and extend the peace structure of Europe, but we are not a party to them. They affect us only as signatories of the Covenant, concerned that the peace of the world should not be broken. Even in the case of the Treaty of Guarantee, Great Britain and Italy, the guaranteeing Powers, must, as permanent members of the Council of the League, be parties to its decision, or in the case of a flagrant violation of the treaty be able to satisfy themselves that there has been an unprovoked act of hostility, and that the circumstances are such as to render immediate action necessary.

The obligation could not be more carefully safeguarded or more certainly directed to the sole purpose of main-taining peace. The treaty forms, to use the apt phrase employed by Professor Gerothwohl in the columns of the

Daily Telegraph, a safety-curtain between Germany and her Western neighbours.

The Treaties initialled *ne varietur* at Locarno on October 16th, 1925, were signed in London on December 1st of the same year. In the interval they had been submitted to and approved by the Parliaments of all the countries concerned in them.

In the British House of Commons the Treaty of Guarantee met with general approval—only thirteen members were found to vote against it—and when the Imperial Conference met the next year, the assembled representatives of the Empire gave their blessing to it in the following resolution :

" The Conference has heard with satisfaction the statement of the Secretary of State for Foreign Affairs with regard to the efforts made to ensure peace in Europe, culminating in the agreements of Locarno; and congratulates His Majesty's Government in Great Britain on this successful contribution to the promotion of the peace of the world."

The conclusion of these treaties, in the negotiation of which this country had taken a leading part, undoubtedly enhanced British influence, but it did much more than this; it produced an immediate *détente* in international relations.

For the first time since the War Germany had been admitted to a conference with the former Allies on a basis of perfect equality, and the result had been agreement and the birth of a new spirit in their mutual relations.

At Locarno there had been no question of a dictated peace, imposed by overwhelming force and accepted under compulsion. Germany had voluntarily renounced all desire for the reconquest of Alsace-Lorraine, and of her own free will had guaranteed the inviolability of the frontiers of the

West and as freely accepted the establishment of the demilitarized zone.

What had once been dictated by the will of the conquerors had now been confirmed by treaties which owed their existence to a German initiative, and were the result of free and friendly discussion. As an earnest of the new spirit, the evacuation of the Cologne zone was begun on the day on which the treaties were signed and was rapidly completed, whilst large alleviations were introduced into the conditions prevailing in the two zones in which the occupation still continued.

But this was not all. If the Western treaties had stood alone, their conclusion might have increased the sense of insecurity in Eastern Europe.

It would have been unreasonable to expect Germany to renounce all desire for change in her Eastern frontiers, as fixed by the Treaty of Versailles—as unreasonable as it would have been, say, in 1875 to expect France to renounce all hope that she might one day recover her lost provinces. No such demand was therefore made, but Germany undertook never to attempt that alteration by force of arms, and to resolve all differences with her Eastern neighbours by peaceful means.

Again, the first suggestion of such agreements had come from Germany, and the treaties themselves were freely negotiated by her representatives and approved by her Parliament. To the Eastern Treaties Great Britain, as I have said, was not a party; they impose no obligation on her. Her guarantee was confined to the West, but her influence was used to secure their conclusion as an additional guarantee for the peace of the world.

We are now told that all this was a mistake, that Government and Parliament were alike wrong, and that the Treaty of Locarno, on which they received the congratulations of the Imperial Conference, will, if maintained, destroy the Empire.

What concern have we, it is asked, with the Continent of Europe, what interest in the frontiers of France and Belgium? What business is it of ours whether there is peace or war in Europe? Let other nations stew in their own juice and let us revert to a " splendid isolation."

It might be sufficient to reply that we have signed the Covenant of the League, and cannot divest ourselves of the responsibilities it imposes; that the Dominions and India share those responsibilities, for they, too, are members of the League, and that they have throughout shown, and continue to affirm, their attachment to the League.

It might be recalled (for memories are short) that the signal for the Great War was given by the murder of the Archduke at Serajevo, and that remote from our shores as the origin of the conflagration was, it spread like a prairie fire after a summer drought, and quickly involved not only these islands and the Empire, but even the United States.

It is true that we have no direct interest in the Polish Corridor or Upper Silesia, and certainly we are not called upon to assume any particular responsibility in regard to them. But who can predict with confidence that if they gave rise to conflict, we should remain entirely unaffected, and that the experience of 1914 might not be repeated?

It is a truism of politics that Peace is a British interest— almost the greatest of British interests. Since that is so, we do right to use our influence to maintain it, though it is no part of our duty to make ourselves in every case its guarantors.

Our concern with the West is far more direct. There have been many fluctuations in British foreign policy, perhaps many inconsistencies, but through all our long history from the time of the Spanish Armada to the present day there has been one principle to which we have persistently clung. Separated as these islands are from the western shores of the Continent only by the narrow waters of the English Channel and the North Sea, it has been a cardinal principle of British policy in all times, and under all governments, that we could not allow the Low Countries to be dominated by the greatest military Power of the day.

For this cause we fought Spain under Philip II and France under Louis XIV and Napoleon. It was the invasion of Belgium which united this country in the early days of August 1914, and finally determined our intervention in the Great War. From first to last the independence of the Low Countries has been recognized as a British interest, for, in truth, their frontier is our frontier, and the destruction of their independence would be a fatal blow at our own.

The lesson which we learned in the days when sea power was a secure defence is doubly impressed on us when aviation has annihilated space and bridged the waters. Our safety lies not in abstention till war has broken out but in throwing our weight beforehand into the scale of peace.

It may well be—German as well as French authorities assert it—that if the German Government had known in time that this country would join in repelling any attack on France or Belgium, the Great War would never have been begun.

Germany, though at present disarmed, is still potentially the greatest military Power on the Continent. It is from that quarter, and that quarter alone, that danger has menaced us since 1870, or might menace us again.

The fate of Belgium is inextricably bound up with that of France, our safety with both. All must be in danger if war should again break out in Western Europe.

Is it not better to recognize the danger in time and guard against its occurrence, rather than sit idly by until the world is again in flames?

Of one thing we may be sure. There could be no more perilous policy than to declare that we were henceforth indifferent to events in Europe. The British Empire covers a vast area of the globe. Its growth has been watched not without envy by other nations; it offers splendid pickings for the hungry. The one thing which might make possible Napoleon's dream of a Europe combined against us—a dream which haunted also the Kaiser's imagination, as his notes show—is that we should announce our intention to take no further interest in the affairs of the Continent.

In such a case other nations might see their only chance of salvation in union, and we might well awake to find that we had to pay the costs of their feast of harmony. In truth, our choice is not between participation and isolation, but between helping to shape events and becoming their victim.

It is objected that by the Treaty of Locarno we obtained no guarantee for the United Kingdom in return for the guarantee which we gave to France, Belgium and Germany —or, in other words, that we took additional risks without gaining any additional security. It is true that we neither sought nor obtained any reciprocal guarantee; it is not true that we gained no additional security.

As long as the existing territorial settlement of Western Europe is maintained these islands are in no danger. Our peril would arise only if that settlement were upset, but then it would arise immediately. We made by the Treaty of Locarno a great and significant contribution to the peace of the world, but in making that contribution I have never pretended that our motives were purely altruistic and that we took no thought for ourselves. On the contrary, it was because the peace and security of these islands and their immunity from attack are closely bound up with the independence and integrity of the Low Countries and France that we felt justified in giving in that sphere alone a guarantee which we refused to make general. In guaranteeing those frontiers we insured our own.

There remain two specific allegations to which it may be worth while to give the answer.

First, it has been alleged that the Treaty of Locarno, though it does not guarantee the maintenance of peace between Germany and Poland, does indirectly commit us to war if war breaks out between those two nations.

The argument, as I understand it, is as follows: If war breaks out between Germany and Poland, France is bound by her alliance to support Poland and will attack Germany in the West. In that case the Treaty of Locarno obliges us to go to the assistance of Germany to repel the French attack.

If this be the argument it rests on a double fallacy, for if Poland makes an unprovoked attack on Germany the Franco-Polish Alliance, as modified at Locarno, absolves France from any obligation to go to her aid. If, on the other hand, Germany wantonly attacks Poland, in defiance of her pledges at Locarno and of her signature of the Kellogg Pact, no sane man will suggest that the action of France in going to the assistance of Poland is an act of unprovoked aggression such as alone brings our guarantee of the western frontiers into operation.

PRAISE FOR THE BOOK

the last time that cinema served as a catalyst to social
ia can never forget how *Rang De Basanti* fuelled action
mous Jessica Lal case. This is the true power of cinema.
Rakeysh Omprakash Mehra for being a conscience keeper
right. This book is co-authored by Reeta Gupta, someone
ell. She understands the power and potency of language and
on the reader. Their combination makes for a powerful and
book.

—**Arundhati Bhattacharya**, Former Chairperson, SBI,
Current Chairperson and CEO, Salesforce, India

ursuing films in Hollywood when I saw Rakyesh's film, *Rang
anti*. It was incredibly moving with a strong sense of purpose
eaning. From then on, I have been a huge fan of his work,
d everything he's done. It's tough to constantly infuse your
with your own belief systems. Success or failure, Rakeysh has
ntly done that. And that makes him a passionate and a true

—**Shekhar Kapur**, Filmmaker

e is no difference between a David Lean set and a Rakeysh
rakash Mehra set. I'd say that Rakeysh has that same
ordinary ability when it comes to choosing his shot.

—**Art Malik**, Actor

keysh's success is important because it is based on his integrity.
er than his obvious achievements, he is an icon because he has
pired millions of Indians to believe that cinema has integrity and
ul.

—**N.R. Narayana Murthy**, Founder, Infosys

discovered *Aks*, *Rang De Basanti* and *Bhaag Milkha Bhaag* through
ord of mouth. Each film is different, drawing you into its complex

The Stranger in the Mirror

When was
justice? In
in the infa
Kudos to
in his own
I know w
its impact
importan

I was p
De Bas
and m
watche
films
consta
artist.

Ther
Omp
extr

Ra
Ot
ins
so

characters through beguilingly simple story lines. Rakeysh's sensibilities are appealing—he understands glitz, glamour, polish and middle-class audiences, having directed ad films selling lifestyle products including Coke and American Express cards. None of this prepares you for the way he captures the moment in the celebrated *Rang De Basanti*! He captured the angst of an economically empowered generation who knew nothing beyond self-gratification. However, when awakened, they are willing to sacrifice everything for their beliefs. *Bhaag Milkha Bhaag* blended adversity and heroism into a rare biopic, capturing the youthful longing to break out of the ordinary and forcing audiences to reach beyond their TikTok reality. A master of the storytelling oeuvre, he has brought to life alternate narratives, whose success lies in their being relevant irrespective of the continuum of time.

—**Sanjoy Roy**, Producer, Jaipur Literature Festival

I resonate strongly with the fearlessness in Rakeysh Omprakash Mehra's films and his approach. He goes boldly into subjects that others would think twice about. He bats from the front foot! Also, he has scored his own triple hundred for India, with the films *Rang De Basanti*, *Delhi-6* and *Bhaag Milkha Bhaag*. I wish him many more centuries!

—**Virender Sehwag**, Cricketer

On the surface, it can be said that Rakeysh Omprakash Mehra is one of India's finest directors. But that would just be what is obvious. When one sees his movies with attention (as I usually do), one realizes that he is not just an artist but also a thinker. This was even more obvious to me when I met him for the first time a few years ago. For Rakeysh, his films aren't just a means of showcasing the work of a talented actor or to display brilliant shot composition but also a way to engage the audience to think and reflect on issues. Whether you agree or disagree with the viewpoint presented in his movies is not important: what is important is that he makes you think. That is truly rare in a filmmaker. And that's what makes Rakeysh a genius. Read this book to understand the making of a genius.

—**Amish Tripathi**, Bestselling Author

The Stranger in the Mirror

The Stranger in the Mirror

rakeysh omprakash mehra

with REETA RAMAMURTHY GUPTA

RUPA

Published by
Rupa Publications India Pvt. Ltd 2021
7/16, Ansari Road, Daryaganj
New Delhi 110002

Sales Centres:
Allahabad Bengaluru Chennai
Hyderabad Jaipur Kathmandu
Kolkata Mumbai

Photos courtesy: Author Archives
Illustrations: Mohit Suneja
Icons: Mischoko via Getty Images
Book design: Bena Sareen

ISBN: 978-93-90547-99-9

First impression 2021

10 9 8 7 6 5 4 3 2 1

Printed at Thomson Press India Ltd., Faridabad

Ek Din
एक दिन

Toh, ek din nikal pada main
aap hi apne ko dhoondne.
Pagdandi mili, nikal pada,
chaon mili, toh so gaya,
taare soye toh uth pada,
fir chal pada.

One day, I set out
In search of myself
Found a random walking track
Slept when the sun was slack
Rose when the stars slept
And set out again.

—RAKEYSH OMPRAKASH MEHRA

~

I dedicate this book to my mother Annapurna
and my father Omprakash who showered my
childhood with love and gave me the wings
to soar.

~

Bharathi, Bhairavi and Vedant,
you are the light of my life.

~

Contents

xiv

Foreword
A.R. Rahman

When you're working in the world of Hindi cinema, you cross paths with many different kinds of filmmakers. Some of these directors come from a background in theatre. Others are artists that have chosen to make movies. And then, you have writers who've decided to venture into the realm of visual storytelling.

Rakeysh Omprakash Mehra came from the ritzy world of advertising. And he did have something extraordinary about him right from the beginning, both in a visual sense and in spiritual sense. My professional relationship with Rakeysh started right after his first movie, *Aks*, came out. I saw parts of *Aks* and I was blown away by the visuals. I met with Rakeysh not long after and he showed me the storyboards he had with him for four other movie concepts. One of the ideas that he shared immediately struck a chord with me. Many years later, this idea would go on to become *Rang De Basanti*.

One thing I really loved about the story was that it continually went back and forth. It shifted between the past and the present. Much like Rakeysh himself, it was a film that was rooted firmly in the values and ideals of a bygone age, but dared to hope for change and a brighter tomorrow.

For *Rang De Basanti*, Rakeysh wanted music that would make his rather dark subject into a movie that would stand the test of time. So, as a composer, I was always trying to interpret and go up against every situation in a way that was artistically beautiful. For instance, I wanted to take the heart-breaking death in the film and make it more about liberation than loss. That was the foundation for the song 'Luka Chuppi'. With that track, I created music that was metaphoric and symbolic rather than real and literal. In that sense, it was kind of going against the whole spirit of the movie, which was grounded in hard realities. But Rakeysh immediately and completely understood what I was trying to do.

It's very rare to find a filmmaker who accepts radical ideas. Rakeysh is always willing to experiment. His courage and conviction allowed us to come up with inventive path breaking ideas. When I was working with him in the mid- to late 2000s, there was always a huge amount of trust between the two of us and enormous joy in the jamming whenever we were in the studio. *Delhi-6* was our next project and this too was a movie that had a sense of social awareness about it. It spoke to me in its own way. And what I took away from the film was: we always want people to change for us. Why can't we love people for who they are, is the question the film raised in my mind.

Things always seem evident in retrospect, but the point of this story is this: Rakeysh is a bold creator. He's never afraid to hit the pause button or backtrack in order to explore new ideas. For me, that's what makes him special.

One of the toughest things to do as an artist is to not be closed. When I come up with musical ideas for filmmakers, many of them say, 'Oh, that's not what I'm looking for' or 'I don't need this'. And something that could potentially be a great piece of work is nipped right in the bud. They set parameters and never cross them. They say, 'We want to do this and nothing else.' When you do that, you sort of limit this amazing medium that is the cinematic language. If you're too caught up with trying to make what you think people want, you risk missing out on all the possibilities that come from going into the unknown and the unexpected.

In sharp contrast, Rakeysh always says, 'Alright; let's try this and see where it goes.' He's an explorer—a great explorer. He knows his destination, but he's completely open to taking different roads to getting there.

Personally, the Rakeysh Omprakash Mehra I've had the pleasure of knowing over the years is a man with a great sense of humour and a deep sense of spirituality—spiritual not in the divine sense of the word, but rather someone whose thought process is in a different realm altogether. His stories have the spirit of '60s and '70s rock: the spirit of Ken Russell's *Tommy* and Pink Floyd's music. I grew up with those and it made me love his work all the more.

I've been fortunate that Rakeysh has always been willing to go with me on the journey to discover strange and wonderful new things, be it injecting a kind of sound that doesn't seem to fit a certain story or adding a song to a situation that doesn't, at first glance at least, seem to warrant it. He was always open to my wildest ideas. And his imagination and spunk have taken me through doors that I probably might never have walked through otherwise.

When the Story Tells Itself
Reeta Ramamurthy Gupta

It may seem natural for each story to have a primary narrator. However, this autobiographical account is unique, in that it has many narrators.

To understand why this multidimensional, multi-character narration qualifies as an autobiography is to truly understand what it means to be as unselfish as Rakeysh Omprakash Mehra (lovingly called ROM by his cast and crew): a man who gleefully steps back and lets the experts do their job.

There are several anecdotes spread liberally all over the book, and you have to pay attention to understand who is narrating because the plot may have just shifted a little bit—just like his movies.

What really stands out is how effortless his journey has actually been. And herein lies the greatest paradox because there is no lack of perseverance in this richly experiential, multi-faceted account of one of India's greatest directors, an architect who endeavours to build a bridge between Indian and world cinema.

The miraculous manner in which things fall in place naturally, like pieces of a pre-ordained puzzle, with the universe acting as the *sutradhar* (narrator), making light of the struggles, is the fulcrum around which the joy of this journey is built.

The chai–biscuit college days are every bit as exciting as the popping of the proverbial champagne.

I wish you a happy ride.

■■■■■■■■■■■■■■■■■■■■■

The real voyage of discovery consists not in seeking new landscapes, but in having new eyes.

—Marcel Proust

■■■■■■■■■■■■■■■■■■■■■

A for Apple

Historically, the alphabet 'A' is said to resonate with the ideas of confidence, independence, courage and leadership. It is resolute and purposeful.

Thankfully, my life has been dotted by many such As.

Annapurna, who gave birth to me.

Aks, a film that gave birth to a director.

Amitabh Bachchan, a supreme artist who gave voice to the director in me.

I must quickly add B for Bharathi, my partner in the journey called life!

But let's think about another 'A', my guru who is no more with us, Ashok Mehta. I have had the pleasure of making several ad films with him. Like me, he was self-taught. A two-time national award winner, Ashok Mehta could caress the visuals with his lens, as he did in films like *Utsav*, *Mandi* and *36 Chowringhee Lane*. He could provoke you, as he did in *Bandit Queen*. *Teen Thay Bhai*, produced by me, was his last feature in 2011.

Mehta relied on his eyes and hands rather than manuals and textbooks, and his do-it-yourself credo persisted even after he attained legendary status. Known to be extremely nimble and nifty during shoots, changing the 35 mm reels, cleaning the lens, puffing the shutter, hammering nails into the walls of a set himself and constructing platforms on which to place equipment: he had an agile energy about him that made him a kinaesthetic worker.

Bollywood: The Greatest Love Story Ever Told (2011) was my swan song with Ashok Mehta. The docu-feature was a montage of around 200 Indian feature films and a dozen documentaries spanning India's independence in 1947 up to that point. Mehta made it all look like one, an unenviable task for any cinematographer in the world. He performed a miracle on the colour grading and merged a uniformity in the archives, making them all look seamless as one. That's what the story demanded and that's the genius he was. The feature was an official selection at the Cannes Film Festival in 2011 to celebrate 100 years of Indian Cinema.

Through the film, I proposed the obvious—that the Indian film industry *is* the definitive culture that holds India together. And that ironic to the title of the film, there is no such thing as 'Bollywood', a term I have always felt ashamed of. You see, there is nothing original about the title Bollywood; it's just a 'me-too' monkey shadow of Hollywood.

In contrast, Mehta was a paragon of originality and his genius was that he didn't even know the sheer brilliance of what he was creating. Not one for words, he was never able to discuss his art in depth, but very few understood storytelling with the camera like he did.

I miss him.

'Let's Do It'

It was the winter of 1998. I had given Amit ji (Amitabh Bachchan) a script that he was supposed to read over an evening flight to Delhi (Hope springs eternal!).

I was quivering like a fiddle string, excited with anticipation, about what he would think. Unexpectedly, my phone rang at 11 p.m.

A hushed voice spoke to me, whispering and yet managing to drown the mechanical, oddly piercing background noise of a plane making its way after landing.

AB: What were you drinking?

Me: Sorry sir!

AB: What were you drinking when you wrote this script?

Me: Rum and Coke, sir.

AB: Let's do it!

And just like that, the greatest star in Indian cinema, probably world cinema, was going to be a part of my first film, *Aks*.

1.

3.

Early
Influences

✳

1. The winner takes it all—Receiving the best athlete
award in Class four
2. Maa and Bauji share a smile in Manali
3. A young me, just out of college

CHAPTER I

The Pursuit of Innocence

'Junglee libas!' I shouted passionately.

'Meri aankhon se mere khwab na cheeniye, Shehzaade, main marr jaoongi', joined in my sister Mamta.

Our thin frames could barely contain the excitement of being able to listen to the full audio track of *Mughal-e-Azam*, a film we had not seen but heard countless times. With a splendid star cast and music that had a perennial appeal, Mamta and I were beyond thrilled to have the soundtrack of this masterpiece in our hands.

All of four years younger to me, born in 1967, my sister Mamta bonded with me as a friend: we would swim together, play pranks together and basically live happy carefree lives as children. However, my birth fell on the night of a lunar eclipse, which an astrologer would call a rather inauspicious night. Fortunately, I was born two minutes after the eclipse at 4.15 a.m., on 7 July 1963 to Annapurna (Maa) and Omprakash Mehra (Bauji). Both Mamta and I were oddly reverential—at least she was—to my older brother Rajan, who was born in 1958.

Bauji, Maa and siblings Rajan, Mamta and I were happy residents at the staff quarters of New Delhi's very British the Claridges Hotel. Over 35 years of service, my father, who started as a dishwasher, rose to the food and beverage (F&B) manager and eventually the go-to management person in all crisis situations. As children, we were blissfully unaware and unaffected by the fact that the auspices of our home lay within the servant quarters at the rear of Independent India's first few five-star hotels in 1952.

We enjoyed little covert mischievous perquisites that added up to the kind of joy that only kids can experience. One New Year's eve, I remember sneaking into the banquet hall, hiding under a table and watching a cabaret performance through the gaps in the table cloth. Sure enough, I was caught by a waiter, but the kind man smiled and let me go, assuring me that he wouldn't tell Bauji.

I distinctly remember another occasion, 31 December 1971. At the Claridges, it was time for another New Year party. I was eight years old. These were tumultuous times: India–Pakistan had just fought a 13-day war, triggered by Pakistan's airstrikes on 11 Indian airbases. All three armed forces fought in unison. Despite India's victory, the war shook the country. War teaches us the value of peace, so every bit of fun was cherished tenfold; people craved safety and were kind and generous to each other.

There was a game of raffles with numbered tickets that was being played, and the grand prize was a shiny new Philips mono-record player. The winner of this grand prize was the maharaja of Bharatpur, who was so happy with Bauji's services that he gave away his prize to him.

As Bauji carried this priceless piece of entertainment to our plebeian doorstep, I was thrilled. We had no TV, no fridge, no air conditioner, no scooter and no telephone at home. But we had new Philips mono-record player, and I had a ticket to ride!

I would have limited rides, however, as the records were expensive. Bauji, in those days, enjoyed a meagre salary of ₹450, in addition to the luxury of the staff quarters and the customary tips. Truth be told, I had no idea what a record looked like! The Connaught Place market was a five-mile walk from our home and it had a gramophone shop. But the records were priced upwards of 20 bucks. Steep! Understandably, the mono-record player remained a show piece for a while at home. But I was restless.

I had heard about the famous Chor Bazaar (literally 'thieves market') behind Red Fort, which resurrected itself on the sidewalks every Sunday. It stocked all kinds of second-hand riff-raff, probably contraband loot! I checked out this bazaar and discovered a vendor selling old records. I knew we could bargain because the Chor Bazaaris (vendors at the flea market) were always eager to get rid of their underhanded merchandise. Legend has it that this bazaar was so bizarre it once sold a platypus too! How this endangered species from Australia reached Old Delhi is anyone's guess! The bazaar was illicit with a capital 'I', and all of us had steals and bargains we could discuss with glee as part of our growing up years.

So one Sunday, I pestered and dragged Maa along to check out the bazaar. My prize catch was a four-disc, eight-sided record of the complete soundtrack of *Mughal-e-Azam*, which Maa bargained for ₹10—a major discount on its marked price. Suffice to say, at that moment, a regular Delhi boy, growing up around South Delhi's iconic landmarks, was delivered to art and cinema unknown to him!

Mughal-e-Azam fired up my imagination; I could hear the dialogues verbatim in my head and imagine any scene I wanted, in whatever way I chose, to complete my visual experience. The freedom to imagine was also bolstered by the fact that I had never seen the film. Needle on record, night after night, falling asleep to the dialogues; I memorized every dialogue, every sound, and every song. The roar of '*Mera jism zaroor zakhmi hai, lekin meri himmat zakhmi nahi*' and the intense pathos of '*Meri aankhon se mere khwab na cheeniye, Shehzaade, main marr jaoongi*' would reverberate in my ears and my heart for years to come.

It captivated my family as well and, for almost a year, you could call *Mughal-e-Azam* the official lullaby of Omprakash Mehra's family. The funniest part was how Mamta and I managed to misinterpret and mouth incorrect dialogues with heartfelt passion. So '*jangee libaas*' (the costume of a warrior) became '*junglee libaas*' (tribal dress), though it didn't make sense at all! I use to wonder why Emperor Akbar the Great would go to war dressed as a tribal covered with green leaves, but that's what we heard and that's how we rolled! Thanks to *Mughal-e-Azam* and my mother's melodious singing voice, to this date, I think in Hindi.

While *Mughal-e-Azam* was firing up my imagination, the cross-cultural, post-Partition stories of Old Delhi and the emotions they gave rise to, found in the immersive conversations among colony members, continued to tie our childhood friends and extended family.

Thanks to *Mughal-e-Azam* and my mother's melodious singing voice, to this date, I think in Hindi.

My childhood and the *kabaadi* (scrap) bazaar behind Red Fort have many fond memories for me. I bought my first pair of jeans there; I would wander aimlessly in the bazaar to check things out. In those days, nobody had telephone lines, and people reached home when they reached home. There was no interim conversation. As for the people who had telephone lines—well, I didn't know any of them. Not in my childhood at least!

5

CHAPTER 2

Maa

Maa's mellifluous humming still rings in my ears. Day after day, there she was, cooking us meals before we left for school, and then staying up till Bauji came home late at night, sometimes as late as 4 a.m. *'Piya aiso jiya mein samaaye gayo re,'* her sweet voice emulated the dulcet tones of Geeta Dutt, alive on the radio, as she attended to her many chores of a homemaker. I never could separate their voices; they became a single soul cooing in perfect harmony. Her name was Annapurna.

From the first day of my conscious life to the day we put my Maa to rest on her journey onward as a soul, I don't remember seeing her resting or taking an afternoon nap. She was awake before any of us, slept after all of us slept and was always available whenever we wanted food or anything else.

One of my earliest memories of Maa is her leaning forward on a *chulah* (stove), making the stubborn coals come alive, so she could sustain a good fire to cook. This was something she had perfected to an art. The coals were kept on the window so the smoke would go out and not get into the lungs of the family members that she lived and cared for.

The goddess of food is also called Annapurna, and fittingly, her cooking was to die for! Let me explain her remarkable skills in context. The Claridges Hotel was famous for hosting innumerable dinners for global celebrities and gourmands. It had the best chefs serving up mouth-watering delicacies to discerning, well-travelled palates. It was also a preferred venue for many film shoots and premieres. I remember the *Upkar* shoot featuring veteran actor Manoj Kumar and the great performing artist Helen shooting the song 'Gulabi Raat Gulabi' there. Functions celebrating successful 100-day runs and silver and golden jubilees of films were often held at the Claridges.

My father ended up making some friends well beyond his means. These included Om Prakash, the actor; Rajinder Krishan, the lyricist and, to a lesser extent, Raj Kapoor, the legend. A secret little binge that brought these superstars of Hindi cinema to my humble home was the exquisite taste of Maa's mutton curry–rice that she served up so lovingly. Imagine my amazement when I realized that the expensive food at the hotel couldn't match what my mother served with her limited resources. Served in an ordinary steel plate in contrast to the expensive silverware in the plush hotel restaurant, she had celebrity guests licking their fingers in glee.

Maa's single-minded dedication to her family, friends of family and even extended unknowns that family brought home occasionally enabled my Bauji to make many friends in his life. My grateful father reciprocated by paying Maa the ultimate compliment—that she was the best chef in the world.

The goddess of food is also called Annapurna, and fittingly, her cooking was to die for!

And here's the funny thing: Maa died a vegetarian, even though she cooked the most delicious *dahi* mutton (a preparation of curd and mutton) for all of us all her life—a recipe I am still trying to perfect for my friends today!

Born to a very poor family, Maa had a rough childhood. Her father died early, leaving her family with no money. She grew up eating congee made of wheat or rice with salt: the food that India's poor eat even today. Coming from those humble beginnings, Maa raised us in an atmosphere of plenty. How she did that is beyond me! She would save judiciously, buy some gold when she had money and pawn them later to pay our school fees. She never thought that pawning a chain or a bangle was something to be ashamed of, and she did it in a very matter of fact way. There is a lesson in this, almost philosophical. She could practice an almost Buddhist detachment: what you possess will come and go; what is more important is what you do with it.

Much later, I shot parts of *Delhi-6* at the Dariba Kalan jewellers market in Old Delhi, which reminded me of my Maa's immense sacrifices. I even wrote a scene where Om Puri pawns jewellery to arrange funds for his daughter's marriage dowry.

Maa's devotion was not just for her small family of five but for our extended family as well. Sometimes, a distant relative we had never heard of would get admitted to the All India Institute of Medical Sciences (AIIMS) Delhi, which was closer to our home than that of our other relatives. By some inspired sense of duty, Maa would make 50 *paratha*s, take them there and feed everyone. In hindsight, how she managed to feed so many people is difficult to imagine. But she was a giver, and she had a reputation for her kindness and dependability. Far-flung kinsfolk, young and old alike, got attracted to her and came to her with their problems. The narrative was that Maa had eight hands like Durga and that she always took care of everyone.

As the middler-meddler among three children, I was at the receiving end of special privileges; Maa always pampered me. I remember that I had this momentary fetish once to play lawn tennis, imagining in my vanity that tennis players were more stylish. The tennis court was just behind the pool, and I enrolled without giving it much thought. My coach asked to buy a racquet and I promptly transferred the demand to Maa. She took me to the Old Delhi brass market and sold a lot of brass utensils to gather some funds. We subsequently went to the sports shop in Connaught Place and bought a racquet for the princely sum of ₹40. These used to be wooden racquets in those days. But like most high school fetishes, mine lapsed in three months.

In a nutshell, Maa could pull rabbits out of a hat, giving us education and experiences we couldn't afford.

The things she had a problem with were more in the ethical domain. 'I will put red-hot coals on your tongue if you lie' was something she was likely to say. A survivor with clear priorities, she felt that loss of character was a much more severe blow than loss of money. She instilled in us the idea of coexistence. Sentences such as 'Give me my space' weren't part of my childhood. Space was a luxury. Living together and caring for everyone else was not called adjustment or compromise. It was the only way we knew how to live.

During her last days, Maa was uncomfortable in the ICU on ventilator. I was shooting my fourth film, *Bhaag Milkha Bhaag* (BMB) in Haryana. During the nights, I used to come back to the hospital to be with Maa. Many a times, she warned me not to make her survive miserably. Mamta understood, but both Rajan and Anupama Bhabhi could not let her go. I had to remind them that Bauji would not let her suffer and she was only going to a better place to join him. I was with her in the room when we pulled the plug and offered her peace on 8 September 2012.

Traditionally, the ashes go to Haridwar, but I asked Rajan Bhai to give me half of our mother's ashes. At 4 in the morning the next day, I took the warm ashes from the funeral pyre and set off for Ladakh. It had always been Maa's wish to visit Ladakh and the universe conspired to fulfil her wish on her final journey. I remember that this was made possible by a friend of mine, George Utpal (he was the line producer for a film I never made called 'Samjhauta Express' and, later, the line producer for the Ladakh portions of *BMB* and *Mirzya*). George helped organize a small ceremony at the Diskit Monastery in the Nubra Valley of Ladakh. I immersed Maa's ashes in Shyok River. In so many ways, Ladakh was an apt, pristine setting to offer prayers to the soul of an angelic, honourable and devoted woman.

By now, the *BMB* schedule had also moved to Ladakh. For seven days, I went for Maa's prayers early morning at 5 a.m. and reported to shoot by 6.30 a.m. Binod Pradhan, the cinematographer who was on location at the film and my very dear friend, was a rock at the time. He comforted me in his own stoic way during those days. I am quite certain Maa blessed *BMB* to be the resounding success that it eventually became.

9

THE ART OF SELLING

During my ninth standard, an advertising professional visited our
school as a guest lecturer. He put a question to the class.
'I have a pen in my pocket, how will you sell it?'
I answered, 'Sir, you can use it to say things you cannot say.'
I received appreciation for the same.
I was told I could express myself well.
This memory stayed with me.

CHAPTER 3

Bauji

There are two kinds of people in the world: those who own the world and those who sneak in.

My father sneaked in and yet owned the world. He was full of life always and taught us to 'live life rather than analyse it'.

He lost his mother early, when he was just an infant. He grew up with a stepmother and siblings, surrounded by both emotional and existential poverty. A narrative from his life I became familiar with was that his school-going days were marked with a rope to hold his shorts, lest they should fall down. He grew up to be something of a rebel.

With not much formal education, he dropped out of school in ninth class and started doing menial work. One thing led to another, and he ended up as a ticket checker and torch man at Jagat Cinema opposite Jama Masjid in Old Delhi.

One incident involving my parents' marriage will always be etched in my mind. There was a ritual that prescribed that the brothers of the bride must go to fetch the groom and bring the *baraat* (groom's wedding procession).

Maa would've been 16–17 years old at the time, and her brothers were 14 and eight, respectively. They went to fetch my father's baraat, all the way to Fatehpuri, Old Delhi, where he lived. It was a 45-minute walk. On the way, the two brave comrades got tired and collapsed to a deep slumber on a bench in the Company Bagh Park, opposite Old Delhi Railway Station.

My father's family kept waiting for them to arrive. On the other hand, Maa's family in Ballimaran was waiting for the groom, who was picked up much later than he was supposed to be. Anxious moments were endured at both ends as the two brothers slept on a bench in a park, their tiny tired selves weighed down by the responsibility of conducting a marriage. Such was the abject simplicity of my parents' union.

Bauji was very driven and wanted to be a good provider to his family. During my early childhood days, I saw very little of him; I just remember that he was extremely hardworking. He used to come back home from his night shift at 2:30 a.m. and would be sleeping when I left early morning for my school. There were times when he didn't even know which class we were in. Annual days, sports days, parent–teacher meetings were all handled by my 'Durga' Maa and her charm.

To his credit, Bauji was exceptionally good at networking and developed key connections to create opportunities for his children with great perseverance and honesty. His unique ability to build relationships was fostered by Maa's willingness to nurture them.

Bauji was very driven and wanted to be a good provider to his family.

Bauji bonded well with the Khannas, the Indian owners of the Claridges. They loved horses, and Bauji too developed a love for horses. He started reading thick books on horse and pedigree details and pretty much became an encyclopaedia. He would often go to the Delhi Race Club, a stone's throw away from Claridges and place small bets to check whether he was able to make the right calls with the knowledge he had. Visitors to the Club, which comprised of Delhi's swish set, observed him and started seeking his help on how to place their bets. How a ninth standard dropout from Girdhari Lal Hindi-Medium School in Old Delhi—with no exposure to English—could hobnob with the elite that dabbled in equestrian matters is beyond me!

I would occasionally accompany Bauji and get a ride at the Race Course stables, where races and polo matches were held. Once, I fell off a stallion and got 32 stitches on my chin. That pretty much cemented the memory of being around horses. The romance lingered years later when I was shooting key scenes in *Mirzya*. Also, the Delhi Race Club was on Race Course Road, famous because 7, Race Course Road (now rechristened 7, Lok Kalyan Marg) is the official residence of the prime minister of India. I placed this landscape in my film *Mere Pyare Prime Minister* (2019) when I found the opportunity.

It was at the Delhi Race Club that Bauji met Air Chief Marshal O.P. Mehra. What began as a simple conversation on betting tips developed into a fond relationship over time. The Air Chief Marshal gave Mamta and I a reference letter for admission to the prestigious and coveted Air Force Bal Bharati School, a massive school with top-of-the-line facilities spread across many acres and large playgrounds.

13

Cinema and I

Cinema and I connected early through some odd coincidences. But the real romance with movies happened through my father. He was an ardent movie fan. He knew all about each and every movie, the technicians who shot it, the songs and the character artists. He had watched too many credits roll by during his early employment at the theatre as a young man. Later, when he made friends from the film industry at the Claridges, he knew enough to converse knowledgeably.

The cinema of those times was magical. It was the mid-'60s and early '70s (with a hangover of the '50s)—the golden era. Along with the birth of a nation was the birth of hope and independent self-expression. I must have been around eight years old, when I saw *Jal Bin Machhli Nritya Bin Bijli* at Regal theatre with Bauji. This was my introduction to the genius of the great master, V. Shantaram. What a magnificent artist!

> **I watched *Pakeezah* for three days in a row at the Chanakya theatre, offering a new 70 mm experience.**

We also had our Sunday and Wednesday evening weekly fix: a movie and *Chitrahaar* on television with Mataji. She belonged to the family that owned Claridges and lived in the bungalow adjoining the hotel premises. She was also the only one who owned a TV. A couple of us kids used to liven up her Sundays and get yummy treats in return.

Stories always excited me and my favourite subjects were History and Hindi. Our Rashtra Bharti textbooks had some brilliant stories, including one of Valmiki the thief, who got transformed when Narada tricked him into chanting 'MaRa' continuously, till he could only say 'RaMa' and one of how Angulimala the dacoit was transformed by the Buddha into a monk.

On our birthdays, Bauji used to treat all of us to a movie, either at Regal, Plaza or Odeon in Connaught place. I remember watching *Guide*, *Johny Mera Naam*, *Jhanak Jhanak Payal Baaje* and countless other films on screen with Bauji. I watched *Pakeezah* for three days in a row at the Chanakya theatre, offering a new 70 mm experience. The storytelling was epic and the music was moving.

Every Saturday, Bauji used to go to the Old Delhi family temple for a *jagran* (religious ceremony where songs are sung all night). I witnessed human behaviour at its funniest: devotees high on *bhang* (a traditional Indian marijuana drink) out-singing each other, replete with body language and histrionics, clanking the *manjeeras* (brass bells) loudly, competing for who would be heard the loudest. I used this memory in a scene in *Delhi-6* that has Pavan Malhotra and Om Puri doing the same as an amused Abhishek Bachchan watches on.

After a point, I wasn't interested in the jagran and would slip off to watch the 9-to-12 show instead. For a year, every Saturday, I watched *Sholay* and *Jai Santoshi Maa*. Bauji used to know the owner of Novelty cinema (where *Sholay* played for over a year) from his Jagat Cinema days, and his best friend, Thakur Balu Singh, was the manager at another theatre, Minerva. So I enjoyed free seats. The occasional fruit chaat was a bonus.

Some of the films I got to see in theatres and later on TV gave me goosebumps. Masterpieces like V. Shantaram's *Do Aankhen Barah Haath* offered a rare glimpse that human beings could change—an idea that stayed with me. It was the story of a reform-minded, idealistic young warden who gets special court permission to conduct a social experiment. As part of the experiment, the warden takes six surly murderers from prison to a dilapidated country farm, where they transition to an open jail system. They have to rehabilitate the farm and their own selves through hard work and compassion. What a soulful idea to focus on the good in people and bet on it! Songs like 'Ae Malik Tere Bande Hum' will always remain evergreen.

15

Sports Quota

I have loved water since I was three years old, again thanks to the Claridges Hotel. It was just another one of those things I had to thank Bauji for. He got permission for his kids to dive into the fabulous five-star pool.

Thanks to this, two things happened subconsciously early in life. First, I lost my inhibition against white skin because I was swimming with the *goras* (foreigners), who were tourists at the hotel. Second, the pool became my playground, and later, I also became proficient in the rare sport of water polo.

My serious engagement with the sport started in the ninth standard and continued till the third year of college, when, for all of seven years, I had access to a fabulous swimming pool—the only Olympic-sized pool in Delhi—at the National Stadium. This was passed on to the people of Delhi by the government after the First Asian Games in 1951. It was a world class sporting facility. My school sports teams—cricket, hockey, athletics and swimming—all practiced at the National Stadium.

Looking back at those days at the National Stadium, we had legends for company, no less. The Indian national cricket, hockey and athletics teams would hold camps there. There were some stories that did the rounds and became part of the oral tradition of the cohort at the stadium: there was one about how Adolf Hitler tested Dhyan Chand's hockey stick for magnets. The legendary brute strength of Dara Singh was another favourite tale. Everyone's favourites were the jokes built around the legend of Milkha Singh—how once he chased a thief and overtook him thinking it was a race. My coach always gave examples of Milkha's hard work on the tracks, how he used to run 100 rounds after everyone else had finished their practice. He would collapse and then people would have to carry him out. Fortuitous in hindsight, but I didn't know it then.

I had built a great ritual. Every morning, I would reach the stadium at 6 a.m., practice till 8.30 a.m., attend school/college, go back to the stadium from 3.30 to 7 p.m. and finally go home. This discipline has served me all my life—till date I wake up at 4 a.m. and get down to my writing. It was evident to me early that investing precious morning hours in hard work is critical to fulfilling your dreams.

I was lucky to be assigned to Khetarpal Sir, who had returned from Germany after intensive coach training. He became my guru and advisor. He observed that I swam fast and convinced me to put these skills to use to play water polo. In no time, I became part of the water polo team and progressed quickly to the Delhi state team as well as the junior national teams. I was considered a probable candidate for the 1982 Asian Games. I even captained the junior national water polo team from North Zone.

Thanks to this, I was eligible for the sports quota, which opened up to me a whole range of educational opportunities that would've otherwise been elusive. I secured admission into Shri Ram College of Commerce (SRCC) after twelfth standard because of my swimming. This was a full scholarship and was an immense relief as I did not have to burden my parents to pay my college fees.

I was the youngest on the team, and made it all the way to the final training camp for the contingent that trained for the Asian Games. My teammates eventually won the bronze at the 1982 Asian Games in Delhi.

> I was considered a probable candidate for the 1982 Asian Games. I even captained the junior national water polo team from North Zone.

Though I never made it to the final national team for the Asian Games, sports was a way of life and continues to be. I have to thank Ms Harbans Baxi, the principal of Air Force Bal Bharati School, for my relationship with sports. She had a philosophy that academics must be balanced with equal emphasis on sports. Under her leadership, we built a very strong school cricket and swimming team. She made sure to be present during the training to demonstrate her commitment. In those days, we had six India under-17 cricket players; players like Maninder Singh, Tilak Raj and Gursharan Singh even made it to the senior team later. Naturally, with such stars, I had no chance of making it even to the school cricket team.

I was very close to Ms Baxi. Even after she retired, we spoke off and on, till she passed away in 2017. She was the one who put my name on the school's notable alumni board. I was overcome with warm nostalgia, happy to have made her proud.

This spirit of achievement in sport and linking my identity to it was reinforced by another mentor much later in life. It was none other than the flag bearer of information technology (IT) in India, Infosys founder

N.R. Narayana Murthy Sir, who told me that if I had to stay young in my mind, I must consciously spend more time with the youth. What better way to do that than sports!

I will be forever grateful to the influences of my childhood years, the neighbourhood, the teachers and all the movies I saw. These helped me create a unique signature as an ad film director and feature filmmaker in my later years.

CHAPTER 4

Rajan, Rakeysh, Mamta

Born in 1958, my brother Rajan was five years older than I and attended St. Columba's, a missionary school run by Irish fathers. My sister Mamta was four years younger than me. We all grew up sleeping under the stars on the terrace because there was not much room in the house. Winters were snug as we all fitted into the space available.

Mamta says, 'I somehow remember that our grandparents were always around, from when I was nine years old to about 14 or 15. That's why we all used to sleep on the terrace, and those were the nights when Rakeysh and I bonded the most.'

Mamta and I completed kindergarten in the Garden School and our primary schooling was at Bluebells school in Jor Bagh. When I joined Bluebells, it was a small school with only 35 students enrolled and had classes only till fourth standard. The school grew with me; as I went to fifth grade, it offered fifth grade, and so on. I finished up to eighth grade from there. Maa was very particular that we go to an English-medium school and she gave us what our parents had missed out in their childhood.

The school was like a small family and under the leadership of Mrs Soni, the principal, a lady with great cultural inclination, the school gave its students an excellent base to build on. Mrs Soni ensured that we got exposed to a liberal way of thinking. In fact, every

We all grew up sleeping under the stars on the terrace because there was not much room in the house.

Independence Day, she used to encourage us to get acquainted with the idea of India by organizing unusual plays. In the seventh grade, I remember playing Jawaharlal Nehru and had to enact his famous 'Tryst with Destiny' speech.

Our peer group comprised kids of rich people, so while my classmates had more than one pair of shoes, we used to wear canvas shoes procured from the army shop. We used to paint them white and extend their shelf life. I had to wait until college to buy my first pair of proper sneakers, after several years of pushing my nose against the limpid glass of the Bata shop and looking at shoes longingly from the outside. Even today, I am subconsciously trying to fill that gap—I own almost 25 pairs of sneakers.

Mamta
in first person

I will never forget the day in 1995 when my husband Sandeep had to undergo an open-heart valve-replacement surgery. My son was four years old, and I was worried to the core. Rakeysh came to visit me in Faridabad from Bombay and asked me to ensure that we went to the best doctor possible. After spending some time with us, he left. As I shut the door behind him and walked back, I saw a bag lying in the room. In it was the money I needed for surgery. And true to form, Rakeysh didn't want the emotional drama of handing it over to me or making a big deal of it. Eventually, we met Dr Naresh Trehan together and understood the procedure. Years later, Dr Trehan would perform the same surgery on Maa.

Rakeysh's biggest strength is that he can look at things with an objective, third-person view and make them seem simple; he is always looking for solutions to problems. He is also extremely emotional but somehow finds inner strength and balance. When Bauji was hospitalized at AIIMS for a stroke, I was only in fifth or sixth standard. These were tense moments for Maa. Rajan Bhai would look after Bauji and Rakeysh, with his simple manner, comforted all of us and listened to everyone who had anything to tell. It was also Rakeysh who, much later, couldn't bear to see Maa suffering from paralysis. He pulled the plug on her ventilator and let her go. Maa had always told Rakeysh not to let her suffer during old age. He obeyed!

We had simple parents who were fiercely motivated to ensure that our childhoods would be very different from theirs. Maa was *barkat* (abundance) incarnated—all the Lord's blessings in a neat package. We were her pride, her reason for living; she always trusted us with whatever we did and had her own way of telling us right from wrong. She spoilt us silly. Bauji, on the other hand, was fun-loving but had very little time.

Rakeysh was by far the most pampered among the three of us. I had to go in the school bus but he had a cycle. As a sportsperson, Rakeysh became a team player, in every aspect of his life. I remember that Bauji was by and large supportive, but not very excited about me swimming. 'Mamta will not travel out of town for national swimming meets' was his diktat! Rakeysh would fight with Bauji and take me for the nationals.

He used to cook the world's best Maggi for me. There was also a tradition of flying kites on 15 August, unique to Old Delhi, which we used to engage in from the terrace of our *nani's* (maternal grandmother's) house. This is how Rakeysh developed his love for kites; he used to love flying them, something you will see the characters of *Delhi-6* indulge in and talk about.

After his twelfth, Rakeysh did his BCom Honours from SRCC. He and his gang—Rajiv Varma, Vivek Bhushan and Rajiv Tandon—were the privileged ones. They had permission to come home late after all their meandering, and Maa would happily make parathas and *rajma-chawal* (kidney beans in gravy and rice) for all of them.

In hindsight, we grew up in something of a cubbyhole in the precincts of a five-star hotel, observing wealth and the lack of it, the reliable strength of familial bonds, at close quarters.

22

MUJHE KUCH KEHNA HAI
मुझे कुछ कहना हैं

Mujhe kuch kehna hai
Aaj ki hawa
Jaise meri saansen nichod rahi hai
Aaj ki tarikh
Jaise mujhse kuch pooch rahi hai
Aur mein chup hoon!

23

(I have something to say!
But the air
is being sucked out of my breath.
The times
are asking me questions
and I'm unable to speak.)

—Rakeysh Omprakash Mehra

FROM THE MAKERS OF RANG DE BASANTI

delhi-6

THE JOURNEY WITHIN

Delhi-6
Brews in
My Belly

CHAPTER 5

The Inspiration for *Delhi-6*

Why am I jumping straight to my third film?

Because for me, *Delhi-6* is and will remain the closest to my heart. And because as a script, it was the first that took shape within me and stayed dormant for a very long time inside my consciousness.

Let us set the context.

As a child, when I stood at the top of Chandni Chowk, the grand avenue in Old Delhi, on my left I could see the Charity Birds Hospital. Next to it is the 800-year-old Gauri Shankar Temple, which has Shri Digambar Jain Lal Mandir as its neighbour. Opposite this temple is Delite Cinema and next to it is the Methodist Church. Churchgoers could see the highly revered Sis Ganj Sahib Gurudwara diagonally across them. And if you stood at the Gurudwara, you could see both McDonald's and Haldiram's (famous Indian food joint). Visitors to these two would not be able to miss the Fatehpuri Masjid that stood at the end of Chandni Chowk, and when you turned around, you would see the Indian tricolour fluttering atop the Red Fort.

What a scintillating cauldron of cultural co-existence! We used to buy our canvas shoes at the army disposable shop in Chandni Chowk and play cricket around the Jama Masjid and Red Fort lawns. This neighbourhood was a reservoir of faith, religion and temporal existence. Vastly varied customs, philosophies, values and traditions

27

thrived side by side and dotted my active and eventful childhood.

My nani's house was in Old Delhi, in an area called Charkhewalan, and my *dada*'s (paternal grandfather's) house was in Fatehpuri. We used to live in Gali Paswan (you will find a reference to this in *Delhi-6*), which was diagonally opposite to Gali Qasim Jan, where the heritage site Ghalib ki Haveli, the residence of the nineteenth-century Urdu poet Mirza Ghalib, is located.

All of us raucous striplings used to play hide and seek all over Ghalib Ki Haveli, which had not been declared a heritage site till 1999. We were blissfully unaware of who Ghalib was. Quite often, we would hang out in Red Fort, sitting on the Peacock Throne (or what was left of it), pretending to be the emperor of India. That particular slice of history was indistinguishable from any other nook or cranny in the neighbourhood.

From this carefree existence to the Babri Masjid demolition on 6 December 1992, the Delhi of my childhood had changed. This ghastly event had long lasting ramifications. The sentiments triggered by the act snowballed into subsequent barbarity that manifested itself in the 1993 Bombay blasts, the Godhra train carnage, followed by the Gujarat riots in 2002 and the 2008 Mumbai terror attacks. This also served as the trigger for the original script of *Delhi-6* in my mind. It left a deep impact on me, and if you've seen the film, you'll know what I'm talking about.

Delhi-6 is and will remain the closest to my heart.

While most liberal Hindus and Muslims condemned the demolition, the frenzy of the moment and the 'possessed' behaviour of the people made me realize that we cannot pretend to be 'accommodating' when we are not anymore. I channelled this disbelief and horror into *Delhi-6*. As a society, we were becoming more and more intolerant. I had too many memories that tugged at my heartstrings and implored me to create a film that took the mirror of cinema and reflected society's behaviour onto it.

This was also the time in my life where I had just delivered my first blockbuster, *Rang De Basanti* (*RDB*), and earned the right to express myself more freely. For a filmmaker with no formal schooling in filmmaking, I was being told that my work was a significant milestone in Hindi cinema.

Internally, I knew if I had to keep making great cinema, I would need a solid footing in picking the right kind of story. My movies had to have a voice. And I wanted to tackle sensitive subjects and make cinema that had a soul. The message of *Delhi-6* is bigger than any individual. Deep within, I felt validated and I knew why I had been chosen by the universe to make movies. Today, the movie has become *even* more relevant than ever before (sadly because communal intolerance is not a good thing but the adverb can be eliminated).

Would I have made *Delhi-6* if not for the immersive secular experiences of my childhood?

THE TITLE

One day, I urged Kamlesh Pandey, one of the most brilliant scriptwriters of our times, to take a tour of Old Delhi with me. I wanted him to taste the food, meet the locals, smell the air and feel the culture. While we were walking on the lanes of Delhi and crossed the very same neighbourhood I had inhabited as a child, I was recounting old tales.

On our walk, we encountered a rather emotional street fight. One boy was getting beaten up by three others. That's when he said, '*Haath na lageeyo, Delhi-6 ka launda hoon*' (Don't you dare touch me, I am a Delhi-6 lad.) The way the boy said that, despite being outnumbered, spoke of his attitude and identity that screamed with pride, a power that came from belonging to Old Delhi.

And in a flash, we had the title of our film—*Delhi-6* (Delhi-110006 being the postal code for Old Delhi.)

It struck me that the city where I spent my childhood had a character all its own. Perhaps that's why, vicariously, I wanted the old city of Delhi to be the third character in *Delhi-6*.

CHAPTER 6

Creating
Magic
on Celluloid

'The wound is the place where the Light enters you.'
—Jalaluddin Rumi

31

Delhi-6 *being my third film, I had built access to some genius talents.*
A.R. Rahman (I lovingly call him AR) was one of them. 'There are
some deep wounds in our society today and I want to put a balm
on them,' I told AR. He understood this and gave me a lovely
composition: 'Rehna Tu Hai Jaisa Tu', which became a huge hit.

Another co-conspirator in my rebellious storytelling was Ronnie
Screwvala; he believed in me. UTV Motion Pictures had grown into
a major studio under Ronnie's vision. The cinema he was supporting
and creating was path-breaking and he was raising the bar with every
attempt. Ronnie unquestioningly enabled me to embark upon this
journey to make a sensitive film about people, their aspirations and
their susceptibility to irrational behaviour when they become part of
rabble-rousing swarms of emotionally charged religious tribes.

The script of *Delhi-6*, which had been alive inside me for many
years, needed a fresh look. I had done a one-to-one script writing
workshop with Hollywood's screenwriting guru Syd Field post *RDB*
and was revisiting the narrative. Kamlesh Pandey gave it his magical

touch. Later, Rensil D'Silva added his dose of realism and Prasoon Joshi finally sealed the script.

The plot that finally evolved had American-born Roshan Mehra (Abhishek Bachchan) bringing his ailing grandmother, who has only a few months left to live, back to India. The grandmother was played by Waheeda Rehman, and her screen name was Annapurna Mehra—my mother's namesake. Maa always yearned to go back to Old Delhi after Bauji passed away, like a fish going back to the waters she was born in. It is a natural tendency and Waheeda ji was such a perfect fit. Roshan Mehra's mother, Fatima, is Muslim, while his dad is Hindu. Little does he know that the quick trip to Delhi will turn into the longest journey of his life. I also cast Sonam Kapoor as the rebellious Bittu, even though it was only her second film, in a very complex part. She essayed the part without a single false note.

Bharathi worked tirelessly behind the scenes and put together the greatest cast I had ever worked with. There was Atul Kulkarni, who had been an integral part of my second film, *RDB*. He has the kind of talent that can hold a frame in thrall. The naturally talented Divya Dutta, with whom I was about to build a lifelong friendship, played Jalebi, an untouchable. Then there are the constantly bickering brothers played by Pavan Malhotra and Om Puri, who are caught in a fight for one-upmanship. One of the most significant scenes to illustrate their relationship is when they out-scream each other during the jagran (a replay of my childhood memories). The thespian Prem Chopra, the gifted K.K Raina, Deepak Dobriyal, Raghubir Yadav, Supriya Pathak, Sheeba, Tanvi Azmi, Aditi Rao Hydari, Vijay Raaz and a special appearance by the late Rishi Kapoor represented a formidable pool of nuanced talent. Add a guest appearance by Amitabh Bachchan and you have a cast that's manna from heaven.

We proceeded to reconstruct Old Delhi in a ghost town called Sambhar in Rajasthan. That gave play to the roof tops—my childhood memories were replete with kite-flying days against a picturesque backdrop of open terraces. Old Delhi is so congested with humanity that there's no room for an apple to fall. So the only space left to socialize are the terraces. This is where Om Puri feeds pigeons and Pavan Malhotra flies kites. We also shot the immensely popular

'Sasural Genda Phool' on the terrace because so many characters reveal their true nature on the rooftops.

One of my favourite scenes in the movie is Waheeda ji being rushed to the hospital. Their cycle rickshaw gets stuck in a traffic jam because there's a cow giving birth on the road. The crowd's reaction captures India beautifully—a very sick Waheeda ji, who has just suffered a heart stroke, is encouraged to get down from her rickshaw to take the cow's blessings. For me, it was a scene of dark humour and a comment on people's blind faith in religion.

Ace cinematographer Binod Pradhan was invited to interpret the story with free-flowing camera work. To linger and capture the flavour of Delhi with a longing touch, I encouraged him to think of the camera as another character in the film, always floating around, always observing, like a neutral buoyant underwater camera. Binod, being Binod, invented a contraption where he suspended the cameras on a bungee rope that gave it the freedom to be with the characters and turn 360 degrees at will. It was a nightmare for the crew but, somehow, we managed. Later, during colour correction, we drained out most of the blues in the frame and that gave the film a very earthy feel. Another important difference in the camerawork of *Delhi-6*

Bharathi was working tirelessly behind the scenes and had put together the greatest cast I have ever worked with.

33

was that we went for subtler contrasts. This was a sharp departure from filmmaking in those times.

To quote Binod Pradhan:

> The director and the cinematographer see the movie before it is shot. Rakeysh gives me about three months for pre-production, which I absolutely enjoy. In order to create the kind of scenes he expects from me, I have to invest time. Almost everything is very clearly shared at the beginning of the film, and our discussions are more intense when we sit on the shot breakdowns. He involves me in the storyboarding itself.

To my mind, the camera artistry in *Delhi-6* is even better than that in *RDB*. We shot the whole film on Arri Alexa (Alexa from Arri, Germany, a leading manufacturer of camera and lighting systems represents cutting-edge technology in film shooting) except for few shots on the high-speed camera, Phantom.

Last, but not the least, there's a pigeon in the script, Masakali—a metaphor for Sonam Kapoor, who wants to escape the environment she inhabits. Her father played by Om Puri takes care of the pigeons and feeds them, but there is a distance. The pigeons seem to like Sonam, though. Unknown to me, this young girl with unspoken fire in her eyes was about to show the world how much the camera loved her. And she submitted herself with reckless abandon.

Sonam Kapoor
in first person

Mehra made me Sonam Kapoor. Period. There's no other way to say it.

I first met Mehra when I was 21. Dad (Anil Kapoor, actor) and I had gone for the trial screening of *RDB* at Yashraj Studio's private screening theatre, hosted by Aamir Khan. I came out of the screening, shell-shocked and moved to tears, and hugged Mehra. I never imagined I would become his muse someday.

The post-*RDB* phase was when everybody wanted to be Mehra's heroine. I was thrilled to sign *Delhi-6* in September 2007, two months before *Saawariya*, my first film, released. There were lots of names being considered for the male lead. But finally, when Mehra settled on Abhishek, it seemed perfect.

I had been forewarned that to sit through a narration by Mehra is very painful—he takes almost eight hours and meanders all over. But I loved his narration—with the caveat that he's naturally spaced out and doesn't need drugs to be that way! His reputation as a rambling narrator has spread though and is legendary now.

> **Mehra made me Sonam Kapoor. There's no other way to say it.**

I am fortunate that he and I got along. He is kind and sensitive. Mehra understands that I am in my own space among my contemporaries. He sees me as this reluctant warrior princess with oodles of unexplored talent.

The sets of *Delhi-6* and the prep for Bittoo Sharma's role are both unforgettable. I was very thin, and Mehra wanted to fatten me up. I was given a quota of chocolates to finish every day. He knew I liked parathas and *gajar ka halwa* (a sweet preparation made of carrot, milk and sugar), and he ensured that his brother, who was doing the catering, spoilt me silly!

Then came the first day of shoot—the day I broke out as an actor. It was a one-take scene where I had to rattle off two pages of dialogues; it was a walking-talking shot on a steady cam facing Abhishek and myself. The cameraman was struggling for some reason, and we were on our thirteenth take. I was faced with a director who refused to direct me and wanted to stand back and see what emerged from within me. I was losing it all and became nervous.

I went to Mehra and complained that I was unsure about the take, my performance and my look! Triple whammy! 'Sonam, if I think you didn't know your job, I would never hire you,' he responded calmly. That was that! From then on, I gave my takes unabashedly. I could ask any number of questions but he refused to direct me like anybody else would. He has his own style that you understand as you go along.

'Think of me as your football coach. I won't intervene in the middle of the game unless I think you're stepping out of line (going off your character); I'm going to let you play,' he said.

Another thing I remember vividly is that Mehra wanted me to cut my hair for *Delhi-6*, up to my hips. *Saawariya* featured my real hair, which was insanely long. I started crying at the very thought of cutting my hair. '*Kyun bachhi ke baal kaat rahe ho!*' (Why are you cutting the child's hair!) chipped in Waheeda ji, my co-star, in my support. But Mehra is very clear about what the character demands.

Every actor has that one song that plays over and over again and makes them a star. For me, it was 'Masakali'. The pigeon called Masakali was a representation of my spirit in the film, and even after so many years, I am remembered as Masakali. During the shoot of the song, the pigeon was supposed to be on my shoulder, but decided to go to and sit on my head and stayed there. That's how the shoot happened. We also shot for two days on the Delhi metro, which doesn't have bathrooms. Ergo, there was no dressing room! Two people used to hold cloth curtains and I would change for the next shot.

Mehra has an amazing aesthetic. He understands the use of costume to convey the character. He gave Bharathi and me the freedom to embody it. Anamika Khanna did my clothes; I borrowed Bharathi's jewellery and became Bittoo Sharma, the character. In the words of the great actor Sir Ian Murray McKellen, 'Every character you play as an actor filters through you as a person.' There's a sieve of Sonam Kapoor through which Bittoo and Biro, my character in *BMB*, have passed. I was delighted in my character, a young Indian girl whose voice could not be silenced, and gave it my own flavour.

During the shooting schedule, we were put up at a gated community called Nandan Greens. I used to drive with Om Puri to the set every day. I also spent time with Waheeda ji, who is my hero. *Guide*, a 1965 classic featuring Waheeda ji, is my all-time favourite film. In which Waheeda ji plays Rosy, an atypical, flawed Indian character, very ambitious and inspiring. I also loved her in *Pyaasa* and was enamoured by her in the song 'Jaane Kya Tune Kahi'. I have always been told I look like her—a fantastic compliment.

There were get-togethers every other Sunday at Nandan Greens, where we stayed like a family. Everyone would get wasted! Bharathi and I gave each other company with orange juice. I must warn you that Mehra starts singing after two drinks and he's the worst singer in the world. This is even more shocking because he has such a great sense of music. How can he sing so badly!

Mehra spoilt me silly as well. The day we wrapped up, Mehra took me to have *chaat* (savoury roadside snacks) on the streets. We went to Paranthe Wali Gali, ate *chole kulche* (spicy chickpeas with Indian styled bread) and chaat with full abandon. Unfortunately, after my street indulgence, I started throwing up and was down with food poisoning. I had no manager/mother/assistant with me, and Bharathi was my support system. We postponed my return to Mumbai and Mehra sent his niece to babysit me at my hotel room. I was barely conscious, but eventually nursed and mollycoddled back to health.

37

Mehra's films are always respected, whether they succeed or not. This is very unique, because the audience recognizes that he channels his idealism and honesty through his cinema. Mehra gets too involved in the shot. He doesn't sit on the monitor—he sees the action live and is capable of walking into a take and saying 'amazing', forgetting to say 'cut'.

Mehra makes me feel beautiful, intelligent and talented. He makes people who work with him feel capable. He's a university by himself; I'm still in touch with his assistants, Sandeep and Collin, who have flourished from there to make films of their own. Mehra is an enabler. He has a unique generosity of spirit that comes from love for family and love for food. *Delhi-6* changed my life. I am very much a part of his contribution to Indian cinema, as are the iconic films he has made. Every director has three–four films that define them. But Mehra is an original. He is a sensitive poet with a soul that recognizes talent.

I will always cherish the magical cast he put together. Abhishek, whom I've known since childhood, was perpetually late to the sets. He's the most naturally talented actor I've worked with. But Mehra was patient with his naughty streak. In Mehra's own words, Abhishek lent his soul to *Delhi-6*.

Abhishek Bachchan
in first person

'Yeh Delhi hai mere yaar,
Bass ishq mohabbat pyaar.'
(This is Delhi my friend,
we are all about love, love and more love)

These lyrics of the title song from our film *Delhi-6* sum up Rakeysh, our friendship and his approach to life. We had discussed another script before *Delhi-6*; it was called 'Samjhauta Express' and was to be my launch. Unfortunately, that got shelved.

When he narrated *Delhi-6* to me, I heard him out but there was no point. I didn't understand a word of what he was saying. Now I know to steer clear of his narrations. Politely, I asked for the script and read it and suggested some changes, none of which he used. But that's him.

On the first day of the shoot, we were both emotional. We had invested a lot of energy in trying to create a project and work together before, and the moment for him to direct me was both an aspiration and yearning within every fibre of our beings. For *Delhi-6*, he had assembled a stellar star cast. But how Rakeysh manages to create magic on screen has more to do with the atmosphere he creates on the sets.

The entire unit was put up at Nandan Greens in Sambhar village, over 70 km from Jaipur. It was an abandoned place that the team had restored. It had small, quaint one- and two-bedroom cottages. The entire unit, including the crew, was staying within this gated community. There was a common club house for catering, a big lawn for cricket and a gym. The unit lived like a family, building camaraderie off camera. Perhaps it was designed so. It was very common to see Waheeda ji going on her evening walk when I wanted to get a coffee from the club house. Deepak Dobriyal would be flying a kite. Rakeysh and I would be cycling.

Unlike normal shoots, where we would be put up in hotels, where everyone goes back to the privacy of their rooms, this camp was meant for mingling. Also, as the roads were not wide enough for trailers,

38

the production team had taken up a marriage hall to support the shooting. They had rooms that were converted into make-up rooms and the hall at the ground floor was for costume and props. From our accommodation to our shoot, Waheeda Aunty, Chintu Uncle (the late Rishi Kapoor) Om ji, Prem Uncle—everybody was always together. Even if it wasn't our shot, we would be hanging around. I remember Supriya Pathak ji would regale me with her stories. Being naughty around Waheeda Aunty is normal. I have played in her Bangalore farmhouse even as a child so she knows me as *badmaash* (mischievous child).

I used to prepare this special concoction with walnut, ghee, *mirchi* and chaat masala for everyone in the club house. Rakeysh and I are incorrigible foodies, so we found a *halwai* (sweet-maker) in Sambhar, who used to make *gajrela* (gajar ka halwa mixed with mawa). We gorged on it.

I can think of several takeaways from the experience of *Delhi-6*. However, I will elaborate three. First, Rakeysh considers the whole concept of cinema sacred. When he comes to direct you, he's intimate about it. No screaming in the mic for him. Rakeysh expects his actors to absorb the circumstances and the atmosphere and react; he counts on an honest response to the situation in the script from the actor, and this called for great self-discovery on my part. The whole build-up before the take is about 'just being', not acting. And he enforces that sanctity with his calmness. I remember we shot the Ram Leela in a trailer inside a green chroma tent in the middle of the night in Mumbai. I was getting many reminders to begin the shot and I kept delaying for some reason. Finally, Rakeysh himself came with a sense of urgency. 'There's a lot of crowd, let's take the shot,' he said with a level tone. I could see he was upset, wondering why I'm taking time. He could've said, 'What the hell!' But he curbed himself and did not lose his cool. To see a creative genius who doesn't hide his flaws behind the word 'temperamental'—it was wonderful.

Second, there is some absolute magic in the scenes Rakeysh creates. There's a quiet scene in which Chintu Uncle and I are talking. I am drinking beer, he's having tea, and he opens up about his relationship with my mother, Fatima (played by Tanvi Azmi), via a beautiful confession of regret, 'I should've said "I love you" to Fatima 25 years ago. That rascal, your father, took her away.' But there's so much grace and dignity to the whole scene. Also, Rakeysh shoots romance in a very real way and my scenes with Sonam were understated but magical.

Third, I liked how he gets the whole unit to discuss things openly but agree to finally do what he wants to do. I remember the entire unit was talking and discussing the ending of the film. Deep down, Rakeysh himself was conflicted about the ending. He felt that Roshan must die because the mob has found the perfect target, who is half-Muslim and half-Hindu, to vent their anger. They lynch Roshan to death, accusing him to be the *Kaala Bandar* (black monkey) who is creating trouble in the neighbourhood. Personally, I liked the idea of Roshan surviving as a metaphor for hope.

In between flying to Mumbai and Delhi for the premiere of my wife's (Aishwarya Rai Bachchan's) film *Jodhaa Akbar*, we shot both versions and decided that we would take a call at edit. We shot the climax all night on the main road of Sambhar. It was cold: the temperature was sub-zero. I was warm and cozy in my monkey suit but the rest of the cast was freezing!

Delhi-6 is my favourite film— it's most personal to him as well.

Rakeysh added a master stroke, with dad himself playing my dadaji. In the end, I meet him in heaven after I am shot dead. He asks me to 'go back' because, in the middle of chaos, there's a hope that 'India actually works'.

There is no doubt in my mind about Rakeysh's intention or his message. *Delhi-6* is my favourite film—it's most personal to him as well. As a friend, I'm happy that *BMB* gave him the success that he deserves. *Rang De Basanti* has already been declared a modern-day classic and was a narrow miss for me. *Aks* revolutionized the way cinema is styled and shot. In my mind, *Delhi-6* is much more layered and nuanced than *Aks*. It is true that box office matters as much as how a film is remembered, but *Delhi-6* will always be relevant to society.

We went for the Museum of Modern Art's (MOMA's) New York premiere of *Delhi-6* together. The MOMA is a very prestigious theatre. You can't just hire it: the curator has to invite you. We travelled on the Emirates Airbus A380 and were chuffed that we could have a shower at 30,000 feet after a night of blissful sleep. After the screening, I took the whole team to my cousin Shiva's restaurant named 'Dhaba' in New

York. It was midnight, but we had a memorable meal.

For the promotion, I wanted to set a Guinness world record. I vaguely remembered that Will Smith made it to three premieres or so within 24 hours for *I, Robot*. We managed seven cities within 12 hours and claimed that record.

Rakeysh continues to be a low-maintenance friend. He's a part of every family gathering and very happy just being by himself. He doesn't want you to fawn all over him. Professionally, I hope we make *Abhimaan* part two, famously after my parents' iconic original. Rakeysh also has this script ready with the title 'Bhairavi' after his daughter's name, written by Kamlesh Pandey ji.

My only regret? 'Masakali' was shot primarily on Sonam.

MASAKALI

Very few people know that AR mouths his own gobbledygook or phonetic language when he composes a tune.

There was no character called Masakali in the original script. AR kept humming and saying 'Masakali', and was literally on song when he made me hear the track in the middle of the night. I was so taken in by the melody and his ingenious muttering that I went back to the script and named the pigeon in the script Masakali.

And that led to how the song was picturized and made memorable.

CHAPTER 7

The Sublime Music

When a movie is sensitive and about to touch a raw nerve, the music has to be very powerful and hold the entire theme together. Fortunately for me, the music of *Delhi-6* was created by the living legend A.R. Rahman with additional Ram Leela tracks by Rajat Dholakia (aka Juku). This was my second outing with AR after *RDB*, which had already been declared a classic. We had an understanding.

I first met AR with Jhamu Sugandh, who had financed a part of my first film *Aks* and presented both Ashutosh Gowariker's *Lagaan* and Mani Ratnam's *Bombay*. He took me to meet AR in Chennai. I narrated a story called 'Samjhauta Express' to AR; he even did a lovely soundtrack but that wasn't meant to be. The next time we met was in London, when he was recording for a musical.

The late '90s saw a shift in Indian sensibilities. A lot of us wanted to take India to the world in whatever we were doing. We weren't apologetic about Hindi cinema and believed that our stories were powerful and original. In hindsight, this was a defining period for Indian cinema. Yes, western budgets were bigger, but budgets are never an excuse for making bad cinema. AR led the bandwagon of India's creators who knew that the only way to export your culture is through art and mass media, be it music, literature, sports or, of course, cinema. He shared Indian culture with the world without expressly claiming

42

to do so. AR's music is fundamentally universal—it cannot be placed within any silo. In that lies his genius. One of the greatest joys of my life has been to be inside the recording studio when AR is creating a song of mine, not because I feel the need to guide but because I enjoy seeing his creative genius at work.

AR understands something very fundamental: there's only one truth when you're making a film—that you're making that one film. Music, editing, cinematography, art direction, wardrobe, lyrics, actors etc. all have to tell that same story. They all have to serve the film and the director's job is to remind each artist of the one vision that everyone is working towards.

In his words, 'You could write the most interesting piece of music, but it's of no use if it doesn't enhance the film.' This is the key: a song that works in one film or one setting is unique to that. To say that 'Punjabi remixes are the rage; lets insert one in our film' is bordering on insanity. The music has to serve the film. The songs are the emotion the characters need to express.

That's why AR always wants to understand the script deeply. As a creator, everyone associated with the film is walking a tightrope because neither the story, nor the music it commands may be the flavour of the day. In fact, it may be set way in the past or much ahead in the future. But an original creation always commands attention and is quite enough to shine through!

> **'You could write the most interesting piece of music, but it's of no use if it doesn't enhance the film.'**

Luckily, I always plan the music of a film even before I start casting. You could say that I start planning the music when I am writing the script. It helps me integrate the songs into the narrative and take the story forward. My role with AR is to transfer my deepest convictions and feelings for the story—why am I making this film, what are my fears, my anxieties, my dreams. He hears me out patiently and then interprets it in his own way.

He understands me, and I have always been in awe of his

unquestionable genius. He knows that my songs are not lip-synched like other Indian films and he respects that. I find it difficult to believe in my characters if they break into a song and dance. I have compromised on this stand of mine on two occasions, once in *Aks*, in which Raveena plays a singer and is supposed to lip-sync and later in *BMB*, when the characters allowed it.

After AR set the music, Prasoon Joshi joined in to pen the lyrics and together we created one of most memorable sound track and songs that the Indian film industry has witnessed. To this day, many call it one of AR's best works. For me, whatever AR creates is magical.

The way AR and I work is that I keep narrating to him and he keeps creating something magical in his head. The essence of *Delhi-6* is of the prodigal son who returns home. I told him that we need a whole new rendition for the qawwali, a musical noblesse conferred upon the world by Hazrat Amir Khusrau, composed in the emotional flavour of 'Mora Piya Ghar Aaya'.

We don't discuss scenes like 'this is the situation, boy proposes to the girl' or such! He knows the entire flow of the film and its ethos and keeps creating. He kept churning melodies for *Delhi-6*.

On one occasion, late at night (its only late at night with AR), we were both in the zone and I asked him, 'Why... Why are humans like this ... divided by religion when all religions are just a route to realizing your own self?' Instead of answering me, he composed 'Rehna Tu'.

He played the tune to me on the continuum, an instrument which sounds like a violin married a piano. The tune captured the need for a secular mindset that respects individuality—'be yourself just the way you are'—irrespective of caste, creed, religious or racial biases. There was so much pain in the tune, but oddly enough, the melody was about self-acceptance. Back in the hotel room, I broke down.

Prasoon wrote the line 'Rehna Tu Hai Jaisa Tu' and we recorded the song. Later, after the song was done, while I was reading Prasoon's notes, I came across a stanza:

Haath thaam chalna ho
To dono ke daaye haath sang kaise

Ek daaya hoga ek baaya hoga
Thaam le haath yeh thaam le
Chalna hai sang, thaam le

Rehna tu
Hai jaisa tu

(It can't be two right hands that walk side by side.
One hand has to be the left hand and the other will be the right
hand. You have to let each hand be.)

I was blown away. I asked, 'Why is this para not in the song?'
   'It is already too long,' came the reply.
   'No way, this para is the soul,' I insisted.
   We re-recorded the song with the additional stanza. The lyrics crafted by Prasoon were the perfect yin to AR's yang and took it to the next level.
   The one song that I wanted—about homecoming was taking time. There were times when I wondered what I could do to expedite the theme song I wanted. I read the poetry of Rumi to him, which both AR and I share in our own way. But AR will

To this day, many call it one of AR's best works. For me, whatever AR creates is magical.

make you see the difference between creation and creativity. He's pure genius. You have to let him be and let him do his thing; the music just emerges.
   I used to land up in Chennai with a one-way ticket, not knowing when I would return. While there, I kept working on my other scripts inspired by the way AR kept working. On another occasion, at 5 a.m., he shook me from the couch where I was sleeping.
   AR: Mr Mehra!
   Me: Hmmm?
   AR: I just had a dream about 'Mora Piya Ghar Aaya'.
   Me: Yeah!
   AR: Yeah!
We were both excited like toddlers set loose in a toy store. He

gave me headphones where he had recorded himself jamming for 35 minutes. I was absolutely bedazzled, in thrall of The Master's work. That is when I understood that beyond the noise of Bollywood, Hollywood, Mollywood, when I'm with AR, I am in the presence of Mozart, Beethoven, Tansen, Bade Ghulam Ali Khan, Chopin, Vangelis all at once, to name a few. His music is transcendental.

In the thirty-second minute of the composition, magic happened! Hidden there, was the theme song of *Delhi-6*: 'Arziyaan'. It took AR one year to build this masterpiece.

> *Maula, Maula, Maula mere Maula*
> *Darareein darareein hai maathe pe Maula*
> *Marammat, mukaddar ki kar do Maula, mere Maula.*

(The creases of my destiny are embedded on my forehead like worry lines, fix my destiny, O Lord.)

To give this perspective, the Taj Mahal took 17 years to build. So we were lightning quick, I reckon! But my favourite track in *Delhi-6* remains the surreal song 'Dil Gira Dafatan'.

> *Dil gira kahee par dafatan*
> *Jaane magar ye nayan*
> *Tere khaamosh julfon ke gehraayiya*
> *Hai jaha dil mera*
> *Uljha huwa hai wahin kho gaya*
> *Tu magar hai bekhabar, hai bekhabar*
> *Dil gira kahee par dafatan, kyon gunj rahee hai dhadkan*

(My heart has fallen somewhere, all of a sudden, unexpectedly. But these eyes know the depths of your silent locks where my heart is entangled. There itself it, the heart, has got lost. But you are ignorant of it all. Why is the sound of heartbeats echoing?)

This is the heartfelt hark from a reticent boy to the firebrand girl he loves. In order to bring out true emotion, AR believes that a singer must be able to act out the song when he's belting it out. For 'Dil Gira

Dafatan', he wanted a blues feel to the music. So he reached out to Ash King, who didn't know a word of Hindi and had never sung a Hindi song in his life. So while I taught Ash King how to speak Hindi, AR recorded a line a day and finished it over 17 days. That's the thing with the man; he never tells you how hard he works.

Now, I had this beautiful song and the next step was how to film it, so I wrote a 'dream' sequence for Roshan. One early morning, Roshan wakes up on the terraces of Old Delhi to discover that the Statue of Liberty is standing tall as a part of the skyline of Old Delhi right next to Jama Masjid. The streets are deserted and when he opens the closed gates to another lane, he enters Times Square. All the characters of our story, including the cow giving birth to a calf, are splattered generously over the landscape: his two diverse worlds had merged, quite seamlessly. The symbols now get mixed up as the Ram Leela parade that one would see in Chandni Chowk travels down Times Square led by break dancers. There is Vincent van Gogh painting a portrait of Bittoo (Sonam Kapoor). As he looks for her, Roshan, now aka King Kong or Kaala Bandar of Delhi-6, finds her on top of the Empire State Building. They kiss in his world.

47

I envisaged Kaala Bandar to be a metaphor about the evil within in the film. I sent the edit to AR and got the best compliment I have ever got. 'Mr Mehra, you are a genius!' It was a classic case of Rahman being gracious in praise; it is his talent that's exemplary.

The second part of the music of *Delhi-6* is my dear friend Juku. *Delhi-6* features a parallel music track—that of the journey of Lord Rama depicted as folklore and enacted as Ram Leela, the traditional street theatre of our land, and played out in Old Delhi every year in all its grandeur. Juku composed the additional tracks of the Ram Leela scenes for *Delhi-6*.

Before starting to make movies, I had made over 200 ad films. Many of my relationships are thanks to that decade in advertising. Juku is one of them, whom I met when I walked into Bombay's Grand Centre restaurant one evening with Rajiv Kenkre, one of the finest sound engineers India has ever produced. For the uninitiated, sound engineering is a highly technical skill and can make all the difference to how the audience experiences music. Rajiv ushered me to a table where

I met Paresh Rawal, Shafi Inamdar and a very jovial gentleman named Rajat Dholakia. With Juku's absolute command over the minutiae of music, the evening took an unexpected turn. I started to understand his passion for music and the expression of emotion through music.

I will never forget what happened when I first met Juku.

Me: I will give you ₹1.25 (*sawa rupaiyya* is auspicious in Indian culture) and am signing you for a film I will make sometime. I don't know when, but I will make it.

Juku: Anytime! The purity with which you have offered me sawa rupaiyya is evidence enough for me that we will work together on hundreds of projects.

Unknown to me, this gem of a man, an inventive virtuoso with a yen for music, had also taken a liking to me.

Juku says,

> Before I met Rakeysh, I had composed music for 400 plays for theatre and films like *Mirch Masala* (1987). But that evening was a date with destiny at Grand Centre Restaurant and Bar. Later, when Rakeysh was contracted for a commercial, Rajiv Kenkre and I worked on the music and that's how our musical journey together began.

Juku was pure magic. He went on to win National Awards for *Dharavi* (1992) and *Sunday* (1993 [best music direction for non-feature film]). I looked out for every possible opportunity to work with him. So after composing music for over a hundred commercials for me, Juku and I built an unbelievable equation. He was to be a guiding force in my life. Juku was the one who scored the music for my first documentary, *Mamuli Ram: The Little Big Man*.

Rajat Dholakia
in first person

Arre re re! What should I say about Rakeysh!

(The emotional 'arre re re', a common Hindi exclamation that can mean a whole range of things depending on the tone, resurfaces every 5 minutes!)

Rakeysh and I have made more than 100 ad films together. In fact he gave me a break into the world of ad commercials. It was the '90s, when ad films were his bread and butter and his Tardeo office was full of positive energy. But from the very beginning, I could spot that Rakeysh's ambition was to make films.

Somewhere in the mid-'90s, Rakeysh had started expressing his keenness to make a feature film; he wanted to make 'Samjhauta Express', a beautiful story about a train from India to Pakistan. He was contemplating the script with Kamlesh Pandey and Abhishek Bachchan. This was to be his first movie and I know every scene of this movie. But it was not to be.

What I truly find remarkable is that even after so many years and making successful commercial films, Rakeysh continues to be the god of pure cinema. There is an aching purism in his work. Despite the obvious distractions, he does not pander to the superstar culture or to any sycophancy. He's not here to bootlick egos or to help create a larger than life image for anyone else. If anything, he deconstructs life itself threadbare and lays it out for his viewers.

I still remember the docu-drama that Nita Bhabhi (Nita Ambani) asked him to make, to surprise Mukesh Bhai (Mukesh Ambani) on his fiftieth birthday in 2007. Rakeysh captured the core 'involvement' of Mukesh in the business, his knowledge of the concepts of Arthshastra and Arthaneeti as well as his human side effortlessly. He focussed on Mukesh Bhai's love for the family and close-knit friends and beautifully wove it into an endearing personal narrative.

Having known him for so many years, I can say that Rakeysh is an idealistic wanderer held together by his wife, Bharathi. What a woman! During *BMB*, I remember that they were not able to raise funds. Bharathi said, 'Let's keep the properties on mortgage and produce it ourselves.' What a wife! Unlike other wives who hold the husbands' ambition back by worrying about kids and security, Bharathi provides the energy and confidence to Rakeysh that everything will be alright; he should go and chase his dreams.

I feel connected to Rakeysh and would like to believe that I have been part of all his films, even though Ranjit Barot and Anu Malik set the score to *Aks* and Shankar–Ehsaan–Loy composed for *BMB*.

I have also acted in *Delhi-6*. I am the *fakir* in the film who carries a mirror every time he appears on screen and shows it to the characters saying '*Jhaankh le*' (look inside yourself). While most people dismiss me as a tramp, later in the pre-climax, Abhishek shows the same mirror to the key characters who have now divided themselves to Hindu mobs and Muslim mobs. He tells them in the same mirror they will each find their God—Hindu's will find their bhagwan and the Muslims their Allah. He is inside us and does not reside in a mosque or a temple; so what are we fighting about?

What I truly find remarkable is that even after so many years and making successful commercial films, Rakeysh continues to be the god of pure cinema.

The classic 'Sasural Genda Phool' from *Delhi-6* is credited to me. But it's a folk tune, an original Chhatishgarhi number, introduced to us by Raghubir Yadav and delivered in true Bundelkhandi style. 'Sasural Genda Phool' was a surreal experience. Rahman was in Mumbai for work and on his way to the airport. We were all at Ranjit Barot's studio. Rahman came in, and within 10 minutes, gave us the 'oye hoye hoye' refrain in the beginning and said that nothing else needed to change. Rakeysh, Ranjit and Raghubir—all of us were present and received Rahman's input—were stunned, bedazzled and ecstatic. We had a song of the kind Hindi cinema had never heard before. In fact, Bharathi was so kicked about it that she wanted to use the original version of the lyrics in the film.

'We have to do this in Hindi,' Rakeysh beseeched her.

'I won't talk to you if you change anything,' pat came the reply from Bharathi.

But somehow, Rakeysh, Ranjit, Prasoon and I prevailed and Rekha Bharadwaj gave us her sublime voice to maintain the rustic feel of the song. We all know that the music in Rakeysh's films is out of this world! The secret to that is that Rakeysh is a poet at heart. And Rahman is a master who brings Rakeysh's poetry alive.

1.

The Depression after *Delhi-6*

✳

1. On top of the world—Framing Jama Masjid at the
far end of the labyrinth of terraces.
2. Incendiary emotions take root—Hindu vs Muslim.

Aeene Mein Dekha Toh
आईने में देखा तो

Ganjo ke shahar mein main kanghi bechney nikla tha
aeene mein dekha toh pataa chalaa
duniya ne merey hi baal noch daley!

(I set out, like a fool, to sell a comb in a city of bald people.
When I looked in the mirror,
The world had shaved my head too!)

—Rakeysh Omprakash Mehra

CHAPTER 8

The Fate at the Box Office

Every artist had put their heart and soul into Delhi-6. *For the cover* design of the soundtrack of *Delhi-6*, we embedded an actual mirror on the CD cover and also when the first teaser poster of the movie was released. The idea was for society to take a good hard look at itself in the mirror. In the end credit roll, we had the entire cast appear on screen one by one and take a bow looking at their own reflection. I asked each actor to give that one emotion that defines their character: it was just amazing to see their talent emerge like a fountainhead.

The film opened on Friday, 20 February 2009, to a great response at the box office. By Sunday, we had done over 40 crore of business, but then came Monday, and the audience just vanished from the theatres. The collections that started dropping on day four never picked up. I was devastated. Was it too dark a reality for them? Were they unable to identify with the protagonist?

I was in the line of fire! Was *Delhi-6* an actualization of the proverbial love's labour lost?

The box office debacle, and my own conflict with what ending was appropriate, shook me deeply. Was I capable of producing great cinema consistently? Was *RDB* a fluke? As I have said before, this period was after the runaway success of *RDB*.

Over a live radio interview in Delhi, a caller announced a death warrant for me: 'Bastard! How can you say Allah and Bhagwan are both inside you?'

The National Commission for the Scheduled Castes summoned me to their office. 'How can you refer to Jalebi [Divya Dutta] as lower caste?' they asked.

I implored them to see my intention in context: in the beginning of the film, when Roshan (Abhishek) accidentally touches Jalebi, an untouchable, Gobar (an upper caste Brahmin played by Atul Kulkarni) wants to pour a bucket of water over his head to cleanse him. In the end, Gobar himself holds Jalebi's hand. This is an ideological win. The commission was led by a very senior Congress leader who was in Parliament. They threatened to throw me out of the fourth floor of the window where the meeting was taking place at Khan Market in Delhi.

Thankfully, Ronnie stood steadfast by my side. He had lost a lot of money but never complained. Instead, he kept asking me about my next film. But my senses had deafened. The audience and critics that had loved me and showered praises post *RDB* were taking me apart piece by piece.

The reviews read thus:

'The shockingly graceless final stretch, which implodes under the treacly burden of its good intentions,' wrote blogger Bharadwaj Rangan.*

'It's hard to qualify *Delhi-6* as an actual film,' wrote Raja Sen in a review titled 'Yeh Silly Hai Mere Yaar' on rediff.com. 'If dying means I get to wear white and sit next to Amitabh Bachchan and eat jalebis, I really wouldn't mind being run over by a bus.'**

'Ultimately then, the film is a noble failure. *Delhi-6* is ambitious and well-intentioned, but good intentions don't always translate into good cinema,' said Anupama Chopra in her review on NDTV.***

I was going deeper and deeper into a dark hole.

Unable to take it anymore, I drowned myself in alcohol. Not that I had never drunk before. In fact, I am infamous for getting drunk

---

*https://baradwajrangan.wordpress.com/2009/02/21/review-delhi-6/; accessed on 27 April 2021.
**Raja Sen, 'Yeh Silly Hai Mere Yaar', *rediff.com*, 20 February 2009. Available at https://www.rediff.com/movies/2009/feb/20raja-review-delhi6.htm; accessed on 27 April 2021.
***https://www.ndtv.com/video/shows/picture-this/anupama-chopra-reviews-delhi-6-57106; accessed on 27 April 2021.

on my third drink, and post that, my behaviour is all about being footloose, singing songs, hugging and kissing my friends and so on! It's how several people express their joy—for me, having a good time is also a manifestation of my love for my cast and crew and friends.

This time, my relationship with alcohol and the reasons for which I was getting sunk in its stupor were different. I wanted to drink myself to death—to sleep and never get up. Now, alcoholism is a very weak character trait! We all know that. We give excuses for our own shortcomings and become lesser human beings when we hit the bottle. I could see how much pain I was bringing to Bharathi and our daughter, Bhairavi, who was now in her pre-teens. My son Vedant was observing and things were eroding between us. I remained careless and insensitive to my closest ones, the people I loved the most. As I let myself drown, a part of me started to look for a float.

It was Bharathi who spoke to me and made me see reason. She told me:

They threatened to throw me out of the fourth floor of the window where the meeting was taking place at Khan Market in Delhi.

You have to see the low of *Delhi-6* in the context of the high of *RDB*. While it is normal for actors to be asked for autographs, post *RDB* when we were walking down Soho, London, people approached you for your autograph. Your fame was heroic. From that standpoint, the debacle of *Delhi-6* seems catastrophic. But look at the film with fresh eyes: did the characters we created fail? Was the message of *Delhi-6* not important enough? Maybe some parts failed but some parts succeeded too! We also have to think about the kids. Bhairavi knows what has happened, but Vedant is small and confused about why you're so traumatized. How will the children have the courage to fail if you react so badly to it? No failure is final unless you decide it to be. Who will make the films that need to be made if you don't?

As I heard Bharathi, I realized I couldn't let down the woman who had always chosen me over every material comfort in life. I had to rise!

57

The Depression after *Delhi-6*

CHAPTER 9

Delhi-6
Lives On

Six months later, one morning I woke up with a clear head.

I had taken up a canvas and painted it, now I wanted to add some colours to it. I called Binod Pradhan.

Binod: You are still alive!

Me: Kind of.

Binod: Ready with your next?

Me: Not yet. I'm not done with *Delhi-6*. I want three days from you to finish it.

Binod: Sure, tell me about it.

I told him that the original script begins with a scene in which the ashes are being immersed by Roshan's father in the Ganges. Roshan's voice says,

Those are my ashes. The earthen urn you see that holds them: dadi had bought for herself for 101 rupees, but I got to use it. I am dead now! They mistook me for a kaala bandar and killed me. Speaking of monkeys, I came to Delhi...

It is after this that the plot opens up.

From the very first frame, the audience knows that the hero is going to die, and his commentary narrations (was recorded in the past tense since Roshan will die) lead us through the story, underlining key moments. It was a completely different experience. So six months after the film was released, we spent three days shooting a new beginning and modifying the ending. Bharathi put her heart and soul into the new edit. She was rewriting the screenplays on the editing table while dealing with a wreck of a director and a husband.

The new edit went to the Venice International Film Festival. We got a late night slot but the main theatre and the red carpet. The morning after the screening, there was a small crowd and press reporters in my hotel lobby. They somehow had my photographs and wanted autographs. There was this senior critic from *Variety* and we got a front full page article for *Delhi-6*. The headline said: '(UN) BOLLYWOOD'.

This was heartening, more so because none of the popular awards back in India recognized either the story or the direction of the film. Then came the announcement of the national awards. *Delhi-6* had won in two categories: the national film award for best production design (Samir Chanda) for the brilliant re-creation of Old Delhi and the Nargis Dutt Award for best feature film on national integration. Suddenly, the dark humour came back full circle: how could I get death threats for making a film about national integration?

> I would love to see my version of *Delhi-6* with the newly shot ending in theatres again—we fondly call it the Venice cut. I want to share it with my audiences so they can see the story I wanted to tell.

I would love to see my version of *Delhi-6* with the newly shot ending in theatres again—we fondly call it the Venice cut. I want to share it with my audiences so they can see the story I wanted to tell. Modern platforms like Amazon Prime and Netflix are ideal for this because the mindset of the audiences has changed completely.

As recently as 2020, 11 years after the release of the film, there was an article in *The Hindu* by editor Namrata Joshi. She quoted *Delhi-6* and the song 'Rehna Tu' and its relevance at a time when once again the nation stands divided between the right-wing Hindus and extreme Muslims.*

Delhi-6 lives on, because of me and in spite of me. And I have filled the vacuum I had left in the film long ago.

---

*Namrata Joshi, 'Why "Delhi-6" Resonates Even More Today than It Did 10 Years Ago', *The Hindu*, 24 January 2020. Available at https://www.thehindu.com/entertainment/movies/why-delhi-6-resonates-even-more-today-than-it-did-10-years-ago/article30643596.ece; accessed on 27 April 2021.

———————————————————————————

Stop acting so small
You are the universe in ecstatic motion.

—Jalaluddin Rumi

———————————————————————————

1.

The Colours of My Youth

✳

1. Vivek Bhushan and I attempt a trek to the perilous
   Manimahesh Kailash peak (Himachal Pradesh)
2. I take guard as Rajiv Tandon kicks, just for kicks
3. Vivek Bhushan and Rajiv Varma pose as I click
   them in Dalhousie (Himachal Pradesh)

FOUR FRIENDS

Vivek Bhushan: *Kya karna hai*? (What should we do?)

Me: *Bhooth dhoondne chalte hain.* (Let us look for ghosts)

Rajiv Varma: Gin and lime *hai*? (Do we have gin and lime?)

Rajiv Tandon: *Badkhal Lake ke peeche ek burial ground hai, wahaan dhoondte hain*! (Let's go to the burial ground behind Badkhal Lake and look for ghosts!)

CHAPTER 10

Friendship

If my adventurous childhood was laced with a caring family and wonderful opportunities, my youth was laced with friendship and mischief—as it should be! I've been fortunate to have friends thick as banyan tree trunks through college days and after. We were four notorious rats—Vivek Bhushan, Rajiv Verma, Rajiv Tandon and I.

Bhushi (or Vivek Bhushan) was senior to me by three years when I first met him in 1980. He was on the sports selection committee of SRCC. In Vivek's words,

> Rakeysh was 17 and was trying to impress the hell out of me, seeking admission on the basis of his swimming credentials. Not shy of using his oddly energetic yet languid 'I've come up the hard way' appeal to worm his way into my approval, I liked him from the very first moment I saw him. I supported Rakeysh's admission on two grounds: he was a gifted swimmer and his oddly wired brain saw solutions, where others could see only problems. Over time, I knew I had made the right decision. With Rakeysh, I learnt how to live in the moment and enjoy it.

At the prestigious SRCC, it was roll-call time on the first day of college. The professor asked students to stand up and introduce themselves and share their twelfth grade percentages. Everyone who stood up before my turn had scored above 94.6 per cent as that was the cut-off mark for admission into SRCC.

'Rakeysh Mehra, 56.6 per cent,' I declared rather shyly.

The professor thought he hadn't heard correctly, so he asked again.

'Rakeysh Mehra, 56.6 per cent,' I repeated.

The professor was ready to drop dead!

'How?' he persisted.

'Sports case sir,' I replied.

'It is students like you who spoil the name of SRCC. It is not a leading college in India but also in the world, and known for its esteemed faculty,' the professor was livid with rage.

I was in tears. A hand reached out.

'Sir, My name is Rajiv Tandon. I have topped in Economics in twelfth grade at Frank Anthony Public School. I have got into SRCC because of my merit, and Rakeysh has got in because of his.'

I could literally see the colour drain from the professor's face.

And Rajiv Tandon—from back then till the day I was felicitated recently by the SRCC college faculty as one of the five most distinguished alumni—has had my back. He is my producing partner in ROMP Pictures to this day.

In a way, it was sports that got the four of us together. I was the college swimming captain, Varma was the athletics captain and Vivek Bhushan was the national champion in track—800 metres. Rajiv Tandon, the mildest in our crazy cohort, was the college football captain. And we were all born in different years: Bhushi in '60, Varma in '61, Tandon in '62 and I in '63.

We loved frequenting a ramshackle joint, something of a small thatched hut on the banks of the Yamuna called 'Majnu Ka Tilla' (can it get cheesier than that?). In those days, we could only afford rice beer, also called chhang, the cheapest alcohol available, and we shamelessly frequented the place because the ladies who waited on us at the tables were seriously pretty!

Bhushi elaborates cheekily,

Rakeysh had a way with the lady owner of Majnu Ka Tilla and all its beautiful hostesses. The three of us were notorious for never attending any class, piggybacking on the notes of Tandon, whom we have already established as our saving grace. We bullied him into doing our work and held him responsible for our collective grades too!

In those days, Bhushi was the only guy with any serious money. His father, retired Lt Col Kul Bhushan, used to run a garment export business. The middle class was represented by Varma and Tandon. Varma's mother ran a garment fabrication factory and Tandon's father worked in Peerless Insurance. As for me, well, I had just bought my first pair of sneakers in life.

We wore each other's clothes, drank our rum neat but were completely serious and dedicated about our respective sports.

We thrived in absolute aimlessness and bonded only because of that. We wore each other's clothes, drank our rum neat but were completely serious and dedicated about our respective sports.

Shri Ram College of Commerce was extremely well known for academics but had no presence in highly competitive sports at Delhi University. This gave us an opportunity to work hard for three years, practise tirelessly all day and prove ourselves. We fought with the management and increased the sports quota. In the University Games, aside from our own individual sport, everyone took part in events like long-distance running and marathon among others, as it earned us one point for participation. It seemed our small drops were good enough to fill the ocean, and by the end of my third year, it was nothing short of a miracle that SRCC won the prestigious vice-chancellor's trophy which was awarded to the best college in sports in Delhi University. This taught me early in life that hard work and perseverance can make your dreams come true.

CHAPTER 11

The Seeds of
Rang De Basanti

Our youth could very well be the youngsters in RDB: *crazy, riotous* and uncontrollable!
Varma chips in:

68   You could add two more people to our group. Jagdeep and Jagdev were brothers who had been with Rakeysh right from his Air Force Bal Bharati School days. Jagdev, one year senior to us, was a serious TT player and a Hanuman bhakt, and you could see shades of him in Sharman Joshi's character from *RDB*. I could see myself in Atul Kulkarni, a political worker, itching to change the system through ideological protest and patriotism. Jagdeep, three years senior to us, was a hopeful for the Indian cricket team along with Vivek Bhushan. Both contributed shades to the iconic DJ of *RDB* played by Aamir Khan. Both flunked exams and had their identities closely linked to a sense of belonging to Delhi University. Their comfort zone was their claim to fame. Siddharth's character was borrowed heavily from Tandon, who stood no bullshit ever! I think Rakeysh would be closest to Madhavan (air force fighter pilot)—idealistic and action-oriented, always wanting to change the system. Kunal Kapoor's character was representative of the rustic flavour of Old Delhi and its biases. *Rang De Basanti* has at least 20 scenes from our raucous, irreverent times. Case in point being Vivek Bhushan's red Gypsy,

driving around at night and the complete lack of seriousness with which we looked at life itself.

Even though we were quite footloose and fancy free, in hindsight, we were fortunate enough to find girlfriends at every party. The thumb rule was that on any given day, three of us could get drunk and the fourth had to give us a ride home.

Most nights, Varma would borrow his elder brother's scooter or Tandon would borrow his father's scooter (unwittingly). Vivek had a bike and that's how all four of us would meander around.

More often than not, the gang ended up at my house. After all, Maa would always have food ready!

Vivek Bhushan narrates further:

Having drinks with Bauji and having Aunty's rajma chawal was the ultimate treat! Mamta always wanted to be part of the fun. She was our favourite little girl, a collective outlet for all of us to show we could actually be good, caring folks.

Rakeysh was the ladies' man amongst us, and here's the funny thing about it! He could juggle up to three girlfriends at a time while openly discussing them with each other. There were mornings when he didn't recognize the girls we had partied with the previous night, and yet girls loved him most of all!

> **Even though we were quite footloose and fancy free, in hindsight, we were fortunate enough to find girlfriends at every party.**

Few things bothered him. And since he wasn't hiding anything, he never felt any shame either. All this while the rest of us found it difficult to handle the one girl we were loyal to at the time! Very early, I realized that behind all the tomfoolery, Rakeysh's mind was wired differently.

When I look back today at Bhushi, Tandon and Varma, I realize that I did not fit in economically into this group. But they never made me feel that. In our initial days, I used to feel embarrassed to call friends home. Right outside our staff quarters at the Claridges was a staircase that led to a garbage dump, with a caustic stench that spread out for at least half a mile.

After our many romps at night, my friends used to cheerfully ignore the garbage dump and climb that staircase, behaving as if the malodour simply did not exist! All they could smell was the rajma chawal my mom made.

I could've never found more giving or grounded friends. And yet, I knew that work would take all of us in separate ways soon.

During those days, there was a Jumbo-point (where one could watch international flights take off and land) outside the wired boundary of the Palam airport on the Delhi–Jaipur highway. We would sneak in through the barbed wire and run towards a plane that was about to take off: trying to reach higher and higher and pretend to touch the rising plane.

Bahut dino se hai ye mashgala siyasat ka,
Ke jab jawan hon bachay tou qatal ho jayen.

(For many days it has been the ploy of the establishment
To kill the young when they find their voice against the rulers.)

—Sahir Ludhianvi

Official poster of *Rang De Basanti*
Courtesy: ROMP Pictures

Rang De Basanti

✳

Koi bhi desh perfect nahin hota ... use behtar banana padta hai.

(No country is perfect, we have to make it better.)

—Flt Lt Ajay Rathod in *RDB*

CHAPTER 12

The Story of
MiG-21s

Rang De Basanti *was my second film. Rooted in my youth, inspired* by the unique traits of my friends and revved up with purpose, it had the unlikeliest of beginnings.

My journey to making films was through advertising and one of my assignments in 1996 was a docu-drama called *Mamuli Ram*. I was cooped up in Gujarat, in the village of Anand for almost three months. Kamlesh Pandey often dropped by and stayed with the crew for a couple of days. Gujarat is a dry state (prohibition), and the villages of Kheda district had no nightlife. The shoots were mostly in the day time and we got some time in the evenings to hang out and recite poetry over endless cups of chai. A common love was the work of Sahir Ludhianvi, Kazi Nazrul Islam and Dharamveer Bharti.

Kamlesh and I would talk at length about the armed revolution of India and resistance against the British Empire that had enslaved India for over 200 years. Young students transformed themselves into fiercely patriotic revolutionaries and sacrificed their lives in their early 20s with their heads held high.

He narrated that when it was time for Bhagat Singh to be escorted to the gallows, he asked the jailor to wait till he finished his book on Lenin.

'Wait a minute Jailor Saab, one revolutionary is meeting another.'

Kamlesh would also talk about Bhagat Singh's famous last lines to the jailor minutes before his last breath: '*Hamare baad aur bhi aayenge*' (There will be more rebels/revolutionaries after us). Many years later, I used it as the opening scene of *RDB*.

I used to wonder what made these young guns drop their aimlessness and give their life for the country! To quote George Bernard Shaw, it's a pity that youth is wasted on the young.

My mind went to Gore Vidal's *Billy the Kid*, the classic 1989 western starring Val Kilmer, who played an outlaw named William Bonney, a cold-blooded killer and an all-American boy rolled into one. 'Let's make a Billy the Kid (patriotic) version of Bhagat Singh,' I suggested. 'And let's keep it realistic,' I added.

The story captured the essence of Indian armed resistance against the might of the British Empire between 1919 and 1935.

After a few months, Kamlesh ji gave me a script titled 'The Young Guns of India'. The story captured the essence of Indian armed resistance against the might of the British Empire between 1919 and 1935. I was as excited as a drone honey bee that's about to mate—deep down I felt the same way the revolutionaries felt. They wanted to end exploitation of one human being by another, and this equality was as important as the absence of the British from India!

The question on my mind was, 'Can the youth of today relate to this?' I asked a friend of mine in an ad agency to help me run the script through a focus group of youngsters. We hired a small banquet hall in Parel in Mumbai and invited 30–40 college kids. I started talking to them about the script 'The Young Guns of India'. To my shock, they completely rejected the idea. The MTV generation wasn't interested in revolutions. They wanted to wear the latest denims and perfume, go out on dates, wear Nike shoes and go to the US for studies. Eventually, they would find work with a multinational and settle abroad. These were the professed aspirations of young India.

But I didn't want to believe it. I said, 'Maybe we picked the wrong sample.'

So I repeated the focus group exercise in Delhi. I felt that perhaps I would be able to connect to those youngsters better. Imagine my shock when I realized that at least the yuppie crowd of Mumbai heard me out and sat in the room for two hours. The Delhi folks rejected my idea within five minutes. In fact, one of the guys asked me, 'Was Chandrashekhar Azad grandfather of cricketer Kirti Azad?'

Another had the opinion, 'If Bhagat Singh was born today he would at best join the Indian Army or the State Bank of India.' Someone else objected, 'I would rather join Citibank than the Indian Army! Why serve a corrupt nation?'

This hurt more than I thought it would. Kamlesh ji too was very upset.

'This is not happening, Rakeysh. The generation is just not getting it. Let's work on something else.'

But 'The Young Guns of India' never left my consciousness. I continued making several ad films and also my first film, *Aks*, in 2001. But during this time, the charged atmosphere in the country brought back the relevance of the script Pandey had created. India's MiG-21 fighter planes were bursting into balls of fire. These were trial flights, not war, and we were losing our young men to training! Media had started dubbing the MiG-21 the 'widow maker'.*

As for me, the MiG-21 wasn't just another plane. Entering the Air Force Bal Bharati School gate every day, we would see the shell of a MiG-21 on the front lawn. This aircraft was embedded in my consciousness. My teachers were the wives of the air-borne warriors, the fighter pilots, and their kids were my friends. During school, we were taken to tours of air shows. There was a stage in my life during which to be a fighter pilot in the Indian Air Force (IAF) was a dream of mine. The MiG was an iconic symbol of the IAF. To put things in

77

---

*Ninad D. Sheth, 'With 28 Fighters Lost in 1999, IAF's Flight Record Plummets. But Is the MoD Listening?', *India Today*, 7 February 2000. Available https://www.indiatoday.in/magazine/defence/story/20000207-with-28-fighters-lost-in-1999-iafs-flight-record-plummets.-but-is-the-mod-listening-777048-2000-02-07; accessed on 27 April 2021.

context, I'll refer to a brilliant *New York Times* article that came much later in 2013, but chronicled the scandal at the time surrounding the aircraft. Here's the extract.

> The MiG is the most-produced combat jet in aviation history since World War II ... The aircraft has participated in every major conflict involving India since 1963, and was the bedrock for most of the air force's operations. However, the availability of spare parts and maintenance was a major concern for India's ageing fleet, and the country has looked at various cheaper options in countries like Israel and former Soviet states like Ukraine. This prompted the defense authorities in Moscow to warn India not to cut corners in purchasing authentic parts. The Russian ambassador in New Delhi, Alexander Kadakin, said, 'India should not be surprised if aircrafts meet with accidents if it continues to use spares from outside Russia.'*

The article went on to state that 170 IAF pilots were killed in MiG-21 accidents, as also 40 civilians, during the period between 1970 and 2013. Families of some of the pilots killed in MiG-21 crashes met President A.P.J. Abdul Kalam, the supreme commander of the armed forces, and appealed to him to ensure that country's soldiers were not killed by their 'own weapons'. According to news reports at the time, a citizen named Kavita Gadgil and her husband Capt. Anil Gadgil (retired), who lost their son, told reporters that they had submitted a petition to Kalam for action to make 'flying safe'.

'We are not anti-Indian Air Force nor are we calling for grounding of the MiG-21 fleet. We know it is the backbone of our Air Force,' Kavita said. 'The MiG-21s at present are unsafe and we want the problems in the fighter aircraft to be solved.'**

In response, in 2003, Defence Minister George Fernandes

---

*Kabir Taneja, 'The Trouble with India's MIG-21 Fighter Jets', *The New York Times*, 8 August, 2013. Available at https://india.blogs.nytimes.com/2013/08/08/the-trouble-with-indian-air-forces-mig-21-fighter-jets/; accessed on 27 April 2021.
**Onkar Singh, 'Don't Let MiG-21s Kill Our Sons, Kalam Told', *rediff.com*, 5 August, 2003. Available at https://www.rediff.com/news/2003/aug/05mig.htm; accessed on 21 April 2021.

undertook a 25-minute sortie on a MiG-21 in a bid to dispel fears about the IAF's fighter jet following a series of mishaps. The minister further declared that the MiG-21 is safe or why else would he have flown in it. What a charade! What enraged me further was the planted propaganda articles, which said that that 45 per cent of the accidents are due to human error. There is also the hazard of bird hits, accounting for around 10 per cent of the accidents that involve IAF planes. The IAF claimed that it was doing its best to cope with this danger by creating a bird-free environment around airfields. This called for modernization of slaughter houses, proper garbage disposal and building of sewage systems, which was beyond the ken of the IAF and the defence ministry.*

Fernandes's flight in a MiG-21 was a gimmick. I could feel my body shivering with hatred towards such politicking! The entire emotional impulse of revolutionary fervour hit me again. I was drawn back to 'The Young Guns of India'. The apathy of the political system demanded it. And the idea of *RDB* started taking shape once again!

What if 'The Young Guns of India' were to be born again in today's India? Would they have kept silent against the indifference of the establishment for its own soldiers who had pledged their lives for the country?

Kamlesh ji heard me out and the genius in him started ticking. Within three days, he turned the idea on its head, and *RDB* was born. I felt a compulsion to get the music going. As soon as we finalized the script, I flew to London to meet Rahman, who was working there on a West End musical. He loved the story. Late that night, he even composed the theme music for *RDB*, which we used in the climax of the film five years later.

London was also a revelation of another kind. At the British Council Library, I was researching the British Raj in India for the film. One must admit that the British have preserved their records amazingly well. But then I also realized that one nations' patriot is another nation's terrorist. Bhagat Singh, Rajguru and Chandrashekhar

---

*John Cherian, 'Falling and Flying', *Frontline*, 25 May 2000. Available at https://frontline.thehindu.com/the-nation/article30244989.ece; accessed on 21 April 2021.

Azad were terrorists as per British literary records. In my mind, the British were undoubtedly oppressors. I felt compelled to contribute to the moral urgency of explaining to today's Indians why colonialism was the horror it turned out to be and why we need to wake up and fight even today. A fight for freedom from corruption and apathy in Independent India is as important as our freedom struggle itself.

I was consumed by the passion of bringing back patriotism. This seemed even more important, given that my initial focus groups revealed that the youth of my country did not relate to what it is like to give their life for their country. Imagine the gumption of Bhagat Singh, Rajguru and Sukhdev, who marched to the scaffolds with a smile on their faces to the chant of *Inquilab Zindabad* (Long Live the Revolution). They were aided ably by the wily Azad, who led the movement with complete fearlessness, along with Ram Prasad Bismil and Ashfaqullah Khan. Durga Devi Vohra, better known as Durga Bhabhi, posed as Bhagat Singh's wife to help him escape from Lahore under the guise of a family man. She managed this miracle on a day when 400 cops were searching for Bhagat Singh at the railway station!

Could I make the youth of today relate to that revolutionary sentiment? Deep down I believed they all had it; it was just lying dormant and needed to be shaken up. Because not so long ago, in 1990, the infamous Mandal Commission (27 per cent reservation for Other Backward Classes candidates in all government services) had brought the youth to the streets. Rajeev Goswami, a Delhi University student, son of a postal clerk, had set himself on fire, sustaining 50 per cent burns. He survived the self-immolation bid (but died in 2004), but the spark of revolt had been ignited. In cities and towns near Delhi, more than 159 people attempted suicide and 63 died. I was 27 at the time and, in Bombay, when the news of the Mandal Commission protests broke out. On one of my travels to Delhi, I got to see some censored film footage of a video news channel—the student protest against the Mandal Commission was being crushed brutally. The police was actually shooting at the students. They weren't rubber bullets but real ones. The female students were being mishandled and beaten with batons. People on the streets were saying, 'Our own government is firing at us—this is Jallianwala Bagh all over again!'

I was reminded of Ludhianvi's famous poem:

Zulm fir zulm hai, badhta hai to mit jata hai,
Khoon fir khoon hai, tapkega to jam jayea.

(When atrocities become unbearable, they have to end
When blood falls, it is bound to become solid and rise again.)

Inspired by the same, we wrote the lyrics 'Khoon Chalaa, Khoon Chalaa' for *RDB*.

I decided to be a part of an all-night peace protest at the same square of AIIMS where Rajeev Goswami immolated himself later. We sang all night while friendly neighbours from Sarojini Nagar sent food and hot tea to us in support. Pandey reminded me, 'Bhagat Singh said that freedom does not mean that the white rulers get replaced by non-white ones.'

To further steel my resolve, I went to Jallianwala Bagh and sought to channel rebellion within myself, the anger that would serve as rocket fuel for *RDB*. Standing at the site, I played the incidents of the unholy massacre of 13 April 1919 in my mind's eye.* The bullet marks were still on the walls. For those who have seen *RDB*, 'reel was going to imitate real.' The Jallianwala Bagh massacre is a key moment in *RDB* that impacted the young viewers who watched the film.

I now had my story and had found a way to say it through the

81

---

*For those who may not have read about the Jallianwala Bagh massacre, it was one of the darkest days in the history of the British Raj in pre-Independence India. On the day of Baisakhi, the Sikh festival, many villagers had gathered there peacefully. Many of them probably weren't aware that the Rowlatt Act had just forbidden public gatherings. Gen. Reginald Dyer, a tyrant of unimaginable proportions, came to know that a meeting had assembled at Jallianwala Bagh. He proceeded there with Gurkha, Baluchi and Rajput troops, blocking the main entrance after them. The troops took up position on a raised bank and fired 1,650 rounds on the crowd, which included women and children, for about ten minutes, directing their bullets largely towards the few open gates through which people were trying to flee. More than 1,000 people were killed. The sheer brutality of the act, the targeted firing at peaceful civilians and the guiltless justifications offered by Dyer were condemnable. Rabindranath Tagore renounced his knighthood in protest.

eyes of an expatriate student Sue McKinley (played by Alice Patten, daughter of Lord Chris Patten, chancellor of Oxford University and the last governor of Hong Kong. Interestingly, the Oxford connection to the film continues with Soha Ali Khan, an alumna of the university, whose father is the nawab of Pataudi, who captained both Oxford and India, and mother is the legendary actress Sharmila Tagore). Sue was coming to India to make a documentary on the fearless revolutionaries she had read about in her grandfather James Mckinley's diaries. James McKinley had served the British Empire and walked Bhagat Singh, Rajguru and Sukhdev to the gallows. (This was created to suit the narrative.) His opening lines in his diary were, 'I always thought there were two kinds of men: one who walked to their death crying and the other who walked in silence ... until I met the third kind.'

When I had first conceived the project, the film was to be made both in Hindi and English. The English version was to be titled 'Paint It Yellow'. The plans for the English version were dropped subsequently. For the Hindi name, I sought inspiration in the fact that in India, the colour of saffron represents sacrifice. When someone says, *Mohey Rang De Basanti*' (paint me saffron), it means that person is ready to be sacrificed for a great cause.

Excited to begin, I realized that there was just one slight problem. Like Sue in the film, I didn't have any money to make *RDB*. But that wasn't going to hold me back. I would find the money. My search, however, led me somewhere else.

CHAPTER 13

Glamour, Grace and Gumption

I was raised by a tough mother, and subconsciously, I began to admire courage and resilience in women early on. And of course, my wife Bharathi is as tough as they come. So when I was penning the script of *RDB*, I visualized the character of a very strong woman who first sacrificed her husband for the country and then her son. I was drawn to Waheeda ji as a perfect fit to depict this immense fortitude.

As I contemplated reaching out to her, I realized that this period of my visualization was at a very sensitive time in Waheeda ji's life. After *Lamhe* in 1991, she had moved to Bangalore to stay there for good. Her husband's illness, however, brought her back to Mumbai in 1999.

As word spread that she was back in Mumbai, Bollywood came calling. She had just started working on *Kabhi Khushi Kabhi Gham*, but had to abandon this role after the first day of shoot due to her husband's demise in the year 2000. After this personal tragedy, she decided to accept a few films to keep herself busy. However, at this point, she wanted the comfort of working with people she knew personally, like her *Lamhe* co-stars Anupam Kher and Anil Kapoor. So when Anupam Kher offered her *Om Jai Jagadish*, she gave it a nod.

As for me, a fan of Guru Dutt's classics, I knew deep down in my belly, that I badly wanted Waheeda ji in my film—this one, next one, any one.

In Waheeda ji's own words, 'One day, this new director Rakeysh came and narrated *Delhi-6* to me and disappeared for six months.' This had been in early 2001. In the meantime, *Aks* released in July 2001 and gave Waheeda ji a peek into my language and sensibilities. I was very serious about working with Waheeda ji, and soon enough, I went back to her.

This time I visited her in her Bangalore farm and narrated *RDB*. I got scolded. '*Pichli baar to aapne kuch aur sunaya tha!*' (You narrated something else to me the last time around!) She said this with great dignity, probing whether I was serious after all. But I could see that she was taken in with the script. And I was so sure that I wanted her that I threatened to put up the sets on her farm if she didn't come back with me to shoot. She indulged my persistence.

'I was very hesitant but I loved the script and did not want to waste my time sitting idle. So I said yes,' Waheeda ji confessed later.

It was a role integral to the script, and in hindsight, one can see that Waheeda ji's candlelight march is the turning point in the film. A bunch of young boys become serious about their lives and purpose after seeing her grieve—a potent broth of dignity, helplessness and patriotism glistening through her wet eyes. Till date, she tells me that *RDB* will always be special to her as she got to be part of another iconic film in the twilight years of her career. But the ultimate compliment to Waheeda ji came many years later, when the entire cast gathered to celebrate the success of *RDB* at my home.

The conversation centred around how the greatest actors of the world have, at best, five films that everyone remembers. We proceeded to apply this theorem to several actors; it proved to be quite accurate. In fact, the jump from the fourth film to the fifth itself was quite challenging for many. It wasn't till we started counting for Waheeda ji that we crossed five effortlessly and then some: *Mujhe Jeene Do, Pyaasa, Kaagaz Ke Phool, Guide, Sahib Bibi aur Ghulam, Khamoshi, Teesri Kasam* and, of course, *RDB*.

84

Waheeda Rehman
in first person

A few things I must say about Rakeysh. He is very cool and calm on the set and knows how to respect elders. I was nervous to go on his sets because I didn't know his style. However, I was able to focus when I saw the relaxed, creative environment he offers, helping everyone give their best. He doesn't make you do loud acting. And like the hallmark of every good director, he is sensitive.

Rakeysh has a lot of understanding and depth; he has his own way of understanding a subject, the characters and each individual artist. Rakeysh is also a perfectionist—for the candle light scene in *RDB*, we had to get up at 2 a.m. and get ready to get one good shot just before sunrise. He wanted a particular light and wouldn't compromise.

I have worked with many directors. Asit Sen directed me in *Khamoshi*. He could accommodate the individuality of the artist, and perhaps that was his greatness. Satyajit Ray was a genius but a one-man show. Guru Dutt was also one-man show, but in so many ways, Rakeysh reminds me of Guru Dutt because of the sheer variety of movies that he has made, one so different from the other, constantly hungry for new creative expression, refusing to repeat himself. Basu Bhattacharya was another genius I worked with in *Teesri Kasam*. He used to dress the part of an artist too, always in complete disarray with crumpled clothing and spaced out about his work. Rakeysh, fortunately, is always well groomed as a mark of respect to his work and colleagues.

> # Satyajit Ray was a genius but a one-man show. Guru Dutt was also one-man show, but in so many ways, Rakeysh reminds me of Guru Dutt...

85

Rakeysh introduced me to the concept of workshops for script reading much prior to the shoot of the film. In the '70s and '80s, there were no bound scripts. *Director ke dimaag mein kahani thi* (The script existed in the mind of the director). Till I turned up on the sets, I never used to get the dialogues either. So, I was very inspired with

Rakeysh's commitment to preparation. Also, in my career spanning so many movies as a lead heroine, I was not willing to spoil my record at this late innings in my life by doing two-bit roles. Rakeysh understood this and has given me my swan song till date.

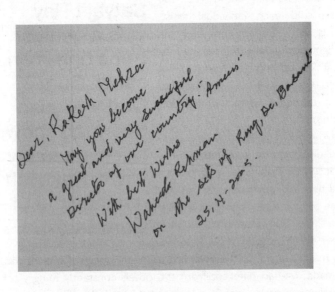

Dear, Rakesh Mehra

May you become
a great and very successful
Director of our country "Ameen."

With best wishes

Waheeda Rehman
on the sets of Rang De Basanti
25.4.2005.

CHAPTER 14

The Blessing That Was Aamir Khan

Aamir had done about 30 films when he said yes to RDB. I couldn't believe my luck, and yet, it all seemed so natural that Aamir should be the one to 'understand' this script instinctively.

I didn't know him at all at the time. One day, I sent him a text message.

'I have made a film called *Aks*. I want to narrate my next film to you.'

Twenty minutes later, he texted back.

'I am in London. Should be back on third. We can have it thereafter.'

I waited till the fifth and sent him another message.

'In case you're back, can we meet?'

Twenty minutes later, came the punctual response.

'Yes I'm back. Can we hear it on this date at this time?'

I went to his office.

AK: What would you prefer? Giving me the script or narrating it?

Me: What do you prefer?

AK: It's not about me, it's about you.

Me: How much time do you have?

AK: It's your pace. If you need 15 minutes, they're yours. If you need a day, it's yours. I want to listen to your idea.

I marvelled at how this man, whose body of work ranged from *Jo Jeeta Wohi Sikandar* to *Lagaan*, a focussed artist who could solve the Rubik's Cube in less than 20 seconds, was only interested in what I wanted to create, not who I was! At an early age, he had shown contempt for conventional education and chose to learn only about cinema. His unusual choices and dedication have made him an iconic actor who had the pulse of his audience.

I started narrating to him. My plot was an unusual one that moved between the 1920s and 2005 played by the same set of actors. A bunch of university students become part of a documentary featuring real-life revolutionaries. Initially, they don't identify with the characters or have a full understanding of their own history. They know little about their forefathers who fought for the rights they take for granted, and yet, as the film progresses, they find a cause worth dying for.

Aamir is a visionary and understands everything that is going wrong or right with the creative process.

There were two parallel stories and wherever they crisscrossed, there were sparks—until they overlapped and the lines blurred. It was a new narrative to say the least and very difficult to imagine. All one could do was to feel it and take a leap of faith. I needed a man who believed in the risk he was taking. I was helming a tumultuous ship!

Three hours later, both of us felt good about it, but there was both anticipation and caution.

AK: I haven't seen *Aks*.

Me: I will arrange a screening for you tomorrow.

Aamir saw *Aks*. I was on tenterhooks till I heard back from him.

Aamir says in *Ru Ba Ru* (Face-to-Face), a 2011 documentary on the filming of *RDB*:

This was around 2002 and I was already part of *Mangal Pandey*, which was also a heavy historical film—the story of a freedom fighter. But I loved the screenplay and the inspiration behind *RDB*.

In the book *I'll Do It My Way: The Incredible Journey of Aamir Khan* by Christina Daniels, Aamir is quoted in this context, 'I didn't know whether it was going to work or not.'

But he put himself firmly behind my unorthodox idea and became the character—something he is known to do. And I don't mean it in a superficial way. He imbibed the soul of DJ and Chandrashekhar Azad and gave his own interpretation to it, ranging from the sublime to the mundane qualities of the character. Bharathi had given me a quote which she had read, 'There are two primary choices in life. Either you let things be the way they are. Or take responsibility for changing them.' I sent Aamir the same as a one-line brief for his character impetus.

Avan Contractor created a more urban hairstyle for his character DJ. This was immediately post the period film *Mangal Pandey* and was a whole new look. Arjun Bhasin, the stylist, worked on the entire cast's look. Aamir rehearsed his Punjabi dialect and twang to perfection. He became one with the cast and crew—every supreme artist understands that the entire crew has to be elevated to another level to make magic happen. He was paired opposite Alice. She observed his command over the cast when she told BBC, 'It's only when you notice how people talk about a person that you realize how important or famous they are. Everyone looked up to Aamir, including the younger actors. He's a lovely man, incredibly generous and funny.'

Aamir is a visionary and understands everything that is going wrong or right with the creative process. Sometimes, tough decisions like 'let's shoot for 10 more days' became easy because Aamir backed the need to do it. Also, he had no ego about whose scene it was. If the scene belonged to the other boys, he would happily stay in the background because the film's narrative was the Bible that could not be tampered with. Aamir's cinematic understanding remains unparalleled in our industry. Without his nod, *RDB* would have been another dreamer's script gathering the dust of apathy and inertia.

While signing on the dotted line, Aamir included a clause, which was the reason I ended up making the movie on time in the first place. Here's an example: 'If my fee is 4 crore and you don't pay me on time, then you'll have to pay me 8 crore for defaulting,' he had said.

I had never even seen 8 crores till then.

CHAPTER 15

Grasping
at Straws

Aks *had released in 2001 and* RDB *released in 2006. This long gap of* five years was because passion was high, but money was scarce.

Thankfully, despite the fact that *Aks* had not done well at the box office, I was being hailed as a new age writer and director. Angad Paul and Nilesh Dadhich were the initial producers for *RDB* and it was their job to raise the money. Unfortunately (or fortunately), they never managed to do it. There was no cash to be seen despite alliances, promises and whatnot.

I had already taken the leap so there was no stopping. Bharathi didn't bat an eyelid when I suggested to mortgage our small little bungalow, bought after 20 years of ad-filmmaking, to Citibank.

However, we kept moving on and finalized the cast and crew. AR and Binod Pradhan (director of photography [DoP]) were already in and the first actor to be cast was Atul Kulkarni, even before Aamir Khan and Waheeda Rehman. Almost every person in my film— Sharman Joshi, Kunal Kapoor, Siddharth and Soha Ali Khan—came through auditions. They were all newcomers.

Kunal Kapoor's role of Aslam is a throwback to my friend Zulfikar, a very good left-arm bowler. We used to call him Zullu. He was from a traditional Muslim household. 'How can you have friends who drink sharaab?' was the question his father would ask. He would get beaten up regularly and often meet us with a black eye. Things had

91

reached a point where he wanted to kill his father. We channelled all of this into Aslam's nuanced character.

Every known actor kept declining the role to play Karan Singhania. I had first offered it to Farhan Akhtar. This was a time when he had never acted in a film before and was one of the most respected young directors. He was both surprised and amused. When I narrated it to Abhishek, he told me point-blank, 'I thought you are crazy but after hearing your narration I think you are completely nuts.'

I requested Aamir to put in a word with Hrithik Roshan. Aamir even went to Hrithik's house. 'It's a good film—*kar le*' (do it). But it wasn't meant to be. Finally, Siddharth signed on the dotted line in January 2005, one month before the shoot. He had never done a Hindi film before. Bharathi had seen the Tamil film *Boys*, starring Siddharth, a couple of months before the shoot, and his energy and unique combination of innocence and naivety came through. She thought he could pull off the conflict in Karan's character well. The senior actors accepted the smaller parts with grace—Om Puri, Anupam Kher, Kirron Kher, Mohan Agashe and K.K. Raina are all masters of their craft and formed a dependable unit on which we built the movie.

I wanted to create world cinema and wanted the backend to be managed like world cinema is done—with perfection and discipline. I was drawn to David Reid and Adam Bowling, who had two cult classics behind them as executive producers—*Lock, Stock and Two Smoking Barrels* (1998) and *Snatch* (2000). They shared the same office as Shekhar Kapur in Soho, London. They loved the script, gave up their homes on rental and shifted to India to set up the film, which meant supervising the production and helping cast the foreign actors along with Bharathi and P.S. Shyam.

Adam and David brought along a boxer from Manchester—Mick Ward—as the first assistant director. They were responsible for casting Alice Patten and Steven Mackintosh for the parts of Sue and James McKinley, respectively. I remember vividly that one of the people who auditioned for the part of James McKinley, the young jailor who walks Bhagat Singh, Rajguru and Sukhdev to be hanged, was none other than current James Bond, Daniel Craig. He, too, came through my producers David and Adam.

Daniel Craig was my first choice but he requested if we could allow some time as he was also being considered to be the next James Bond. The rest, as they say, is history.

Samir Chanda, the incredible production designer, was brought on board the project and was shortlisting locations with Binod Pradhan. We had talent like Nakul Kamte (sound designer) and Allan Amin (action director) on board and, of course, Bharathi, the creative producer and editor. The criteria for every department was to stay as real as possible, whether it was the spoken word, acting, look and feel, camera and lighting or anything else.

However, there was one small thing. The money from the producers was still invisible. The clock was ticking: July 2003 became January 2004—still no money! And the shoot was around the corner. My crew stood behind me for reasons I still don't know. They were patient and gracefully postponed their remunerations to 'payable when able'. I went to meet Kishore Bajaj, who owned the fashion label named Bada Saab, often frequented by film stars. I requested him to help me with some stopgap money so we could begin the shoot. Like an angel, he gave his personal guarantee and arranged for a loan of 2.5 crore at 36 per cent interest from a private financier. Since our bungalow was already pledged, I gave the lien to be first out on the film (he would get paid first when the film made money) as a mortgage.

93

Simultaneously, we had created a writing room at our cottage in Bandra. Bharathi, Rensil D'Silva and I put all our energies into working on the final draft. Rensil took the screenplay to the next level, making it more contemporary and relatable to the youth then. He was moonlighting between his role as an advertising copywriter and a scriptwriter for *RDB*. We had worked on *Aks* earlier, so we understood each other pretty well.

'Why do we have such big dialogues in our movies, we must speak normally,' he would say. Rensil is the key reason for the film's connect with the youth! The dialogues he wrote were effortless and simple spoken words.

It was October 2004 and yet no sign of the moolah. Adam and David were already here, along with their families and kids. There was no turning back, so we worked out a 15-day budget holiday for them in Goa, which got extended to a month as we still did not have the money to go on the floor. Meanwhile, Aamir was getting more and more offers.

'If I back out, *yeh* film *banegi nahi fir se* (*RDB* will not get made),' was his line. In the meantime, I kept the wheels churning. I took a flight to the US where Shah Rukh Khan was shooting for *Swades* at NASA to sign him up for the part of Flt Lt Ajay Rathod. This was the shortest and most challenging role around which the whole film revolved. He loved the script but could not give the dates from his busy schedule. Looking back, I think the part was meant to be played by R. Madhavan and what an outstanding role he played!

I requested Aamir to put in a word with Hrithik Roshan. Aamir even went to Hrithik's house. 'It's a good film—*kar le*' (do it).

In the US, I met Ashok Amritraj (Hyde Park Entertainment) in Hollywood to finance the film. In all my naivety, I had some strange notion that since he had connections in India, he would help me out. He was not ready to expand into the Indian market yet. However, we ended up becoming friends. I was down to my last dollar, so I borrowed $100 from my brother-in-law Srikanth, who was employed there at the time, to take a cab to the airport.

Back in Mumbai, we all had a meeting, where Aamir suggested we enforce his contract and sent a notice to the producers (which included Angad, Nilesh and me) to pay double the amount of 8 crores for defaulting. I now understood Aamir's foresight. To keep me going, Aamir sent me a text message—the same one I had sent him earlier as his character brief for DJ:

There are two primary choices in life. Either you let things be the way they are. Or take responsibility for changing them.

On 28 December 2004, I requested Adam to fly back to London and get Angad to sign a contract, which said they relinquish their rights on my film. I had earlier paid off Nilesh to exit. Adam, an ex-British Marine, parked himself in Angad's office and only budged once the paper was signed.

Finally, Ronnie Screwvala stepped in. From that day onwards, there was no looking back. Ronnie stood behind me like the Rock of Gibraltar. I thought we were all a crazy lot in attempting this film but Ronnie beat us all when it came to 'crazy'. He vetted the budget which Adam and Shyam in production had prepared, cut out a few things and added resources where he felt we needed them most.

All through this and right up to the release of the film, Ronnie led us from the aisle and gave me the freedom to express myself and, of course, the money to make the film. We got the first cheque of 5 crore from UTV Motion Pictures (Ronnie's production house). Immediately, I repaid the loan sharks and set up the shoot. Aamir Khan even offered to reduce his fee. I told him, 'Our boat is sailing. Let's keep it in our back pockets in case we need it later.'

95

Rang De Basanti

CHAPTER 16

Murphy's
First Law

We were all set to go on floors on 1 February 2005. We had 30 days and the entire mood had changed! We hired a larger office to accommodate all the departments. It was in the same building as Sony Music (which eventually published the sound track). I had started sharing the story of *RDB* over coffee with Shridhar Subramaniam, then CEO of Sony Music. The advance team of Samir Chanda, Adam and Shyam departed for Punjab to set up the first schedule. I had already shortlisted the locations many times over along with Samir.

Aamir and the boys got into the new look; costume designer Arjun Bhasin took a quick trip to Bangkok to pick up wannabe, aspirational, cool but fake brands. As luck would have it, on 15 January 2005, I got jaundice and was briefly hospitalized for two days. But then, there was always a larger reason in everything that happened. Instead of rushing into the shoot, it gave me 'my time' on the hospital bed to think things through. My eyes were yellow, I had severe abdominal pain, my body was tender and I was tired easily. Senior director Lekh Tandon, who was also playing a cameo as Aamir's grandfather, said he knew someone who could cure jaundice. Every morning, he would come to my house in Bandra at 6 a.m. from Chembur and give me herbal medicine that was concocted the same morning and had to be swallowed fresh. He said I would be fine in seven days.

The shoot had to be postponed yet again due to my health. I took this as an opportunity to run a workshop in a shutdown recording room of Mehboob Studios. This was the same room where master musicians and directors, not to mention Mehboob Khan himself (he had an Oscar nomination for *Mother India*), had created memorable soundtracks and songs. The energy in this shut down studio was palpable.

Day one, I read the script. Day two onwards, the actors started reading their parts.

Alice surprised us all by picking up Hindi in no time. The entire cast, including Waheeda ji, was holed up at Mehboob Studios rehearsing. No one wanted to go home. On day seven, Nakul recorded the entire sound rehearsal, edited and cut it into a two-and-a-half hour audio movie. Nakul remains the legend who introduced sync sound into Indian cinema in *Lagaan*; before him, our movies were always dubbed.

I took the audio track to AR, he took it a step further and added songs and original track wherever he felt instinctively. It was like a workshop experiment never done before. Regaining my health, I took the flight to Punjab with the rest of the crew.

We were going to shoot *RDB*.

On 22 February, we were scheduled to start the shoot. On 21 February, I got a massive relapse of the jaundice, but I did not tell anyone. To hide the yellowness in my eyes, I wore dark glasses. Bharathi was very concerned. David, Shyam and Adam managed to juggle four more days, but it was impossible to cancel the shoot that was planned for 26th.

The location was the Golden Temple, the most sacred place for the Sikhs. In those days, they wouldn't allow shoots and had turned our request down. But I met with the Shiromani Gurdwara Parbandhak Committee and implored that I am making a film on Bhagat Singh and the spirit of Punjab's youth, that every mother in Punjab sent one of her sons to the Indian Army and pledged their lives to the mother land. They gave us permission for just a few hours and that too only on the appointed date of 26th. And on that day, the first shot of *RDB* happened. Wahe Guru blessed our film.

Rang De Basanti

The bonding was exceptional, and it showed on screen.

The joke on the sets was that 'the director is literally dying to make the film'. The line producer's wife started cooking my jaundice-recovery meals separately. I could not have non-vegetarian food for a year. I added alcohol and smoking to the delete list, so in every way, *RDB* was a *tapasya* (penance) for me. All my cast were together for four days without shooting before 26th and this served its own purpose—the cast started hanging out together. At night, the entire cast and head of departments would gather in Kunal Kapoor's room till 4 a.m. The bonding was exceptional, and it showed on screen.

From then on, for 108 days, a crew of 200 people travelled across Punjab, Delhi and Rajasthan and back to Mumbai on sets to create *RDB*, which had a very different vibe. It was almost as if everyone knew something special was happening. Bharathi says, 'Even a spot boy would occasionally say, "*Aaj accha kaam hua na?*" (Today's work went well, right?).' This energy could not be forced by us. The fact that everyone resonated with it and believed that we were creating something of importance and deep significance was palpable.

It all happened because of Ronnie Screwvala, a simple, happy man who believes that a box of cupcakes can overcome every problem in life.

Ronnie Screwvala
in first person

I came to the industry as a Screwvala from South Bombay, a rank outsider. I retained the 'outsider' tag because I felt it gave me objectivity. I was keen to find success on my own terms in disruption and pushing the envelope.

I wanted to build something in the media outside of the animation channels and the news networks that I had already built. If I had to take UTV to the next level, I would have to move on to movies.

Today, I know from painful experiences that blockbusters don't just happen. Back then, all I knew was that at UTV, we were pushing to go against the grain. So when Rakeysh and *RDB* came into my life, I was fresh from three to four failures but still had not become a cynic. Thank God for that!

I have always evaluated a business proposal on its merits. Hence, whatever problems Rakeysh was going through, I was only keen because I loved the script that Rakeysh narrated to me. He was an outsider, despite his filmy Pali Hill tag. In an industry where references are revered and knowing people personally is important, I could see that Rakeysh was different. When he talks, either you get it or you don't.

I wouldn't say that he's very articulate: Rakeysh is not the man to be put on a podium to belt out a vision statement, but he is pensive, thoughtful and pumped up with deep-seated conviction. If memory serves me right, Rakeysh first called me through a mutual friend, Bimal Parekh. After an initial meeting at my office in Worli, we met at the Breach Candy Club afterwards. His vision for *RDB* was crystal clear. I said yes!

Almost immediately, I was surrounded by an avalanche of naysayers. All the Bhagat Singh (also a part of *RDB*) movies had flopped, one-third of Rakeysh's movie was supposedly a flashback and he had just delivered a flop in *Aks*.

But I believed that Rakeysh knew what he was doing and it helped that Aamir was already part of the film.

That being said, the movie involved incredible hard work and was a high risk–high reward project. But as I've said in my book,

'The difference between predator and prey in a business ecosystem is determined by the strength of one's next idea.'

When Rakeysh showed me the first and second cuts, I had my hand in my mouth. I realized that you had to see the whole film to get it because his style and his vision are very unique; they are a patents by themselves and quite fantastic.

I tried to contribute in the edit room and endeavoured to lessen the duration of the film. But both Aamir and Rakeysh were very insistent about what they had created and I was clearly outnumbered.

My conviction as a producer was called in much later though. When it was time to get the censor certificate, the chair of the censor board said, 'We are not ready to issue it.'

Given that the movie involved an unpalatable military angle, we now needed an approval from the IAF and Ministry of Defence. *Rang De Basanti*, at an investment of ₹400 million, was our biggest gamble till date. The news was unwelcome as much as it was unavoidable.

We rallied the troops and gathered at Aamir's house in Bandra when I received another update: 'We are trying to get a special screening organized on an emergency basis with the Air Chief Marshal,' said the censor board chairman.

I have described these times vividly in my book, *Dream with Your Eyes Open: An Entrepreneurial Journey* (Rupa Publications, 2015). Aamir took a strong stand. 'We have made the movie with a clean heart,' he said. Rakeysh added, 'We are as patriotic as the next guy and if they want us to cut a single frame, I'm not going to allow it.'

Despite having skin in the game, I agreed. Rakeysh had given his heart and soul to making this film and I wasn't going to be the one person to bail out on him. But the risk of the ₹400 million was daunting.

The all-important screening to get the censor certificate was set for 11 January 2006. Two hundred members of the press were waiting outside. We went to Delhi and held the screening as scheduled. Not only was the head of the air force in attendance, but the heads of the army and the navy, as well as the then defence minister, Pranab Mukherjee.

Two-and-a-half hours later, when the lights came up, Rakeysh, Aamir and I went in front of the group to answer questions. The heads of the army and the navy both liked the film and had little to say. 'I really enjoyed the movie, too. What's the problem?' the defence minister asked with a shrug. In *RDB*, much of the blame for Ajay's death falls on the shoulders of the defence minister. Clearly, Pranab wasn't bothered by the parallel.

The last to speak was the head of the air force. 'There is nothing derogatory about the IAF in the film. It is a very good film and as far as we are concerned, it can be released. Now the ball is in the court of the censor board,' Air Marshal P.S. Ahluwalia said, soon after a special screening for the defence ministry.

Further, the air force gave us some data, which we were asked to add as a slide at the end of the film:

> MiG fighter planes have served our country since 1964 and have been instrumental in winning us wars. However, over the last 15 years, 206 MiG planes have crashed and 78 pilots have lost their lives. In their memory and in honour of our Air Borne Warriors who have laid down their lives for our country.

With this text placed in the closing credit rolls, the movie became an authorized version of the IAF's concerns and that lent further credibility to the film.

I'm sure Rakeysh was one breath away from losing his mind through it all. Ironically, the publicity that this high-profile, potential-death-knell screening gathered served the film.

Perhaps Rakeysh didn't understand it then, but the success of *RDB* was not just UTV's first big league film, but also a gift of courage to many directors who were waiting on the sideline to tell their stories, to go ahead and take a chance.

Rakeysh's *RDB* was a blockbuster at another level: one of the top five hits of all time. To celebrate, we released quarter-page ads on the front pages of all the national dailies. I got a call from Aditya Chopra and Karan Johar asking for a meeting at the former's office. I was half expecting a reprimand for bringing out competitiveness by comparing *RDB*'s success and trying to put it on some rank. However, both of them were convinced that my intentions were pure and they spoke of the film with admiration. The non-formula movie had arrived and I realized that this kind of movie was what I actually meant when we set out to push the envelope.

The music was a cult hit with AR doing what only he can do. *Rang De Basanti* became India's official entry for the Oscars and further won a BAFTA nomination. Regardless of whatever I might say now, it is true that we are all infatuated by the American awards. Today, I believe that they're very insular and that if America truly has to acknowledge world cinema, there needs to be more than one 'blanket award' for foreign film. For me, *RDB* will always be the best friend I made in high school: an eternal favourite. Part of the reason the film looked so good was that every actor in the film delivered their best performance.

Over to the cast of *RDB*.

Atul Kulkarni
in first person

After the release of *Chandni Bar* in 2001, I received a call from Rakeysh Mehra's office. It was P.S. Shyam on the line. 'Rakeysh wants to meet you,' he said.

I was excited. I had always wanted to meet the director whose style and finesse had powered *Aks*. Even before that, Rakeysh was a big name in the ad world. I was two-films-old post *Hey Ram* (2000) and *Chandni Bar*, and didn't know the ways of the industry. My apprehension was compounded by the forewarning that Rakeysh would 'just stare at me and expect me to navigate his indecipherable silence'.

We met at his Tardeo office. While I have no recollection of the specific details of our meeting, we broadly spoke about the political climate of the country, social consciousness, state of democracy—everything relevant and irrelevant. What I distinctly remember is feeling comfortable. Rakeysh engaged at a deep, intellectual level, which was my comfort zone. I had been an avid reader since childhood, rushing home from school to read the newspaper rather than to play. Perhaps because Rakeysh and I are almost the same age, with the same political and social exposure, I was spared his famous stoic silence.

The script he wanted to offer me was *RDB*. I proceeded to read at least eight to nine drafts of the same. He never shied away from sharing an updated draft with me. A bunch of brats getting inspired by freedom fighters to set off a revolution on their own could be absolutely phenomenal or absurdly far-fetched, depending on who made it and how. But for a Karnataka-born, Solapur-bred engineering dropout who switched lanes to arts, English literature and finally National School of Drama (NSD), I was prepared to play the role of a lifetime! Then Kunal Kapoor, who was assisting Rakeysh in *Aks*, did a scene with me for the audition. I could sense something momentous shaping up. Rakeysh allowed me to discuss his script openly; every comment of mine on the script was taken seriously. His team used to sit down and note down everything. I must confess, they had no reason to listen.

Finally, we started shooting.

103

Rang De Basanti

Very early in our interaction, I realized how Rakeysh works. Hence, when the shoot began, there was a human connect. Comfort, respect, space—everything amalgamated to provide a creative space where each artist could flourish. This style worked for me. I don't know what it means to be a director's actor. The director cannot tell you what to do—where is my contribution then? Besides, a good director will never lose the 'individuality' and 'originality' brought in by an actor. The cinema only stands to gain. Yes, if an actor strays from the path, there is space for the director to intervene. An actor oscillates between these two boundaries—the limitlessness of his own talent and that of his director's vision. That's why Rakeysh prepares extensively. Our readings of the script in front of all the actors and Binod Pradhan was followed by a 10-day rehearsal in Mehboob Studios, Mumbai, with all the actors and all the key scenes. Every character is made to marinate in the mood before cooking on the sets.

Rakeysh's belief in the process is so immense that every actor on the set knows the whole script as well as their part. So, on the sets, the DoP has a final say on the look of the shot. And, of course, Rakeysh is too involved to be stuck behind the camera. I love that about him. Some of us actors, a minority breed, are of the opinion that the monitor is a barrier. I want my director to look at me when I perform. The most remarkable thing about Rakeysh is that most guys have a sense of superiority or an inferiority complex: Rakeysh has an equality complex. This becomes the culture on the sets, which is usually absorbed and translated further by the senior-most actor. On the sets of *RDB*, it was Aamir.

The chemistry you see in the film, the ease among the friends: the entire credit goes to Aamir. We hardly ever had lunch in our individual make-up vans/rooms. We always ate together. Aamir's van became the common *adda*. Everyone would get ready and end up in his van. Rakeysh had crafted this unique atmosphere without asking for it. When Kunal's dad passed away, we all went together to pay our respects. I remember the day we shot the scene where Madhavan is carried on the shoulder in the bar—we shot it over three days and went back to Aamir's or Rakeysh's place every night for a meal. The togetherness helped us stay bonded and project it on screen. There was an ideological sync. We all believed in the way our characters transformed in the movie, and this was important for the success of the film. My character faces disappointment when his political mentor appears fallible. Similarly, every person's ideology relating to their religion is very important. When I go to Aslam (the character played by Kunal Kapoor) and say sorry, I had to understand it.

Much later, when I worked with Roland Joffe in *The Lovers* and Chuck Russell in *Junglee*, I could draw a parallel. Rakeysh casts the person as well, not just the actor: a well-known Hollywood trend. People with similar temperaments come on board and create magic. I remember auditioning for Bernardo Bertolucci's *Little Buddha*, which was released in 1993. All it involved was talking to the director. The other beautiful interactions on the set had to be with the legendary Waheeda Rehman, an actor-dancer par excellence whom I've grown up watching. To this day, thanks to the equation created on the sets by Rakeysh and Aamir, I still consider myself part of the *RDB* family.

105

R. Madhavan
in first person

When I got a call for *RDB*, I was working on a Tamil project, *Thambi*, and my hair was shoulder length. I read the script and was blown by it. It was the most comprehensive document I'd ever seen. Every shot was described in exact detail. For example, you would see a screenplay that went thus:

> Against the close up of a broken window was a finger applying *kajal* to the eye—you see the reflection of the eye in the broken window, inside the jail, as the camera pulls out.

I remember these lines despite the fact that I read it 15 years ago. This man was onto something. I agreed immediately. They had sent the script to my assistants as well, so my entire team was prepared. There was no insecurity about the script. When I came for the reading, there was a reverence to it. Everybody, all the artists—Aamir, the cinematographers, sound, the foreign AD—were there during the readings. I was initially offered Siddharth's role but the role required changes between the 1920s look and the 2000s look and I was already committed to *Thambi*.

Then Rakeysh called me and said, 'You have to be part of this.'

He then asked me to take up the pilot's role, which was for all of eight days.

I responded with a stupefied 'Look at my hair!'

They organized a wig for me: an expense of about ₹70,000 at the time. Rakeysh said, 'We will manage to make you look like an Air Force pilot.'

They were so committed to having me that it was embarrassing to refuse. Besides, when I read the story again and my new role, I had an intuition. Somehow, when this story is released, I will be as much a part of the film as many others who were spending nine months together. And all I had to give was eight days. The math was working out for me. But the role was very demanding!

I asked Rakeysh, 'Do you know what you're asking me to do?'

ROM: What?

Me: In a total screen time of 10 minutes, I have to be a good boyfriend (where the woman is ready to kill for him), a good son (pathos), a patriot (with conviction) and a friend (worthy to give up your life for). Now if such a pilot exists and the audience is to believe the role, how am I going to manage? Actors render one of these roles in a film, and that too barely so.

ROM: That's why we have you!

He gave me his monk smile!

Me: Swell!

I went into major thinking mode on how to portray this character. The audience had to feel the indignation over my character's death, that it was injustice personified. What happens to my character was unfair. After much thought, I told Rakeysh, 'If they think Flt Lt Rathod has died, the impact will be less. I want them to feel *Maddy* died.' Rakeysh allowed me to do it my way.

I saw that Rakeysh does not have an ounce of malice in his body. He is the very definition of liberation. Honestly, nobody realized how impactful my character was going to be, including me. Rakeysh was the only one who believed that it was a pivotal character. The rest of the cast was extremely supportive, but to many, my flash in the pan appearance was limited to the line '*Koi bhi desh perfect nahi hota. Use behtar banana padta hai*' (No country is perfect, we have to make it better). I wanted to channel indignation against *arajyam* (poor governance) through the few dialogues that I had.

The way Bharathi edited it, Rakeysh placed it and the music Rahman gave made the impact gargantuan. *Rang De Basanti* served as an inspiration for so many public movements afterwards. Today, when they speak of *RDB* to me and say 'your film', I feel validated as an actor.

I took away significant learnings from the sets of *RDB*, the first being silence because every department already knew what to do and took ownership for it. I asked Rakeysh, 'Why do you give out such a script to every department of the project?' He said, 'Because I don't want my thought flow to be interrupted by stupid questions, while I am directing.'

Second, the comprehensiveness of the script itself precluded any disjointed execution. I understood that when you give your team respect, they give you the response of being committed. Rakeysh does not believe in *chupchap apna kaam karo* (follow instructions blindly). Every department knew when to pick up the baton. I have implemented this with missionary zeal in my own film, *Rocketry: The Nambi Effect*.

Third, allow your actors to perform freely in the way they want to. My first scene was the proposal to Soha and I was to smooch her. The only thing I could think of was Saif (Soha's brother, with whom I had worked before in a tense movie as rivals) socking my face. But I had to establish that I was an ideal boyfriend. This was probably her first on-screen kiss as well. Rakeysh could sense the discomfort and he subtly kept the shot in a silhouette, and Soha made it easier for me by getting into the character herself. I understood 'evolution' on the sets.

There is a kind of cinema that's relevant to one generation. And there's a kind of cinema that is timeless. Those directors who make cinema on the basis of 'what's working' at that point in time become obsolete over time. But visionary directors create timeless cinema. *Rang De Basanti* went on to make an entire generation of directors obsolete in 2006. The audience begins to understand that if the same ticket price can buy them an experience like *RDB*, why should they settle for anything lesser?

The new-age directors did not need item numbers or six packs. They had powerful stories to tell that changed mindsets and redefined social impact. Rakeysh is and will always remain one of these 'originals'. And that's why I'm so proud of him and so incredibly lucky to have been part of *RDB*.

Sarita and I also love Bharathi, a fellow South Indian. Meetings are few and far between, but there's a heartfelt smile, an artistic oneness that flows like water between us. Also, Rakeysh has the ability to make you feel special. He calls me a lucky son of a bitch! 'Most people in life want one iconic role, you *&%$#! You've had *Alaipayuthey*, *Kannathil Muthamittal*, *Anbe Sivam*, *RDB*, *Three Idiots* and *Tanu weds Manu*, and that's at first count!' Rakeysh is always generous with his praise.

And the icing on the cake for *RDB* will remain having Waheeda ji as my mom. She's the female counterpart of Amitabh Bachchan, a lady with the same grandeur.

One day, I told my assistant, '*Rendu coffee; Ammaku seriya potu kudungo.*' (Get two coffees, make sure you mix it well for the elder lady.)

Waheeda ji responded, '*Parava illai, avarukku kudukaradu enakku podum.*' (Don't worry, I'll have what he's having.)

The Stranger in the Mirror

I had my 'Aiyyayyo' moment! Born in Chengalpet, Waheeda ji knew her Tamil exceedingly well. I was suddenly wondering what else I might have blabbered in her presence unknowingly. And the mother–son bond only became stronger!

I'm sure some day, Rakeysh and I will do another film together. Will it be a big-budget film? I don't know. I have to fit in. He did offer me another film under his banner but the dates didn't work out.

CHAPTER 17

The B's of
Rang De Basanti

If Aamir and AR were the A's of RDB, *then Bharathi and Binod* Pradhan were the B's. Bharathi's scripting inputs and editing and Binod's cinematography were key contributors to *RDB's* runaway success. Binod and I had bonded on the theme of *RDB* much before we shot it. This film was to be the journey of a group of boys and girls who discover meaning in their life. Capturing the progression of the film on camera was always a challenge.

All screenplays are split into three parts: the setup ('base'), the conflict and the resolution. *Rang De Basanti* had all of this but not in this order or any order; I wrote the screenplay with an emotional progression as it was a story told seamlessly across two different eras. This is not something audiences could point out but only feel. When we were establishing the setup, which is the first one-third of the film, we shot on wider lenses, ranging between 24 and 35 mm and mostly tried to frame all the boys and girls as a group and not as individuals. Slowly, as the story progresses, the characters deepen and the conflict begins to emerge, we shifted to 35–50 mm. The last one-third of the film, as individual characters start emerging, we entered the minds of the audiences by staying closer to the actor's face using long lenses. It was almost as if the camera was choking the frame and making the scene feel claustrophobic.

The audience could relate to what each character was feeling individually, yet never departing from the fact that they were complete only as a group. Finally, in the last sequence in the mustard fields, we opened to a wide lens.

In fact the colour of mustard is the colour 'basanti' and we used this colour palette only once, as an after-life experience! The mustard fields were very important to me in telling the story. Almost nine months before the shoot started, Atul, my assistant, had found this beautiful fort close to Ludhiana, Punjab. This is where the boys and girls hung out. Next to the fort was the air force station (created on VFX) from where the MiG-21 fighter planes took off. This is also the spot where Ajay Rathod (Madhavan) proposes to Sonia (Soha Ali Khan). We also set the transition between the boys of *RDB* and the revolutionaries of the 1920 against this background.

After the death of Rathod, the four boys, Atul and Soha gather at the fort. This is where their helplessness gets converted to resolve, where Sonia saying, '*Maar daalo*' (kill [the defence minister]) is shot. It was a pivotal moment in the film and the beginning of the climax that would last for the next half hour.

'*Hum kisi ke khoon ke pyaase nahin hain*! *Sawaal insaaf ka hai*!' (We are not murderers. But we want justice!)

This is when the spirit of the revolutionaries from the past takes over the consciousness of the present-day characters. This was the moment in the story where all lines converge. I wanted to do it as simply as possible without any VFX and achieve it in-camera. Binod designed a beautiful shot where the camera pans back and forth between the revolutionaries from the past and the boys and girl in the present. I remember it was so much fun to execute the scene. It demanded complete focus from the actors and the entire crew. While the camera was repeating the moment twice for each pan between the six boys and girl, the actors had to run to the make-up van and change into the retro-look with a complete hair, make-up and wardrobe change, then run back and take the same exact positions, and now perform in a completely new avatar. The energy was electrifying as we had to achieve it all without wasting much time or the sun would shift and the light would change. It all came together on the editing table.

After the assassination of the defence minister, the establishment strikes back and brutally kills the boys by unleashing black cat commandos on them. Each one is shot dead. But I never wanted to show them dead. Because their spirit had just come alive. Hence, they continued to smile in a surreal world where they meet the young Bhagat Singh who is playing in the mustard field while his father (played by me) is sowing mangoes. We had to do some advance planning to shoot the after-life scene in the same location as the fort. Four months before the shoot, we rented the entire location. Within the fort was a large empty space that the local farmers used for cultivation. We planted yellow mustard and prayed that on the day of the shoot, the crop would have blossomed perfectly. Samir Chanda had learnt from the locals that it takes approximately four months for a perfect blossom. So the team planted the yellow mustard and the local line producer would send us photographs of the crops every week.

Bharathi stitched all together seamlessly and infused her magic, or if I may say, cooked it slowly on low flame.

Three months in, a freak rain destroyed the crop. We were a month away from the shoot and were staring at an indefinite delay beyond our control. That's when Shyam came up with a brilliant solution. He met with agriculture experts in Chandigarh and did what has never been done in the world before—he transplanted an entire mustard field of 6 acres. The crop was three months old. By some divine design, we got the perfect shot I had envisaged. There were tears in everyone's eyes because after taking that one shot, we had to cut the crop in order to film the other scenes which came earlier in the story.

We had a wonderful script, great actors and soul-stirring music. But I'd like to believe that the screenplay was finally re-written on the editing table by Bharathi. It was complicated story-telling that went back and forth, but we did not want the audience to feel lost. There had to be a sense of continuity for the film to work. Bharathi stitched all together seamlessly and infused her magic, or if I may say, cooked it slowly on low flame.

Top: Maa and Bauji had the simplest of unions.
Middle: Bauji, a first-rate chef himself, was specifically asked by Prime Minister Jawaharlal Nehru to prepare his favourite dishes.
Bottom: Film functions were common at the Claridges Hotel. Here, Bauji poses to the left of Raj Kapoor.

Top: Rakeysh and Mamta, standing in the second row, extreme right. Ms Harbans Baxi, the principal of the Air Force Bal Bharati School, is seated in the centre of the first row.

Middle: Shaking hands with President Fakhruddin Ali Ahmed on 25 January 1977, a day before the Republic Day parade.

Bottom: Mamta with Bauji—A typical Indian 'stern but stemming from love' father–daughter equation.

Top: Participation certificate for the selection camp of the Indian swimming team at the 1982 Asian Games.
Bottom: Rajiv Varma, Rajiv Tandon and I at our boisterous best at Malini and Vivek Bhushan's (seated) wedding reception.

Top: With Abhishek Bachchan and Rishi Kapoor—The green screen was replaced by Times Square in New York for the dream sequence of the song 'Dil Gira'.
Bottom: Divya Dutta seems to be mulling over her fate as the untouchable, Jalebi.

Top: Dazzling dames of *Delhi-6*—Waheeda Rehman, Aditi Rao Hydari, Supriya Pathak and Sheeba Chaddha (L to R).
Middle: Nudging the genius Om Puri as he absorbs the scene.
Bottom: Goofing around—With Sonam Kapoor and cinematographer Binod Pradhan.

Top: Role reversal—Abhishek directs me with some intensity.
Middle: Threading it together with production designer Samir Chanda (in white cap), who added realism to the movie.
Bottom: Sonam and Abhishek play with the iconic Masakali.

Top: Hair designer Avan Contractor working on the look of Waheeda Rehman as Sonam and I look on.

Middle: Getting Jalebi's 'look' right. It used to take Divya Dutta two hours to get tattoos on her body.

Bottom: In the groove for the seminal song, 'Sasural Genda Phool'.

Top: Sonam takes a good look at Kaala Bandar (Abhishek in costume).
Bottom: Heaven's gotta be paradise with Amitabh Bachchan and his favourite sweet jalebi in it! The green screen was replaced by ethereal clouds.

57वें राष्ट्रीय फ़िल्म पुरस्कार 2009

57th NATIONAL FILM AWARDS 2009

फ़िल्म Film	दिल्ली 6 (हिन्दी) DELHI 6 (Hindi)
वर्ग Section	फ़ीचर FEATURE
पुरस्कार विजेता Award Winner	निर्देशक : राकेश ओमप्रकाश मेहरा Director: RAKEYSH OMPRAKASH MEHRA
पुरस्कार Award	नरगिस दत्त पुरस्कार : राष्ट्रीय एकता पर सर्वोत्तम फ़ीचर फ़िल्म NARGIS DUTT AWARD FOR BEST FEATURE FILM ON NATIONAL INTEGRATION

सचिव
सूचना और प्रसारण मंत्रालय
भारत सरकार

Secretary
Ministry of Information & Broadcasting
Government of India

The Nargis Dutt Award for Best Feature Film on National Integration meant more to me than any other award. It was a massive encouragement to keep going.

Receiving the national award from President Pratibha Patil as Ambika Soni, Minister of Information and Broadcasting, looks on.

Top: Taking a silent moment at the Golden Temple on the first day of the shoot of *RDB*.

Middle: Authentic all the way—Sharman Joshi, Kunal Kapoor and Soha Ali Khan in the title song.

Bottom: Who's the craziest? Siddharth, Kunal Kapoor, Aamir Khan, Sharman Joshi and Atul Kulkarni (L to R).

Top: Alice Patten seeks much-needed balance as Aamir looks on.
Middle: My Alfred Hitchcock moment in *RDB*.
Bottom: Changing fast, changing slow. With the cast—Aamir, Kunal, Soha, Atul, Sharman and Siddharth (L to R)—as they pause between shuffling characters.

Top: Inquilab Zindabad—The cast of *RDB* living the writing on the wall.
Middle: A young Bhagat Singh filling a bottle with blood-soaked mud to avenge the massacre at Jallianwala Bagh.
Bottom: At the recording of the song 'Luka Chuppi' with the legendary Lata Mangeshkar (seated) are Prasoon Joshi, me and A.R. Rahman (L to R).

Top: Soha, Alice and Kirron Kher recite the soulful prayer 'Ek Onkar'.
Middle: All in a good day's work—Alice emotes as I sneak in from behind.
Bottom: Let's do it—Setting the context for a scene with Kunal, Aamir, Soha and Siddharth.

Top: Friends for life—Siddharth, Aamir, Madhavan, Soha, Kunal and Sharman share a light moment.

Middle: Soha, Siddharth and Waheeda Rehman (L to R) grieve the loss of a loved one. This irrevocable anguish turned ordinary boys into revolutionaries.

Bottom: The incredible support cast of *RDB*—Mohan Agashe, K.K. Raina, Anupam Kher, Om Puri, Kirron Kher and Steven Mackintosh (clockwise).

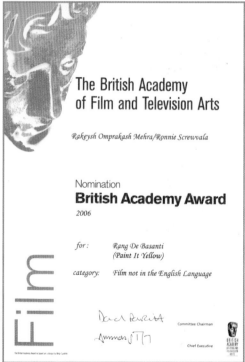

The British Academy
of Film and Television Arts

Rakeysh Omprakash Mehra/Ronnie Screwvala

Nomination
British Academy Award
2006

for : *Rang De Basanti*
       (Paint It Yellow)

category: *Film not in the English Language*

Committee Chairman

Chief Executive

Top: Visions of visionaries—With DoP Binod Pradhan at India Gate.
Bottom: Awards are an important part of every film-maker's journey. I'm fortunate to have had my own share of national and international recognition.

53नफि 53वां राष्ट्रीय फ़िल्म पुरस्कार
53rd National Film Awards

2006

प्रमाणपत्र
Certificate

फ़िल्म — रंग दे बसंती (हिन्दी)
Film — Rang De Basanti (Hindi)

वर्ग — कथा चित्र
Section — Feature Film

पुरस्कार विजेता — राकेश ओमप्रकाश मेहरा
Award Winner — Rakeysh Omprakash Mehra

पुरस्कार लोकप्रिय एवं स्वस्थ मनोरंजन करने वाली सर्वोत्तम फ़िल्म
Award — Best Popular Film Providing Wholesome Entertainment

सचिव
सूचना और प्रसारण मंत्रालय
भारत सरकार, नई दिल्ली

Secretary
Ministry of Information and Broadcasting
Government of India, New Delhi

53नफि 53वां राष्ट्रीय फ़िल्म पुरस्कार
53rd National Film Awards

2006

प्रमाणपत्र
Certificate

फ़िल्म — रंग दे बसंती (हिन्दी)
Film — Rang De Basanti (Hindi)

वर्ग — कथाचित्र
Section — Feature Film

पुरस्कार विजेता — पी.एस. भारती
Award Winner — P. S. Bharathi

पुरस्कार — सर्वोत्तम सम्पादन
Award — Best Editing

सचिव
सूचना और प्रसारण मंत्रालय
भारत सरकार, नई दिल्ली

Secretary
Ministry of Information and Broadcasting
Government of India, New Delhi

Top: Winning a national award is always special. *Rang De Basanti* won the Swarna Kamal in 2006.
Bottom: The National Awards also recognized Bharathi's brilliant editing by honouring her with the Rajat Kamal.

CHAPTER 18

A for
A.R. Rahman,
Again

I had almost finalized Peter Gabriel to work on RDB, *but something* inside me said that AR should be doing it. The music of *RDB* was the soul of the film; the songs AR created became de facto national anthems.

113

When I was narrating *RDB*, I asked AR, 'What's the sound of a rebel?' He introduced me to rap song writer Blaaze, who has an uncharacteristically long name: Lakshmi Narasimha Vijaya Rajagopala Sheshadri Sharma Rajesh Raman. He wrote the rap in English:

I am a rebel...
To the Mahal of the Taj
To the Minar of Qutub
To the Kumari of Kanya

AR developed this rap and gave me an uplifting tune. A rebel does not have to be angry every time. He can be inspired! It's humbling to know that AR considers me as one of the directors who understands music and the joy of making it, as mentioned by him in the book *A.R. Rahman: The Spirit of Music* written by Nasreen Munni Kabir. For *RDB*, Rahman had fused Western classical and Indian folk in a very distinct style, and created a new language in world music.

Rahman's studio is a temple; words are not enough to describe his approach to his work. His involvement is any director's delight. 'Luka Chuppi' was never meant to be a song in the film. Rahman came up with the idea of a mom looking for her son as a take on Bob Dylan's 'A Hard Rain's A-Gonna Fall'.

'Luka Chuppi' became a miraculous song, also because of who sang it. Lata Mangeshkar asked us if she could come to Chennai three days in advance. We thought she might have some other work; turns out she wanted to rehearse for three days. Such humility can only make one stop in their tracks and pray. Lata ji finally rendered the song for five hours, trying to get it right and standing non-stop in front of the mike at the age of 70 plus. She had recorded more than 25,000 songs for Indian films, but she treated 'Luka Chuppi' as if it was her first. What a legend! The other crazy creation was 'Khalbali'. AR composed and hummed 'Ya Ali' in Arabic. When we shot the film, we only had an Arabic recording. Later, Prasoon wrote the Hindi lyrics.

AR has made many global composers redundant because of his prolific genius.

But the soundtrack for the climax left us flummoxed. We still didn't have the theme track for it. Way back, almost four years ago when I had met AR in London for a narration of *RDB*, he was so taken in by the plot that he created a tune and said, 'Keep it.' I had luckily saved it on my laptop. I heard it again and again, but then both of us forgot about it.

Eventually, it was to become the tune for our climax.

'You remember the first tune?' I asked AR.

'Yes,' he replied. We'd had an 'Aha' moment! 'Let's hunt for it.'

We looked everywhere before we remembered where it was all this time—on my laptop! We slapped it on the climax of the film and it worked like magic.

AR has made many global composers redundant because of his prolific genius. To be able to involve a mind like this in your film is itself a privilege. He writes tunes in his own time. It is unlikely that Rahman will sit down to compose with ready lyrics. The emotion and the tune precede everything else. I have never told him, 'AR, let's make a romantic song or a patriotic song.' Because I start the process of integrating the music into the film so early and AR gets so vested in the story, we keep going back and forth, trying to understand what kind of songs are needed to bring out the story. The process is both elevating and liberating. AR understood that the screenplay was actually two screenplays: one in the 1920s and one in 2000. He created music in line with that.

Prasoon Joshi wrote some insanely catchy lyrics, including 'Masti Ki Paathshala'. Many viewers felt this was the Indian answer to Pink Floyd's famous 'We Don't Need No Education'. In hindsight, this was also one of the first mainstream experiments in Hinglish.

One-and-a-half months before the release of the film in December 2005, AR was finishing the original soundtrack that we call background music in Indian cinema, and simultaneously Bharathi was giving final touches to the edit. I was shuttling between Mumbai and Chennai, a two-and-a-half-hour flight in those days. As it worked out, AR works only at night and Bharathi edits only in the day, so my bedroom was my seat on the flight. Later, we realized that I had taken 22 flights back and forth in those 30 days. Imagine my surprise when I came to know later that AR was under immense pressure to join the musical team of the Broadway version of *The Lord of the Rings*. He made a choice and told the producers of the musical that they may fire him because he was committed to finishing *RDB*. That's AR for you.

At the same time, Ronnie was running trial shows. Somehow, I would manage to drop by and get reactions. Aamir was getting married to Kiran at the end of December 2005, Binod was finishing the colour grading and Nakul was mixing the final film. But deep down, I kept feeling I am missing something when one morning the coin dropped. I told Bharathi and Ronnie I need to shoot some more.

Just like the revolutionaries from the past, the boys had avenged the death of their friend Ajay Rathod by assassinating the defence minister. Karan Singhania (Siddharth) even killed his own father (played by Anupam Kher) who was involved in the corruption scam of buying faulty parts. The boys did not run away but surrendered, and then were brutally killed by the establishment. Had the sacrifice of the boys been wasted? Did their message reach the masses?

I called Mrs Radhika Roy, the founder of NDTV who had also partnered us in the film by lending their real reporters and staging a show 'We the People' around the MiG-21 crashes. I requested her that I wanted to shoot with the NDTV news crew around the country and get reactions from the youth of India. She agreed immediately. I took a flight to Bangalore and went to an engineering college with the NDTV crew and broke the news to the students (just like in the movie) that five students from Delhi University had shot the defence minister who was guilty of extreme corruption; they owned up their crime at the All India Radio station but were shot dead by the government in a fake encounter at the radio station itself.

The students believed me and started reacting emotionally. What I was getting on camera were real heartfelt reactions. Later, I did reveal that their reactions were for a movie. It does not matter, they said, corruption in their country needs to end. My assistant Sunil Pandey flew to Kolkata, Kashmir and a few more cities across India. I flew to Lucknow, Delhi and back to Mumbai where we repeated what we staged in Bangalore. Between us, we covered 8–10 cities in four days. The material we got was gold dust, the real reaction got edited into the climax of the film and *RDB* was now complete.

Bharathi and myself could not attend Aamir and Kiran's wedding that was in Panchgani (a hill station barely four hours from Mumbai) as we were caught up finishing the film. Instead we sent Bhairavi, our daughter (eight years old then) to represent us. We were told that Bhairavi and her friend Kasif put up a skit where she enacted Kiran's part while Kasif played Aamir and it was quite endearing.

The film was now complete and we got a censor certificate with a rider, subject to approval from the Ministry of Defence. Like Ronnie narrated earlier, the release had its own melodrama. Later, I was told that the air force chief had been informed that I was an alumnus of the Air Force Bal Bharati School.

Rang De Basanti opened in theatres on the Republic Day of India, 26 January 2006. It was meant to be a tribute to the Constitution of India, which was written 52 years ago on the day—a Constitution that envisaged that the people of India would enjoy freedom of speech.

Madhavan recalls:

Two days before the release of the film, Rakeysh said, 'I can't do this anymore.' It was 24 January 2006. Aamir, Rakeysh, Ronnie, Kunal and I were in Delhi for the publicity drive for *RDB*. As we were seated together, feedback was coming in from a distributor's show in Mumbai. The report was not good. Distributors were predicting a lukewarm run at the box office and wanted to reduce the price they had bought the film at. 'I am not cut out for this. I want to go away,' said Rakeysh with heavy eyes. He was sitting tight on a chair, his hands hugging his knees, ashen, pale and dejected. Ronnie and Aamir, who had lived many such moments before, tried to reassure him. But Rakeysh stared into emptiness, stunned and still, as if he'd seen a ghost.

Two days later came the day of reckoning. If Indian cinema is a sentence, Rakeysh had introduced a new punctuation with *RDB*. Rakeysh Omprakash Mehra, one of Indian cinema's finest directors, had arrived.

117

Touching
New Highs

*

Real imitates reel.
Photo courtesy: *Ru Ba Ru*

CHAPTER 19

The *RDB* Effect

Rang De Basanti was chosen as India's entry in the best foreign film category at the 79th Academy Awards in 2007. We missed an Oscar nomination, but joined *Pan's Labyrinth*, *Apocalypto* and *Black Book* among other nominees in the category of best non-English film at BAFTA. The film travelled to festivals across the globe and broke box office records at the same time.

It won the golden lotus at the National Film Awards for best popular film providing wholesome entertainment. It also won three silver lotus awards: the first for best audiography (Nakul Kamte), the second for best editing (Bharathi) and the third for best playback singing (Naresh Iyer for the song 'Rubaru'). But the irony remains. As Kamlesh Pandey beautifully puts it, 'As long as the State remains the enemy of the nation and politics keep killing its young, *RDB* will remain relevant.'

In the aftermath of this film, there were a series of events that took not only us but the nation by surprise. The tag line of the film was 'a generation awakens'. While writing it, I had no clue that *RDB* was so much more than a movie; it had become a movement.

The film served as a catalyst to civic justice in the horrific Jessica Lal case. To the uninitiated, here's what happened: on the night of 30 April 1999, Jessica Lal, a 34-year-old fashion model, was doubling as a waitress as part of a publicity campaign for a newly opened fancy New Delhi restaurant. At around 2 a.m., Manu Sharma, the young son of a powerful Haryana Congress leader and member of the city's elite brat pack, entered with his friends and demanded that Jessica serve them drinks. It was past closing time, so she refused. He then pulled out his gun and fatally shot her point-blank, in the presence of 300 of the city's glitterati.

He was shockingly acquitted on the grounds of insufficient evidence in February 2006. This was four weeks after the release of *RDB*. A day after the acquittal, *Times of India* headline screamed, 'No One Killed Jessica'. *The Week* expressed its disgust with a cover story titled 'How the Rich Get Away with Murder'. This appalling verdict unleashed a vehement public outcry: this was a departure from the indifference and apathy that greets injustice in India.

About 2,500 people, many of them students, who typify Delhi's insular population, gathered for a candlelight rally at India Gate. The protest itself was a replica of the scene we had created—an on-screen candlelight vigil at India Gate—in *RDB*, which had been released six weeks prior: it was firmly alive in public memory. The students had painted *RDB* tattoos and were wearing *RDB* T-shirts, quoting lines from the film. The media had coined a term called the '*Rang De Basanti*' effect, and it did not die there. Candle-lit protests inspired by *RDB* continued to become a symbolic method to express public outcry. Perhaps the youth of India had found its voice.

Five years later, the April 2011 Anna Hazare fast that shook the government and led to the genesis of a new party—Aam Adam Party (AAP)—also reprised the shades of 'awakening' first sown by *RDB*. An NDTV report at the time titled 'Echoes of "Rang De Basanti" at Mumbai's Azad Maidan' stated that amid patriotic slogans like *Vande Mataram* and Inquilab Zindabad, the crowds also sang 'Yeh Desh Hai Veer Jawaanon Ka' and 'Rang De Basanti' in protest against Anna Hazare's arrest.*

The film evoked reactions in Pakistan too. This was a pleasant surprise beyond border lines, religion, cricket and politics that had traditionally polarized the people of the two nations. Nine months after the release of the film, a reputed Pakistani newspaper *Daily Jang*

---

*IANS, 'Echoes of "Rang de Basanti" at Mumbai's Azad Maidan', *NDTV*, 16 August 2011. Available at https://www.ndtv.com/india-news/echoes-of-rang-de-bas-anti-at-mumbais-azad-maidan-464644; accessed on 29 April 2021.

launched a news channel called Aag (Fire) TV. The channel was envisaged to focus on civic issues and create mass awakening.

The MiG-21 story in the film was my interpretation of real to reel. But the youth of India took over *RDB* and real imitated reel for years to come. Summing up, I can say that an idea that was first named 'The Young Guns of India', then 'Ahuti' and finally 'Paint it Yellow' (English for Rang De Basanti); changed my life forever.

Bharathi went on to direct a documentary on *RDB* called *Ru Ba Ru* that captures the shift in the consciousness that cinema can create. It took her eight years to make it. After all, she is a perfectionist, trained under none other than the visionary adman, Prahlad Kakar (PK).

Candle-lit protests inspired by *RDB* continued to become a symbolic method to express public outcry.

123

Prahlad Kakar
in first person

With *RDB*, Rakeysh had arrived.

What made me truly happy about Rakeysh's success is that he's a good man and generous to a fault. He tends to compensate for lapses in concentration and poor delivery on the part of others.

Rakeysh's greatest advantage as a filmmaker is that he is an outsider. Most super achievers are, including Shah Rukh Khan and Amitabh Bachchan. They have struggled for several years before getting accepted. Outsiders have the will to experiment; they understand hunger, not privilege.

If I had to ask Rakeysh one question, it would be: how did he convince Aamir to do *RDB*? He's the most difficult person to convince. When I shot the Pepsi ad commercial with him, I had to literally tell him that if I've said the shot is okay, *then it is okay*. He wants to do more takes even after the director is happy.

Aamir and Rakeysh coming together—two absolutely gifted creative artists who are never satisfied—had to be iconic. And it was. Their collaboration has created a new language in Indian cinema.

It delights me immensely, vicariously of course, that Rakeysh belongs to the ad world. And I was there when he started.

▰▰▰▰▰▰▰▰▰▰▰▰▰▰▰▰▰▰▰▰▰▰

Every act of creation is first an act of destruction.

—Pablo Picasso

▰▰▰▰▰▰▰▰▰▰▰▰▰▰▰▰▰▰▰▰

1.

2.

3.

The Mad
Ad World

*

1. My first advertising job at Media Communication
Systems, during which I was sent to Japan for an
induction for the client Mazda.
2. This ad produced by me has Kunal Kapoor directing
Aishwarya Rai for Palmolive.
3. My mentor and guru Ashok Mehta
in a pensive mood.

CHAPTER 20

The Taste of
Earning Money

Much before the heady success of RDB, *I learnt my first lessons in* effective storytelling during my stint in the advertising world. It was my training ground for making cinema.

After we graduated, I started selling vacuum cleaners for Eureka Forbes. That was my first job in 1983. I vividly remember that my salary was ₹418, but I got a good commission for selling every piece. I was building my muscles carrying a gargantuan vacuum cleaner box around in Delhi Transport Corporation (DTC) buses. I must've been a funny sight—wearing a tie like a salesman and lugging a massive suitcase.

But in the next three months, I earned approximately ₹25,000 in commissions. It was a great insight into human behaviour. All I had to do was sell to institutions like the railway hospital that bought 11 machines, the tent houses of Delhi to clean their carpets during the marriage season and the wives of the rich and famous living around the Claridges hotel. I built each sale to make someone else feel that they were lagging behind. Herd mentality came to my rescue.

But I got bored soon. It was then that Bhushi's father Col Kul Bhushan gave him some money to start a business. Vivek offered me partnership and then compelled me to take it, like a true friend! We found a deserted factory that had closed down three years ago. It had around 30 sewing machines but were in bad shape.

The factory itself was in ruins. This was at Khanpur: a notorious neighbourhood in Delhi suburbs. We took over the factory, rebuilt it from scratch and Super Garments ('Su' being the initial of Bhushi's unrequited lady love in life) was born. We were to fabricate garments for export houses, meant to be sold all over the world.

I had great fun for around 18 months at Super Garments. We appointed a classmate from college to do accounts. We grew from 30 to 200 machines in three months, and I couldn't believe how well we were doing.

The tailors who came to work for us were off-season farmers—migrants from Rajasthan, Madhya Pradesh, Uttar Pradesh and Bihar. They had these two-in-one cassette players on which they would listen to music, mostly folk styles like Ropni Geet, Katni Geet and Awadhi. Thanks to this, the environment in the factory was like an introductory course in the appreciation of folk and regional music. Later, this induction would come in handy for the sound of my films. Some days, I would wonder why these farmers had left their family behind to stitch garments at a mere ₹2 per piece. Much later, when I watched fashion shows on FTV, I realized that the First-World models wore the garments the Third World stitched but obviously with very different price tags. This always made me conscious of the gap between the haves and the have nots. Today, when I go to a GAP showroom anywhere in the world, I still pick up 'Made in India' jeans and T-shirts, as an ode to the migrant workers from Indian villages.

Interestingly, among these tailors, some were dacoits too! This was revealed when one of my masterjis (colloquial for skilled tailor) came to me and declared, 'I'm going to my village for a marriage.'

I was about to congratulate him, when he added, '*Hisaab pura karna hai. Meri bhai ki shaadi mein do maarey thei, hum jaake baraat mein chaar maarenge!*' (I need to get even. Those guys had ambushed us and killed two of our people at my brother's wedding; we will kill four of theirs!)

I snuck back into my seat. Basically, this nasty little dacoit was going back to extract revenge by attacking a wedding procession.

In my brief stint as a garment fabricator, what struck me was that petty rivalries aside, these folks were happy in their simple

The environment in the factory was like an introductory course in the appreciation of folk and regional music.

interpretation of life, the aching pain in their music and their longing for better days, blissfully unaware of how the fashion world used their work to profit in an unfair manner. I was enchanted by their stories, their music and their lives. Many years later, when I was making *Mirzya*, I also worked on a script called 'Casual Kamasutra', inspired by these tailors from the hinterland. And thanks to their music, I continue to be in thrall of the passion and pathos of folk artists.

Fortunately for me, Bhushi could see that my mind wasn't fully ready to commit to the garment business and that my dreams lay elsewhere.

Says Bhushi:

Loyal to the core, Rakeysh knew that continuing with me would be the biggest disloyalty because his dreams lay elsewhere. So one day he told me, 'Let me go.' That was it! He met some people, joined an ad agency and got totally obsessed with making ad films. I am proud, because he had the guts to follow his dreams.

Rajiv Varma sums up:

Inderpal Singh, a Sardar in our neighbourhood, was an art designer. He helped Rakeysh get his first job in a small ad agency called Media Communication Systems. From there to Ulka was purely on merit.

CHAPTER 21

New Waters
to Swim In

It was 1985. I was 22 years old and there was nothing holding me back! The only way was forward. My dear friend Inderpal, the captain of our cricket club, and I were part of a new agency called Media Communication Systems and I was in the client servicing team. Over the next year and a half, I learnt about advertising pretty much from bottom-up!

As a fledgling agency, our roles were not defined and I was expected to do everything from buying sugar for the office to chasing payments and meeting clients. The only experience I had with an ad agency before this was my part-time job during college, where, as a glorified peon on a bike, I was delivering stuff to clients or spending nights at the printing press watching the next-day publication of *The Times of India* or the next edition of *India Today* being printed. I built some harmless transactional relationships in return for just warmth and friendship, and would somehow always ensure that my client's advertisement got a proper position at no extra cost. My petrol expenses were taken care of by this internship and that had been enough for me back then.

At Media Communication Systems, we had the prestigious Swaraj Mazda account. This was just before the opening up of the Indian economy in 1991. Our task was twofold—we were asked to create an outdoor campaign as well as a radio jingle to launch Swaraj Mazda's light commercial vehicles in India. I was sent to Bombay, the only city in the country that had backlit hoardings at the time. I met with an agency in Tardeo that was in the hoarding business, called One Up Sites. Here's how the conversation went:

Me: Where do you have hoardings?

Agency: All over western India.

(Oh goody! That was sorted then. But the song?)

Me: Do you know who the best music composer for radio and TV jingles is in Bombay?

Agency: You must contact P.P. Vaidyanathan (P.P.V.).

Cool, I said to myself. I had a name to chase for the jingle. I asked around, and figured that P.P.V. had R.D. Burman-like, cult status in the advertising trade. He was the man behind Cherry Blossom's 'Chalte Chalte Joota Chamke', Boroline's 'Khushbhudar Antiseptic Cream Boroline', 'Rang Jamaa De Coca-Cola', etc.

I made persistent enquiries and landed up at P.P.V.'s house. As I entered his apartment, a monkey jumped on me. He had a pet monkey, a pet parrot, a cat, a dog and some more colourful birds, who kept contributing to the sounds in the house.

PPV: When do you want to record a jingle?

Me: Today?

He laughed and made me some tea, a happy bachelor living in a zoo! He also dialled Vinod Sharma, who was referred to as 'Panditji', to lend his voice and Rajesh Johari to write. He suggested that we record at Western Outdoor, the iconic studio where Gulzar recorded all his songs with Lata Mangeshkar. There I was, with blank cheques, giving advances to people I had just met, and creating a jingle for Swaraj Mazda.

This was the final jingle:
Swaraj Mazda T-3500
Chalana aasan, bhare bhaari saaman,
Japaani technique *ka poora faayda.*

Day four, I was back in Delhi. I drove to Chandigarh and made it just in the nick of time for Swaraj Mazda's all India dealer conference. Mr B.S. Devgan, the CEO of Swaraj Mazda India, his Japanese counterpart and their 200 odd dealers—all of them loved the radio jingle. I was an instant hero. **I was kicked** Barely a month ago, I was a partner in a **about** garment factory. Today, an advertising **advertising,** jingle I had put together was good enough **advertising,** for a Japanese MNC. I was kicked about **and how!** advertising, and how!

So impressed was the management that they picked me to be sent to Japan to learn first-hand about Mazda Motor Corporation's manufacturing as well as the marketing and advertising processes and to understand Mazda's corporate philosophy. Japan was a very early influence in my professional and emotional life. The discipline, the hard work, the technology, the food and the people—I fell in love with Japan. Later in life, the mesmerizing works of Grand Master Akira Kurosawa, Japanese film director, screenwriter, and producer, inspired me endlessly to make movies.

Many years later on another visit to Japan, I spent a whole day with Akira Kurosawa's assistant, Takashi Koizumi, who has now become a renowned Japanese director. We even visited Kurosawa's quaint house on the outskirts of Tokyo, where he would bury himself while writing his movies. The pathways of his home were made of rough black stone and there was a small pond. When I was building a country home in Pawna in 2015, I remembered the pathway and the pond in Kurosawa's country home. I have tried my best to re-create the same.

But much before Kurosawa, another inspiration was about to enter my life. It was time to meet Prahlad Kakar.

CHAPTER 22

Prahlad Kakar:
My Irreverent Mentor

After tasting some initial success at Media Communication Systems, by 1985, I soon found myself at Ulka Advertising Delhi. Inderpal Singh and I had been working together at Media Communication Systems, and when he got a job at Ulka, I requested him to get me an interview. I was selected as well. This was a move up for me, as Ulka was a well-established advertising agency with branch offices in all the major cities in India.

I got a chance to work with a talented copywriter named Vikram Uberoi. Once again, I was in a client servicing role and my client this time was Honda's Indian automotive venture, Hero Honda. Honda motorbikes had just come into the country and they wanted to speak about their revolutionary Japanese technology—the four-stroke, 100 cc CD100 motorcycle. Our brief was to convey the extraordinary fuel efficiency of this bike.

After much deliberation, we figured that a total of four ad films were to be made and decided to shortlist the famous Prahlad Kakar. I had to make the trip to Bombay to meet him. Time was of essence!

In hindsight, I was fortunate to be touched by greatness so early in my journey.

Prahlad was and remains a legend; many referred to him as the busiest ad film director in the world, one of the reigning emperors of advertising commercials. He was notorious for doing what his instincts told him to do. All the top brands—Coke, Pepsi, Bullet, Cherry Blossom, Bombay Dyeing—and the biggest agencies loved him for what he was. This, despite the fact that he never listened to them! Simply put, his commercials managed to sell millions of worth of goods and services. His strokes were bold and fearless, yet the simplicity of his work was pure mastery.

He was also invisible: nobody could meet him. One had to go through a secretary, three assistants, his producer and, if you survived all of them, there was Dumbbell, the Doberman. Who brings a Doberman to client boardroom meetings?

Prahlad does.

After much perseverance, I met him and narrated our idea.

PK: Find someone else, I'm not free.

Me: I will not go back to Delhi without you as the director.

PK: My production crew is not free for next six months.

'Production is not a problem,' I blurted!

The films were to be set in Delhi and I told Prahlad he need not worry about production since I am a Delhi boy. Truth be told, I had no clue about the P of ad film production! But I was standing before *the* Prahlad Kakar and I figured I would learn soon enough—and I fully intended to!

PK: Okay, Vikas Sivaraman will be our cameraman. Show him around. I will land a day before the shoot.

His assistants arranged models from Bombay. One of the models was a young, aspiring actor named Salman Khan. There were also two twin models from Delhi. We were to shoot at the Bhatti sand mines in Mehrauli. The big idea was that the models, named Bunty and Sunny, were to start riding their bike 400 km away from Delhi, and that they would still have fuel left in their bikes when they reached India Gate.* The tagline was: What a bike!

PK joined us on the day of the shoot and promptly took the bike for a ride. As we were waiting for the genius adman to return, little did we know that he had met with an accident along the way. He broke his wrist, dislocated his shoulder and was on his way to the hospital.

135

---

*https://www.youtube.com/watch?v=gVWp7O5PJ7U; accessed on 28 April 2021.

We were fully ready to shoot, with a deadline over our head and no director. We packed up and went back to Jukaso Inn in Sunder Nagar, where PK and the crew were staying.

There I saw PK, happily lying in bed, his arm in a sling, surrounded by his beautiful modelling friends from Delhi, pampering poor Prahlad with the broken arm.

You can imagine these beautiful models feeding him grapes as if straight out of an Egyptian tale.

PK: I can't move right now. We need to cancel the shoot.

Me: That's not an option.

PK: Why don't you guys go ahead and shoot with Vikas?

That's when I realized that I had no choice. Every day we would shoot what PK asked us to do. Every evening, we would show PK what we shot, and this went on for four days.

As for me, I was tasting blood.

On the fifth day, PK joined us, but we were more or less done with the lion's share of our ad film shoot. Our footage went to a lab in Bombay, and 25 days later, after due edit and packaging, PK came back with the films. There was a preview room at the Taj Palace Hotel in Delhi where we were to show the final version to the client. The response was lukewarm. After the preview, I was told it was my job to ensure PK was on the Indian Airlines flight at 5.30 p.m. back to Bombay.

For the second time on the trip, I had no clue where he was!

Some investigation revealed that he had gone off to meet the beauteous Feroze Gujral in Lajpat Nagar. I went on the bike in pursuit to ensure that I deposited him at the airport. I reached Feroze's home and was met by an ethereally beautiful woman. To my young mind, it seemed that she was made out of porcelain and had to be one of God's favourite creations. Her demeanour, her conduct—everything seemed impeccable. I still remember that her red brick house was full of paintings; after all, her father-in-law was none other than Satish Gujral, the legendary painter.

I had to snap out of my reverie to remind PK that he was due to return to Bombay.

PK: Give me 10 more minutes.

Me: But sir, the gates will close.

As he finally took leave of his hostess, we hailed a cab.

PK: *Sardarji, kitna time lagega?* (How much time will it take?)

Cab driver: *Kuch bhi lag sakta hai ji!* (There's no way to predict this accurately!)

This exchange wasn't very encouraging.

PK: Let's go on your bike.

Me: You want to ride pillion with me?

PK: At 100 km per hour!

I rode like there was no tomorrow and dropped him off. Just when I thought he was beyond the gates, he came back and looked at me straight in the eye.

PK: You don't belong to Delhi.

I wondered why he said that. And I stood there long after, deliberating over what he implied.

We released the video advertisement soon after. The CD100 was one of the first four-stroke bikes in India and found very few buyers as the two-stroke market was very strong at that time. Our campaign failed miserably. The 'you don't belong to Delhi' remark, however, succeeded.

One of the models was a young, aspiring actor named Salman Khan.

The client was on the verge of sacking us. But Vikram and I decided to give it one more shot. We got working on a print ad and an inspired Vikram came up with the iconic line: 'Hero Honda CD100— Fill it. Shut it. Forget it.'

I could feel that this would work instinctively. We convinced George John, my boss at Ulka, to give us a budget of ₹25,000 to make a new ad internally. Rahul Kansal, my immediate boss, also supported me because Hero Honda was a marquee client for the agency.

Vikram would direct and I would produce—now that I knew what it was about. I scrambled for talent that would work with fire in their bellies. Vikram and I assembled a motley crew: a cameraman who was shooting a TV serial named *Fauji* for DD National and a self-styled band named Dudley 5 to compose the music. We recorded it at a very simple set up called Studio Synthesis owned by a friend, Lokesh.

We shot the whole film in and around Delhi. I was so obsessed that I stopped an army convoy for 25 minutes to get my shots! Then we roped in the Bedi brothers—Rajesh and Naresh Bedi—for editing. They were known to make serials for Discovery Channel. Finally, when I saw the result, Vikram and I thought the ad film looked good! The ad went back to the Munjals, the owners of Hero Group.

'Fill it. Shut it. Forget it' played for two years and is probably one of the most memorable campaigns in two-wheeler history in India.

138

CHAPTER 23

Flicks and Hard Kicks

'You don't belong to Delhi!' PK's words till echoed in my head and gave me sleepless nights.

I told Vikram, 'Let's go to Bombay and set up a company.'

There was one thing we needed to do before that. In order to really leave Delhi, we had to tell our boss George John, who had just given me a double raise.

Me: George, we are going to Bombay.

GJ: Why?

Me: To make ad films.

GJ: We?

Me: Vikram will direct and I will produce.

GJ: Doesn't work like that!

Me: We will work it out.

GJ: Don't do it!

George talked me out of the entrepreneurship bug, but I was restless for the next few months. Vikram and I went back to him. Finally, George saw our conviction and agreed to let us go. George was a great guy and a lovely human being. As a parting gift to us, he gave us an ad film to be produced for Beltek televisions. 'If you're going to Bombay, go with a job,' he said, while giving us the project. Such incredible generosity has always dotted my life.

In 1986, we established Flicks: The Motion Picture Company, starting our career as advertisement filmmakers. We registered the firm in Delhi. Vikram was the son of Col I.S. Uberoi and he had a solid financial background. Together, we jazzed up the new company name with a logo designed by Inderpal Singh. Life suddenly looked full of possibilities.

I landed in Bombay with three buttons of my shirt open and went straight to PK's office. After all, he was the subconscious force that had brought me here. I was 23 and I had the world at my feet.

Me: I'm making a commercial. Can I use your office?

PK: Of course! The staircase outside, that's your office.

And that was Bombay: a reality check within two minutes flat. I genuinely thought I had made it in life with a couple of successes under my belt and my own company. But at Genesis Film Production Pvt. Ltd (Prahlad's outfit), for the first time, I saw how a full-fledged studio looked—with lighting, sets, an art director, wardrobe, sound studio, editing rooms, film lab, the works! The only recording studio I had known so far was Western Outdoor. I went berserk.

We lost money on our first ad film for Beltek televisions. The losses and pressures of being away from Delhi in a fast city where I didn't have a home hit me with full force. Vik helped me find a PG accommodation at a measly ₹400/month. Our landlady was Rose Aunty, and she managed to pack 16 of us in one room.

If you paid more, you could stay in the balcony converted into a room, but who on earth could pay more! One of my crazy roommates in those days was the magnificent singer Lucky Ali, with whom I found instant brotherhood. We used to sing songs and we were all a tribe of aspiring actors, editors, cameramen and directors, with dreams larger than our wallets and a hunger deeper than just food.

One day, I shot till 2 a.m. and came back, stumbling all over sleeping roommates. After much hopscotch, when I finally reached my bed through clotheslines and bodies, someone was already sleeping there!

I shook up the mysterious intruder.

'This is my bed *yaar*,' I asserted.

'Who are you?' he asked.

'Who are you?' I retorted with double the vehemence.

'I'm Mukherjee, I am an editor. I've been here for more than a year. I had gone to Calcutta, my hometown, for a month.'

Indeed! Then what was my status? I wondered. Had Rose Aunty double-crossed me? But Mukherjee was kind; he could plainly see the plot!

'You can take my pillow and find a place somewhere,' he offered.

But I was indignant and proceeded to ask Rose Aunty about the intruder. She lived on the floor above. I rang her bell at 2 a.m. When I explained the situation, her response was quite wise.

'Aah, Mukherjee is back,' was what she said.

This conversation was now getting dense and absurd.

'Can I sleep in your living room?' I asked, putting on my most innocent face.

'No! Go to the terrace,' came Rose Aunty's reply. She gave me some extra bedding.

I took the bedding and stomped off to the terrace. As luck would have it, it started raining. In a bid to prove to myself that I was capable of earning money, I checked into a good hotel with a clean bed, slept the night, had a lavish breakfast the next morning. I blew up ₹2,000.

Happy and broke, I took my customary trip back to Delhi, waiting for another ad film to happen under Flicks. Soon enough, I was back.

Clearly, recording at Western Outdoor in the past had made me ache in a whole new way.

The magic of music had me in its thrall. I wanted to meet Gulzar and hustled to make it happen.

'Why did you agree to meet me?' I asked him, eventually.

'Because I never discourage a young man who wants to make a movie,' he said.

How noble is that!

> The magic of
> music had me
> in its thrall.
> I wanted to
> meet Gulzar
> and hustled
> to make it
> happen.

141

CHAPTER 24

Gulzar

Gulzar is a Persian word with its origin being 'gul', which literally means rose. Gulzar is literally a garden that is flush with blossoms, a pen name for Sampooran Singh Kalra, the magician-lyricist-poet-director who began his career with the legendary S.D. Burman and has enriched our lives with soul-stirring poetry ever since.

Gulzar Sahab and I have collaborated so far on three films: *Aks*, *Mirzya* and *Mere Pyare Prime Minister*. However, he is at the genesis of my film journey. My meeting with him was my first meeting with any bona fide member of the film industry—that too a living legend!

Today, Gulzar recognizes my desire for variety, that I simply cannot repeat myself. He says:

> Rakeysh is a lovely child who is also a go-getter. A strange
> combination indeed! What a man lacks in knowledge can only
> be compensated by a disarming mix of honesty, innocence and
> passion. Rakeysh has this, and that is why he is not afraid to try
> new things and he will not repeat himself. I think he won over
> Kutty Sahab (my secretary) because of his innocence.

I was barely a year old in Bombay when, sometime in 1988–9, I tricked my way through the gateman at Cozy Home housing society in Pali Hill, Bandra, to secure my first ever meeting with the eternally young Gulzar.

As I entered Pali Hill, I couldn't suppress a tingling feeling of awe. One moment, I was passing Raj Kapoor's bungalow, Krishna Raj, and

142

the next moment I was across Dilip Kumar's, Nasser Hussain's, Sunil Dutt's bungalows. I felt as though I was in the Beverly Hills of India.

I made a decision. 'I will live here some day!'

I rang the bell with a swagger that overtakes rationality in my head from time to time and makes me do strange things. The reliable Mr Kutty, Gulzar Sahab's efficient manager, a straightforward South Indian, opened the door.

'I have an appointment,' I said.

'Really? I give appointments and I know you don't have one. It's not in my diary,' he said.

'Then please write it in your diary,' I replied.

'*Baith jaao*,' he said, clearly exasperated but not willing to turn me away for reasons I am still not clear about.

'Sahab is writing,' he told me.

I waited. After all, I was metres away from whatever magic Gulzar was weaving with words. I could feel an aura around me.

Around lunch time, I got my five minutes.

I don't think I will ever forget the first time I actually 'saw' Gulzar.

There was a painting of Meena Kumari (the legendary actress and Bauji's favourite) behind him. Clad in pure white, Gulzar Sahab seemed to emerge from the picture in some unexplained spiritual way. I almost saw a halo behind his head. It was all a blur, even when I was walking towards him, half conscious, half in stupor. The thrill of meeting this man, and that I had tried to hoodwink his manager to meet him, struck me. I felt a pang of guilt: for a minute, I thought I was going to be scolded.

I immediately gave him the book of Sarat Chandra Chatterjee's *Devdas* that I was carrying with me.

'Will you write "Devdas" for me?' I blurted.

I was barely making two ends meet with my advertising and Flicks. But my mind was thinking into the future.

'*Chai piyoge?*' came the indulgent reply.

As chai took its time, I couldn't care less. I was in the presence of greatness. Over four cups of tea, I interpreted my understanding of *Devdas* for him.

'Who's your producer?' he asked.

I swallowed. I hadn't thought about it.

'Actors *kaun hai*?' he asked.

I swallowed again!

'*Yeh tumhari pehli picture hogi na*?' he probed gently.

'*Main seekh loonga*,' (I will learn) I said quickly, so that he wouldn't turn me away.

'I also wanted to make "Devdas",' he revealed. 'I shot for seven days and then realized it wasn't for me.'

I was mesmerized. He went on to share that Kailash Chopra, the older brother of actor Prem Chopra, had come on board as producer. Dharmendra was to play Devdas: Gulzar felt that the actor was perfectly suited to embody the perennial adolescence epitomized by Devdas. Regrettably, the shooting got stalled and 'Devdas' remained an unfulfilled dream.

The thrill of meeting this man, and that I had tried to hoodwink his manager to meet him, struck me.

I was wondering if I could make 'Devdas' with Gulzar; it was a secret desire. I was in love with Sarat Chandra's character—the adolescent who never matured beyond his petulant love. In sharp contrast, the women in the novel were very mature. Paro, the childhood love of 'Devdas', circumspectly agrees to be married off to an elderly man after his orthodox family rejects their proposal of marriage. He doesn't fight for her then, but lives to regret it. Later, he meets Chandramukhi, the courtesan, a social outcast whose love he mocks because she is known to entertain paramours for a price. His drunken vulnerability and naivety make him the object of love of these very beautiful, very different women and lend nuances to their characterization. The story of 'Devdas' was sheer magic for both of us.

Little did I know, that much later, Gulzar Sahab confided in my co-author, Reeta Ramamurthy Gupta.

Rakeysh is the right man to make 'Devdas'. Rakeysh himself is the adolescent boy who hasn't grown up. Bharathi is far more mature. His innocence is intact and, therefore, he will never take no for an answer.

Going back to our first meeting and many grateful cups of tea, I felt privileged to know whatever Gulzar Sahab was telling me. I was certainly drinking in far more than just the tea.

'You're the first person who has understood Devdas correctly,' he acknowledged.

If I were a bird, I would be flapping my wings excitedly. My body was trembling. I mumbled something incoherently.

'Let me work things out and come back,' I assured him.

My next meeting with him was 12 years later in 2000 to write the lyrics for the songs of *Aks*, my first feature film. Those 12 years also saw my struggle: from being a novice in the advertising industry to an integral and acknowledged part of it. Slowly, my trips between Delhi and Bombay became lesser and lesser as Bombay made room for me.

And then there were matters of the heart.

1.

2.

3.

B for Bharathi:
The Reason to Be

*

1. Taking in the fragrance of togetherness at
   Manori beach near Mumbai.
2. The joy of being together.
3. Bharathi's love for dogs comes to the fore during a
   trip Scotland. Seen here kissing a giant sheep dog.

CHAPTER 25

The Girl in the Polka-Dotted Skirt

Bombay was now a part of me and what I wanted to do.

In PK's office, while trying to make ends meet, I had seen this beautiful, shy girl in a polka-dotted skirt, with a 6-inch wide red leather belt, a freaky hairstyle and chunky roadside jewellery—big earrings, lots of bangles.

P.S. Bharathi was like no girl I had ever seen before. And she was Prahlad's all-important 'production person'. This absolutely divine girl was making her way into my heart.

Little did I realize that my furtive glances at Bharathi hadn't escaped Prahlad's notice. Office gossip revealed itself shortly;

In Prahlad's own words, 'My office had three resident virgins (RVs). Bharathi was RV1: the good girl with good values, who had to be pursued.'

While I was slowly falling hook, line and sinker for this girl with big eyes, the losses and pressures of real life were mounting. Thankfully, Prahlad allowed me to hang around and I was cutting 10-second promos for a living that Prahlad outsourced to us at Flicks. Vikram and I kept doing whatever ad films came our way, but Bharathi's allure now kept me quite persistently in Bombay. This Bangalore-born, Ooty-bred girl—the RV1 at PK's office—was walking all over my heart.

PK chips in:

I have known Bharathi and Rakeysh since their early days. They've both grown as professionals in front of my eyes. They're very different from each other: while Rakeysh forgives laggards and gives them more chances, Bharathi will at least convince him to put them in a job where they can't do damage. Bharathi treasures the lessons from lapses, those of others and her own and treads carefully. Rakeysh is far too giving. He often blurs the lines between professional and personal, whereas Bharathi is acutely trained to spot and eliminate professional lapses. I can imagine that this is one thing they fight about as a couple.

There was another catalyst in our story: the magnificent genius Arun Gogate. He was PK's editor at Genesis and he allowed me to watch him work. Bharathi would assist him often. I can gratefully say that both Bharathi and I have inherited an acute sense of detail from Gogate Sir.

Slowly, Bharathi became aware of my existence in a sharp 'stay away from Delhi boys' kind of way. Though I wasn't boisterous in the least, I guess I had this whole 'stamp' of North Indian boy who loved onion, garlic and mutton imprinted all over me.

Born to Amruthakala and P.S. Anantha, Bharathi's early years were influenced by a most traditional upbringing, guided by centuries of rich legacy. To truly understand the ethos of conservatism and culture flowing through Bharathi's veins, you have to look at her father's background.

Bharathi says:

My father's ancestors were the rajgurus at the Parakala Mutt in Mysore, which had a close relationship with the maharajas of the Mysore Kingdom since 1399. The rulers of Mysore hold the Mutt as their official gurukul, and even today, the royal lineage has a close relationship with the Mutt and royal ceremonies continue to be monitored by the Mutt.

Things were smooth till the period from 1956 to 1973, when the geographical boundaries of several neighbouring states around Mysore underwent some re-definition, and eventually the state of Karnataka was formed. Consequently, in the late 1950s, Bharathi's grandfather faced an uncertain future under the patronage of Mysore's maharaja and moved out of the Mutt's premises. He became the vice-chancellor of the first Sanskrit college in Mysore, functioning as a professor of logic. Eventually, he settled in Bangalore, where Bharathi's father P.S. Anantha was born.

P.S. Anantha was the first person in the family to be born outside the protective precincts of the Mutt and gain an education in a normal environment. After his education, he was employed with the Government of India ordnance factory (explosive-making unit) and was transferred to a couple of places. He had a traditional arranged marriage, just like my parents, and in 1967, Bharathi was born in Bangalore. The picturesque place called Aruvankadu between Coonoor and Ooty was her home for 18 years.

Her childhood was predictably high on cultural education. Mornings were spent listening to Lalitha Sahasranamam, setting the tone for the day. She was one of four siblings. Srikanth Srinivas, Padmashree, Bharathi and Shyam, in that order of age, were children who led a simple 'school to home to club to home' life. The club in question is the Aruvankadu Ordnance Factory Club that had courts for badminton, table tennis, billiards and snooker, and it also hosted other family activities. As soon as she could, she received extensive training in Carnatic music and, of course, Bharathi and Shyam had the additional job of taking the cows out for a walk.

Yes, Bharathi grew up with cows, dogs, hens and butterflies!

There was linguistic diversity too, with three languages— Telugu, Kannada and Tamil—spoken interchangeably by members in the household. The treat during her childhood was the Radio Ceylon programme from 7 a.m. to 8 a.m. comprising latest Hindi songs. The other thing to look forward to was the screening of M.G. Ramachandran's movies in the *olakottay* (shed in Tamil) at the Club.

Looking back on those days, Bharathi says,

I got my appreciation for art and music from my parents. Appa was the secretary of fine arts at the ordnance factory and he used to invite stalwarts such as Balamuralikrishna, violinist N. Rajam and singer Madras Lalitangi Vasanthakumari to perform. Amma, on the other hand, used to organize Durga *Stuti* and other community pujas for the families at the factory, where we all sang *bhajan*s. Dancers like Chitra Visweswaran would perform at annual events. Adding to this beautiful exposure, the intense reading habit all four of us had developed since childhood was the perfect recipe for our childhood. We were products of a God-fearing, ideal Indian household.

One day, her father's assistant heard Bharathi singing in a temple along with her mother and some ladies. Her voice was mesmerizing and worthy of being a lead singer. The factory was a small community, and encouraged by friends and neighbours, the 'Sangeeta Orchestra' was created. Bharathi became their lead singer, performing famous Tamil, Telugu and Hindi film songs. Her favourite was Asha Bhosle's 'Yeh Mera Dil Pyar Ka Deewana'.

Bharathi's heart was creatively inclined. She was craving for more.

This band of seven–eight youngsters would perform in functions in nearby towns of Ooty, Coonoor, Coimbatore and Wellington. Bharathi would earn anything between ₹15 to ₹20 for each outing. On big evenings, she would earn up to ₹100 and would diligently give her earnings to her mother to add to the family income. Bharathi's voice is very close to that of Geeta Dutt, and I have always requested her to sing for the movies but she remains shy. However, she agreed to lend her voice to the Sanskrit shloka of the sun god which Shankar Mahadevan composed for the moving logo of our film banner, ROMP Pictures.

In the year 1984, her father moved to Khamaria, near Jabalpur, Madhya Pradesh. She reluctantly enrolled for an MSc in Physics at St. Aloysius College situated in the Jabalpur Cantonment area, but the travesty was that there were all of two girls in the whole science college. Most of the girls were expected to do Home Science at the University. Another realization that happened around the time was that despite being an excellent Physics–Chemistry–Maths (PCM) student, Bharathi's heart was creatively inclined. She was craving for more.

CHAPTER 26

Bombay Calling

Luckily, Bharathi's older brother Srikanth, who had taken the probationary entrance exam, got a bank job in Bombay. It was more of a middle-class 'Tam Bram' (slang for the intelligent and studious Tamilian Brahmin community) dream to settle this way.

Under the pretext of taking the IIM entrance exam, Bharathi packed her bags and set off for Bombay along with sister Padmashree (Paddy). Srikanth advised her not to go back and also helped her find a hostel to stay in. Meanwhile, Paddy got a job with an accounting firm. Bharathi, egged on by two working siblings with salaries, decided she could afford to attend Sophia College for a year and pursue a novel course in social communication media.

One can imagine their father's abject consternation, livid that both daughters showed no inclination to return home to Jabalpur. The course was an eye-opener. The conventional environment she was raised in seemed parochial and Bharathi's universe exploded. The PCM degree seemed ancient and she stepped out of her comfort zone. Post this course in Sophia College, this coyly rebellious runaway South Indian landed up as RV1 at PK's Genesis in 1989.

The offspring of a workaholic Appa ('I've never seen him take leave'), Bharathi was a dogged worker and proved herself indispensable to PK's team. 'She was the "production girl" and specialized in preparing for the worst when everyone was hoping for the best,' Prahlad claimed. As a perennial purveyor floating around Prahlad's office, I was taken in by her unique combination of work and personal ethic and, of course, her unique beauty. One day, I came back from my usual jaunt to Delhi. Chatting casually, my eyes were looking for Bharathi but I couldn't find her.

Me: Where's Bharathi?

There was complete silence.

Me: Gogate Sir, where is Bharathi?

Gogate: Bharathi had an accident.

I was shocked to hear this!

Bharathi says,

The whole office had gone to Goa. The Gypsy in which we were riding overturned, and I broke my pelvic bone and was bed-ridden for three months.

I knew only one thing. I had to see Bharathi right away, wherever she was. Prahlad was more worried than ever before. With such a delicate portion injured, would Bharathi actually die a virgin?

> I had to see Bharathi right away, wherever she was. Prahlad was more worried than ever before. With such a delicate portion injured, would Bharathi actually die a virgin?

153

P.S. Bharathi
in first person

I still remember the day Mehra turned up at my place for the first time.

I was quite surprised at his persistence because he had begun his search for me post my accident with one line—'South Indian girl living in Wadala'—as no one at the office knew my address. There was a good reason for that. I had just started living in Wadala with my entire family. After Appa retired in January 1990, he had the option of going back to the comfort of Bangalore, but his children were living dispersed lives in Bombay.

Paddy and I were living in hostels. Srikanth was doing well at his bank but suffered from a severe case of diabetes. In fact, on one occasion, he fell unconscious in the lift in his office building and was in a diabetic coma. Paddy and one of his friends had to rush and rescue him. At the time, Srikanth was living with four other flatmates. Clearly, he needed someone to take care of him. Our unanchored lives made Appa and Amma choose Bombay over Bangalore. They found a central government quarters house on lease in Wadala. Our family was together again and my parents created new routines and settled down. Soon, Appa started taking our dog out for a walk around the society every evening.

Unknown to us, for at least three days, Mehra was knocking on over a 100 doors in Wadala government quarters with the question: 'Do you know a South Indian girl in advertising who had had an accident in Goa?' Every day, he would also buy a fresh bunch of red roses, just in case he got lucky and found me!

It was on the third day that a considerate watchman became familiar with this lovelorn hero and went so far as to share his bidi with Mehra. I have never seen Mehra give up—the word does not exist in his dictionary. On the third day, while sharing a bidi with watchman, he encountered a tall South Indian man taking a dog out for a walk. Taking a last chance, he walked up to him and asked, 'Sir, do you know a south Indian girl who met with an accident in Goa?'

The man simply said, 'Follow me.'

Mehra promptly followed. Soon, they reached the door of a ground floor flat and the tall man rang the bell. Delighted at the prospect of meeting me, Mehra said a very hurried but profuse 'Thank you, sir', but then the man proceeded to enter the house.

Mehra didn't know what to make of it. How can a man ring the doorbell and proceed to enter the house?

'Come in. Bharathi is my daughter.'

It was Appa who had got him home! You have to understand, a friend coming home, male or female, was a perfectly normal thing. Since our childhood, Amma and Appa were used to having our friends turn up at home. The most common refrain among friends, through our growing up years was, 'Aunty, *dosa hai kya*?' (Aunty, is there dosa?). And Amma would make dosas till she ran out of batter.

So when Appa brought Mehra home, I was summoned casually from my room, because a 'friend' had come to visit. It took me a while as I was still weak and limping. I can't say I was surprised to see Mehra, though I found myself wondering how on earth he found me! We spoke for a while, and content that I was alive and recovering, Mehra left. My accident came a year after I had converted my mass communication internship into a full time job for a ₹800 salary at Genesis with PK. After I recovered, I was welcomed back at Genesis with open arms. Mehra was living his life, shuttling between Delhi and Bombay, trying to find work that would support longer stays in the city. Whenever he was around, we would meet.

Here was this absolutely uncomplicated guy who understood complex issues and that life is not always linear. He never used bad language, seemed to have no ego and was easy-going. More importantly, both of us were outsiders trying to make it in Bombay. We connected. Soon enough, Rakeysh decided to spend a majority of his time in Bombay. To put it more precisely, out of our 18-month dating period, he was in Bombay for the last 8 months and took up a PG accommodation in Breach Candy. But we must have met barely for 30 days. I was really busy and he was trying to make it in the advertising world.

He and his partner Vikram were very different from each other, and I used to wonder what made them click as a team. Vikram and his girlfriend had a much more lavish lifestyle than we did. Mehra was unassuming, frugal and our only indulgence was the ₹10 Chinese minestrone soup at Tasty Corner in Worli.

One of the TV commercials Mehra made was for LML Vespa. He retained the vehicle used for the shoot, though it did not have a legal number plate. I'm not sure it was even tested for quality. So there he

155

was, almost every evening, picking me up and taking me home, in the LML Vespa. As for me, I loved gifting him Archies stickers.

Our journey back home would at times also include street Chinese food outside Dadar East station. We were not into clubbing or wining and dining clients. We were keen on the early morning classical performances at Bhuleshwar back then or the odd Kishori Amonkar show that we would save for. In those days, I had seen ad filmmakers partying late night, hoping to get work. Mehra's ethics forbade it. During our dating period, his love for music became very evident to me. In fact, he bonded with my father over Naushad's 'Prem Jogan Ban Ke', the classic from *Mughal-e-Azam* and the stirring melodies composed by Bade Ghulam Ali Khan, while having filter coffee and *rasam* at home. My family was familiar with him now. On the work front, he was working very hard and got a few breaks with some well-paying ad films.

Soon enough, Mehra suggested that we get married. I wasn't looking for a provider and Mehra's situation was not very stable. He insisted on speaking to my father and I kept telling him off under some pretext or another: 'My father's not in a good mood', 'This is not the right time', etc.

Soon enough, it was time for Mamta's wedding (Mehra's sister) in Delhi on 26 November 1989, and Mehra insisted that I attend. They were living in a 2BHK in Sarvodaya Vihar back then. I planned a four-day visit. Arrangements for my stay were made at Malini and Vivek Bhushan's house. Bhushan was the first in Mehra's gang to get hitched. I received a warm welcome from his friends and family. I heard stories of their trekking, multiple girlfriends and exploits—the usual banter that makes for initial conversations.

Mehra's Maa was on the quieter side. She spoke little, but often found the simplest solution to a problem. She didn't like anyone to do anything for her; she was very independent. His father was a very emotional person. I saw him cry a lot during Mamta's *bidaai*, a farewell function associated with weddings in the North.

After the marriage, we came back to Bombay. I was happy to have seen where Mehra got his roots from and was savouring the simplicity of his origins. Part of me was wondering what his family thought of me because Mehra was my first boyfriend. I was told that *Chotu Maama* (Mehra's mom's brother) had commented '*Baal chote hain*' (her hair is short) and there was a general consensus that '*Thodi saanwli hai*' (she's on the darker side). At the same time, I knew that he had dreams to make feature films of his own someday, and I found myself believing in him.

What happened next was quite unexpected. One day, the doorbell to my Wadala home rang. Mehra's Maa and Bauji had come to discuss our marriage. Mehra always had his own way of doing things. I was in a proverbial soup, as I had not told Appa that we were a couple.

After a pleasant but slightly awkward visit, Appa promised that we would think over the proposal and get back soon. I knew exactly the ruminations on Appa's mind. Paddy, my older sister was still single. To get me married before her was mildly heretic, as per Indian customs. Srikanth too was unmarried, but that was somehow okay in the scheme of things. No one in my family had married outside the caste. I was only 23. My younger brother was still in college and he needed financial support. Appa had his pension and it was enough, but my salary was only ₹1,200 and Mehra didn't have any savings to speak of. How would we make ends meet?

Clearly upon Mehra's insistence, his father called again. 'Bacchhe kar lenge' (the kids will manage), he said. The matter advanced when Amma too jumped on to the bandwagon and declared, 'We can't hold one daughter for the other.' Finally, my father yielded and it was time for us to tie the knot. This was January 1992. The Panditji gave us a date 11 months later for December. But Mehra was up to his own mischief. He went to the Sri Sringeri Sharada Peetham Mutt in Vasant Vihar, Delhi, and bribed the Panditji with ₹500 to advance the wedding date. The playful Panditji apparently confided to him, 'The date doesn't really matter. I also had to get married a second time.' Talk about kindred pranksters! Our wedding date was set for 17 April 1992.

It was a match made in heaven.

Waheeda ji says:

Bharathi and Rakeysh are a great couple, made for each other. They know how to make you feel special and cared for. They have an eye for the small things. Bharathi always ensured that her mom made *avakkai* (raw mango) pickle for me during the making of *RDB*. On another occasion, when we were shooting *Delhi-6* in Jaipur, I casually remarked that the weather was ideal for *sarson ka saag* (a regional delicacy of Punjab made from mustard leaves). Bharathi got it flown overnight from Delhi. Mehra and Bharathi complete each other—he keeps making and she keeps cutting.

1.

2.

Marriage, Mehnat, Kismet

✳

1. Partners for life in joy and sorrow
2. Bharathi and I share lunch with jawans of the Indian
army during our honeymoon at Dras in Kargil,
at a height of 10,800 ft

CHAPTER 27

'Can You Postpone Your Wedding by a Day?'

Bharathi just about made it to her own wedding! In hindsight, it's hilarious. However, back then, my family's anxiety was palpable.

Bharathi's family reached Delhi on 14 April, three days in advance. At this time, my family was living in the DDA flats in South Delhi. Kapil Varma, a friend of Vikram Uberoi, had given us his guest house to use for the wedding. Bharathi's family was put up there. It was a simple wedding, with about 50 people in attendance, a *Mehndi* (henna ceremony), a *Sangeet* (song-and-dance ceremony) and the *Shaadi* (wedding) itself. My conscientious bride happened to be working on a Tata Coffee campaign pitch and missed her own Mehndi on the afternoon of 15 April. The unspoken buzz around was, 'We hope she's coming!'

Thankfully, her family was with me in Delhi, and assured my folks that she intended to come. She looked every inch a prime candidate for a runaway bride to all the Delhi-ites. As for me, I knew her ways so it was all cool. Bharathi took the last Air India flight out of Bombay and reached Delhi for her wedding at 7.30 a.m. the next morning. This, after her boss teased her earnestly, 'Can you postpone your wedding by a day?' Thanks to Kapil Varma's resourcefulness, we found a mehndi *wali* (henna tattoo artist) at the nearby Hanuman Mandir. A half-asleep lady put mehndi on Bharathi's hands at midnight.

An impromptu sangeet had taken place on the night of 16th in typical Delhi style. In continuation to the festivities, my friends and I got sloshed barely a couple of hours before the wedding. We all knew that the wedding was at 7.30 a.m. on 17th, but somehow, the early hour had not sunk in for my friends. As is custom, the South Indians were up, bright and early, on the morning of the 17th for their rituals. The North Indian bridegroom and his friends were snoring. Srikanth was sent to fetch me, with strict instructions to get the smell of alcohol off me in whatever way best possible. Thankfully, I survived the inspection of the 25 wedding guests from Bharathi's side of the family.

There was the *Oonjal* (swing) ceremony, during which Bharathi's grandmother sang very beautifully. My friends, who had laughed at the idea of a wedding at 7.30 a.m., thankfully missed it. They would've never been able to behave themselves that early after the night we had! With great courage, they turned up later.

Meanwhile, Bharathi was fighting the battle of the *pallu* (the end of a saree that can be draped in many ways). She turned up for the *varmala* (garland ceremony) in a beautiful blue saree draped in Mangalorean style. This meant that the saree was wrapped around her bosom like a towel, and not like the traditional demure style that goes across the shoulder. My horrified aunts grabbed her aside and draped the saree in a more conservative style. Later, I learnt that one of my cousin sisters was expressly instructed to ensure that Bharathi kept her pallu down through the ceremony.

My father personally supervised the preparation of a lavish-yet-simple fully vegetarian meal for all the wedding guests. During lunch, Bharathi called out 'Mehra' to say something to me. About half-a-dozen people, all Mehras, turned to her immediately! By North Indian standards, such a hark was inappropriate, given that most of the Mehras there were older to both of us. My father indulgently said, 'We are all Mehra, whom do you want?' And that was the end of any further analysis of her salutation. Even today, Bharathi still calls me Mehra.

The night of the wedding was the *Antakshari* (a parlour game where teams compete by singing songs beginning with successive ending letters). The South Indian bride's team, comprising her friend Mamta Bishnoi and siblings Paddy, Srikanth and Shyam and his friends, beat the North Indian groom's team hollow! We took it for granted that we knew Hindi songs better but came out losers against the inspired South Indians.

Bharathi and I contributed 7,500 bucks each to the marriage, which took care of everything. We took no gifts and insisted on a simple wedding. The night after the wedding on 18 April, Bharathi and I took the Gypsy bought on loan under my company Flicks and left for Chandigarh. It was Anita and Arun's wedding. (Anita is like a sister to me. I call her Rinku.) We were so casual and unpretentious about our own marriage that it seemed perfectly normal to saunter off to another wedding. After attending their nuptials, we came back to Delhi on 20th. On 21 April, we took the early morning flight to Leh. After paying for the tickets, my credit card was almost maxed out: we had only ₹400 left. I was used to going to the mountains without any money because we had planned to camp. My experience told me that if we roughed it out, we could survive the honeymoon. For me, it was not about the accommodation or bottles of wine; I really wanted to share Ladakh, my favourite place, with Bharathi. The opportunity to do it empowered and emboldened me in a magical way.

During lunch, Bharathi called out 'Mehra' to say something to me. About half-a-dozen people, all Mehras, turned to her immediately!

163

CHAPTER 28

The ₹400 Honeymoon

We had gotten married and we were happy. Nothing else seemed to matter. I had this exotic-looking bride by my side, wearing the traditional *chuda*, the colour and fragrance of henna taking their time to leave her hands. Her eyes were open and honest as a child, and she looked at me with a trusting warmth and earnestness.

Raised by a mother who personified Durga, here was my very own Purala, a reflection of Durga. Purala, in Indian mythology, is the guardian of fortresses, and sure enough, Bharathi would become that in my life with time. I was in seventh heaven.

I was determined to give my bride the honeymoon of a lifetime. Ladakh was wild country, and I knew from my trekking days that Ladakh wasn't big on tourist infrastructure but had everything that nature could offer. Nestled in the arms of the Himalayas, majestically jagged, arid mountains enfold Ladakh.

On the first day, we stayed in a homestay kind of inn for ₹35 and spent another ₹30–40 on meals.

That 'pockets empty faster when one is really happy' is a time-tested hypothesis. I realized we needed to conserve cash. At that time, Ladakh did not witness much tourism, and all administrative and health services were provided by the Indian Army. It was a sensitive zone as it shared disputed boundaries with China and Pakistan. There were more army camps than civilians.

We had just visited the Spituk Monastery and were walking back, passing the army camp of Border Roads Organisation (BRO) under project Himank. Himank's work ensures access to sensitive military areas including Siachen Glacier, the world's highest battle-ground, and the Pangong Tso Lake, whose waters span the de-facto India–China border.

On a hunch, I wanted to say hello to the officer in command, so we entered the camp and were received by a very warm Sikh army officer, Col I.S. Bindra.

'How do I get to meet Gen. Vombatkere?' I asked with as much confidence as I could muster. S.G. Vombatkere was the general officer commanding (GOC) in Ladakh. Unknown to me, he was travelling to Chandigarh at the time. Gen. Vombatkere's name was given to me by Col Uberoi, my partner Vikram's father. He had said, 'Son you are going to Ladakh, please pay my regards to Gen. Vombatkere, and don't hesitate to ask the army for any help. After all, you are going with Bharathi.' We were readily accepted as the General's guests, thanks to Bharathi lending some respectability to me and welcomed with open arms.

The BRO gave us a place to stay and even free rides to visit remote corners. Some team of theirs was always on the move from one camp to another and we would jump on the army vehicle. In the nights, we would return to Col Bindra's camp in Leh.

A few days passed and Gen. Vombatkere returned from Chandigarh. We immediately went to meet him. He didn't recognize me. No surprises there. In fact, he might've seen right through me.

'Col Uberoi told me about you,' I ventured my ace. Thankfully, he decided to indulge me and opened his heart to this unusual bride and her audacious husband. And this was the beginning of the best honeymoon gift that even a million dollars couldn't buy—the warmth and the hospitality of the Indian Army.

In my rucksack, we were carrying some cans of KC Das *rossogolla* (sweet cottage cheese dumplings in sugary syrup; a speciality from Calcutta), assorted sweets and loads of *namkeen* (snacks) that were left over from the wedding. We moved around army camps, opening rossogolla cans for the soldiers. Food was the way to people's hearts, as my mother had always demonstrated.

We were driven to the picturesque hamlet of Dras, situated about 60 km away from Kargil, on the road to Srinagar. The chiselled, glacial landscape of Dras valley touched our souls.

Word had spread about the 'honeymoon couple' who was meandering about as unofficial guests of the Indian Army. It was almost as if we were a welcome distraction to their schedule and harsh life. I remember Maj. Porus (in Kargil), a Parsi gentleman who was one of the most gracious hosts we encountered. He assigned us the cottage of Gen. Cariappa for the night. That was a night to remember. Maj. Porus sat us down at the army mess. He was having rum and warm water.

'Lady, what can I offer you?' he asked Bharathi.

'Rum and coke,' she replied.

His face fell. His chivalry was deeply wounded.

Bharathi and I couldn't touch each other for the first few nights!

Stoically, Maj. Porus said, 'Lady I'm sorry, but there's no coke!'

All of us laughed heartily and wormed our way out of an awkward moment.

We feasted on rum and warm water. As it turned out Maj. Porus was an ardent Mirza Ghalib fan, as was I. We recited his poetry all night. Several deeper realities hit me with full force. The borders were ruthless, with inclement winds and snowstorms. And yet, for our brave Indian Army, onions and fresh tomatoes were a luxury. Coca-Cola was unheard of.

There were stories of emotional loss. I met Col Pratap at the camp, and was shocked to know that he was a victim of short-term memory loss. He got an extension of four years. 'Call my home. I have forgotten my wife's name,' he used to say.

One day, on an impulse, I decided to cook my famous *dahi* (curd) mutton curry for the soldiers, and they feasted on the barkat my mother had bestowed upon my hands. We shared food and we shared friendship. On the ice-decked table at Zoji La pass, I opened the last can of rossogolla. Till date, Maj. Porus's singing comes to mind, reciting Ghalib like no one could, before or after!

Our honeymoon was curious in more ways than one. It was so cold and the blankets we used had induced some kind of static electricity. Bharathi and I couldn't touch each other for the first few nights!

We returned to Delhi after about two weeks and then drove back to Bombay in the Gypsy. What seemed like my solo ownership of the vehicle was a portent sign of things to come.

167

P.S. Bharathi
in first person, again

Within a week of our marriage, Vikram suggested to Mehra, 'Let us split.'

Now if you're in the advertising TV commercial business, you will know that the director is the face of the unit. Everyone knew Vikram but no one knew Mehra, the invisible guy who handled production and finances behind the scenes. Moreover, their company owed industry vendors a lot of money. In 1991, a ₹14 lakh debt was a big deal. But Vikram was clear that the person who keeps the name 'Flicks' will also keep the losses. Mehra decided to keep the name and take up the losses. He was emotionally attached to Flicks. To date, his email id has the word 'Flicks' in it.

I was earning ₹4,000 per month at that time, and could not see the wisdom in the decision. But we were just married and Mehra had big dreams. So I played along. All his decisions are emotional, to say the least. The second week after our wedding had another surprise in store. We were living in a rental in Shivaji Park at Konkan Cooperative Housing Society. Mehra had taken the lease as a bachelor, and the landlady was not comfortable with our marriage, fearing that we would in some way usurp her property. So, we were thrown out.

As it turned out, within two weeks of our marriage, Mehra had no company to run, no house to live in and no money to put fuel in his Gypsy.

Mehra gave up the Flicks office and started occupying a table on the eighth floor in the business centre of Everest Building. In those days, Everest Building was a happening place, and somehow, the energy there kept the fire in Mehra alive. There was Shyam Benegal on the first floor, Prahlad Kakar on the sixth floor and NEO films, the makers of *Tamas*, on the seventh floor, where Govind Nihalani used to keep visiting and the *Midday* radio and newspaper office. That's where Tariq Ansari (editor and owner of *Midday*) and Mehra became friends. And when Tariq started his FM radio, Mehra was among the first guest speakers.

Mehra was acutely aware that Flicks owed money to people. As a first step, he spoke to everyone the company owed money to: Guruji brothers, the art directors; the Western Outdoor studio and Natraj canteen (caterers for our shoots). He gave everyone a written IOU (I owe you) and they somehow believed in him and supported him by asking him to pay them when he could. That was a massive relief, but while it was very reassuring, Mehra went without work for almost eight months.

So he did something which no advertising film production house in India had done before. He outsourced directors to complete the work that came his way. The likes of PK, Kunal Kapoor (son of legendary actor and producer Jennifer and Shashi Kapoor), Ashok Mehta and Vikas Desai were enlisted. He did not have a director but a panel of freelance directors. While they all had their thriving businesses going, they supported Mehra wholeheartedly by coming on board to direct some of his projects.

This was a particularly busy period for me. I was working with an agency called Rediffusion now, and my life involved shooting, travelling and making advertising TV commercials and short films. I kept working without any break, learning, earning and supporting us as a couple. Things were so hectic for me that once I had absent-mindedly gone off with the house keys for an important project in Hyderabad. Mehra was stuck outside the house and he slept in the Gypsy.

He continued playing the role of a producer with his panel of directors. After a big, dry patch, Abhinav Dhar gave him the Pepsi commercial in 1993. PK helmed this now iconic commercial with Sachin Tendulkar and maverick batsman, Vinod Kambli. Thanks to the success of the first one, a second commercial for Pepsi followed in 1994. This had the captain of the Indian cricket team, Mohammed Azharuddin, taking away a bottle of Pepsi from Sachin and Kambli. Mehra was still very much a producer and working behind the scenes.

The success of the Pepsi ads made Rediffusion offer Mehra the Palmolive campaign. This was the first time my agency had given Mehra any work. He approached Kunal Kapoor to direct it. This was Aishwarya Rai's (Miss World winner who went on to become an iconic film actress) first beauty product advertisement. It was received well and I could feel the tides turning. In fact, Mehra met a majority of the people he knows today—including Binod Pradhan and Shankar, Ehsaan, and Loy (SEL), who went to shoot and give music for his feature films—during his advertising days. Lady luck started smiling on Mehra as LML Vespa came back to him for a commercial. He stayed producer for many commercials during the period 1992 to 1995.

In those days, directors owned their production houses and were the most visible entity in the entire advertising ecosystem. But when Hero cycles came, again thanks to Abhinav Dhar, something shifted within Mehra and he decided to don the director's hat. Mehra spoke to Abhinav. It was a short and sweet conversation.

ROM: Can I direct it?

Abhinav: Sure!

Mehra went to his trusted buddy and cinematographer Vikas Sivaraman and created a completely new language in the world of advertising. I was moonlighting for locations for Mehra at the time. I used to be a big fan of the British series *The Jewel in the Crown* featuring Art Malik (whom we worked with later), which was shot in picturesque locales in Bangalore and Mysore. So I recommended the same location to Mehra. With his love for the outdoors, he hauled the cycle up to unyielding slopes and shot a visually arresting ad for Hero Tribe that demonstrated the versatility and safety of the bike on various terrains. The budget for the ad was ₹3.5 lakh. Without batting an eyelid, Mehra spent ₹8–9 lakh to make it; after all, he had cleared the loan of ₹14 lakh and had now grown in confidence as well as reputation. As far back as I can remember, he has never compromised on quality.

> The success of the Pepsi ads made Rediffusion offer Mehra the Palmolive campaign. This was the first time my agency had given Mehra any work. He approached Kunal Kapoor to direct it. This was Aishwarya Rai's first beauty product advertisement.

Thanks to the success of the Hero Tribe cycles campaign, my soulmate, the uncomplicated, sincere man whose struggles I had seen up close, had found his calling. There was no looking back. Mehra had become a legit director.

CHAPTER 29

The Tag of an Ad Film Director

The early '90s were a massive learning experience for me. There was a sense of positive anticipation: that good things were on their way. A little earlier, India had a young prime minister, Rajiv Gandhi. He was dynamic and represented hope. I remember his speech: 'I am young and I have a dream'. His face had promise and his words had a leadership quality that stirred the dreams of millions of youngsters in India.

As the '90s dawned, the country was going through massive changes. The socialist mindset was shunned and market was being liberalized. This new outlook of the government attracted more and more foreign investment. For the first time, global brands were taking a good, hard look at India as a market.

This was the time when I was flying solo as a producer and then director in the advertising business post my marriage. There was an unprecedented boom in the advertising industry. I was definitely in the right place at the right time. Advertising films, though restrictive in duration (30–60 seconds max), demanded very fine and lucid narrative techniques. They offered an outlet to my creative expression. Technically, there were several masters of the craft in India who had also learnt from the best in the world. Interacting and competing with them allowed me to stay relevant and informed. After I turned director in 1995, whenever the opportunity provided itself, I also started working directly with global talent, especially taking my post production to London and Singapore. With no formal training whatsoever, I had so much catching up to do.

In hindsight, I feel like destiny's child, having had the opportunity to direct over 200 ad films. Other than learning the craft of storytelling itself, I made some of my most enduring friendships during this period.

I have already spoken about Rajat Dholakia (Juku) and Rajiv Kenkre. Till date, Rajat is among the first with whom I share the rough cut of my feature films to get his precious views. There is also Ranjit Barot, the best drummer in the world. Besides being a great stage musician, he is a very close collaborator with A.R. Rahman. There's Binod Pradhan, with whom I shot countless ad films and went on to shoot three feature films; Samir Chanda, who designed all my films until we lost him in 2011 to a heart attack. He was only 54, and I have often consoled myself imagining that perhaps the gods needed a fresh design for the heavens above!

Then there was Vik, who has shot more than 50 ad films for me. I had offered him *RDB*, but his dates were not available. I am so looking forward to shooting a feature with him. It's an ongoing thirst that both of us have and we know it's going to be so much fun. In Bombay, Vik was my first buddy. He still remains a very close friend. His family, PK's family and we routinely spend Christmas and bring in the New Year together every year. There's Amit Ashar, who is an incredible photographer. His portraits speak to you. We became inseparable soulmates and shared Ashok Mehta as a common mentor.

This cluster of inspired souls who were seeking redemption in creating edgy, contemporary ad films were all pushing their own limits. Perhaps that's why this breed and I bonded at a very different level. Most of them knew Bharathi and me even before we got married.

One of these was the loveable trio of SEL.

In Ehsaan's words:

Rakeysh and Vikram used to come down to Bombay from Delhi to record with Louis Banks, and I used to play the guitar. Soon, Rakeysh started directing and built a name as a good ad filmmaker. We worked together on his first ad film for Hero cycles. But I had no idea that Rakeysh would make full-length feature films one day.

The best thing about working with Rakeysh in an ad film was that he was the only one who wouldn't tell us what to do, in sharp contrast to at least ten others on the sets who would overload us with instructions and expectations. He wanted to 'create' a new language every time, a new kind of music or something courageous that only he could sell to the client. There was a commercial for GSL Yarns with African music that we shot in the Andaman Islands—underwater and all. It was way ahead of its time. Around the same time, Bharathi used to work with the agency Rediffusion as an advertising executive. I have worked with both of them separately.

In hindsight, I feel like destiny's child, having had the opportunity to direct over 200 ad films. Other than learning the craft of storytelling itself, I made some of my most enduring friendships during this period.

Loy, the jazz and western classical maestro within SEL, was originally from Delhi. Pretty much like me, he was meant for Bombay too, and as fate would have it, he teamed up with Ehsaan. The duo started working together on advertising jingles. Soon, Loy and Ehsaan started roping in the talented Shankar to sing their jingles, initially as a freelancer. Shankar has lent his voice to iconic lines such as 'Bole mere lips, I love uncle chips' in ten different languages and also the early version of 'Hey utterly, hey butterly' for Amul.

Shankar claims:

I was a singer floating around every studio with every composer. I had sung for many ads for the composers that Rakeysh used to work with, such as Ehsaan, Juku, Ranjit Barot, Louis Banks, Loy etc.

My first encounter as a composer with Rakeysh was for a project for the Aditya Birla Group. They wanted an anthem derived from the Vedic chants. I saw their corporate logo, and in a moment of inspiration, asked if we could use the Aditya Hridaya Stotra.

Now Rakeysh was the director and he could've rejected the idea completely. But that's the thing about him: though he is the captain of the ship, he values your creative input. He never lets you feel your idea is bad. He first accepts your suggestion. Whether it works or doesn't is a different thing altogether. We delivered world music with a uniquely Indian flavour, which till date is valued by the folks at Birla.

That period was clearly a remarkably creative, burgeoning age of Indian advertising. Creative geniuses by day used to turn party animals by night. Nightlife was heady. Our getaway was PK's diving school in the Kadmat Island of Lakshadweep. In 1995, PK introduced me to deep-sea diving. I felt that I had experienced the truth that 75 per cent of the Earth is underwater. Imagine that we are missing three-fourths of the planet we inhabit. Deep-sea diving also was a lesson for me in coexistence: as long as you were not troubling any other living creature, they would also let you be. Later in life, family holidays became diving holidays, and both my daughter Bhairavi and son Vedant became certified divers the moment they turned 11 years old, the minimum age requirement for a diver.

By 1995, I had given in to the intoxication of the advertising world and was subconsciously honing my craft for a future in cinema. I had completely surrendered to the flow and was going where the water was taking me—to a man called Amitabh Bachchan.

1.

2

3

Bachchan: A Blazing Barnstormer

✳

1. Amitabh Bachchan's first-ever ad film was for BPL.
I was fortunate to direct it. This is the first shot.
2. Amitabh Bachchan shoots for the BPL ad.
3. Should we be making this ad at all—I seem to be
asking the legend.

CHAPTER 30

Believe in the Best

I owe my biggest successes as a director in advertising and my relation-
ship with the legendary Amitabh Bachchan to ad guru, Abhinav Dhar.

Somewhere back in the '90s, when I was still only producing and
not directing, we were shooting an ad film that involved a swimming
sequence at 2 a.m. in a desolate suburb of Bombay. The director
mumbled to me that it would have been nice if we had an underwater
camera for a particular sequence.

I have never questioned a director's instincts. Quietly, I got down
to it and woke up some sleeping vendors. Two hours later, at about
4.30 a.m., we were shooting that same sequence with an underwater
camera. This was back in the days when there were precious few
underwater cameras in Bombay.

Unknown to me, Abhinav was watching all of this from the
sideline. He was the man behind the iconic line that epitomized the
year 1990—'Yehi hai right choice baby, aha!'—the launch of Pepsi
India. Abhinav also invented a whole new language, 'Hinglish' (Hindi
plus English), that would become *de rigueur* soon.

As the creative director at Hindustan Thompson Associates (HTA)
Delhi, Abhinav not only gave me my break as a director for the Hero
cycles ad but also partnered with me to create some memorable films
together. Later, he floated his own agency Dhar & Hoon. We worked
together on the iconic commercial made in 1993 for BPL Televisions,
with the tagline 'Believe in the Best.' The plot involved elephants
breaking down the walls of a house and stealing a television set when

they hear an abandoned baby elephant screaming for help on the screen. The idea was that the picture and sound were so real that even the elephants were convinced that their baby was trapped!

The success of the film gave Abhinav even more confidence to work with me. I, for one, was truly excited to work with him. He had a global aura about him, what with being educated abroad—in New York—a rarity in the '80s and '90s. He gave me the freedom to explore.

One day, Abhinav sat me down.

AD: There is this set of ad films, will you do it?

Me: If you write them, I'll do it.

Amitabh Bachchan shifted the paradigm and paved the way for celebrities to come forward and claim their stardom in commercial terms.

AD: They're for BPL Sanyo and it's with a big name.

Me: Who?

AD: Amitabh Bachchan.

Me: ... (goosebumps!)

AD: And we are meeting him tomorrow.

Me: Chance *hi nahi hai!* (No way!)

I don't know what made him think that I could do justice to these ads with Mr Bachchan. Later in life, I surmised that we probably connected because both of us were rule-breakers. The central idea of the ad film was bigger than our own job security, losing money on the film, losing a client, etc.

In October 1995, BPL engaged Amitabh Bachchan to front a new campaign called 'Believe in Yourself'.*

While celebrity endorsements are routine these days, back then, this deal was significant, as the '80s and '90s were exploratory times for such associations and celebrities considered it beneath themselves to endorse brands.

However, the size and nature of endorsements given by actors in Hindi cinema was about to change forever. Amitabh Bachchan shifted the paradigm and paved the way for celebrities to come forward and claim their stardom in commercial terms.

---

*https://www.youtube.com/watch?v=PCMRhXAsdMo; accessed on 28 April 2021.

Abhinav Dhar
in first person

I had known Rakeysh, the young, dependable boy, as the production partner of a Delhi-based ad filmmaker, Vikram Uberoi. In those days, production and execution was a lot more valuable than just direction skills. Too many things could go wrong, and when the Bachchan project for Sanyo landed on our doorstep, the stakes were very high, given that it was Mr Bachchan's first foray into ads.

Rakeysh just happened to be the hardest working man I'd ever met in the ad film industry. When he buys into an idea, he fully commits to it. It goes into his soul. He is also humble enough to allow people to poke holes and question his assumptions. He had a way of understanding the gist of an idea very quickly and delivering more than what was required.

Rakeysh has always been the ultimate Mr Reliable, and his biggest strength is his simplicity. He doesn't hide behind bullshit. If he doesn't know something, he isn't afraid to admit it. And yet, he has a way to bring a larger vision together by bringing out the best in all the people involved. For him, the idea is bigger than everything else, including his ego.

Even in the advertising days, Rakeysh never hid his love and passion for movies. It was a driving force for him, egging him on, even during the subsequent stages in his career, when he wasn't quite sure what he wanted to do next.

CHAPTER 31

A for Amitabh,
B for Bachchan

I stood in front of the mirror and stared at myself for a long time. I had a meeting scheduled at 10 a.m. with Amitabh Bachchan at the AB Corp office in Juhu. My hero, the hero of an entire nation, walked in wearing a blue shirt, denims and a baseball cap.

'Hi, I'm Amitabh Bachchan,' he said, shaking hands.

'Can you come again?' went my silly head! But then, let's not push it.

'Rakeysh,' I said meekly.

We started discussing the BPL Sanyo ad, shared the creatives and said our goodbyes. This was a Friday morning. Over the weekend, I felt uneasy, and on Monday met Amit ji again and shared my deep feelings!

Even though getting the opportunity to shoot the BPL Sanyo ad with Amit ji was a cathartic experience, I was not only creatively nervous, but also gripped with an uneasy conscience.

'I'm really excited, but I don't think you should do this ad,' I said.

Mr Bachchan looked at me and smiled indulgently.

I continued, 'You have died and come back from death in real life.' I was referring to 1982, when this great man met with a near-fatal accident on the sets of the film *Coolie* (1983) that landed him in the hospital battling for his life. It is believed that along with the doctors, it was the entire country that brought him back to life with their heartfelt tears and prayers. I was among the millions praying.

I have no idea what overcame me or where my presumption that I needed to protect this colossus came from. I insisted, 'All our lives in cinema halls, we've seen you 60 feet tall, you have controlled us, entertained us, mesmerized us. But on television, you will be 6 inches tall. I could insult you by merely changing the channel. How can I shoot these TV commercials?'

I tried very hard to dissuade him from doing the ad. But his mind was clear.

'Rakeysh, this will be the future. You will see more and more celebrities endorsing products. Don't worry on that account,' his baritone rang.

However, sure enough, Abhinav understood the sentiments behind what I was saying and his brilliant copy writer Syed Usman laboured on the script until we got what felt right. In 1996, we worked on a set of five commercials; the first one was meant to ease his entry into the world of product endorsements. It began with him saying something like, *'Shaayad aap mujhey TV par dek kar hairaan hongey'* (You may be surprised to find me on TV).

He goes on to say that he has been offered to endorse BPL products and while he has done theatre, sang songs, acted in movies, there was no harm in trying this new thing out. What followed in the next four commercials was ground breaking. One had Amitabh Bachchan emerging from the escalator of Piccadilly Circus Tube Station, earnestly vocalizing that he was seeking an Indian name that had a reputation outside India.

As he moves away, a signage with BPL appears right behind him, making a bold statement. That was the Indian brand he was looking for. I had a vision to employ some breakthrough technology. In the next commercial, there was the real Amitabh Bachchan walking through his own retro films and interacting with his own iconic characters from *Shahenshah*, *Deewar*, *Anand* and many more.

Kehte hain ki international naam ho to sab kuchch chalta hai.
Humme wo baat kahan! Hai koi Hindustani naam jisme
koi dum ho... Kuch wazan ho... Kuch baat ho?
Sunaa hai woh naam B se shuru hota hai...

(It is believed that only foreign brands work. We're not up to the mark. Is there an Indian name that can stand up to the world? They say there is one and the name starts with B [a pun on B for Bachchan and B for BPL].)

I decided to spend the last penny available to ensure the highest quality and took the final post production—colour grading and VFX—to London, the hub of the world advertising back then, to achieve something new. Our VFX supervisor, Paul Sims, was from a leading post-production house in London. Bharathi and I rented an apartment near Soho square for four months to finish the job. I was very clear from the beginning that our advertisement had to be at par with, if not better than, the best in the world.

Coincidently, Amit ji happened to be in London while I was there. One day, right in the middle of our work, Amit ji dropped by to say hello and asked:

AB: What are you doing later in the evening?

Me: I'm available.

Of course I was!

Amit ji took me to a recording studio where, along with Bally Sagoo, he was creating an album. I heard some of the music; it was path-breaking fusion to say the least.

Amit ji and I were eager to cross the threshold of what we had done before. Perhaps that's why I was able to bond with a legend two decades and several paeans senior to me. Later, I realized that innovation was a constant for Amit ji. He's a visionary with tremendous foresight. In those times, in his mind, he was imagining the future and wanted to be part of shaping it. In 1996, he founded Amitabh Bachchan Corporation Ltd. (ABCL), the first ever attempt to corporatize the Indian film industry. I remember thinking how full of energy he was, always forthcoming, always thinking at least a 100 steps ahead of anyone else.

After wrapping up the BPL commercial, I returned to India, when I got a call from Rosy Singh (Amit ji's dependable executive secretary) for a meeting. Here's how that went.

AB: Remember the music studio in London?

Me: Yes!

AB: Here's what we created.

He proceeded to play me some songs.

AB: I've composed Babuji's (Harivansh Rai Bachchan's) poetry in my own voice with Bally Sagoo. Maybe we should do a music video. What do you think?

Me: Amazing!

Mentally, I started compiling a list of the best pop video directors from the US and London who were best suited to make such a video. Each song deserved out-of-the-box thinking!

He prodded me, exploring my thoughts.

AB: What are the songs you like?

I shortlisted three: The first was the rustic 'Eir Bir Phatte', which brought alive folk storytelling in Awadhi. The sound was new and unheard, thanks to Bally Sagoo's modern reggae flavour. Then the lilting romantic ballad 'Sone Machari' and finally, the intoxicating lyrics of Sahir Ludhianvi and 'Kabhi Kabhi' in AB's own voice.

AB: Good choices. Will you direct the songs?

Me: I have never done music videos, but why not?

AB: Then let's begin with 'Eir Bir Phatte'.

Suffice to say, we proceeded to make a dent in the universe with the album *Aby Baby*. India had never seen anything like 'Eir Bir Phatte' before.

I needed a choreographer who could think differently. Young Raju Sundaram's work in Mani Ratnam's *Bombay* had blown my mind. For the first time in India, we brought in professional, international dancers from the London School of Dance. For the second song 'Kabhi Kabhi', I took a totally different approach. The elegant and accomplished danseuse and national award-winning actress Shobana Chandrakumar played AB's muse, with him as a sculptor, trying to recreate her poise and grace in stone. 'Sone Machari' was a rustic track set to rhythm in rap style. To my mind, it was a truly unique song but we never made a video for it.

I realized that innovation was a constant for Amit ji.

The album was released in 1996, with BPL credited as sponsors (printed on the album sleeve). I was very nervous and then realized so was Amit ji. Thankfully, it worked out well. Every television channel wanted to play 'Eir Bir Phatte'. It started a trend of fusion music: music videos for independent songs that were out of the feature film space and for a world music vibe. For the first time, a collaboration with international dancing talent was showcased and it blew everybody's mind. The bar had been raised. I had lived up to what I wanted to create for my idol. As for Amit ji, he normally hits the ball out of the park.

This was a very prolific creative period for me: I was highly in demand by now as an ad filmmaker. I was hungry for more. But even in my wildest dreams, I couldn't have imagined that Amit ji would be the hero of my first film.

But this exciting, path-breaking journey from ads to films, however, had an interlude called *Mamuli Ram* in between.

186

Mamuli Ram:
The Little Big Man

I was itching to tell longer stories.

In April 1996, just before *Aby Baby* released, I directed a 75-minute docu-drama called *Mamuli Ram: The Little Big Man*.

It was inspired by the story of the 'milk revolution' in India led by Amul (Anand Milk Union Limited). The documentary narrated the story of ordinary villagers led by Tribhuvandas Patel, who employed an America-returned Dr Verghese Kurien, to bring about an economic revolution and make India self-dependent in the field of milk and dairy products.

Post India's independence in 1947, the dairy industry was non-existent. We depended on heavy imports from Denmark and New Zealand and aid from the UNICEF. It was Amul that took strident steps in making India self-sufficient in milk production, leading to the white (milk) revolution.

The foundation for *Mamuli Ram: The Little Big Man* was built around a thought: 'if a pinch of salt got India its independence, imagine what a drop of milk can do'. This reprised Mahatma Gandhi's famous salt Satyagraha against the British Raj. Bharathi came on board as editor, Rajat Dholakia gave the music and Jehangir Chowdhury, one of the most senior and respected cinematographers, shot it. To lend an authentic flavour, I studied the Bhavai folk form from Gujarat and found an 80-year-old Bhavai exponent. We

187

constructed a tent near the Narmada River and recorded the music under this tent.

The cast of *Mamuli Ram* was truly exceptional. There was the brilliant Raghubir Yadav, who played the role of Prime Minister Lal Bahadur Shastri. The intense, emerging theatre talent Ashish Vidyarthi, whose debut film had established him as an actor to watch out for, gracefully accepted the part of Dr Kurien and Kamal Tewari, with whom I had done some ad films, played Tribhuvandas Patel. Sardar Vallabhbhai Patel's role was enacted by thespian theatre actor Manohar Singh and Morarji Desai (who went on to become India's prime minister) was played by the eccentric actor, Virendra Saxena.

Making *Mamuli Ram* gave me the confidence to direct a feature film. I had to wait for several years to make it, though, because my first venture in the world of cinema was destined to be *Aks*. But *Aks* was not the first film I wanted to make. It was 'Samjhauta Express'.

Doodh pyar hai, ki doodh hathyar hai?
Doodh sarkar hai ya doodh vyapaar hai?
Bhook ka jawab hai ya sirf ek khwaab hai?
Doodh sailaab hai ya doodh inquilab hai?

(Is milk love or is it a weapon?
Is it the government's job to provide milk or is it a business?
Is it a solution to hunger or just a dream?
Is it a flood or a revolution?)

Now when I look back at *Mamuli Ram*, it surprises me that there were so many real life political characters in a single docu-drama who were among the original authors of the idea of Independent India. Kamlesh Pandey, who penned the script, gave us these wonderful opening lines that defined milk revolution in India; and its role in society.

188

Making *Mamuli Ram* gave me the confidence to direct a feature film. I had to wait for several years to make it, though, because my first venture in the world of cinema was destined to be *Aks*. But *Aks* was not the first film I wanted to make. It was 'Samjhauta Express'.

CHAPTER 33

'Samjhauta Express':
The Train I Missed

To understand the difference between posturing and friendship is to understand the rocky but rock-solid journey of Abhishek Bachchan and me. A cursory look at the phonebook of Abhishek Bachchan will reveal a contact named Liaquat. Dial the number and it will connect to me. On my phone, Abhishek flashes as 'Hassan Sarhadi', even today, after 20 years.

These names are characters from 'Samjhauta Express', a film we wanted to make together: it was to be Jr Bachchan's debut film.*

Kamlesh Pandey had already written the script. I have said previously that when I first met AR, I had narrated 'Samjhauta Express' to him so that he could begin work on creating the music. Binod Pradhan, Samir Chanda and I took a long trip to Ladakh to find the locations to shoot the film. As usual, I am halfway around the world with an idea once I commit to it.

Abhishek was equally invested in the film. 'Samjhauta Express' was the third 'being' in our lives for almost a year in the period 1996–7. He

---

*Abhishek adds, 'I wanted to be an actor and Rakeysh wanted to direct. There was an honest moment where both of us felt: "let us team up and do something together." Suffice to say, Rakeysh and I threw ourselves at "Samjhauta Express", our dream movie, together. Rakeysh has this creative magnetism to his ideas: Maa, Kamlesh Pandey and I were party to his crazy, organic, imaginative process.'

maintained a diary for the character and used to enter Hassan's daily routine every day.

We were all set to shoot our first schedule in Ladakh, when one fateful day in Bangalore, during Shyam's (Bharathi's brother) wedding, Mrs Jaya Bachchan called me to say, 'After much thought, we have decided that *Refugee* will be Abhishek's first film, and not "Samjhauta Express".'

I understood the decision rationally. My script involved Abhishek playing a Pakistan-sponsored terrorist in his first film, which was against the grain of how Indian audiences perceive their hero. Our heroes were seldom grey at that time. They were caricatures of an unattainable ideal, defeating evil villains. I was deeply disappointed and crestfallen. I wanted to argue that the journey of my hero was that of a braveheart, who finally gives up his life for peace and brotherhood and leaves us with a life lesson to love each other. I couldn't help but wonder: what is the right launch pad for an actor with a gargantuan legacy like Abhishek?

'After much thought, we have decided that *Refugee* will be Abhishek's first film, and not "Samjhauta Express".'

Lost and frustrated, I declared that I would never make 'Samjhauta Express'. I took the script and all the research work, location pictures, wardrobe trials and burnt them in a bonfire on my terrace on the barbecue stove. I was too attached and had to let go. Deep down, I knew what I was venting was not anger but grief, and this was the only way to move on.

In hindsight, perhaps I was meant to begin my journey in cinema with *Aks*.

Official poster of *Aks*
Courtesy: ROMP Pictures

SECTION ELEVEN

Aks

*

■■■■■■■■■■■■■■■■■■■■■

Na koi marta hai, na koi maarta hai.
Yeh main nahin ... main nahin kehta;
Gita mein likha hai.

(There is no killer,
And no one is killed
It's not I, who says this;
It is written in the Bhagavad Gita.)

—Raghavan's dialogue in *Aks*

■■■■■■■■■■■■■■■■■■■

CHAPTER 34

The 70 mm Leap

There is only that one first film. The act cannot be repeated, not in this lifetime at least.

I'd like to believe that the making of *Aks* was a conspiracy. The universe conspired and I ended up making my first film. I vividly remember the playful days of my childhood at my nani's house in Old Delhi, when we would fly kites and nani would tell us stories from Indian mythology.

Her favourite was the Ramayana, an ancient Indian epic about the exile and return of Lord Rama, the prince of Ayodhya, and his battle with Ravana, the evil demon king of Lanka. However, my nani didn't have a straight-laced interpretation of the epic. She had never gone to school, but her wisdom and life lessons were as deep as an ocean.

She would often say, 'All these stories and their characters are symbolic. Both Ram [good] and Raavan [evil] are inside you.' The seed of the idea *'accha aadmi, buraa aadmi; ik hi sikkey ke do pehlu'* (good and evil are two sides of the same coin) was planted by her.

In the winter of 1998, Rensil D'Silva and I had written what we thought was a script. We titled it 'Good vs Evil'. In any case, it was much more than a TV commercial, because it was 25 pages long. One evening I was hanging out with Abhishek at their home when Amit ji peeped in:

AB: Bye guys, I am off to Delhi.

Me: Please read this as in-flight entertainment.

He indulged me and took the 25 pages of 'Good vs Evil'.

Unexpectedly, the phone rang at 11 p.m. The ensuing conversation has been described earlier in the book. Basically, Amit ji wanted to know what I had been drinking while writing the script. In his inimitable style, he agreed to be part of whatever I made out of 'Good vs Evil'.

I felt a strange hollow in my stomach that grips someone when an impossible dream comes true. Now I had to mount a film that featured this towering titan of Indian cinema. Amit ji was to play Inspector Manu Varma, an honest law enforcement officer. His nemesis in the script was to be Raghavan, a ruthless killer whose dialogues were laced with spirituality. I had to cast Raghavan next: someone who could match the prowess of Amitabh Bachchan, if such a thing was indeed possible. I was chewing the cud on this when I saw a performance by Manoj Bajpayee. He was the toast of those times post his hugely acclaimed role as gangster Bhiku Mhatre in Ram Gopal Varma's *Satya* in 1998 and a powerhouse performance in *Shool* in 1999. I narrated the storyline to him, and I still remember his reaction.

MB: Mehra Sahab, *aap* film *nahi* philosophy *bana rahe hai.* (You're not making a film, you're propounding a philosophy.)

He was perfect to play Raghavan. Another crucial part to be cast was Neeta, a strip club dancer, a first for Indian cinema. She is also Raghavan's love interest. When Raghavan is shot dead and his soul enters the body of officer Manu Varma (Amitabh Bachchan), Neeta is the one to sense this paranormal shift and her love for Raghavan finds completion in Manu Varma's avatar. I needed an actress who could pull it off and I found my Neeta in the ravishing Raveena Tandon. She was the reigning queen of the box office and this part was very much against her projected persona. But in my first meeting with her, I knew there could be no one else. This bold part was written for her.

The support cast had to be stellar as well. My association with K.K. Raina began with *Aks*. Critically acclaimed actresses Nandita Das and Tanvi Azmi and senior actors Dr Mohan Agashe and Amol Palekar elegantly accepted support roles as guest appearances. Kamal Tewari from *Mamuli Ram* played ACP Pradhan, Manu Varma's senior and friend. The find of *Aks* however was the character Yeda Yakub played by Vijay Raaz (*yeda* means crazy in Marathi), a relatively new talent at the time. Bharathi had shown me a stage play on a VHS video cassette of an actor playing a 70-year-old man. He was amazing, to say the least.

Me: Where has he been hiding?

Bharathi: He is just in his early 20s.

Vijay's performances have always blown my mind and we went on to work together in *Delhi-6* and *Toofaan* as well.

Samir Chanda and Kiran Deohans from the advertising world joined the crew as production designer and cinematographer, respectively. One of the most challenging departments was prosthetics; both Amit ji and Manoj were to impersonate each other wearing face masks.

BAFTA award-winning British make-up effects and creature designer Nick Dudman, who was part of the *Harry Potter* series and *The Fifth Element*, joined the crew. Paul Sims, my VFX supervisor from advertising days, flew in from London for the VFX sequences. Anu Malik, the most sought after music director of the time who was delivering one blockbuster after another, was signed up for the music. He teamed up with Ranjit Barot, another throwback to my advertising days. It was a unique experiment as both of them have different temperaments. While Anu brought in the timeless melodies, Ranjit interpreted the sound and design in a new-age manner. Both of them collaborated gracefully and that is why the music of *Aks* is both memorable and path breaking. But one of my biggest fantasies was about to come true: a decade after I knocked on Gulzar's doors for the first time, he wrote the lyrics for *Aks*. The film was Bharathi's first baby at the edit table.

Now, I had never gone to a film school or assisted any one. And here we were going to make a full-length feature film. But before anyone could talk sense into me, I had already taken the leap. I was so involved in the idea of making the film that I missed a crucial ingredient completely—the money needed to make it.

Initially, ABCL was to fund the film with Flicks Motion Picture Company Pvt Ltd. But this was not to be, given the delicate phase ABCL was going through. The company was Amit ji's dream to corporatize and clean up the Hindi film industry. As is the norm, this first attempt is usually a sacrifice to the cause. Amit ji levelled with me.

'These are tough times. How do we make this film?' he asked.

And as he was speaking with me, Canara Bank was all set to auction his house. Many people were writing him off as finished around the time. Amit ji was on the cover of a magazine with the headline screaming 'A Legend Falls'. I noticed that he had kept that magazine on his desk for four years. It might have inspired him to reverse the flow that was against him. Eventually, he sprang back and rose like the proverbial phoenix.

Finance was a challenge but I was determined to make the film myself. I would make one ad film at a time, and shoot *Aks* for a few days with whatever money was earned from it. My contemporaries in advertising were buying penthouses; Bharathi and I stayed in a one-room apartment in Prabhadevi with the old Gypsy. I did not want to worry about how things would happen; I just wanted to make them happen.

Like I said earlier, the universe conspired. I was offered to make a commercial for Red & White cigarettes, a shoot that involved hot air balloons, in Budapest. The opening sequence of *Aks* was to be shot in an Eastern European nation as well. What a coincidence! My personal life had also taken a new turn. My beautiful daughter Bhairavi was born on 8 February 1999. We left a three-month-old Bhairavi with Bharathi's mother for the Budapest schedule.

So we took the same crew that was shooting *Aks* to shoot the commercial. Later, Amit ji and Manoj joined us. *Aks* was rolling. I couldn't believe it. It was a week-long schedule and we got some exceptional aerial shots on the very first day. Action director Allan Amin (who had choreographed the Yamaha bike commercials) and Kiran Deohans managed some great footage. When we saw the video output of the material we were creating, it was very exciting. We felt we were on to something.

In the opening sequence of the film, we were to shoot the defence minister (Amol Palekar) and his chief of security (Amitabh Bachchan) travelling in the same car, which was part of an impenetrable security convoy. They are aware that there is a death threat on the defence minister. The shoot team was on the move, there were cars and bikes rallying around and more crew was following with all kinds of camera equipment. Raghavan (Manoj Bajpayee) was to assassinate the defence minister as the car emerged from a tunnel.

Powering up the light equipment was a small generator van following the shoot. Deohans and I were in the 'action' car and our video feed led to a van from which Bharathi was watching. We kept shooting, took several rounds around the block to get the perfect shot.

Finally, when we came back to the base, we realized that someone had shut the van doors that Bharathi was sitting in. To everyone's horror, the smoke from the generator set had filled up the interior of the van and Bharathi and my assistant were trapped and had fallen unconscious. Bharathi, however, took the brunt of it and suffered acute asphyxiation. Oxygen levels in her blood stream had fallen to critical levels. The emergency ambulance arrived and Bharathi was immediately put on oxygen. I was at my wits end and we had no idea if she was going to make it. Amit ji reached out to Laxmi Puri, the then ambassador of India to Hungary. She went out of her way to help us. Bharathi was unconscious for about 10–12 hours. They even arranged for a priest to read prayers to her. Later, we got to know that the wing in which Bharathi was admitted was for suicide victims.

> Often, when I was shooting with Raveena and Manoj in the nights, Amit ji would come to the shoot, unannounced and sit around there.

On the same day, we had scheduled a night shoot as well and it was an expensive location: a museum. As the hours passed, I kept whispering 'Bhairavi' into Bharathi's ears, as if to remind her that we had left a three-month-old back at home. Finally, Bharathi opened her eyes. Her first question was, 'Mehra, what are you doing here? Why aren't you shooting?'

'Kiran is setting up the lighting,' I lied.

Bharathi insisted that I finish the shoot, which we had scheduled with money we didn't really have. I was shuttling between the shoot and the hospital for the rest of the night and the next day. This was the time Amit ji became a huge admirer of Bharathi. He saw her for what she was—a pillar of resilience in my life. Through the years, I then saw them bonding in a very different way.

After this, the entire unit felt connected at an emotional level. Everyone came through in their own way. Back in India, we had set up a huge stunt sequence near Nasik: it was a 300-foot waterfall and Amit ji and Manoj were to jump off this waterfall. Amit ji stayed with us in a small hotel along with rest of the crew.

Looking back, I don't know how we did it. I didn't have the money for fuel but I was making a film with Amit ji and the rest of the stellar cast.

Samir Chanda used his wealth of experience to create sets of Topaz Bar (Neeta's strip club) in a broken down studio at Filmalaya. It was the cheapest studio floor we could afford. We had to shoot three songs at the Topaz Bar at Filmalaya. It was a 30-day schedule but we ran out of money in 15 days. The crew stood by me and we finished the schedule. I still remember Mr Shetty of Nataraj catering services fed meals to the crew on the promise of 'payable when able'. Many years later, I was able to repay the debt by contributing in my own humble way to his daughter's wedding.

Every single schedule of *Aks* was built on the foundation of some advertising film project that I had taken up. Amit ji was a force of nature, pouring his immense talent and commitment; giving his 100 per cent to *Aks* as ABCL's debacle took a toll on his own financial life. The company had approached the Board for Industrial and Financial Reconstruction (BIFR) for bankruptcy in March 1999. The Bombay High Court restrained him from selling off his bungalow *Prateeksha* and two flats till the pending loan recovery cases of Canara Bank were dealt with. Often, when I was shooting with Raveena and Manoj in the nights, Amit ji would come to the shoot, unannounced and sit around there.

'If I'm not on a shooting floor, I'll go insane,' he would confide in me.

I cannot explain what I felt towards him. All I knew was I couldn't let this great man down. Amit ji saw what was happening. He gave me his personal savings of ₹1 crore. At this point, 70 per cent of the film was shot. This was an incredible gesture of generosity. Everyone in the crew was borrowing on their goodwill from the vendors. Shyam and Guru (our line producers from my first Hero cycles commercial in Bangalore) kept the ship sailing somehow.

We were knocked sideways. Amit ji made one final call to Jhamu Sugandh, a well-known industry financier who came on board on a 'last in first out' basis and financed the rest of the film. When *Aks* released, he was paid first. We could never pay ourselves back. It was my first-hand exposure to film finance.

'Welcome to filmmaking,' said the universe that had got me so far.

The film opened to mixed responses at the box office but garnered much appreciation among cinema lovers. It did not set the box office on fire like we hoped. I recovered only partially from the film and had to keep covering my losses over the next three years with ad films. As we kept selling the rights—VHS rights, satellite rights, digital and television rights—I was able to recover 80 lacs more, which I was able to return to ABCL. Creatively though, something gnawed at me. *Aks* was an incomplete product; I had to complete it in some way. Perhaps with the next film?

Aks had made me destroy myself and recreate a new me. The end result empowered me in some way. I was now a feature film director. That profession was perceived quite differently from being an ad film director.

Aks also brought in several accolades and I was happy to win awards for my first film. Manoj won the Screen Award for Best Actor in a Negative role in 2002 and Paul Sims won the IIFA for best special effects in 2002. At the 47th Filmfare Awards in 2002, we won the critics award for best performance for Amitabh Bachchan, sound design for Rakesh Ranjan, best background score for Ranjit Barot and a special award for actress Raveena Tandon.

Raveena and I share some common history. She had also worked with PK in Genesis as an assistant. This star actor and heartthrob of millions was also extremely energetic and hugely successful, doing multiple shifts every day. Neeta was an edgy, bold role that would redefine a mainstream heroine's paradigm, and there could be no other better suited for the role than Raveena.

She was ready and how!

Raveena Tandon
in first person

When Mehra came to narrate *Aks* to me, I was aware of him as a successful ad filmmaker. Despite a common connection with Prahlad, we had never met. It was perfect timing, portentous almost, as I was looking to make a shift—be a part of different cinema—to add a new leaf to my filmography and challenge my limits.

Those were times when cinema with slapstick comedy and obnoxious dance numbers were doing well. It would be perfectly normal for people to say 'music *ke upar nikal padi* picture' (the film succeeded because of the music), with no thought to the storyline whatsoever.

Mehra met me at a studio where I was shooting one of the three films to which I was committed. When I heard the visceral, deep-throated Shubha Mudgal track 'Raat Aati Hai, Chali Jaati Hai' (the night comes and it goes), I was hooked to both the intensity of the plot and the passion of the man. We continued the narration all the way home.

At home, we sat at a sliding door adjacent to the ledge of the balcony, facing the sea and the mangroves. He was so tranquil, and yet there was a maniacal glint in his eyes when he narrated the film. I agreed to be part of this soft-spoken, silent genius's debut directorial venture. And I'd like to believe that Mehra has given me one of my most celebrated performances till date.

Another thing I will never forget about *Aks* is that I was supposed to be comfortable seducing Amitabh Bachchan. I have foot-in-the-mouth disease when it comes to that man. I've grown up seeing him and I have something of a record of inexplicably goofy behaviour around him. I was 17 when I set the stage for a lifetime of blundering. *Stardust* magazine was hosting an MTV party and I was the presenter for the evening.

Thoroughly pumped up with my new-found identity, I was on song!

I looked playfully into the camera and rolled, 'Guess who we have here: we have Aby Baby.' Then I turned to the man himself and asked, 'Hi Amit, how are you doing?' My debut on camera was rolling well up to that point. My casual salutation was received with an icy cold stare!

'Excuse me, who are you?' he asked.

I stood there like an inflatable that had just been pricked.

On another occasion, I blurted, 'I loved your album "Eir Bir Phatte"!'
'No, the album is *Aby Baby*,' came the restrained response.

I had learnt my lesson—don't mess with the Loch Ness. And now Mehra was asking me to seduce this man on screen, confront him and basically be this diva who knew her bearings around him. I panicked, 'Mehra, what are you making me do?' I buried my head in my hands.

Mehra looked back at me with a serenity that wasn't particularly appealing at that time. I scrounged around for some steely resolve within me. I decided that if I focussed on Mr Bachchan, he would chew me up and spit me out in every scene. I devised a strategy to isolate myself and focus. I would reach the sets, greet everyone and then read a book or pretend to. Thankfully, I was comfortable with Manoj as we had done *Shool* before. I had to summon nerves of steel to see me through those days.

Amit ji would constantly tell everyone on the sets, '*Yeh mere ghutnon ke neeche, thee. Lekin aaj ise dekh kar mein jhep jaata hoon*' (I have seen her grow up in front of my eyes. She wasn't even as high as my knee, but when I see her today, I'm astounded).

When I look back at *Aks*, what stays with me is Mehra's assurance and faith in his actors. He discussed every scene with Manoj and me and then he would allow us to unfold, to find a way to bring out the scene from within our conscience. I also remember Raju Sundaram for breaking my knees during the dance rehearsals. But most of all, I will thank Mehra for re-inventing my glamour. For someone who does not depend on an item song to salvage a senseless film, Mehra really knows how to ramp up the seduction quotient when it's a part of the script.

When he suggested a striptease to me, I was uncertain. But he explained his vision to me—it was sophisticated and classy. Between him and Kiran Deohans, they conjured some magic with the lighting in 'Yeh Raat', written by Gulzar. There was no nudity and no vulgarity; it was purely performance-oriented glamour, pivotal to the script. Every day on the sets, Mehra was crystal clear on what he wanted. Was it really his first film?

When the film released, I saw the opening scene and was astounded. No one had seen anything like it in Indian cinema. For me, Mehra is an integral part of redefining Indian cinema. My favourite scenes would have to be the interrogation and the one in which I put Manoj in jail. I won many awards for *Aks* in the following year. I hope Mehra is writing another script for me.

CHAPTER 35

Raghavan:
The Devil Incarnate

And then there was Manoj Bajpayee. I have been privileged to work alongside this raw, powerhouse method actor.

I call him one of the finest actors in the Indian cinema-scape. A young boy from Bihar, who idolized Amitabh Bachchan and wanted to grow up to be like him, had shaken the world of Hindi cinema with an uninhibited performance in *Satya*. I didn't know what to make of him, except that he threw himself into his roles and ceased to exist as himself. My vision for Raghavan, the maniacal killer who wanted his audience to love him despite how horrific he was, was about to come true.

Manoj Bajpayee
in first person

One day, Anurag Kashyap called me. He was the assistant writer in *Satya*, a film that had helped me achieve recognition as an actor. He told me that Rakeysh Mehra, a big ad filmmaker, was looking to cast me opposite Amitabh Bachchan.

I was aware that it was Rakeysh's first film, and that he already was a known name in the advertising industry. I had watched his song 'Eir Bir Phatte', which was doing very well on TV. Rakeysh knew the craft of filmmaking—he was adept with the camera and well-trained in how to execute a scene: that was evident from his past work. So I went to Rakeysh's Tardeo office. We sat there, and later even went out for a drink to discuss the film. I entered *Aks* with hope, looking forward to a great ride. The presence of Mr Bachchan was the icing on the cake.

But then there was the narration. Due to Rakeysh's persistence, I decided to hear him out instead of reading the script. We sat together for three hours but we barely reached the interval. He is slow and deliberate when he talks. I had to excuse myself saying, 'I'm more of a read-the-script-myself person.' I proceeded to bury myself in the script.

Initially, the screenplay wasn't ready. But the script helped me prepare extensively. My process is private and individual. I work in my own way and was happy that I had six months to prepare myself for the role. I was asked to portray pure evil. I didn't know how to approach my part. Besides, doing that character needed a kind of thought process. We wanted to make my character Raghavan a seductive and attractive embodiment of evil. Raghavan chases and hunts wolves. He is the devil incarnate. But the glassy, cold evil often portrayed in cinema lacks layers for me. I think evil is a shade, therefore, my performance of Raghavan has elements of both Raavan and Krishna. The person who is evil is human too and, hence, there have to be moments when even a villain is loveable and humorous.

Rakeysh's brief to me was nuanced:

Saare kaayde kanoon hata do toh har aadmni Raghavan banna chahta hai.

(If you take away all the rules from society, then deep inside, everyone wants to be a Raghavan.)

Every human being wants to feel liberated. And pure evil lacks accountability and, hence, is fully liberated. I channelled evil from the cry of the hyena, the lure of the striptease, the deceptive sexuality of a bottle of alcohol. The crazy laughter I created came from a place of magical realism. And like any *nasha* (intoxication) that you can never completely leave, evil is an addiction.

I used to end up at Rakeysh's house at least thrice a week for over six months to show him how I was imbibing the character. I challenged the heinous into me. Kamlesh Pandey used to admit that sometimes he didn't know how to start my dialogues. Rakeysh used to call me and then we would write some dialogues together. On other days, Bachchan Sahab and I used to read our lines together often at his home and Rakeysh sat through the process like a moderator, guiding the course of the rehearsal. Then one night, in 1999, I was at home and my phone rang. It was Amitabh Bachchan. He said, 'I'm playing the part where your character gets inside me. Can you please come and show me how you did it?' I rushed to the sets and did my best to demonstrate. After all, Bachchan Sahab wanted to learn something from *me*! I was going to do better than my best. He kept me in the loop about the development of his character. The journey of working with him on the sets of *Aks* was my greatest reward.

We shot at various locations. Rakeysh visualized incredible sequences: the waterfalls, the caves, the wild outdoors and the cryptic interactions between Varma and Raghavan. He wanted to create something original. Cinematographer Kiran Deohans's contribution to *Aks* is as much as any of us actors: he oozed genius. And Rakeysh, the ringleader, used to listen to everyone but always knew what he was creating.

In hindsight, Rakeysh was the first of the cohort that emerged from the rebellion against formula cinema in the '80s and '90s by Shekhar Kapur (*Masoom, Mr. India, Bandit Queen*), Ram Gopal Varma (*Rangeela, Satya, Company*) and Mani Ratnam (*Roja, Bombay, Dil Se*). He, along with Vishal Bhardwaj and Raju Hirani, had the courage to experiment on the path laid by these three people.

Rakeysh will always lead the pack of directors who brought 'original' content into mainstream cinema. He relies on the believability

His courage, the character dynamics, the cinematic leap he was taking in 2001 were all ahead of their time.

of the stories he is telling. I've invited him to the screenings of my movies and he always comes whenever able. As Delhi boys, both outsiders, we keep giving each other feedback. He speaks less, but I always know what he's saying. *Aks* is a film which has given me a lot of respect as an actor and I would place it among the great 50 films in the last 50 years. I feel *Aks* is very difficult to recreate.

Having said that, I have several complaints with Rakeysh. Let me outline two if these.

First, why doesn't he talk about *Aks* as often as he talks about his other films? His courage, the character dynamics, the cinematic leap he was taking in 2001 were all ahead of their time. Second, where's the Rakeysh Mehra who made *Aks*? This is Manoj Bajpayee calling.

Top: My identity card as a young executive at Ulka Advertising.
Bottom: He's the man—With ad guru Prahlad Kakar.

Top: Solidly behind me is adman Abhinav Dhar.
Bottom: Ace cinematographer Ashok Mehta (in the grey hat) offers valuable lessons on camera-handling to me as Bharathi looks on.

Bharathi taking Rahul Dravid through an ad script.

Top: A Samsung ad I directed in the '90s featured the following: Top row (L to R)—Mohammad Kaif, Zaheer Khan and Harbhajan Singh; middle row (L to R)—Rahul Dravid and Anil Kumble; bottom row (L to R)—Dinesh Mongia and Ashish Nehra.

Bottom: An elephantine endeavour—On the sets of an ad for BPL televisions.

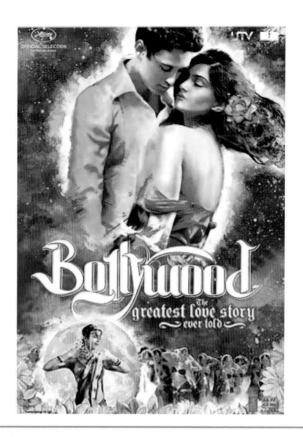

Top: The official poster of *Bollywood: The Greatest Love Story Ever Told*.

Bottom: It was a matter of great pride when our documentary was the official selection at Cannes, celebrating 100 years of Indian cinema.

Top: Marriage as per South Indian customs, as I struggle to stay awake.
Bottom: Lost the ring already?

Bharathi makes for a beaming, blissful bride.

Top: The adventure that was the honeymoon at Fotu La Pass in Ladakh.
Bottom: At the Rome Film festival 2018 for the world premiere of *Mere Pyare Prime Minister.*

30 years later.

Top: Manoj Bajpayee is evil personified as he performs the last rites of Vijay Raaz after killing him.
Middle: Here's looking at you—Amitabh Bachchan and Raveena Tandon in a still from *Aks*.
Bottom: Good vs Evil—Manoj Bajpayee stands up to his idol Amitabh Bachchan.

Top: Nandita Das, Tanvi Azmi and I on Juhu beach, rehearsing a scene as we walk along.

Middle: With my trusted VFX supervisor Paul Sims of Soho 601, London.

Bottom: With celebrated writer Kamlesh Pandey, who wrote *Aks*, *RDB* and *Delhi-6*.

Top: *Aks* unmasked Manoj Bajpayee's celebrated talent in newer ways.
Middle: The unusual pairing of the legend Amitabh Bachchan and critically acclaimed Nandita Das.
Bottom: Amitabh Bachchan channels the devil within in a surreal song sequence choreographed by Raju Sundaram.

Setting the stage for a bravura performance—With Raveena Tandon.

Top: Is this your normal temperature?—Manoj and I share a light moment.
Bottom: Nick Dudman getting the prosthetics right with Manoj for the face mask in *Aks*. Make-up artist Vikram Dada is seen in the reflection.

Top: I'm leaning on you here—With Amitabh Bachchan. The DoP, Kiran Deohans, looks on.
Bottom: Raveena won several awards for her bold and convincing role in *Aks*.

Top: Stunt director Allan Amin chooses an umbrella in the rains as Manoj and I choose a hot cup of tea.
Bottom: One of my favourite moments with Amitabh Bachchan and Gulzar.

CHAPTER 36

Dance like
No One Is Watching

When Mani Ratnam's Roja *released in 1992, Raju Sundaram's nifty* leg movements in the hit song 'Rukmani Rukmani' took the nation by storm.

Bharathi, who was familiar with his work, told me that Raju had learnt at the feet of his father, dance-master Mugur Sundar, since his teenage days. It was Mani Ratnam's *Thiruda Thiruda* that turned the tables for Raju in South cinema, and from then on, there had been no looking back for this talented artist.

He and his brother Prabhu Deva again danced together in the 1993 runaway hit song 'Chikku Bukku Railey' from the movie *Gentleman*. Bharathi has always had a penchant for bringing new talent into our work and it was her idea to involve Raju in the choreography of 'Eir Bir Phatte'. The best camaraderie on the sets I've ever seen is Amit ji's banter with Raju, which started with 'Eir Bir Phatte' and continued on to the sets of *Aks*.

He brought freshness and depth to my work that even I could not have imagined.

Raju Sundaram
in first person

Rakeysh Sir was new to me as I was to him on the sets of 'Eir Bir Phatte'. Here was a director who wanted the song to look like a story. That was the first challenge. Second, he did not like lip synching: he thought it was too far-fetched for heroes to suddenly start singing songs unless they were performers in the film. From an established Chennai mould, where I had to match the steps to the beat, I had to now match the picturization of the song to its meaning.

I am grateful to have been a part of 'Eir Bir Phatte'. Amitabh Bachchan Sir has made only one music album in his life, directed by Rakeysh Sir and choreographed by me. These are memories that can give an artist goosebumps.

So when Rakeysh Sir called me to direct the songs of *Aks*, I was excited but extremely anxious. Unless you know the entire script and pulse of the film, you cannot work on a Rakeysh Mehra set. It is a very daunting task. *Aks* had three challenging songs. The first one was 'Yeh Raat', a striptease to be performed by Raveena Tandon. We had to establish Raveena's character with it, so I had to focus on her facial expressions to a great extent at the same time the song had to be sensuous.

The second was 'Banda Yeh Bindaas Hai', in which Amitabh Bachchan dances with Nandita Das. The aim was to establish his shades of grey, the evil that had been embedded in him as the song progressed. We called a famous dancer from Spain and gave a flamenco touch to the song.

The third was 'Aaja Guffaon Mein Aa', in which Amit Sir is completely taken over by Manoj Bajpayee's spirit and is behaving totally out of character. This too has trained international dancers and a sinister appeal. The song received rave reviews for its slick choreography and the lyrics once again took the story of the film forward.

Working with Rakeysh Sir was a completely new learning experience for me. I am an entertainer but he demanded layered entertainment combined with deep meaning. I will never forget the backslapping game that Amit Sir seemed to enjoy with me. I couldn't make head or tail of it but was too intimidated to object.

I will never forget the backslapping game that Amit Sir seemed to enjoy with me.

After seeing my work with Rakeysh Sir, other big stars and directors also started calling me to choreograph Hindi songs. This expanded my universe and I got to experiment with another language and audience. Subsequently, I also worked with Rakeysh Sir on *RDB* and *Mirzya*. Each moment in the music has to contribute to the story. That's how Rakeysh Sir wants it.

My humble advice to him is this: Rakeysh Mehra should not try to be 'Rakeysh Mehra' because he already is. He is a path-breaking director. Talents like him are rare and original. The southern film industry respects him as a prudent technician and an iconic visionary; we know there is no one like him or ever will be. When he fails, many originals lose courage and have to start from zero. That's bigger than just individual failure.

But then he is not afraid to fail.

211

CHAPTER 37

Rakeysh
Omprakash Mehra
Is Born

Bauji passed away on the last day of the Aks *shoot. It was 12 October* 2000.

I left the sets, mumbled something to a very perceptive Amit ji and rushed to cremate my father in Delhi at the Nigambodh Ghat near the Yamuna River.

After the cremation, we all stopped to have *aloo puri*, my father's favourite dish, and remembered him. My brother Rajan and I proceeded to carry the ashes to Haridwar.

As I immersed my father's ashes in the holy Ganga and took a dip in the waters, Rakeysh Omprakash Mehra was born. Even though my college degree reads Rakesh Mehra, every film of mine is a tribute to my father.

Years later, Mamta called me one day and said that she wanted me to add a 'Y' to my name. *Aks* had flopped and it had been almost three years since I had released a film.

I asked her why. She said that since I had already added our father's name 'Omprakash' to my name, her close friend, who was a numerologist, had recommended highly that I convert Rakesh into Rakeysh.

I didn't see any harm coming out of it.

So out of respect for Mamta's love and to keep the peace (she can be quite persuasive and insistent), I became Rakeysh.

I have a thirsty fish in me
That can never find enough
Of what it's thirsty for!

—Jalaluddin Rumi

213

1.
2
3

SECTION TWELVE

Understanding Myself

✳

1. In love with the waters.
2. Fulfilling dreams does involve standing on your
head. Swimming and yoga are a way of life.
3. Seeing through the noise.

CHAPTER 38

The Birth of a
Dream Weaver

With Aks, I discovered that cinema is my calling. That I love telling stories on celluloid. Directing actors was second nature to me; my cinematic technique and camera work was intuitive, organic, visceral and I enjoyed creating music with my composers and lyricists.

Essentially, cinema is stories told in moving pictures. It is different from novels and plays: a novel plays out in our headspace and every reader has a different imagination of the same story; a play unfolds on stage. But the core of cinema is a great screenplay. It is a very different art of writing.

My biggest shortcoming in *Aks* was the screenplay and I understood this instinctively. The key is that a screenplay is not written just once; it is always re-written. It is re-written for the last time on the edit table by the director and the editor: this is when a story comes alive visually. I needed to master this art.

The urge to make films had now become an obsession. But first I had to hone my skills as a film writer. I wanted to learn how to write a screenplay.

I didn't have formal training and, luckily, didn't know what to look for. Hence, I explored and discovered the beauty of cinema, music and art in my own way. I would edit a lot in the Soho area of London for my advertising films. Virgin Records at Oxford Street and the HMV store were a stone's throw away from my apartment at the Groucho club on Dean Street, Soho. Set over three floors, HMV had made it into the Guinness Book of Records as the world's largest music store. In the basement was a wall dedicated to world cinema: the genius of Federico Fellini, Akira Kurosawa and Krzysztof Kieślowski, among many others, lit up my imagination. I discovered all kinds of expression there.

Organically, I started exploring and discovering master filmmakers whose work I could relate to. I started reading books on screenplay writing. One of the writers from whose books I learnt a lot was Syd Field. He is revered as the original master of screenplay story structure, and his book *Screenplay: The Foundations of Screenwriting* has expounded on the essential structure of emotionally satisfying screenplays.

The pattern started unfolding in my head: the idea of a storyline, the setup, the conflict and the resolution; how the real and the surreal come together; balancing flashbacks and the flash-forwards. I learnt that the rule of telling a story is that there is no rule. It is an individual's expression of what they want to say and how they want to say it.

I wanted to meet and learn from Syd Field one day; this wish got fulfilled post the success of *RDB*...

This knowledge was liberating; I felt a lot lighter. I wanted to meet and learn from Syd Field one day; this wish got fulfilled post the success of *RDB*, when I made some serious money and could afford a one-on-one interaction with Syd in his Beverly Hills home for a good 21 days.

I also realized that Western culture had created a divide. There were art films and commercial films; there was Hollywood and then world cinema, and somewhere, this bifurcation had crossed borders and reached India. I had a good mind to question this divide through my work.

I discovered Ingmar Bergman's *Cries and Whispers*, a hypnotic film. I revelled in Federico Fellini's decision to replace Italy's image as bombed-out, post-War landscape with a hip, thriving, modern culture in all its glory in *La Dolce Vita* in 1960. The narrative captures

217

not just the characters but a city's tensions—between tradition and modernity, morality and hedonism, fantasy and reality.

I encountered the work of Polish director Krzysztof Kieślowski, who persevered for decades without recognition. His 1991 film, *The Double Life of Véronique*, explores the story of two young women, Weronika and Véronique in Poland and France: both singers, born on the same day and physically the same in every respect. They don't know each other but unconsciously sense a spectral companion. He raises the questions: are all of us truly unique? What happens when we find out we are not?

The Krzysztof Kieślowski trilogy, *Three Colours: Blue* (1993), *Three Colours: White* (1994) and *Three Colours: Red* (1994) captivated me too. Then there was his anthology called *Decalogue*—10 one-hour films—inspired by the Ten Commandments. Now this was as bold as it could get, as fearless as it could get, as imaginative as it could get.

I encountered the brat pack of Hollywood of the late '60s, '70s and '80s: Brian De Palma, Martin Scorsese, Oliver Stone, Frank Darabont, Steven Spielberg, George Lucas, Woody Allen and Francis Ford Coppola. There was so much out there to be soaked in. These filmmakers and many others of their ilk had challenged traditional mindsets and re-invented cinema from that part of the world.

Akira Kurosawa was the grand master, and his archetypal work impressed me the most. He would tell stories that were deeply set in Japanese culture and mirror the changing times. His work was marked by intoxicating cinematography. He told stories like nobody had ever done before him. I am yet to see anyone emulate his style. He remains an inspiration for generations of filmmakers who went on to become masters in their own right.

Back home, I revisited the cinema of Chetan Anand, V. Shantaram, Vijay 'Goldie' Anand, Guru Dutt, Raj Kapoor, Mehboob Khan, Hrishikesh Mukherjee, Asit Sen and Bimal Roy. Their movies were incredibly soul satisfying.

I was happy as a clam with this journey of discovery. I started writing screenplays, adapting stories and collaborating with my co-writers. I wanted my films to tell a story inside out. I had no strategy to get my films into festivals or make them blockbusters—that was about merit and all I could hope for was to earn my place.

I once entered a theatre one week after the release of *Aks* in Jaipur. There were only half a dozen people in the theatre. I learnt to give myself permission to fail not just in a philosophical way but in a practical way. Failure is the only way to evolve, to make cinema that is more meaningful.

My philosophy towards filmmaking has evolved over time, over the films I've written and directed. There were films that never got made. I've been understanding my motivations, navigating through massive successes at the box office and tremendous critical acclaim as well as big flops at the ticket window.

The enduring friendships along the way have made the journey even more special. Syd Field became a friend and a mentor and even came to India on my request. Ronnie did not blink an eye and hosted Syd's masterclasses.

219

CHAPTER 39

Real-Life Fountainheads

I was fortunate that my cinema enabled me to meet and learn from some extraordinary human beings. In our line of work, we get consumed, but I learnt from my real-life heroes that each one of us has to discover meaning in our own way, that each one of us was thirsty and searching.

Dr Verghese Kurien was a great man: he taught me the meaning of sacrifice. Post the independence of India, he gave up a thriving career in the US to serve the villagers of India and founded the Amul cooperative. He was a change-maker and a rebel. He transformed the lives of the poor and exploited villagers and paved the path for their economic independence. I remember him telling me, 'Rakeysh, life is too short. You need to pursue that one thing all your life; only then you can bring about a change.'

Another person who has touched my life in a very deep way is the late Pranab Mukherjee, former president of India, whom I lovingly called Pranab da. As the then defence minister of India, he saw *RDB* at a special screening hosted for him. That was the day I felt his blessings. Many years later, I was having lunch with a diplomat from Bangladesh when he received a call from the president of India. After they had spoken, Pranab da got to know that I was there.

He asked, 'Can I speak with Rakeysh?'

I took the phone.

'Rakeysh, when are you going to make something where humanity is above religious fanaticism?' he asked me.

'I will,' I committed obediently.

Pranab da had a lot of anguish and concern for the religious divide in India.

Then there's Arvind Kejriwal, an engineer turned politician who became the CM of Delhi in 2013 riding the wave of the Lokpal Movement led by Anna Hazare in 2011. This was a watershed moment in India's political history, scripted at the Ram Leela Maidan, a place we have spoken about in reference to *Delhi-6* in the book. I first met Kejriwal on a TV debate were we spoke about the 'idea' of India—it was a year after the release of *RDB*. Since then, I have always looked up to him. Whenever we speak, we share the same feelings and pain about this huge chasm between the haves and the have-nots.

I got to meet Mrs Sudha Murty, the richest lady in the world, whose account in the bank of life is overflowing.

A few years ago, I started mentoring Yuva Unstoppable, an NGO in Ahmedabad, and actively structured their activities. The goal was to raise money to build and renovate toilets in municipal schools and slums. This triggered my decision to make *Mere Pyare Prime Minister*. The movie was made 100 per cent out of corporate donations and, in turn, is raising more funds for the NGO to make toilets. I had to give up commercial filmmaking for a good two years to make this happen.

Post the release of *RDB*, I got calls from people who quit corporate jobs to start NGOs. Jasmine Shah, an alumnus of IIT Madras and Columbia University, gave up a comfortable position at ITC and joined the Janaagraha movement. Later, he got a scholarship to study International Relations in the US and returned to India. He continues to do ground-breaking work in the field of social reform. Jasmine went on to join the Aam Aadmi Party under the leadership of Arvind Kejriwal.

Ramesh and Swati Ramanathan touched my life with their grace, purpose and dignity. The couple had come back to India from the US where both had flourishing careers in banking and urban design, respectively. They started the NGO Janaagraha and the campaign, Jaago Re. In Ramesh's words, 'Jaago Re One Billion Votes' stood for social awakening and empowering the youth of India to lead the change themselves. The initiative was to awaken the youth to get the entire nation to vote.

The campaign's advisory board at Janaagraha comprised N.R. Narayana Murthy (founder, Infosys), T.S. Krishnamurthy (former chief election commissioner), Tariq Ansari (MD, Midday group) and me.

As the meetings for Janaagraha continued, my conversations with Murthy Sir, the original poster boy of India's success in IT, became more and more personal. One of the things Murthy Sir insisted I do was spend a lot of time with youngsters. I also acquired a desire from him to create a signature—a kind of cinema that would become a 'Rakeysh Omprakash Mehra' film. He became an enduring influence in my life.

I got to meet Mrs Sudha Murty, the richest lady in the world, whose account in the bank of life is overflowing. Not because she accumulates but because she gives, not because she keeps but because she shares. She once hosted Bharathi and me at the Infosys Campus in Mangalore to screen *BMB*.

She drove down from Bangalore early in the morning and served breakfast with her own hands. Her foundation—the Infosys Foundation—is the torch bearer in bringing about social change and, more importantly, change in the mindset of society. Incidentally, Murthy Sir is the only person who called me 'Omprakash' when he was being interviewed by my co-author.

N.R. Narayana Murthy
in first person

My wife and I already knew about Rakeysh through his extraordinary work with *RDB*. It had all the ingredients of an inspiring piece of cinema that could enthuse millions of Indians. Janaagraha, a movement to encourage the country to vote, brought us together, and I am grateful for that. I have great respect and affection for idealism, and Janaagraha provided a platform for Rakeysh and me to explore that. Rakeysh was one of the few people I have met who speaks even less than I do. However, at Janaagraha, I realized that even by speaking very little, he could come up with very innovative ways to solve a problem. What I could see in him was that he had the potential to create a brand doing unusual things. The unique blend of patriotism, idealism and power of youth that he had served to the nation via *RDB* had left an imprint on my mind. I knew that he was going to leave an indelible mark on Indian cinema, but I counselled him to develop his own trademark.

Rakeysh is one of the few relationships I have outside my work, again because I'm somewhat reserved. My personal relationships with cricketers—Rahul Dravid, Javagal Srinath and Anil Kumble—are mostly thanks to them being based in Bangalore. The only people I knew in Mumbai other than Rakeysh were Yash Chopra, a man with whom I used to spend time whenever I visited the city, and Sachin Tendulkar.

I encouraged Rakeysh to spend as much time with youngsters as possible. Young people have imagination: they understand technology faster than us. They also understand other cultures better than us. Therefore, if one has to understand the world better in a contemporary sense, their company is a good source.

Rakeysh's success is important because it is based on his integrity. Other than his obvious achievements, he is an icon because he has inspired millions of Indians to believe that cinema has integrity and soul. Ethics are above all else for him and Rakeysh has made people believe that great cinema can be made even with nothing in the pocket, given his own humble origins. By recreating the immense sacrifices of our freedom fighters in *RDB*, he awakened the proud patriotic Indian within each of us and held us accountable. Rakeysh also conducted a talk with me as part of the business forum during the IIFA weekend and awards

223

in 2014 in Tampa City, USA. The year before, he had released *BMB*, another extraordinary masterpiece about the triumph of the human spirit. Milkha's moving story swept away all the awards.

His passion to tell inspiring stories is his greatest contribution to Indian cinema.

CHAPTER 40

Bin Gogh

Take a grinder. Mix cinematographer Binod Pradhan and the legendary painter Vincent van Gogh and what you get is Bin Gogh! Don't forget to sprinkle a bit of Italian cinematographer Vittorio Storaro for best results. That's my friend for you!

There's the stillness of a Buddhist Lama about Binod, a calm he's carried with him despite three decades in the hysterical, high-octane world of films. Binod comes from the milieu of pure cinema. His work on *Parinda*, *Jaane Bhi Do Yaaron* and *1942: A Love Story* moved me very early in life. What followed was our collaboration on *RDB*, *Delhi-6* and *BMB*.

Born in 1953, with the majestic Kanchenjunga Peak as the backdrop to his life, he lived amidst the detailing of nature: the northeastern part of the great Himalayas. Pradhan's father had a photo studio and gifted him a box camera at a very early age. The cinematography bug bit Binod when he was all of eight years old. Naturally, he grew up with a great understanding of colour and picturesque shots and went on to do a photography course at the Film and Television Institute of India (FTII) Poona. After he passed out, he came to Bombay in 1975. In many ways, I think Binod and I were destined to work together. It happened when I started directing ad films.

Binod says:

> I vaguely remember that Rakeysh directed me in a jeans ad, a BPL
> Sanyo ad and another ad film for Limca that we shot in Mauritius.

225

There was also one ad with Asian Paints in which he asked me to experiment with very unusual visuals. When Rakeysh saw what I had shot, he said, 'This is sex on toast.' We discussed 'Samjhauta Express' and even took a long trip to Ladakh for locations, but the film did not happen. What attracted me to Rakeysh was that he was as soft-spoken as I was. When someone talks aggressively, I tend to go into my shell. When Rakeysh speaks, he seems to see things that are not obvious. He also gives the listener space to think. So while working with Rakeysh, you get the freedom to figure things out within what that means and explore within the perimeter he sets. That's the real magic with Rakeysh. When he narrates a script, I don't feel that I'm doing a commercial Bollywood film; I feel like I can cross the line and go somewhere else. I can experiment technically. Beyond just good-looking visuals, Rakeysh understands technically strong visuals.

Binod shares my hunger to create something 'never done before' on screen. The compelling question for me was—do we need to follow the art vs commercial route or can we create a new cult of cinema that can transcend all boundaries? Can I tell Indian stories to the world?

And I wasn't the only one thinking about it. I spoke extensively to AR and Binod about it. We all had a common thought: that Indian cinema was rendered inept and hollow by its own vicious circle of lip-synched songs and deliberate choreography, thereby shrinking a potential global audience. I felt strongly that the more Indian we get, the more global our cinema would become. I desperately felt the need to break away from pots and pans and create films that would be eternal in some sense.

Rang De Basanti was my first attempt to build this new alternative cinema, doing away with sound-assisted, bombastic hero fights, misplaced dance sequences and, most importantly, lip-synced songs. And yet, nobody could label *RDB* as arthouse or commercial.

'*Tu sahi kar raha hai, Mehra*,' (you're doing the right thing) Aamir always used to tell me. Binod, AR and Bharathi were always egging me on. All of them were only concerned about the beauty and sanctity of the product we were creating, and not worried about whether it would be a hit or flop.

'How can you make a hit?' Binod would ask me.

'True that, Bin Gogh. You can at best make a movie you believe in,' I would reply.

Binod adds:

Rakeysh knows what he wants but has his own way of getting it. I always thought Rakeysh worked with me because he respected me as a cinematographer. When I started getting calls at odd hours, I took it to be a sign that he wanted our friendship to grow.

Binod shares my hunger to create something 'never done before' on screen.

He would come home and my beautiful Gujarati wife Sonali would prepare her signature chicken momos for him. This continued for a while; we were working and eating momos together. All was well with the world. Imagine my surprise when I discovered that secretly, he was enlisting my wife's help to get a house help from my hometown. And just like that, the meetings disappeared—because now someone else was making the chicken momos for him! Here's my big tip to you—the way to Rakeysh's heart and life is through his tummy.

227

CHAPTER 41

Food + Friends = Films

My love for food and cooking is genetic. Bauji could cook exquisite Peshawari cuisine, a legacy from the North West Frontier Province. Rustic and robust, my brother Rajan inherited it and went on to open his own restaurant, Bauji ka Dhaba, in Delhi. And as I've said earlier, Maa could whip up a meal in no time that not only filled your stomach but fulfilled your soul.

Food is the common thread with everyone else. In Chennai, AR's mom Kareema Begum always used to send breakfast sharp at 6 a.m. in the morning after a night's recording session. There was also the indulgence of biryani for the night that she used to make for us.

Shankar Mahadevan and I also share a unique bromance over food, and thanks to this, we have a strange subliminal connection. If two grown men can WhatsApp videos of gravy simmering in the pan, it's us. One day, I called Shankar from a Thai restaurant in Mauritius. Bharathi and I were sitting on this beautiful candle-lit table in the middle of a restaurant surrounded by a pond overlooking the ocean. I shared with him a photo of the dish I was having and our location. Shankar responded, 'Try the Thai ginger pepper fish at that restaurant. And pay my regards to the lady chef if she is still around.' Another time, he was in Germany trying out a particular traditional beer with his beautiful wife, Sangeeta. He called me from there. I knew exactly where he was because I had been there too! We tend to end up visiting the same places thanks to our insatiable taste buds.

228

Shankar says:

Rakeysh is very functional and active in the morning and we often call each other by 7 a.m. every alternate morning discussing what we must try. We call Rakeysh to our studio for a narration before we start working on the music of a film, mostly because he brings food.

Bharathi's mom is an encyclopaedia on South Indian dishes. Bharathi and Shankar share her secret recipes of pickles made out of gongura, tomato and red chilles, *amla* (Indian gooseberry) and green chillies: the list is endless. When I head for recording sessions, Bharathi always sends jars full of mouth-watering chutneys made by her mom for Shankar.

Moving on to another foodie, PK is someone who can cook anything. By anything, I mean that his knowledge of food, recipes and the subtle art of cooking is endless. Few people know that Govind Sandhu, Meghna Gulzar's husband, is a gifted chef. Whenever he cooks his favourite green chilli mutton, a portion promptly arrives at our doorstep in a casserole. We have always joked that if our films fail, there is always the highway *dhaba* (restaurant) business!

Whenever Bharathi travels to Europe, she is only looking out for different varieties of cheese to bring back for Gulzar Sahab. The best *shami* kebabs come from Waheeda ji's kitchen—she is a master chef. I think she mistakenly believes that there are 10 members in our family because every time food arrives from her house, it's plentiful.

Aamir's mom has absolutely spoilt us with her kebabs and mutton rogan josh during our reading sessions. Every Id, his house is the place to be. The only gift Paweł Dyllus(my DoP from Poland on *Mirzya* and *Mere Pyare Prime Minister*) brings for me are strips of thin Polish sausages. In return, I give him *motichoor ke laddoo* (a spherical sweet preparation made of gram flour) He loves them. I still remember mom would send *gajjak* (Indian sweet made of jaggery and sesame seeds) for Amit ji and Jaya ji.

My venture *Toofaan* with the colossus Javed Akhtar and his son Farhan Akhtar involves gastronomic indulgences as well. Our sessions at Javed ji's home to discuss the script involve lunches that

229

last for three hours. When I enter his house, where he also has his writing studio, I am not even remotely thinking about the script. I am consumed by the spread of pure Awadhi and Mughlai dishes that will be laid out.

Bhairavi has surprised us all with her culinary skills, but unlike my desi preferences, her dishes are global and fusion. The shopping list that she would hand me on my foreign travels would include: books on baking and baking ingredients from Melbourne, miso and wasabi from Tokyo, hand-pressed olive oil and parma ham from Italy, sausages from Germany and so on. Her favourite though, is *rasam*-chawal made by Bharathi's mom. Vedant is not far behind. He takes three hours to marinate a single piece of chicken, dipped in Italian spices, honey and tequila, and then takes another hour to turn it on slow fire. Perfection is not to be rushed.

When we built our second home overlooking the Pawna Lake, Puran Kumar, designed the house around the kitchen. Sharing food is an inseparable part of who we are as a people.

When we built our second home overlooking the Pawna Lake, Puran Kumar (who had earlier designed and built our home Mamta Bungalow in Pali Hill and our studio in Pali Village), designed the house around the kitchen. Sharing food is an inseparable part of who we are as a people. To this day, every Saturday evening at home is open house for food. Ellen, our housekeeper, makes the most delicious dimsums and friends drop in unannounced bringing in their contribution.

But I discovered that food can be a motivator too. Who can forget the legendary Milkha Singh's love for a glass of *dudh* (milk) and two raw eggs?

Mere apno ka khoon hai us hawa mein
Main saans nahin le paaonga, sir.

(The air in Pakistan is sullied by the blood of my ancestors.
I won't be able to breathe there, sir.)

—Milkha Singh in *BMB* to PM Jawaharlal Nehru when asked to
lead a contingent to Pakistan for the Indo-Pak Friendship Meet in
Lahore in 1960

Official poster of *Bhaag Milkha Bhaag*
Courtesy: ROMP Pictures

Bhaag Milkha Bhaag

CHAPTER 42

Milkha Anoints Me

In 1947, the British left India, but left it divided. They drew a line of hatred and split India into two nations: Pakistan was born. Things would never be the same again. The formation of an Islamic nation caused the migration of millions of Muslims to West and East Pakistan (the latter now known as Bangladesh), while several others chose to stay back in India, their motherland, and millions of Hindus and Sikhs who were in Pakistan at the time of Partition headed to India. The bloodshed and ethnic violence left indelible scars on the psyche of the citizens of the newly formed countries.

Across the Indian subcontinent, communities that had coexisted peacefully for almost a millennium attacked each other in a terrifying outbreak of sectarian violence, with Hindus and Sikhs on one side and Muslims on the other. This mutual genocide was as unexpected as it was unprecedented. The mindless revenge that ordinary Sikhs, Hindus and Muslims wreaked on each other hardened our social sense, distorted our political judgements and deranged our understanding of morality.

I had been toying with the idea of making a film on Partition for a very long time. To understand why, let's go back to my youth. When I turned 18, my family shifted to a rented place in Lajpat Nagar. My landlord's family had come over from Sindh, and their kids were the first post-Partition generation growing up from birth in India. They were Indians who came to live in Delhi from Lahore and were nostalgic about their birthplace.

Now Lajpat Nagar is a colony of post-Partition migrants, predominantly Punjabi refugees. There was a lot of fond nostalgia in their conversations. '*Lahore mein jaisi patangen udti hain, Lajpat nagar mein kya udengi!*' (The kites in Lajpat Nagar cannot match those in Lahore!) Listening to their tales, I understood the difference between *watan* (the land one belongs to) and *desh* (the country one belongs to). At the same time, they hadn't forgotten the horrors of Partition. Their tales of bloodshed were graphic and disturbing. Many of them were permanently scarred (like Milkha Singh) with memories of people they had lost and the remorseless carnage they had witnessed at close quarters. As I heard these stories, they became part of my subconscious.

I also started reading different stories about Partition. In fact, some of the most poignant literary works of India are set in the context of Partition. I was deeply moved by Saadat Hasan Manto's 'Khol Do', 'Toba Tek Singh' and 'Tetwal Ka Kutta', among others.

Another legend I am personally close to is Gulzar, whose family migrated to India at the time of Partition. Gulzar was aged 13 when Partition took place: he is a living legend with a personal narrative of the holocaust. He was separated from his parents, while making the journey to India from Lahore, on a train that was swarming with densely packed people. He wrote 'Raavi Paar and Other Stories' ('Across the Raavi River and Other Stories' [Raavi River now also forms a natural boundary between the two nations]).

To this day, Partition is an integral part of what defines the emotions at play between India and Pakistan, even in a game of cricket. Sadly, more than seven decades later, the two-nation theory has never really worked. India and Pakistan have fought four wars, a third nation Bangladesh has been created and there is a perpetual proxy war all the time. Elections have been won and lost by politicians on both sides by fueling this hatred and further exploiting ordinary citizens.

One day, a young director, Aditya Dhar, visited me to narrate a script. This was a comedy which he wanted to direct and my company to produce. At the end of our meeting, he gave me the autobiography of Milkha Singh. Aditya went on to make *Uri: The Surgical Strike*, one of the biggest blockbusters of 2019, which Ronnie Screwvala produced.

I picked up the book only to realize that it was an autobiography written and self-published by Milkha Singh in Gurmukhi (Punjabi script). I immediately gave it to Rajiv Tandon to figure out if he knew someone who could read it. Tandon's uncle Babbu Mama knew Gurmukhi. He read it and the very next day came to office and started telling me the story in the book.

Milkha had lost his childhood to Partition. He escaped and went on to cross the border and somehow reunited with his sister. What inspired me was how a 12-year-old, who witnessed the massacre of his family, was pushed and shoved into India and lived with no roof to sleep under and no food in his stomach. He then went on to create a national record in athletics that remained unbroken for almost 40 years! He also won a double gold medal in the Asian Games, broke the Commonwealth Games record with a gold medal and then set a world record in 400 metres.

I knew that I had found my story and that night wrote the opening scene of the film and the last scene of the film.

Milkha used to practice running at the National Stadium in Delhi, the same place where I would practice my swimming 40 years later. My coach would always inspire us with stories of the legendary Milkha, Dhyan Chand and Dara Singh. I called up Lokesh Sharma (Loki as we call him), my classmate and close buddy from SRCC. Lokesh, a former sports journalist, is the author of the *Wills Book of Excellence: The Olympics* (1984), among others, and is now a giant name in sports management in India. He connected me to Milkha. A couple of days later, I took a flight to Chandigarh to meet one of India's greatest athletes and his wife Nirmal Kaur (Nimmy Aunty for me).

I had a 5.30 p.m. flight back the same evening, but when I heard what Milkha had gone through in his own words and his journey to becoming an Olympic-level athlete, I ended up staying for another seven days. He gave me a Hindi translation of his autobiography. As for me, I hadn't even carried a toothbrush. I bought kurta pyjamas from Khadi Bhandar and a few other essentials and checked into Taj Chandigarh.

Bhaag Milkha Bhaag

I was completely engrossed in his story. Every morning, at 11 a.m., Milkha would finish golfing at the Chandigarh Golf Club, wear his signature suit, red turban with a matching red tie and sit down with me at noon sharp. We would both have our first beer. We would speak over lunch until 4 p.m., then meet again for an early dinner and talk some more. I would go back again the next day. Nimmi Aunty would spoil me with home-cooked meals. The couple was both receptive and courteous. Gradually, he started trusting me and poured his heart out. During these narrations, I noticed tears in his eyes on two occasions: first, when he spoke about the massacre of his family during the ethnic violence that followed Partition, and second, when he lost the gold medal in the finals of the 400 metres at the Rome Olympics in 1960, where he was one of the favourites to win.

He was leading in the 400-metre race up to 250 metres. That's when he committed a tactical error and looked back to see by how much he was leading. In that one fraction of a second, three athletes overtook him. I knew that I had found my story and that night wrote the opening scene of the film and the last scene of the film.

The film opens with Milkha flying off the blocks at the 1960 Rome Olympics. Around half way, his coach shouts, '*Bhaag Milkha, bhaag*' (run Milkha, run). The voice of his coach reverbs and morphs into his father's voice from the past: bhaag *puttar*, bhaag (run son, run). Milkha remembers the words his father had screamed, urging him to run for his life during that fateful day of the massacre.

Milkha has a déjà vu moment: he looks back to see a militant on a black horse chasing him with a sword. But that reaction costs him the race. As past and present merge into a single moment, the man on the black horse cuts off his father's head from his torso in one swift slash of the bloody sword. Milkha shudders to the finish line, incapacitated mentally by his own demons, despite being the fastest runner that day.

Then, I wrote the last scene: Milkha at the peak of his running career goes to Pakistan reluctantly at the behest of Prime Minister Jawaharlal Nehru. This was in 1960, when President Ayub Khan of Pakistan and Prime Minister Nehru announced an Indo-Pak Friendship Meet between the two countries to be held in Lahore.

In Pakistan, a day before the event, he goes to visit the village he had fled 13 years ago and re-lives the moment of tragedy of his family's massacre. As he allows himself to cry, the ghosts of the past are set free and washed away in his tears. He comes back to Lahore and runs the race of his life. He wins the race and celebrates it with a victory lap. In a surreal moment, the 12-year-old Milkha and his battered childhood run alongside the now healed, grown-up Milkha, who finally comes to terms with his past. It is an out-of-body experience. His past lets go of its heinous hold on him, the child smiles at the adult winner: all the hatred which Milkha had nurtured inside him for Pakistan melts away in that one moment. Metaphorically, it's time we let this hatred melt away too.

Gen. Ayub Khan garlands him with the gold medal and declares that the world from here on will know him as 'the flying Sikh', a title by which we all lovingly still call him. For all his trials and tribulations, Milkha was a hero.

Prasoon Joshi took the baton from me and wrote some riveting scenes. In hindsight, he overwrote because he was so deeply involved with the material that he wrote almost two films for me. I don't blame him as there was so much material in Milkha's own words. Prasoon's interpretation was deep and layered.

I had broken the narrative in a non-linear way. I was getting better and better at jumping back and forth in time after *RDB*. Subconsciously, it was also a style I was developing. Binod Pradhan (DoP) kept hearing various drafts and when I bounced a non-linear approach, he immediately liked it. Shankar, Ehsan and Loy were the first people on board for *BMB*. I trusted them to tug at some soulful adrenaline strings.

However, I still hadn't found my Milkha. I narrated the story to Hrithik Roshan, whom I have always seen as a very intense actor. Hrithik sent me a beautiful message, 'You've completely screwed my life upside down.' However, he passed it as he was already committed to his franchise, *Krrish*. Aamir Khan too heard the narration. 'Yaar Mehra, this one is not for me,' he said. I started screen testing for Milkha and found Ranveer Singh to fit the bill. He was thrilled with the part and so was I with his audition. But then even he passed it for

239

reasons I will never know. I have always respected the decisions of another artist—we all have our own head spaces.

Bharathi has an important point here:

> Mehra and I saw Milkha as a winner who had conquered his own fears and overcome personal tragedy. However, he did not really win a medal at the Olympics for his country. Many of the actors must have not been able to 'see' this as a heroic story and hence, turned it down.

I kept searching. Unknown to all of us, there was someone out there who would not only play Milkha but become Milkha, and leave an indelible mark on Indian cinema with this performance.

Farhan Akhtar
in first person

Rakeysh and I used to meet on and off at the Otters Club, where we both train. I was familiar with him. However, the first script he gave me was not *BMB*. I was working out at the club one day in 2003 when he came and handed over a script to me; it was called 'Paint it Yellow' (Rang De Basanti). He asked me if I would play the role of Karan Singhania. My first reaction was fear. I hadn't thought of acting back then, and when I got to know that Aamir was also involved, I wondered whether I was biting off more than I could chew. So, I politely declined. The thing that struck me about Rakeysh back then was that he genuinely wanted feedback on his script. If the script troubles you as an actor or you cannot relate to it, he wants to understand why. When I saw the script-to-screen translation later as *RDB*, I was blown away.

A few years later, I received another call from Rakeysh. He came over and told me the story of *BMB*. In his calm way, he said, 'I would like you to consider being Milkha.'

I had to first appreciate that, as a director, Rakeysh was able to visualize me in such a difficult role. At the time, I was aware that he was making a film on Milkha, but I had never reached out to him or seen myself being able to play it. That's the magic of a director's vision. I was delighted that despite all the urban roles I was bringing alive, Rakeysh could visualize a small-town athlete in me, and that too a rustic Sikh. I could see he was in love with his script. After a 15-minute narration, we shook hands on the project. That was it.

Looking back, Rakeysh brought alive the same soul-stirring magic of *RDB* in *BMB* as well. He put together a stellar team. There was cinematographer Binod Pradhan, who is a master of the craft. The minute you have a man like that on the visuals, you can surrender completely. Binod has elevated storytelling through visuals to a fine art. The beauty of the shot he captured for the last race in the film, in which I defeat the Pakistani athlete Abdul Khaliq, is timeless. They were rolling at 1,000 frames per second, and this was the race. After the third take, Binod screamed, 'This is it!' All of us ran to the monitor. I couldn't believe what I saw—I had accidentally managed to touch my nose to the finish line, and the ripple of the thread was visible. Had my chest touched the finish line, the ripple wouldn't have been so pronounced. It was magic.

Then there was Prasoon, who had worked on the script. I was playing a village boy with no education, no exposure to any other culture and unable to speak English. I relied on Rakeysh's help to flush the Mumbai city sensibilities out of me, so I could become Milkha. I had a dialogue coach—he kept working on nuances with me to unlearn everything I knew. I was supported by sprint coach Melwyn Crasto and sports nutritionist Samir Jaura. Melwyn asked me to take up a speed target so we could be more focussed. I aimed to run the 100 metres below 12 seconds. Melwyn finally timed me when I was running with others and, at my peak, I touched 11.4 seconds, which was truly liberating. There was Divya Dutta, a fine actor who raises everyone's game just because of her dedication to her craft.

As for me, I immersed myself to serve the film. Rakeysh's love for the script and the real Milkha Singh's expectations of the film were always at the back of my mind. I wanted the audience to say, 'We didn't know that Farhan could do this.'

I was possessed by Milkha. I isolated myself from everyone else. I didn't want to be an actor who was hired to play an athlete. I lived and trained like an athlete, became one, so that it would be easier to act like one. All sporting champions, whether Usain Bolt or Mike Tyson, have a certain body language. They exude energy that they own their arena. I knew I couldn't fake that. When we shot, I wasn't bothered about things like will my stamina hold up or will I look like I belong. I trained like a beast to belong.

Rakeysh has said often that he didn't choose Milkha but Milkha chose him. That's because he takes his work seriously but himself lightly. Even though the boy coming to him with a Punjabi book on Milkha could've been fate, what he did with the book was his own karma.

I think what makes Rakeysh and me click is that we are yin and yang. Our energies are quite different. Rakeysh is calm: even when he gets angry on set or decides to take charge because something is not happening the way it should, he conveys it without yelling. He doesn't rush me. On the contrary, I am impatient and raring to go. As an athlete, I didn't want to be around people who were drinking or eating delicious things. But Rakeysh constantly dangled tasty 'naan' in front of

242

me, teasing and testing my willpower. And lastly, off the sets, there's a dormant singer within him, struggling to emerge during the after-hours of a party.

My fondest memory of *BMB* is Rana Sahab, who used to tie my *pagdi*. Talking to him helped me tremendously. He had a very endearing gesture—whenever he made a mistake, he would stick his tongue out. I used that gesture to portray the simplicity of Milkha.

CHAPTER 43

Off the Blocks, Finally

During 2009–10, I was consumed with scripting BMB. *For Prasoon,* it was his first script. He had done lyrics before. The first thing I wanted both of us to do was to spend as much time as possible with Milkha. So, once again, Chandigarh became a frequent destination. In the beginning, Milkha was wary of Prasoon and whispered discreetly but innocently in my ear, 'Yeh sports *nahi samajhta*' (he does not understand sports)!

I reassured him that I could relate very well to sports and Prasoon understood human relationships beautifully, and that this was the balance we needed. My wonderful assistant Nikita Deshpande and I would spend as much time as we could get with Prasoon Joshi— he was the top boss at McCann World group, a multi-million dollar advertising agency—juggling and finding time for my script. Many times, it became frustrating as Prasoon had very little time, but I kept my trust in him. He would give me handwritten scenes, which Nikita would then make sense of, edit and give them to me. She went on to write her first book post this.

My job was to put the screenplay together and I went with my instincts with a non-linear and abstract screenplay, where the continuity of storytelling was the emotional line and not the timeline. On paper, it was hard to comprehend, but in my head, I was seeing the film. Most importantly, I already had the beginning and the end of the film from my first meeting with Milkha and I was completely convinced about that. In a metaphysical way, Milkha's story had some connection to *Aks* and *Delhi-6*: all were about the demons within. I told Binod and Bharathi that *BMB* is the final part of the trilogy. The common message was not to fight or run away from your demons but to face them. Binod and Bharathi were always there with their critical opinion. They were not attached to the material yet, so I had a third person's objectivity. Their mastery over their respective crafts—cinematography and editing—only elevated the writing process.

With the script done and dusted, it was time to raise funds. I was not aware that this would be the beginning of another marathon. Nobody was interested in a movie on the life of a Sikh athlete, with his sister (played by Divya Dutta) as the heroine. The movie had just a sprinkle of fleeting romance, but that too was unfulfilled. There was no action either. I didn't blame the studios or the financiers—there was no precedent for a film like *BMB*. What added insult to injury was that my previous film *Delhi-6* had not worked at the box office.

I approached Ronnie at UTV Motion Pictures to produce the movie. We both shared a massive comfort level after *RDB* and *Delhi-6*. But Ronnie was in the process of handing over the baton to the new management of Walt Disney Co., which had acquired UTV. This did not help my cause.

'I don't want to play Farhan's sister. I have a huge crush on him.'

I kept narrating and looking for a producer. There was a phase when people started questioning my passion for the script itself. 'Who will give you money to make a film about a Sardar athlete who did not win at the Olympics?' was a common enough question.

Sports biopics weren't invented back then. Some of my friends even told me: 'I feel for your passion, but don't make it.' Bharathi stood by me like a rock, saying that we would pawn our house yet again and make the film if no one gave us any money. In fact, my Pali Hill home, which was bought from my advertising money, had already been mortgaged before for *RDB*. So why not for *BMB*?

After much persistence, Viacom18 Motion Pictures finally agreed. I am thankful to Vikram Malhotra, who loved the script. He fought

245

Bhaag Milkha Bhaag

with the board and the management and put his neck on the line. After all, he was a national-level tennis champion and understood a sportsman inside out. I had my film and I had my finance.

I may have struggled a bit to find Milkha, but for the key part of Isri Kaur, Milkha Singh's sister, my first and last choice was the talented Divya Dutta.

But there was a twist, albeit a fawning one.

'I don't want to play Farhan's sister. I have a huge crush on him,' said Divya Dutta.

Divya Dutta
in first person

There are two kinds of directors—one who sets an example, the other who follows them. Rakeysh Mehra is clearly among the former. And I get withdrawal symptoms if I don't meet him or talk to him for over a month. He met me when my career was in a strange position. I had just had a massive hit in *Veer-Zaara*, and I was the new Punjabi *kudi* (girl) in tinsel town.

The most renowned production houses offered me roles in the mould of the vivacious, *chulbuli* (perky) 'Punjaban'. The artist in me was disappointed by the banality of it, and I sat at home for a year. My earnest mother kept telling me that 'audiences will forget' and that 'I would become extinct.'

Then one fine day, I got a call from Rakeysh Mehra.

ROM: I'm making *Delhi-6*. I want you to play 'Jalebi'.

Me: Is it a Punjaban's role? Is that why you're offering me the role?

'No,' he sounded surprised at my suggestion. 'But I think you can play it. Come to the office and I'll narrate you the role,' he added.

I went to Rakeysh's Tardeo office. The first thing that struck me was how rooted he was: a man from the soil. And the role he narrated was so wonderful; I never thought I would play it. Jalebi has a gypsy look and essays the role of a local hottie who uses the typical '*mardon ki bhaasha*' (street and slang language of men), tone and dialect. The film got pushed and, in the meantime, Rakeysh offered me a Samsung ad with the Indian cricket team. When we arrived on the sets, the cricket team and I were assigned separate 'coupes'. Not a single word was exchanged.

In his quiet, observant and unassuming way, Rakeysh saw that the ice needed to be broken. He called Harbhajan Singh (a key spin bowler in the Indian cricket team, who knew Punjabi).

'Do you know Divya? She just did the film *Shaheed-e-Mohabbat Boota Singh* with Gurdas Mann (Indian playback singer, songwriter and actor and a legend among the Punjabi diaspora).' Harbhajan, who was stoically maintaining his distance up to that point, opened up very warmly. He held my hand playfully and took me to meet his teammates. There was banter and laughter and the shoot was a breeze.

Bhaag Milkha Bhaag

247

Rakeysh knew just the right buttons to push.

Finally, we worked together on *Delhi-6*, a film I'm very proud of. I had to take training in Haryanvi to do the role. I play an untouchable and reform a very orthodox character in the film, played by Atul Kulkarni.

We had detailed script-reading sessions and rehearsals for every scene. However, Rakeysh never tells you how you should act. At the end of a scene, the actor is expected to think and produce their own version of performance. When you look at him for feedback, a *'badhiya hai'* (looks fine) after a long gap of silence is the best response you can hope to get.

He unconsciously builds chemistry on the sets. There are games, laughter, camaraderie being built off the sets too, which adds organic gravitas to the film. During the shoot of *Delhi-6*, senior cast members Rishi Kapoor and Om Puri were asked to teach me 'abuses' so I could become more comfortable narrating my lines.

I could see that Rakeysh was just absorbing my performance quietly. The best thing about him is that he listens, absorbs and responds in the most human way possible. He is also a gentleman who invests time in every character of his film. There is no frivolity to be expected from him.

Soon enough, we met again. He was really excited. 'Your next role is ready,' he smiled. This was the character of Isri Kaur, in *BMB*, an anchor role that can challenge any actor. I am blessed that I was able to re-imagine the stereotypical sister who is rarely more than an insignificant prop or object of pity for the protagonist via my role in the film.

My only grudge with Rakeysh is that I still have not received the mutton curry he promised me long ago.

CHAPTER 44

Champions in
Their Own Right

Divya's eyes speak a lot. I knew that she had this arterial understanding of what constitutes a powerful performance. And she was the heroine of *BMB*.

Sonam Kapoor benevolently accepted to play a guest appearance for a princely sum of ₹11 only for her brief portrayal of Biro, a fictional muse that is the object of young Milkha's adolescent affection. She lights up the screen every time she appears in the movie. Sonam, too, fondly looks back and says, 'I'm the *tadka* (spice) in the film,' knowing that *BMB* will remain part of her filmography and history for posterity.

Sonam understood that the film was not a love story—it was about a Partition survivor's tryst with his horrific childhood, and that Isri Kaur, the sister, was his only connect to a past that he was reluctant to both own and discard. Pavan Malhotra, K.K. Raina and Yograj Singh (father of celebrated Indian cricketer, Yuvraj Singh) joined the gang to complete a stellar cast. I first spoke to Yograj on the phone and he humbly came down to Mumbai for a complete narration. He too had played for the Indian cricket team as a bowler and understood the script we were dealing with very well. After his career was cut short by an injury, Yograj had started acting in Punjabi films. He knew sports and he knew the art of performing, and both of these reflect in his fine performance in the film.

Among the crew, the young Pranav Shukla joined in as the sound designer. An alumnus of Whistling Woods, Pranav had worked with Nakul Kamte before, but this would be his first film as the head of a department. 'Within two-and-a-half months, I got fired thrice. But I knew that Rakeysh sir was testing me, checking whether I would succumb to the pressure or stand up to it,' Pranav told my co-author later on the sets of *Toofaan*. The brilliantly experienced Dolly Ahluwalia designed the wardrobe and gave complete freedom to Abhilasha Sharma, her chief assistant. Abhilasha went on to become not only my designer but an integral part of my films thereafter. Vinay Waikul was my support in the direction department, along with Yatharth Awasthi, who assisted him. Yeti, as I call him, went on to become my associate director in *Toofaan*.

Vikram Dada, Avan Contractor and Allan Amin continued to helm the makeup, hair and action, respectively. They were like extensions of me and had been a part of three consecutive films I had made along with Binod and Bharathi. The sensitive Sumeet Basu (production designer) stepped into Samir Chanda's shoes.

The script spans Milkha's life from the age of 12 to 30. So, while there were countless documentaries, archives and statistics available on Milkha's sporting life, we wanted to delve deeper into the man behind the athlete and what went into making him.

The schedule had us jumping into deep waters from day one. We started shooting the pre-climax of the film in Ferozepur, Punjab, a town on the Indo-Pak border. There was barbed wire separating the two countries: we actually filmed that and the existing border post at Hussainiwala, bang opposite the Pakistani village of Ganda Singh Wala. The armies manning the borders on both sides helped us and, for a shot, even let us place the camera on the other side. P.S. Shyam and Rajiv Tandon, who is a driving force at ROMP even today as a producer, somehow managed special defence permission and assistance from the Border Security Force. Since there were no hotels, we created homes within the army barracks, government circuit homes and even the open fields under the stars.

Hussainiwala was also where we pictured the scene when Milkha visits his childhood home in Pakistan and breaks down, remembering the massacre that killed his family. He meets his childhood friend, who speaks to him in the language of their playful past as they embrace each other. The friend's wife offers him his favourite drink—a glass of milk—and their son, who has a newspaper clipping of Milkha framed on the wall, asks, '*Aap wohi Milkha Singh ho na, jo daudta hai?*' (Aren't you the same Milkha Singh who runs?) He also gets to know that his friend survived Partition because he was raised by a Maulvi (Muslim priest) in Pakistan. The dialogue in the film, by Milkha's friend, '*Log bure nahin hote; halaat bure hote hain*' (It's not people who are bad, but the circumstances that make them act like savages), captures a beautiful sentiment.

We treated the last 20 minutes of the film with almost no dialogues. I did not want to lose my first thoughts of when I first met Milkha. I wanted the pictures to tell the story. So, we used the radio commentary of the bygone days as it also underlines a period gone by and transports the audiences. Milkha wins the race in Lahore and the entire country rejoices.

We treated the last 20 minutes of the film with almost no dialogues. I did not want to lose my first thoughts of when I first met Milkha.

This was also my first outing with SEL for a feature film. The music sessions with them were a blast, to say the least. It was like a reunion of four friends.

Shankar has this natural instinct to improvise. There was this scene where Milkha is running and his leg is bleeding. An idea struck him during his *Bramha Mahurat* (the sacred time of 4.30 a.m.) that we must use a line from the Gurbani in Daler Mehndi's voice because only God can get you through such situations. We immediately called Gulzar Sahab later in the day. He heard the situation out and then suggested a traditional prayer:

Bhaag Milkha Bhaag

Nanak naam jahaz hai
Chade so utre paar
Jo sharda kar sev de
kurpaar utaaran haare
kurpaar utaaran haare

(Nanak's name is a ship:
Every boarder is taken ashore.
One who serves devotedly,
Guru will drop him across.)

This inspired treatment to the scene remains one of the finest moments of the film.

It was great fun to offer the shy Loy a small role in the film. He plays a guitarist and the singer in the song 'Woolloomooloo Wanda', a song he had composed and actually sung for the album.

About the feel of the film, he says:

> Part of the reason we were able to create great music was because Rakeysh has a habit of giving you a script and leaving you with it. He plants a seed and hopes that it will grow and find meaning within you. He has a beautiful way of extracting work from you, despite his taciturn nature. There's something abstract about the creation process and Rakeysh understands that.

Ehsaan and I are exactly the same age; he constantly updates me about the best international cinema that he has watched. I remember once Ehsaan got this crazy inspiration for a rock-bhangra track called 'Zinda' that went on be part of the film soundtrack and something of a rock anthem. I took the rough composition home and played it for Bhairavi and Vedant. Later, I told Ehsaan, 'My kids have found new respect for me, thanks to your inspired track.' Eventually, of course, Shankar's son Siddharth sung it as his debut and made it powerful!

Ehsaan
in first person

During the making of the film, we were invited to Kargil to perform at the Vijay Diwas celebrations of the Indian Army in 2012.

Rakeysh decided to come along. As soon as we landed, Rakeysh and I were diagnosed with high-altitude mountain sickness. We managed to stabilize and were required to perform under the flag for the army. It was a proud moment. But the most memorable part of the trip was how Rakeysh used to dictate the army mess to make the eggs this way and the parathas that way. Basically, we enjoyed the simple everyday things that life offers to the fullest.

Even today, when we meet him after a really long time, and ask him how he is, his response is always, '*Bas masti kar raha hoon*' (just chilling!). He doesn't take himself very seriously. In fact, Farhan was the man who pointed it out to me. 'I don't get how calm the man is on the sets!' he had remarked.

And it is probably this calmness that lets him accept and run with your idea or suggestion, till the point that you yourself realize that it's not working. He never gives you the feeling that he's interfering with your art. He respects our melodies and our musicality. He doesn't even let his own preferences influence the music of his films.

253

Bhaag Milkha Bhaag

CHAPTER 45

On Your Mark

Early in the first week of shoot, Divya joined the cast and crew on location. I introduced her to the tawny, lean sardar standing next to me. She smiled politely at first but then looked closely again. She couldn't believe the transformation. Farhan had become Milkha. She was clearly frazzled by the unwavering focus with which Farhan had re-sculpted his body and his look. The fine artist that she is, she took it upon herself as a challenge and a fuel for her role.

We had to shoot a scene of her sibling interaction with Milkha, the child. I discussed it with her.

Me: What did you play in your childhood?

Divya Dutta: Pitthu (a game with seven stones and a ball), Kanche (a game with marbles), Chupa Chupi (hide and seek)...

Me: Do you want to try one of those in this scene?

Divya: How about a 'find my thumb' game?

Me: Let's see how it goes.

She demonstrated, and this simple game becomes a signature bond between brother and sister throughout the film.

One of my favourite scenes is when Milkha re-unites with his sister after his military training, wearing a Team India blazer and dark sunglasses. Isri, who is washing utensils, looks up and does not recognize her own brother in this new avtar and says, '*Haanji*?' (Yes?). A moment passes, she realizes who it is and hugs her brother. Milkha offers her his blazer, after which he asks her to put her hands in the pockets. She does this only to find a pair of gold earrings inside. Divya improvised mid-scene by pushing him away and saluting him, with tears of pride welling up in her eyes. We allowed the chemistry that was developing between them to flow—it was both organic and unscripted.

Visually, my favourite location Ladakh, made *BMB* even more beautiful.

Visually, my favourite location, Ladakh, made *BMB* even more beautiful. Binod Pradhan reminisces:

> During the shooting in Ladakh, we were on top of the mountains, shooting the portions where Milkha Singh is training intensely. We captured beautiful shots via angles that conveyed a meaning to the landscape itself. After we wrapped up for the day, Rakeysh and I walked down the valley and didn't take the car with the rest of the crew. Funnily enough, we reached the bottom faster than the cars, and when we realized it, we started running faster to put a greater distance between us and the cars. It was just a spur of the moment thing for both of us.

255

Bhaag Milkha Bhaag

CHAPTER 46

The Gold Standard

Finally, it was time for BMB*'s date with its box office destiny on 12 July 2013*. I knew that this was unconventional fare for Bollywood: a script every studio had turned down. Also, the film was quite long, all of three hours and eight minutes—the length of almost two films put together.

256   We arranged a screening for the inspiration behind the film, the real Milkha, in Delhi once the first print came out. There were only the three of us: Milkha, Farhan and I. He sat in the centre. Once the film was over, it was very hard to say how he felt. It must have been surreal to see your life playing out before you. He had tears in his eyes, held my hands and spoke in a choked voice, '*Beta, jitnee nafrat thi merey dil mein Pakistan ke liye, aaj saab pighal gayi*' (Son, all the hatred in my heart I held against Pakistan has melted today). I have never ever received such a compliment for my work—we had more than achieved what we started out to.

The film premiered in London on 5 July. From here, the cast flew back to promote the film in India and I took a flight to New York to hold a screening for the press on 7 July (my fiftieth birthday) at Tribeca Cinemas. The US press was brave enough to sit through a film much longer than what they were otherwise used to. Fortunately, we had an interval and a 10-minute break.

The verdict was unanimous—they loved it. That night, I kept receiving calls from back home that the industry trials were pretty successful. The best one was from Ronnie, 'The only thing I regret about *BMB* is that my name is not there as the producer.'

It ran and ran in the theatres for the next 10 weeks, breaking many records. It became a cult hit, with Farhan's face even managing to replace that of the legend Milkha Singh in history textbooks across schools. Incredible yes, but such is the fascination with cinema in India. 'Mehra, you're my Ridley Scott,' Farhan told me, like only he can.

'Mehra, you're my Ridley Scott,' Farhan told me, like only he can.

The film went on to receive the president's Gold Medal, two national awards, best film and best director. It swept all the popular awards in India and was invited for various festivals around the globe.

The media hailed the film as the father of the biopic movement in Hindi cinema, especially sports biopics. The bridge between Indian cinema and the cinema of the world was getting built, brick by brick, irrespective of art house, alternate, Indie or commercial labels. As for me, I was trying to tell the story woven around the partition of India and trying to apply a soothing balm on the open wounds that the people of both nations had nurtured for the last 70 years.

257

Daant se kaat le bijli taar
Chaba le tambe ki chhankaar
Phoonk de khud ko jwala jwala
Bin khud jale na hoye ujala
Lipat hai aag Milkha, aag Milkha, aag Milkha
Ab tu bhaag Milkha.

(Cut the electric wires with your teeth
Chew the vessel of bronze
Throw yourself into a volcano
There's no light without burning yourself
Milkha, there's fire around you
Just run, Milkha.)

—*Bhaag Milkha Bhaag*

CHAPTER 47

The Business
of the Box Office

The success of BMB *was very important for me. Besides giving me* wings to experiment with my craft further, it also gave me a lot of love from the people.

A few years later, I was returning home from Italy, where I was invited for the inauguration of the National Museum of Cinema in Turin. It was an Air France flight via Paris. For some reason, the flight was grounded due to technical reasons and we were off loaded. There was some chaos, and the authorities were not able to give us a sense of when we would be able to fly out again. There was an Indian couple travelling on the same route, who recognized me. They went to the airline office and insisted that I be treated well. The airline authorities organized for me to have a shower. The family told me to sleep and that they would let me know when the flight took off.

At the end of the flight, the couple came and introduced themselves. Every compliment was about my work. 'We love your films,' they said. Then they added, 'Please carry on doing what you are doing. Don't worry about hits or flops; we relate to your work even after a few years.' The wife went on to say her favourite, among all my films, is *Delhi-6* and not *RDB* or *BMB*.

I don't know if I managed to hide my tears. Many people in India and around the world have shared the same sentiment with me. I had managed to make a box office blockbuster *BMB* after *Delhi-6*

259

had not done well. The best of us know that if we don't deliver at the box office we will become irrelevant to the market. However, the audience is more discerning today than they were in the '80s or the '90s. They have access to more mediums to watch your film: television, satellite, digital platforms. They also have unlimited access to regional and world cinema, not to mention mini series and serials that run for many seasons.

But audiences in India are also driven somewhat by the star system. They go to the theatres to watch their favourite stars, not necessarily an actor but an entertaining star performer. Great actors have been able to balance the actor and the performer and win hearts. But for me as a director, the journey is very different; it's more internalized and yearning for the limelight is not the main motive. There is a sense of massive responsibility about what one is feeding the audiences. There is always a fight to be true to yourself, your own sensibilities and your own conviction to stay original.

As a creator, you cannot let down those who give you the tools to create, who have believed in your vision in the first place.

The catch is that filmmaking is an expensive proposition and there is a studio or a producer who has invested and trusted you. As a creator, you cannot let down those who give you the tools to create, who have believed in your vision in the first place. The challenge for me has always been to create something new, something original—cinema that can stand the test of time. I have searched and found my answer—I remind myself constantly that I will pursue all these virtues attached to cinema without compromising and yet try and create cinema that reaches the masses, not just in India but all over the world.

For this, I have to give myself 'permission to fail', which again is a contradiction to the box office diktats. It was not going to be easy, but when was it ever easy? Our Hindi movies at large were escapist fares. And since the time the hero started dancing in the mid-'60s, the stories have been a blend of drama, music, comedy, romance and some action, miraculously all in the same film.

But all my successes have been unconventional because somewhere I could connect with my audiences; they had always supported me whenever I tried something new, irrespective of my success or failure. And the success I achieved with *BMB* gave me the freedom me to make my first musical, very different than any film I had made before.

261

Official poster of *Mirzya*
Courtesy: ROMP Pictures

Mirzya

*

―――――――――――――――――――――――

Ye Waadiyan Doodhiya Kohre Ki,
Inmein Sadiyaan Behti Hain
Marta Nahi Ishq O Mirza...
Sadiyon Sahiban Rehti Hain.

(These dense, milky fog–filled valleys,
Have witnessed the passage of time.
But love is immortal, O Mirza.
And so is Sahiban!)

—*Mirzya*

―――――――――――――――――――――――

CHAPTER 48

The Legend of Mirza–Sahiban

I had read the story of Mirza–Sahiban in my college days and was attracted to the idea of an unexpected kind of love story. It is a folklore that is etched into the consciousness of Punjab, Kashmir and the North West Frontier Province (now in Pakistan). As the legend goes, Sahiban's family was opposed to her romance with Mirza. When she elopes with him on her wedding day, her brothers follow in hot pursuit. After riding hard for three days and two nights, they paused to rest under a tree. Dead tired, they both fell asleep. Then Sahiban has a dream where Mirza shoots and kills her brothers one by one. She wakes up re-living the nightmare again and again in her mind.

Then she acts on impulse, caught between her family and her beloved, breaks the arrows of her lover, the ace marksman Mirza, to protect her brothers. When Mirza wakes up to the hoof beats of the approaching posse of Sahiban's brothers, he senses immediate danger and picks up his bow, only to discover that all his arrows are lying scattered and broken into two pieces.

He looks at Sahiban, in abject disbelief. The only question he has: 'Why? Why did you do it?' The unarmed Mirza is lynched and murdered by Sahiban's brothers.

This was a tragedy of Shakespearean proportions. It was the kind of betrayal that could shatter a person completely. What made Sahiban do this?

This gave rise to the question that drove me to attempt this story: 'Why do we hurt those whom we love the most?'

I approached Gulzar.

Me: *Sahiban ne Mirza ke teer kyun tode the?* (Why did Sahiban break Mirza's arrows?)

Gulzar: *Yeh toh Sahiban se hi poocho.* (Why don't you ask Sahiban herself?)

Me: *Mein bahut dinon se dhoond raha hoon! Woh toh mil hi nahi rahi hai!* (I've been looking for her for many days! She has been eluding me!)

Gulzar: *Chalo saath-saath dhoondtey hain!* (Then let's search for her together!)

That sums up my proposal and Gulzar Sahab's acceptance to write the legend of Mirza–Sahiban, with music by none other than SEL.

Gulzar took his time. He was returning to screenplay writing after a gap of 17 years. His last film as screenwriter had been *Hu Tu Tu* (1999). A few months later, I received his version of Mirza–Sahiban, seductively titled 'Mirzya'. He set up three worlds in *Mirzya*: one in current times, the other in an earlier era and the third of gypsy narrators. It was an intricate plot—the trio of the folklore, modern story and the gypsy's tale, all converge towards the end.

The folklore version of *Mirzya* is a story in silence, narrated visually, set in a time you cannot define. It was both surreal and captivating. The present-day version is set in Rajasthan and this time Suchitra or Suchi (Saiyami Kher) is stuck between two lovers, Adil Mirza (Harshvardhan Kapoor) and Prince Karan (Anuj Choudhry).

The character of Adil, at the age of 11, accidentally shoots his school teacher point-blank. He simply cannot tolerate that the teacher has punished and whipped his love, Suchi. Gulzar captured this beautifully:

This was a tragedy of Shakespearean proportions.

Hota hai, hota hai,
Ishq mein aksar hota hai
Chot kaheen lagti hai jaakar
Zakhm kaheeen par hota hai.

(It often happens,
in love it often happens
that someone is hurt,
and someone else suffers the wound.)

I was in thrall of Gulzar Sahab's writing. I thought about the time when years ago, during my ad agency days, I had wanted Gulzar to write Devdas for me as my first movie. Twenty-five years later, he gave me the script called 'Mirzya'. I was filled with gratitude and reminded him playfully:

'*Gulzar Sahab, aapko yaad hai 25 saal pehley bhi ek ladka aaya tha "Devdas" lekar?*' (Gulzar Sahab, do you remember that 25 years ago, a boy had come to you with a request to write Devdas?)

He indulged me again, '*Bachchu dadhee bada lene se, tum ne socha mein pechan nahi paunga?*' (Son, just because you have grown a beard, you thought I would not recognize you?)

Gulzar says:

How can you forget a man like Rakeysh? He is ambitious, he falls in love with what he's doing. He's a go-getter. I still remember the boy who came to me and said he's from advertising. He had an infectious confidence and I could see that the possibility of failing was not something he was considering at all.

Sense of humour is like ventilation in a room. When Rakeysh and I get together, we do leave a room well-ventilated. Part of the charm of working with Rakeysh is his intelligence. It was a pleasure to write *Mirzya*, though I felt heartbroken when it didn't do well at the box office. Maybe I let him down.

CHAPTER 49

High Notes
of a Musical

Mirzya was not an easy film to execute: the structure was something I had never attempted or even seen before. There was no precedent or a reference point; we had to create everything from scratch. A major part of the film was silent. The characters in the folklore did not have a single dialogue. It was going to be very challenging for the actors, as both Harshvardhan and Saiyami (though she made her debut in the 2015 Telugu film, *Rey,* this was her first Hindi film) were debutants. They had performed brilliantly in their auditions and rehearsals, along with the talented Anuj Choudhry, who plays the third part of the triangle. Exceptional artists like Anjali Patil, Om Puri, K.K Raina and Art Malik joined in as the support cast. All had decades of theatre and cinema between them.

Binod Pradhan had to drop out to direct his own debut film. Paweł Dyllus from Poland stepped in to fill his shoes. Paweł and I immediately hit it off. We had a few loves in common—Krzysztof Kieślowski, a glass of vintage red wine and cheese.

It was a new approach for both of us and our first project together. But on the second day of the shoot, there was such a shared passion towards creating something original that it felt like our tenth film together. Paweł tested various formats and lenses. We were sure that we wanted to create a special look for our movie. Adam Mendry and Shamak (operative cameramen) from his team joined the Indian crew a few days before the shoot. Danny Baldwin, the action director from Australia, was assisted by Indian counterpart Manohar Varma for all the horse stunts. My trusted Allan Amin choreographed the rest of the action.

The visual expression of the film, put together by the world-class team, was fluid and seamless. The most interesting were the mounted archers from Eastern Europe who joined the crew one month before the principal shooting.

Raju Sundaram and Mayuri formed a team to choreograph the dances. We rehearsed at Mayuri's studio in Bengaluru for a month with fusion dancers. Pranav Shukla was on sound design, Niharika Bhasin did the wardrobe and Vikram Dada, who had been my collaborator from my first film, styled the make-up and hair. Sumeet Basu re-imagined the production design (my second film with him after *BMB*). Yatharth was the first assistant director and Shyam was the co-producer along with Bharathi and Rajiv Tandon as producers.

Mirzya opens with dazzling sweeping shots of Rajasthan and Ladakh, immediately foretelling a grand, epic romance. We shot the film across Ladakh, the barren desert of Nubra Valley and Pangong Lake; the majestic Mehrangarh fort in Jodhpur and the dunes of Jaisalmer in Rajasthan. Like any folklore, the story of Mirza–Sahiban has been passed down generations through oral tradition. I was looking for the right treatment and found inspiration in the Oscar-winning French documentary *Latcho Drom* (safe journey), which was set in the universe of the gypsies of Rajasthan. *Latcho Drom* captures the journey of the Romany nomadic people told through musicians and dancers of India, Egypt, Turkey, Romania, Hungary, Slovakia, France and Spain.

So, I set the narration of the story via the gypsy ironsmiths of Rajasthan led by Mamdu (Om Puri). They form the third character in the film, singing and dancing and narrating the legend of Mirza–Sahiban.

We also sought traditional folk and offbeat singing voices as the narrators who serve as balladeers to supplement this. Daler Mehndi from Punjab, the Sufi musician Sain Zahoor from Pakistan, the folk singer Pathanay Khan from Balochistan on the borders of Afghanistan and the famous Sufi singers the Nooran Sisters—all rendered the folklore. The present-day voices were those of the contemporary genius Shankar himself, Siddharth Mahadevan and the classical singer Kaushiki Chakraborty.

I was completely immersed in this crazy experiment where the different art forms of cinematography, dance choreography, art direction, wardrobe design, editing and, above all, poetry and music were in a very heightened state of creation.

We spared no expense—the horses were of the highest breed and the mounted archers were from Poland and Armenia. *Mirzya* was more expensive than both *BMB* and *RDB*. From the physical production point of view, *Mirzya* was not for the weak-hearted. Imagine transporting 25 horses over the highest mountain pass in the world to shoot action sequences at 18,000 feet in sub-zero temperatures! Juxtapose this with completing the story in the scorching hot dunes of Rajasthan with a cliff hanger of a chase sequence shot in the sand.

From the physical production point of view, *Mirzya* was not for the weak hearted.

All this while, Harshvardhan, Saiyami and Anuj kept their cool. All three had to learn extreme riding, play horse polo and understand the complexity we were grappling with. Harshvardhan went a step ahead and learnt mounted archery. Later, I got to know that Harsh did not even know how to ride a bike. He had catapulted straightaway to mounted archery on horseback at breakneck speeds. I must say he put his heart and soul into the part. Anuj was extremely disciplined and has a curious approach to his role. Besides living the part, he researches extensively. He was playing a present-day, blue-blooded royal and brought immense dignity and realism to the part.

Saiyami was a constant inspiration for all: the amount of hard work she put in won everyone's heart. I still remember it was an extremely chilly night in Udaipur and we were shooting a rain sequence in Rajasthan. Saiyami had to complete a long walk in the chilly rain created artificially. It was a difficult shot and she had to repeat it a dozen times and then get into a dramatic scene with a bare-chested Harsh and end up making love. I was blown away by the unquestioning dedication and hard work the young actors were putting in. They submitted themselves to the common goal of excellence towards the cinema we wanted to achieve.

Paweł and I had established a discipline of watching the 'dailies' without fail every day. The material we were watching was very exciting. The way Bharathi put it together on the table elevated its impact. The recording for the background music went on for six months. Tubby and Parikh picked up from where SEL left and created a haunting background score.

Our labour of love, *Mirzya,* premiered at the London Film Festival and then released worldwide on 7 October 2016.

Top: Sibling—A word that comprises love, strife, protection and friendship. Enacted beautifully by Japtej Singh and Divya Dutta.

Bottom: I believe my ability to connect with and inspire children has resulted in some exceptional performances. Seen here with young Milkha played by Japtej Singh.

Top: On location at the Indo-Pak border in Hussainiwala, Ferozepur, during the making of *BMB*.

Middle: With British actor of Pakistani origin, Art Malik, in a candid frame. The film fraternity has always lived above boundaries.

Bottom: Love at its purest—The sibling revelry in *BMB* was a departure from the usual.

Top: No money for running shoes—Milkha suffers an injury as powerhouse performer Pavan Malhotra, his mentor, attends to him.
Middle: Meesha Shafi, star singer of Pakistani origin, played a cameo that got the mercury rising.
Bottom: Blasted and flabbergasted! With the young cast of the film.

Top: The classic emotional denouement—Farhan runs with his younger self Japtej Singh and unlocks the demons within.

Middle: Milkha secures top honours for India against Pakistan's Abdul Khaliq played by Dev Gill. Also in the frame are K.K. Raina and Shanta Kumar, who played Field Marshal Muhammad Ayub Khan, former president of Pakistan.

Bottom: Getting into Milkha mode as I run between two units on the sets.

Top: The team behind Farhan's transformation (L to R)—Celebrated fitness trainer Samir Jaura, athletics coach Melwyn Crasto and physiotherapist Dr Anand Kumar (standing), alongside an intensely focused Farhan.

Middle: My cameo as a pilot in the film, allaying Milkha's flying fears!

Bottom: Sonam was truly the tadka in *BMB*.

Top: Farhan's incredible training and ripped transformation was one of the key inspirations behind the film's success.

Bottom: Love's labour found in smiles—With Sonam and Farhan during the world premiere of *BMB* in London.

Yuki all the way—In front of an elevator door painted with the Japanese poster of *BMB* in Tokyo. The film was a huge success in Japan.

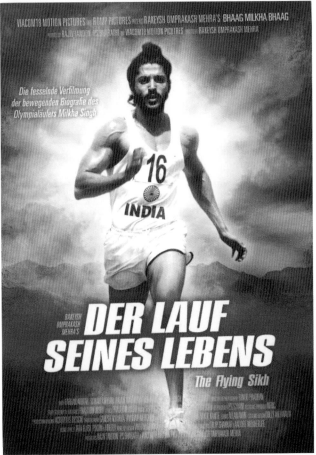

Top: Farhan and I present the *BMB* poster to Milkha Singh at PVR theatres in Delhi.
Bottom: Achtung! *BMB* breaks borders with this German poster.

भारत सरकार
Government of India

राष्ट्रीय फ़िल्म पुरस्कार
National Film Awards
2013

फ़िल्म	भाग मिल्खा भाग (हिंदी)
Film	**Bhaag Milkha Bhaag** (Hindi)
वर्ग	फ़ीचर
Section	FEATURE
पुरस्कार विजेता	निर्देशक : राकेश ओम प्रकाश मेहरा
Award Winner	Director : **Rakeysh Omprakash Mehra**
पुरस्कार	सर्वश्रेष्ठ लोकप्रिय एवं संपूर्ण मनोरंजक फ़िल्म
Award	**Best Popular Film Providing Wholesome Entertainment**

बिमल जुल्का
सचिव
सूचना और प्रसारण मंत्रालय
भारत सरकार

Bimal Julka
Secretary
Ministry of Information & Broadcasting
Government of India

Hattrick! Overcome with a feeling of gratitude, as I won the Swarna Kamal for my third consecutive film, *BMB*.

❝एक महान खिलाड़ी की जीवनगाथा और मूल्यों को समेटती हुई फ़िल्म जो सिनेमा के माध्यम से मंत्रमुग्ध करने वाली कहानी बुनती है।❞

❝For retaining the story and values of a great sportsman and translating it into the cinematic medium with aplomb. ❞

फ़िल्म समारोह निदेशालय
Directorate of Film Festivals

The citation for the film was very meaningful as well.

Top: Receiving the Swarna Kamal for *BMB* from President Pranab Mukherjee. Manish Tewari, Minister of Information and Broadcasting, and Bimal Julka, Secretary, Ministry of Information and Broadcasting, look on.

Bottom: Bharathi seen here accepting her second national award for best editing from President Pranab Mukherjee, as Manish Tewari and Bimal Julka look on. *Bhaag Milkha Bhaag* also won several popular awards.

MOMENTS
FROM *MIRZYA*

Top: Losing ourselves in art—With Saiyami Kher, Harshvardhan Kapoor
and Paweł Dyllus, as we serenade the sands.
Middle: Dilemmas of debutantes—Harshvardhan and Saiyami.
Bottom: It's the shadows that have more to say—In a pensive mood with
young Anuja and Athesham on the sets of *Mirzya*.

Top: The ill-fated marriage—A scene from *Mirzya* featuring Anuj Choudhry as the groom with Art Malik and K.K. Raina on either side.

Middle: Me, Ehsaan, Shankar, Gulzar and Loy (L to R) at a recording studio, making and celebrating music.

Bottom: With Paweł Dyllus at my favourite place—Khardungla, Ladakh, the gateway to Shyok River and Nubra Valley.

Top: Harshvardhan goes for bull's-eye.
Bottom: All is fair in love—Saiyami and Harshvardhan play star-crossed lovers in *Mirzya*.

Top: My feisty leading lady—Looking endearingly at Saiyami.
Middle: Mercy or no mercy?—Anuj Choudhry delivers the goods.
Bottom: The 'forty rules of love' confound Anjali Patil and Om Puri.

Top: Picturesque—Mounted archers from Poland make a dramatic entry.
Middle: A surreal action sequence being captured by a drone.
Bottom: An elaborate rigging of multiple cameras atop tracking vehicles on location in Rajasthan.

Top: Co-conspirators in crime—With Harshvardhan and Saiyami.

Bottom: Sonam, Harshvardhan, Saiyami, me, producer Rohit Khattar, Anil Kapoor and Art Malik (L to R) at the world premiere of *Mirzya*, which was the official selection at the London Film Festival.

CHAPTER 50

Failed Experiment or a Step Forward?

Mirzya *failed at the box office, but what was surprising was that there* was simultaneous praise from serious critics who saw it as a classic.

Journalist Catherine Sedgwick, who watched it at the London Film Festival said, 'With excellent direction, *Mirzya* is a ravishing, tour de force production and a very charming, moving piece.'*

Personally, I grew and learnt a lot.

Amitabh Bachchan was the first person to see it. He compared it to the other classic *Heer Raanjha* made by Chetan Anand. Later, he told me sagely, '*Woh bhi nahin chali thi*' (That film hadn't worked either). Atul Kulkarni came to see *Mirzya* two days in a row, and one of India's finest actors Anil Kapoor (the debutant hero Harshvardhan's father), who was hosting the shows, asked him, '*Tu phirse aa gaya?*' (You are here again?). Atul replied that once was not enough for him.

Mirzya was also a special presentation at the Chicago International Film Festival in the prestigious category of musicals of the world. Some of the greatest musicals of the world had been showcased in this segment in the years gone by. The global praise kept pouring in, with *The New York Times* calling it 'an action romance from India; a contemporary story of star-crossed lovers, which takes place both in

273

---

*Catherine Sedgwick, 'Mirzya', *The Upcoming*, 5 October 2016. Available at https://www.theupcoming.co.uk/2016/10/05/london-film-festival-2016-mirzya-review/; accessed on 29 April 2021.

the real world and in a fantastical, folkloric parallel universe.'*

Mirzya turned out to be a niche film. It was a whole new dish, a completely new narrative. In a compilation of 22 must-watch films around the world, the website Culture Trip wrote:

There's more to Indian cinema than all-singing, all-dancing Bollywood spectacles. Based on a Punjabi folk tale, Rakeysh Omprakash Mehra's *Mirzya* sees Saiyami Kher make her Hindi-language debut opposite Harshvardhan Kapoor (son of legendary actor Anil Kapoor) and proves that Indian cinema is on the rise once more. The sweeping romantic epic blends mythical elements with a modern-day love story to great effect.**

But with the catastrophic debacle of *Mirzya* at the box office, the artist in me seethed. It was like I was back at ground zero, but this time I knew that the box office, though very important, is not the ultimate milestone for a movie.

After the box office verdict was out, Ehsaan, who along with Shankar and Loy had created one of the best soundtracks and songs among all my films, said:

We know that the creative process is enhanced by success, but success cannot be the only measure of it. When we got together to brainstorm for *Mirzya*, the first sentence Rakeysh told us was, 'Let's give ourselves permission to fail on this one, guys; *Mirzya* should be remembered for its bold strokes and not for its compromises.'

Shankar added:

The three of us (SEL) believe that *Mirzya* is the best soundtrack of our lives. We never decided to play safe or recreate the normal

---

*Anita Gates, 'Fall Movie Release Schedule', *The New York Times*, 16 September 2016. Available at https://www.nytimes.com/2016/09/18/movies/fall-movie-releases-2016.html; accessed on 29 April 2021.
**Cassam Looch, '22 Must-See Films From Around The World', *Culture Trip*, 30 November 2017. Available at https://theculturetrip.com/europe/united-kingdom/england/london/articles/22-must-see-films-from-around-the-world-at-the-london-film-festival/; accessed on 29 April 2021.

stuff because if Rakeysh and Gulzar Sahab won't create magic, who will?

Loy said:

No composer, no director, no singer or even cricketer has a 100 per cent success record. We are here to create art, not just deliver hits.

Mamta, my sister, who is the dean and principal of a large school, told me, 'Maybe people couldn't fathom that the young hero could kill his teacher and not get penalized for the rest of the film.' Fair comment, but then I have taken bigger amoral leaps earlier!

The characters in *Mirzya* had shades of grey. The girl who is being dishonest with her fiancé, the prince whose love for her is like an obsession based on possession and not letting her be. On the other side is the hero who internalizes everything and suffers silently. Gypsy folksingers bring out the pathos in their predicaments. All these emotions were a new concoction for our audiences and that too narrated in a stylized way. Maybe I had stretched it too far but then what's too far? Until you try, you will never know.

In hindsight, perhaps the film was too busy—from its structure to its song score, colour palette, silences and multiple narrative strands. Maybe the audience could not submit themselves to the story.

Strangely, post *Mirzya*, I emerged stronger. The anchor that is Bharathi grounded me and the sails in her gave me wings. She has a bigger twinkle in her big eyes when I have a big idea. She understands the fun of executing a challenging idea and the beauty of the risk and has never let me compromise on my filmmaking. Perhaps she thought I was going overboard with *Mirzya*, but she understands that cinema is my religion. We don't have a deity at home; the work we do is our worship.

What *Mirzya* has taught me remains precious and unique—cinema may not be about making money but the business of cinema is about making money. I believe people who tell stories should tell it for the love of it. If I do not express myself, I will go crazy. However, I have to take the financial responsibility for my films and take my audiences along with me. So, I shared the losses with my financing

Strangely, post *Mirzya*, I emerged stronger.

producer Rohit Khattar and his Cinestaan Film Company, co-promoted by the visionary industrialist Anand Mahindra. It was important we did that for more reasons than one. The director has to take ownership of the fate of the film. As I write these lines, I'm also repaying the losses of *Mirzya*.

I went into self-introspection. Why do films work? Why don't they? The entire family takes the brunt of a flop, and yet, I want to keep experimenting. Keep trying to reach where I have not been before.

Am I hurting the people I love the most? Wasn't that what *Mirzya* was all about: the question I was trying to answer through the movie itself? Yet I couldn't recreate a popular folklore for my audiences. For me to turn around and say that 'the audience didn't understand' is a poor excuse. It's my greatest karma as a filmmaker to engage the audience.

Much later, Amala Akkineni (the actress from South India and the legend Nagarjuna's wife) called me to her film school, Annapurna College of Film and Media, in Hyderabad for a masterclass. The maximum questions I faced were about *Mirzya*. Students asked questions about the cinematic aspects and it simply blew my mind! These kids were the future filmmakers and *Mirzya* had touched them deeply.

When I returned to Mumbai, I shared the experience with my daughter Bhairavi. She was in her teens and understood success and failure; in her own signature style, without looking up from the Japanese anime series on her laptop (she watches that for 20 hours a day), she asked, 'Pa what's your next?'

The only other person who would say this to me all the time was Ronnie Screwvala. I had now made up my mind to do my first Indie film next.

276

Mr Prime Minister
Meri arzi karlo register
Dabbey lekar khadi hui
Highway par mother aur sister.

(Mr Prime Minister,
my request you must register,
Defecating by the highway
are our mother and sister.)

—*Mere Pyare Prime Minister*

Official poster of *Mere Pyare Prime Minister*
Courtesy: ROMP Pictures

Mere Pyare
Prime Minister

✳

Bharathi Mehra's
Encore

Mehra and I were on a yoyo journey. Our failures were followed by success. The debacle of *Mirzya* brought us back to square one and yet gave us hope. I remember how keen all of us were to make the film. *Mirzya* was a beautiful story.

We made a major decision, however, that we were not going to put all our eggs in one basket and keep waiting for projects to either succeed or fail every four years. At any point, we wanted to evaluate multiple scripts and have many projects on the floor.

The only way forward for us was to work ourselves out of the situation. I decided to step out of my editor's role and create a bank of content. We envisioned a project titled 'Tara', which was to kick off in 2019 but that didn't happen. But thanks to our new resolve, it wasn't the only one we were working on. We had *Toofaan*, which Rakeysh had put together with Excel Entertainment (Farhan Akhtar and Ritesh Sidhwani's boutique studio) with Farhan in the lead. The OTT platforms were already creating new opportunities for creative people and I bought the rights to two scripts and started preparing them for serialization. Mehra also envisaged 'Karna' with Shahid Kapoor. As a couple, we were firing on all cylinders.

But the important thing was to ensure that Mehra got behind the camera again—and soon. *Mere Pyare Prime Minister* was that project. Mehra did it because of his association with Yuva Unstoppable, an

As for Mehra, he was totally stepping out of his comfort zone to attempt his first Indie film.

NGO. My reasons for loving the script were completely different. Whenever there is a conversation about rape, we assume that the victim is scarred for life. In fact, we practically impose this 'scarred for life' status on the rape victim, and that other men will never see her as a suitable candidate for marriage.

In *Mere Pyare Prime Minister*, the rape victim Sargam (played by Anjali Patil) finds love again. She dares to trust a man (Pappu, played endearingly by debutant Niteesh Wadhwa) despite the horrifying experience. He too falls in love with her. There are no hackneyed lines about him accepting her, despite her rape. A lot of women want to move on after rape; it's their own families and social circles that don't allow them to. They expect her to remain shamefaced and penitent. I was sold on the idea from the get-go. As for Mehra, he was totally stepping out of his comfort zone to attempt his first Indie film.

282

CHAPTER 52

When Reel
Meets Real

I had to now go to the other end of the spectrum and make a film with little money. I wanted to re-invoke what had made me a filmmaker: my youth, my spirit and the passion to make cinema.

Now what I needed was a story. I went back to the times when we were shooting for *Delhi-6* at Film City and had a late wrap-up, at about 3 a.m. I was sleepy and tired and took the back entrance from the Film City, which is a shortcut across a slum dwelling. As my car turned the corner, a dozen odd women got up rather hurriedly. They were defecating in the darkness on the roadside. My car headlights bathed them as they were answering nature's call. The image stayed frozen in my mind forever as I hung my head in shame and looked away.

Years later, when an Ahmedabad-based NGO called Yuva Unstoppable reached out to me, I agreed to be their mentor. I was curious about their work and agreed to visit them. During the trip, I visited Gandhi ji's Sabarmati Ashram and got a glimpse into the original vision of Swachh Bharat that Gandhi ji had envisioned. At 6 a.m. in the morning, the caretaker of the Ashram was kind enough to show me around exclusively before the gates opened to the public. I was fascinated to see the various models of toilets built by the Ashram. They even had a toilet cafe where, instead of chairs, there were toilet seats. One could sit on them and enjoy a cup of coffee. The memory stayed with me.

Amitabh Shah and Parth Vasavada, the founders of Yuva Unstoppable, were doing some exceptional work but were spreading their resources too thin. I advised them to focus only on building toilets in municipal schools and slums. We also laid down an ambitious target to build 10,000 toilets over the next five years. I realized that girls were staying away from school as there were no separate toilets for boys and girls. The economics of it was quite simple: it costs 5–6 lakh per school per year to build or renovate a block of toilets with provision of water and pay for the salary of the maintenance staff. So, the next challenge was to collect funds. I ploughed back on my learnings from Janaagraha and we formed an advisory board. We started a drive to raise money and that has already contributed to about 1,000 toilet blocks so far. Friends and acquaintances like Ian Botham (Beefy's foundation), the Modrich family from the US, Bharat Shah (founder of HDFC Bank), Mohit Burman (vice-chairman of Dabur India) and V.V.S. Laxman (former Indian cricketer) stepped up. They contributed their time and experience to raise more funds.

Our work spread to Rajasthan, West Bengal, Maharashtra and Andhra Pradesh. Yuva Unstoppable grew to over a hundred thousand volunteers.

With my heightened awareness of the sanitation issue, when I was offered a story by a first-time writer from Bihar (Manoj Mairta) where an eight-year-old boy wants to build a toilet for his mother but is unable to do so as he is poor, I found it quite heart-warming. The little boy even writes a letter to the prime minister, which goes unheard.

The image of the women defecating—bathed in my car headlights—flashed across my eyes. I had to make this movie. I loved the central theme and turned the idea around its head, where the eight year old takes on the system because his mother gets raped when she goes out to answer nature's call. *

Young writer Hussain Dalal contributed to the screenplay and

---

*UNICEF figures reveal that 50 per cent of the rapes committed in India are when women go out to defecate.

Mere Pyare Prime Minister was born. The story pivots around Kannu, who writes a letter to the prime minister of India, asking him how he would have felt if his mother was raped while stepping out to relieve herself because that's what happened to his own mother. He shares that they didn't have any toilets at their slum in Mumbai and if he could help them make one. He also adds innocently that he would return the government's money when he grows up. He, along with his friends, then boards a train to Delhi to hand deliver the letter to the prime minister in person.

The exceptionally talented Anjali Patil accepted the role of the young single mother. We discovered the very sensitive eight-year-old Om Kanojia to play the son and debutant Niteesh Wadhwa completed the principal cast.

Theatre legend Makarand Deshpande stepped in, along with Rasika Agashe and Nachiket Purnapatre, into parts that lent key support. As a special appearance, Atul Kulkarni was gracious enough to do a single scene.

Pawel Dyllus came back from Poland with his team; Yeti (Yatharth Awasthi) stepped up as the chief assistant director. Abhilasha Sharma did an amazing job of the wardrobe: she brought in the realism the film needed. Pranav Shukla was the sound designer. I also got to work with the incredibly imaginative Rajat Dada as the production designer.

The image of the women defecating—bathed in my car headlights—flashed across my eyes.

285

Gulzar wrote four wonderful songs, which were composed by SEL. One of the patrons of Yuva Unstoppable financed the film. The idea was to use the film, in times to come, to raise more funds to build toilets. The budgets were limited and we approached it that way. Shooting entirely in the slums of Mumbai with a guerrilla crew, this was my first film outside the studio system and we completed the principal shoot in 36 days.

This film presented an opportunity to me to reinvent myself and to tell a poignant story that was socially relevant with very little resources at hand. It liberated me from the commercial pressures of Bollywood.

The slums of Mumbai, which are spread on hill tops, were not easy to shoot in. I must confess that it was by far my most difficult film to execute, but the cast and crew were totally immersed in it. The climax was filmed in an actual drainage, which was clogged with human waste and infested with pigs and god knows what! The reason to make this film was larger than all of us.

The ordinary Indian slum dwellers—the have-nots who occupy the lowest strata of our society—opened the doors of their hearts. They welcomed us and the shoot was exciting. Their 10 x 10 shanties became our makeup rooms; they cooked food for us, acted in the film and became an extended production crew. Once the filming was over, I took my team from Yuva to build toilets in the slums and the municipal school out there. That was my way to thank them.

The world premiere of the film was held at the Rome International Film Festival, in the same year that they showcased Martin Scorsese's retrospective. The Western audience could relate to the plight of the slum dwellers; the never-ending standing ovation still reverberates in my thoughts.

The film opened across very limited screens but soon found its way to Netflix. Most importantly, it's doing its job to raise awareness and funds for the NGO. It took me 18 months to make it, but when I look back, it remains as one of the most satisfying journeys in my career as a filmmaker.

It was like an interval, a mid-point for me in my journey as a director: a frugal, creative exploration sans box-office pressure.

Anjali Patil
in first person

Early in my life, I knew that cinema and I were joined at the hip. I was studying acting and direction in drama school when *RDB* had just released. It wasn't just another film: it *happened* to us, to all of us. The passion with which *RDB* was made coursed through our veins like blood. It was a perfect amalgamation of the time, the youth, and the idea. My classmates and I were literally 'on fire'.

I fell in love with this original brand of cinema and hunted out *Aks*, another film that had the same maker's name. I was deeply moved by this person who was fearless and making cinema without bothering about the consequences.

After my graduation, I moved to the NSD for direction and design. Then *Delhi-6* happened. I could relate to the layers, the teasing with the timeline and the liberties. The director's dreamscape crossed reality again and again. My classmates and I found hope. We were not alone.

There was this authentic master named Rakeysh Omprakash Mehra who was doing crazy things with cinema, pushing the limits. He had created space for us to express ourselves. Formula was dead. There was room for individual original styles in Hindi cinema that could breathe, find some room. We didn't have to conform.

The struggle of humanity is often the desire to do something substantial, say something meaningful. Rakeysh Sir had created songs that could be heard when people were going through this struggle. You could celebrate so many moments of your life with him.

One of the things you do as a student is to watch cinema and study different styles. At NSD, we studied text, a lot of plays from geographically diverse literary foundations. We watched films—French, German, Russian—and we also learnt about dance and drama— classical and western adaptations, Greek theatre, etc. My roommate in those days was Archana Shinde, who went on to study filmmaking and editing at UCLA. Our favourite pastime in those days was to discuss Rakeysh Sir's films, despite the plethora of choices available. Funnily enough, we didn't need jargon—or couldn't use the existing ones, at least. We always struggled to find new ways to describe it.

287

Mere Pyare Prime Minister

In 2013, I worked on a Telugu film, *Naa Bangaaru Talli*, for which I received the National Film Award (special mention). This was when I first set eyes on Rakeysh Sir. It was at the Delhi airport parking lot and he had come to collect his national award for *BMB*. I stood frozen when I saw him. Later at the function, I had no courage to introduce myself to him. I was just happy to be around him.

Suddenly, one day I got a message on Facebook that ROMP Pictures was looking for Anjali Patil.

I wondered what to do, besides being excited, of course. I wrote an email to Rakeysh Sir, 'I saw you at the national awards; heard that someone from your production house is looking for me.'

He responded, 'Let's meet.'

I went to meet him in his now iconic Pali Village office. We spoke about many things and the casting director of *Mirzya* explained that they were considering me for the part of Zeenat.

There was a look test and auditions: the role was quite small. But I wanted to do a Rakeysh Omprakash Mehra film. It was an adolescent dream come true. To prepare for my role, I was asked to study the book *The Forty Rules of Love* by Elif Shafak.

What I saw during the making of *Mirzya* made me understand why he could produce the kind of cinema that we enjoyed. He allows you to be, thus making room for every actor to perform. He's so particular about each detail, but that's something you have to understand, not something he will tell you. Whatever his vision, he gives time to the other person to arrive to that point. He allows everyone to go through their journey. Whenever we met away from the sets, we would speak about life, art and our relationship with it. I was always happy.

On my last day on the sets of *Mirzya*, he said, '*Abhi aur bahut kaam karna baaki hai*' (There is a lot left to do).

At that time, I didn't know that Rakeysh Sir does not say empty things. He always follows up on a commitment. When I was going to the Berlin International Film Festival with *Newton*, he gave me the script of *Mere Pyare Prime Minister* to read on the flight. I was going to do the film anyway. The day we started work on the film was the same day I saw him for the first time at Delhi airport—just a different year.

Rakeysh Sir's presence itself has been a blessing for me. I have something visceral within me that I can share with him. Talking to him, whenever I return from some travel or exploration, helps me express myself better. He understands my struggle, and both of us try to match our artistic sense with the marketing aspect of Bollywood. A sensitive man like him understands that even our shadows talk back to us. I wish we see the day that Rakeysh Sir's competition does not have to be with the box office but with the next dimension of creative success, untampered by commercial pressures. We cannot afford to lose a purist like him. I want to give something back to him—maybe the performance of a lifetime!

CHAPTER 53

Rekindling
My Own Childhood

I had a whole new realization when I was working with kids: their innocence and playfulness energized me. Om Kanojiya, the child who played Kannu, told my co-author:

> After the audition, we were called for a meeting at Rakeysh Sir's office. My father was very nervous. At the office, I saw posters of some of my favourite films: *RDB* and *BMB*. I got excited. But Rakeysh Sir mischievously pulled my ears very hard: they became red and that made me upset at first. Then he took me to the fridge where he had stocked lots of goodies, which he offered with a smile.

Only a child can tell you playfully and sincerely at the same time, that they've had enough shooting for a day. Even if they were a little tired, my crew would simply pack up.

Om adds:

> I never heard him say, 'We have to finish this scene today.' We were pampered, treated like kings on the sets and our director loved us! We worked when we felt like and rest of the time, we would be having fun. Then one day, he announced a prize: a drone for whichever child behaved the best. We had to reach a thousand points to win the drone, and it was incentive enough for all of us to behave. Directors are always stressed! Rakeysh Sir

was so cool! Also, we would get whatever we wanted: chips, milkshakes, chocolate biscuits, juices. It was the hot summer, after all.

Another child artist, Adarsh Bharati, who auditioned for two parts, Kannu and Ringtone, but got selected to play the latter, says:

Rakeysh Sir knows how to make everyone feel special— that's his biggest gift.

> Rakeysh Sir became my best friend! He's a very simple man with no attitude. Everyone was kind. There was Pranav Bhaiya (Pranav Shukla); Vicky Bhaiya, our spot dada; Yatharth Bhaiya and Abhilasha Didi (Abhilasha Sharma). After pack-up, we would go and sit with them, have snacks and then leave.

Om finally saw the film when it was screened for Sadhguru (profound and pragmatic yogi, mystic, visionary and spiritual master, he is one of the most influential seers in India) in Coimbatore, with a crowd of more than 2,000 people.

Om recalls:

> My mom had also come. Sadhguru congratulated me, removed the *mala* (garland) from around his neck and put it around mine. I felt like a celebrity; even Juhi Chawla ma'am (celebrated actress) was there. But at least for five minutes, I felt like I was the biggest celebrity in the room because all the attention was on me. Rakeysh Sir knows how to make everyone feel special—that's his biggest gift.

Atul Kulkarni
a reprise

I was so happy to be a small part of *Mere Pyare Prime Minister* because, with Rakeysh, one keeps going back to do good work. There's never a full stop.

Part of the excitement to work with Rakeysh is that he shoots each film differently, despite the DoP. He knows so much about the technicalities and about the character that you have to do your homework even to perform. And he looks straight at you, not into the monitor.

> **Part of the excitement to work with Rakeysh is that he shoots each film differently, despite the DoP. He knows so much about the technicalities and about the character that you have to do your homework even to perform.**

When the script first came to me, he wanted me to play Makarand Deshpande's role. I was not able to give the dates, but he insisted. Then he asked me for a day to shoot a critical scene where I play an official from the prime minister's office, who interacts with the kids.

Whether it was Gobar's role in *Delhi-6* or Laxman Pandey in *RDB*, I have seen a family environment on his sets. This is very important because actors sometimes feel uprooted; we are like nomads. We are in one tent for a period of time and then another tent, depending on the length of the role. Feeling like family is critical to the atmosphere Rakeysh is able to weave on the sets.

Rakeysh is also a great producer: he gives so much that he demands a very high level of art in return. Also, on his sets, you will find that all actors are thinking about how to support him as a producer because here's a man who's not doing it for the money anyway! How many directors have made more than three films that change the way an entire generation thinks?

I am waiting for my next casting call from Rakeysh.

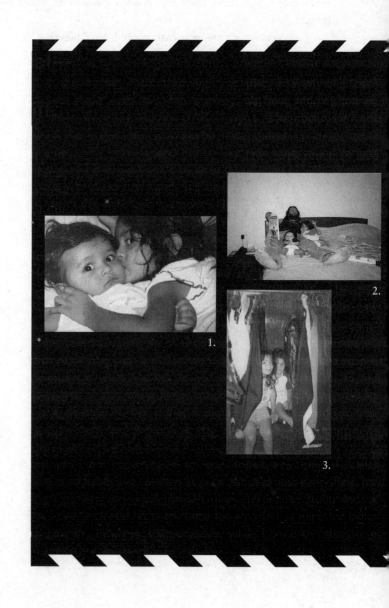

1.

2.

3.

Bhairavi
in first person

Papa and I are similar in many ways. We have the same nose: big, a little wide. Brinjal noses, as named by Mamma. We like our chocolate dark and our coffee black. We are both messy, clumsy people. We spill our drinks and trip on flat ground; our thoughts are always somewhere else. We both love stories. We see them everywhere: the morning news, overheard conversations at the vegetable bazaar, the walk of a stranger we pass on the street, the fables passed down from our grandparents and childhood memories. We believe that stories can be powerful.

When I was small, I was afraid of the dark. Every night, Papa's stories would lull me to sleep. My brother, Vedant, and I were often characters in them. He would take fragments from our lives and transform them. A simple morning walk to the school bus stop became a sci-fi adventure, a race to get to school while battling aliens and monsters. Other times, he would tell us stories of him and Mamma. How, when she was injured from an accident and bedridden, he knocked on countless doors trying to find her apartment simply to deliver a single rose and a 'get well soon' message and their blissful days chasing out cockroaches in their creaky, cramped one-room apartment. Papa is a die-hard romantic and so am I.

As I was mulling over what to write about in this chapter, I realized a lot of things about my upbringing that I hadn't been conscious of before. Growing up, even at the ages of 11 or 13, Papa would always consult me like he would consult a peer. Whether it was the songs for his movies, story ideas or screenplay drafts, he would ask me what I thought about them and how I was affected. Papa wanted to stretch his audience as wide as possible for his work to impact the old, the young, those in-between and even children who aren't quite fully formed people yet. That's what made his stories powerful. He didn't just teach me how to love stories and how to search for them in the mundane but also how to think stories through and reconstruct them and how to make them accessible to all.

Papa and I are both stubborn people. We fight sometimes. Along with Vedant, we often argue about our perspectives and beliefs at the dinner table. Even when we all butt heads, we influence each other. Every time I visit home after a few months at college, I notice that the basis of our arguments has shifted ever so slightly. Even if we disagree, we've incorporated a bit of each other into our own worldview. Growing up, I used to wish that we could just have a quiet meal and talk about simple things like the weather or the sitcom we watched the other night. Papa does not like to spend time on frivolous, empty things. He doesn't cushion his words, or his truth, just because it is different from those around him.

And the best thing about him is that Papa always bounces back. He bounced back from *Delhi-6*, whose failure took a toll on his spirit, by creating *BMB*. Again, *Mirzya* may not have been practical but the experiment was personally meaningful to Papa. And that kind of artistic integrity, the desire to communicate in a new way, is something we can understand. I like that he does not forcefully separate his emotions from his truth. That's what makes his stories so powerful. They are stories of the heart, filled with the feelings and experiences he has drawn from those around him. Papa is the best storyteller I know and, someday, I hope to be one like him too.

Vedant
in first person

I vaguely remember Papa throwing me into a swimming pool when I was three years old. No warning, no float and, of course, no permission from my mother. While I don't remember whether I conquered the water or it conquered me, I never seem to forget the value the story holds for me today. That was my first and earliest introduction to Papa's passionate belief in taking leaps of faith. Growing up, I have witnessed first-hand this unwavering belief being put to the test: from old childhood memories like my first swim to present-day, important decisions about choosing which story to tell the world next on the silver screen. I've always wondered what gave him the confidence to make such decisions.

'Always trust your instincts,' he would say. Nowadays, as I watch and try to learn about my parents' work more keenly, I understand better the barrage of crucial, complicated and time-crunched decisions that directors and producers face. Sometimes, Papa is at a crossroads. Be it about developing scripts or choosing the right project to pursue, he has to walk one path and abandon the other. He has shown me through example what 'instinct' is and why I should trust it. To my father, 'instinct' is not some fancy, magical spell that only Himalayan monks are capable of, but rather a simple feeling in your gut that doesn't allow outsiders to confuse you and grants you greater self-awareness the more you embrace it.

Papa and I are no strangers to long, sometimes tiring, debates. While we're together, we're often at odds about almost everything: his unending optimism vs my calculated realism, his infinite stubbornness vs my relative flexibility, his preference for emotion vs mine for logic. The list goes on. However, paradoxically, while I am with others, my behaviour mirrors my father's instead.

According to my friends, I adopt all of his stubbornness, idealism and penchant for emotion. Ever since realizing that I am subconsciously inspired by his worldview, the one that would often annoy me endlessly at the dinner table, I have grown to admire it hundredfold. His perspectives on giving yourself permission to fail, respecting nature's will and energy, challenging the system and countless more have been ingrained in me, regardless of how much logic and rationality I throw at him in our many heated debates. Papa is my fiercest rival but also my most trusted mentor.

Papa and I are very fluid with each other. There are never any filters, rules or traditional father–son barriers during our conversations. For years now, he has been telling me to see him as a friend and not a father because of how much he dislikes people who are always forcing children to fit some kind of mould or do things they don't like to do. Honestly speaking, I am grateful for the freedom that my parents have given me growing up and a large part of that comes from Papa always encouraging me to take my own, independent decisions, regardless of whether I fail or not.

Sharp instincts, unique perspectives and confident determination: all are a part of how I see Papa as an individual. Yet, none of them are the strongest of all his distinctive qualities. What I respect above all in my father is the importance he gives to family. While Bhairavi and I were growing up, Papa was extremely busy. He worked long hours and would often be back from the office late at night while we were sound asleep. Still, despite his gruelling working hours, he would always try his best to set aside time purely for family.

Most Sundays, despite having meetings to plan for or colleagues to talk to, we would go for brunch and a swim to Otters Club. On days we didn't, he would teach us how to cook for long hours at home (Papa is notorious for making his food insanely spicy, which is the only reason I can tolerate almost any spice nowadays). Beyond that, he'd always be planning at the back of his mind about the next time we could spend a weekend at our home in Pawna, giving us little reminders here and there every few hours near a free weekend. For him, family time is family time and absolutely nothing else. I have never seen him pick up a work call or reply to a text message while he's spending time with us.

Even if he does falter in some ways, I have faith that he will always bounce back when it's for family. Watching his commitment to us makes me believe that strength does not just come from family, but family itself is the embodiment of strength.

The only person we need to change is the one whose face we see in the mirror every morning!

AB MERI SUN
अब मेरी सुन

Tune apni karli manmaani,
Ab meri sun,
Tune duniya ki
Duniya ne teri,
Har baat hai maani,
Ab meri baari, ab meri sun.
Tu duniya se, duniya tere se,
Mein tere se,
Kya tu mere se?
Ab meri baari, ab meri sun.
Mein vahi hoon, mein yahi hoon.
Taak mat, dekh.
Mere andhar jhaank.
Aeena dekh
Mein tere andhar rehta hoon.
Ab meri baari, ab meri sun!

(The poem describes the conflict between the two voices within
each of us.
You've always had your way!
Its my turn!
Am I always to listen?
And never speak?
As you hold the world in thrall!
Am I subjugated? Meek?
I 'am' because you 'are'
Are you because I am?
Do you see me?
In you?
As your reflection?
I am within you.
And I speak for you. Its my turn!)

—Rakeysh Omprakash Mehra

Mirrors

Me: Who are you?
Mirror: 'I' am you.

Me: Yeah! I look like you!
Mirror: I 'am' you.

Me: Why do you feel like a stranger?
Mirror: I am 'you'!

In my dreams, often I see multiples of myself. While they are all flying around, the real me is anchored to the ground, my feet feel heavy and I am not able to move. I want to wake up but I am not able to.

And then I have dreams when I am alone and flying over buildings, rivers and mountain ranges, even in space sometimes. I wake up with a smile.

'I' am what I am. And I can stare into the mirror, look deep inside me and meet my soul, and I become one with myself. It is almost like an out-of-body experience. Many a times, when I am shooting, I get the same feeling. I watch myself playing the director.

There is a movie outside the movie I am making. I don't even know how I will frame my next shot. So, I let go of the feeling of wanting to know. Suddenly, the creation becomes seamless.

And in this process of creation, mirrors have always fascinated me. There was a scene in *Mughal-e-Azam* when Anarkali, the courtesan-dancer, defies Emperor Akbar and expresses her love for Prince Salim. She dances her heart out. The scene is set in Sheesh Mahal (the hall of mirrors), where the ceiling is made of thousands of mirrors. These reflect over thousands of images of Anarkali and her rebellion.

It is a captivating scene, not just in imagery but in the overpowering impact it has on Emperor Akbar, the most powerful man in the world, who feels trapped by an ordinary courtroom dancer.

Mirrors are more than a way to check your make-up. They reveal the innards of your soul.

I have included scenes with mirrors subconsciously into my films as a visual metaphor. Whenever my character faces the ultimate challenge, he/she finds it first in their reflection in the mirror. Because at some point, the only person you are competing with is yourself and this feeling always finds its place in my films.

In *BMB*, the athlete Milkha is India's hope for a medal at the 1956 Melbourne Olympics. But when Milkha meets the gorgeous Stella Hamilton, he submits to a night of beer and light-headed revelry. With just four days left for the race, he misses and turns up late for practice and continues to be besotted by her.

Viewers are aware that Milkha has gotten this far by sheer grit and talent. They see him lose focus. As the race begins, Milkha starts strong but does not have the stamina or single-minded determination to finish first. In fact, he finishes a disgraceful fourth. He lets down his teammates, his coach and his country.

After the race, Milkha stands in consternation before a mirror. He looks at the other Milkha in the reflection—the one who lost the race, the one who let his country and himself down. He does not like this other Milkha so he slaps him, slapping himself on the face again and again! On his face, the audience can see fury and repentant realization as he slaps himself hard repeatedly.

As the mirror reveals to Milkha that he's the only one to blame, he apologizes to Stella and owns up that it's not her fault, it's his. This is the apology that frees him up to heal.

In *Mirzya*, the two star-crossed lovers are destined never to build a life together. A terrible crime separates lovers Adil and Suchi in their adolescence. Many years later, Adil works as a stable hand, while Suchi is on the cusp of marrying Prince Karan, who also happens to be Adil's employer.

While learning horse riding, Suchi realizes that Adil is her childhood love. This realization heralds an avalanche of emotions. Fate has thrown them together again. But Adil reminds her that they can never be together: he's just an escaped convict who murdered his own school teacher and she's engaged to a prince. They couldn't possibly have a future together.

She is torn by emotions, and rushes home and faces the mirror. The Suchi in the mirror shows the Suchi outside the mirror the tattoo on her bare shoulders, the tattoo both she and Adil had got done together as kids. Their childhoods and their shared love bring tears to her eyes as she allows herself to cry.

The Suchi in the mirror is silently egging the real life Suchi to stand up for her love.

In the middle of this moment of naked honesty, Prince Karan joins her in peering into the mirror. The duplicity and dishonesty of marrying one man while being in love with another hits her hard. Suchi turns around and cements this duplicity by hugging Karan and saying, 'I love you.'

We know this love story is destined to be tragic.

This is the lie, this is the truth, this is the contradiction that the mirror just exposed.

In *RDB*, the mirror played a simpler metaphor. Once the boys agree to act in Sue McKinley's documentary *The Young Guns of India*, they have to go through rehearsals and transform their look to get into the character of the early 1920s. This is a period of change and transformation, not just physically but metaphysically. In the reflection, we see the stages of their physical transformation, and in real life, we can observe their own.

I have used the mirror to express my anger and anguish at society at large in *Delhi-6*.

There is a fakir in the film who carries a mirror every time he appears on screen and shows it to the characters saying, *'Jhaankh le'* (Take a look). The residents of Delhi-6 dismiss him as a tramp. Later, the neighbourhood gets divided along communal lines. Roshan Mehra, who is half-Hindu and half-Muslim, is caught in between this madness. He takes the mirror from the fakir and shows it to key characters who have now divided themselves to Hindu mobs and Muslim mobs.

He tells them that in the same mirror, they will each find their God—Hindu's will find their Bhagwan and Muslims will find their Allah. The Almighty is inside us and does not reside in a mosque or a temple, so what are we fighting about?

Humans seem to get agitated and become communal at the slightest provocation. So, is this agitated and provoked character dormant within us and a part of who we are?

When the pretence drops, does the mirror show us who we actually are? The end credits of the film were like a curtain call in the theatres. Each cast member appears in a reflection, projecting a part of themselves: in each of the characters we see ourselves reflected somewhere.

The music of *Delhi-6* was exceptional, so even the music CD had a real mirror embedded on its cover. It was my naive attempt to show it to society at large.

But it was *Aks* that probably had the most complex interpretation of the idea of reflection. The Hindi word 'aks' itself means reflection.

The film starts with the assassination of the Indian defence minister in Budapest. The assassin, Raghavan, disguises himself as Manu Varma, the chief of the minister's security. He actually wears Varma's face mask and murders the minister.

The killer Raghavan is on the run, but Verma catches him. The justice is fast and swift and Raghavan walks to the gallows. Just before he is to be hanged, he tries to escape, and in a dramatic moment, both killer and cop shoot each other.

It's a paranormal moment: the killer dies but his soul manifests itself in Verma's body. Now the evil has the best address in town—he is in the good man's body. Manu Varma, the good guy, turns evil. The killer's soul continues his reign of murder and mayhem, even raping his own wife.

When Manu Varma looks into the mirror, there is Raghavan looking back at him.

Because Raam and Raavan, all reside inside us. Ask the mirror and it will show you because every morning, I see myself as completely new in front of the mirror.

Who is that stranger in the mirror?

Filmography
(as Writer, Director and Producer)

1. *Mamuli Ram: The Little Big Man* (1996)

2. *Aks* (2001)
   Production: AB Corp and Flicks Motion Pictures Company
   Director: Rakeysh Omprakash Mehra
   Written by: Renzil D'Silva, Kamlesh Pandey and Rakeysh Omprakash Mehra
   Dialogues: Kamlesh Pandey
   Lyrics: Gulzar
   Director of Photography: Kiran Deohans
   Production Designer: Samir Chanda
   Action: Allen Amin
   Sound Design: Ranjit Barot
   Re-recording Mixer: Hitendra Ghosh
   Choreography: Raju Sunderam
   Casting Director, Editor and Associate Director: P.S. Bharathi
   Costume: Nakul Sen and Theia Tekchandaney
   Make-up: Vikram Gaikwad
   Hair: Jaya Surve
   VFX Supervisor: Paul Sims
   Prosthetics: Nick Dudman

3. *Rang De Basanti* (2006)
    Production: UTV Motion Pictures and ROMP Pictures
    Director: Rakeysh Omprakash Mehra
    Producers: Ronnie Screwala and Rakeysh Omprakash Mehra
    Co-produced by: Zarina Mehta and Deven Khote
    Creative Producer: P.S. Bharathi
    Executive Producers: P.S. Shyam, Adam Bowling and David Reid
    Associate Producer: Ram Mirchandani
    Written by: Kamlesh Pandey, Rensil D'Silva and Rakeysh Omprakash Mehra
    Director of Photography: Binod Pradhan
    Music: A.R. Rahman
    Lyrics: Prasoon Joshi
    Editor: P.S. Bharathi
    Production Designer: Samir Chanda
    Action: Allan Amin
    Sound Designer and Sound Mixing: Nakul Kamte
    Choreography: Raju Sunderam, Vaibhavi Merchant and Ganesh Acharya
    Costume: Loveleen Bains and Arjun Basin
    Hair: Avan Contractor (BBlunt)
    Make-up: Vikram Gaikwad and Arun Seal
    VFX Supervisor: Pankaj Khandpur

4. *Delhi-6* (2009)
    Production: UTV Motion Pictures and ROMP Pictures
    Director: Rakeysh Omprakash Mehra
    Producers: Ronnie Screwala and Rakeysh Omprakash Mehra
    Co-produced by: P.S. Bharathi, Zarina Mehta, Deven Khote and Siddharth Roy Kapur
    Executive Producer: Smita Bhaliga
    Story: Rakeysh Omprakash Mehra
    Screenplay: Kamlesh Pandey, Prasoon Joshi and Rakeysh Omprakash Mehra
    Director of Photography: Binod Pradhan
    Editor: P.S. Bharathi
    Music: A.R. Rahman

Lyrics: Prasoon Joshi
Production Designer: Samir Chanda
Sound Design: Nakul Kamte
Re-recording Mixer: Anup Dev
Choreography: Vaibhavi Merchant and Saroj Khan
Costume: Arjun Bhasin and Anamika Khanna
Make-up: Vikram Gaikwad
Hair: Avan Contractor (BBlunt)
VFX Supervisor: Craig Mumma

5. *Teen Thay Bhai* (2011) (as producer)

6. *Bollywood: The Greatest Love Story Ever Told* (2011)

7. *Bhaag Milkha Bhaag* (2013)
Production: Viacom 18 and ROMP Pictures
Director: Rakeysh Omprakash Mehra
Producer: Rajiv Tandon, P.S. Bharathi and Viacom 18
Co-producer: P.S. Shyam
Executive Producer: Shivaji Dasgupta
Screenplay and Lyrics: Prasoon Joshi
Music: Shankar–Ehsaan–Loy
Director of Photography: Binod Pradhan
Editor: P.S. Bharathi
Production Designer: Acropolis Design
Sound Designer: Nakul Kamte
Re-recording Mixer: Debajit Changmai
Choreographers: Ganesh Acharya, Vaibhavi Merchant and Shaimak Davar
Action Director: Allan Amin
Costume Design: Dolly Ahluwalia
VFX Supervisor: Pankaj Khandpur and Viral Thakkar
Make-up: Vikram Gaikwad
Hair Designer: Avan Contractor (BBlunt)
Sports Trainer: Melwyn Castro
Fitness Trainer: Samir Jaura

8. *Mirzya* (2016)
   Production: Cinestaan Film Company & ROMP Pictures
   Director: Rakeysh Omprakash Mehra
   Producers: Rohit Khattar, Rajiv Tandon, P.S. Bharathi and Rakeysh
   Omprakash Mehra
   Screenplay and Lyrics: Gulzaar
   Music: Shankar–Ehsaan–Loy
   Director of Photography: Paweł Dyllus
   Editor: P.S. Bharathi
   Production Designer: Acropolis Design
   Sound Designer: Pranav Shukla
   Re-recording Mixer: Justin Jose
   Choreographer: Raju Sunderam
   Action Director: Allan Amin
   Costume Designer: Nihaarika Bhasin, Ellawadi Leepakshi and
   Samidha Wangnoo
   Make-up: Vikram Gaikwad
   Hair Stylist: Avan Contractor (BBlunt)
   VFX House: Prana Studios

9. *Fanney Khan* (2018) (as producer)

10. *Mere Pyare Prime Minister* (2019)
    Director: Rakeysh Omprakash Mehra
    Producers: Rakeysh Omprakash Mehra, Arpit Vyas, P.S. Bharathi
    and Rajiv Tandon
    Screenplay: Manoj Maitra, Hussain Dalal and Rakeysh
    Omprakash Mehra
    Lyrics: Gulzaar
    Music: Shankar–Ehsaan–Loy
    Director of Photography: Paweł Dyllus
    Editor: Meghna Manchanda Sen
    Sound Designer: Pranav Shukla
    Re-recording Mixer: Anuj Mathur
    Production Designer: Rajat Poddar
    Costume Designer: Abhilasha Sharma
    Make-up: Vikram Gaikwad

11. *Toofaan* (2021)

Production: Excel Entertainment and ROMP Pictures
Director: Rakeysh Omprakash Mehra
Producers: Ritesh Sidhwani, Rakeysh Omprakash Mehra and Farhan Akhtar
Executive Producer: Stuti Ramachandra
Co-executive Producer: Darrel Foster
Written by: Anjum Rajabali
Dialogues: Vijay Maurya
Lyrics: Javed Akhtar
Music: Shankar–Ehsaan–Loy
Director of Photography: Jay Oza
Editor: Meghna Manchanda Sen
Associate Director: Yatharth Awasthi
Sound Designer: Pranav Shukla
Re-recording Mixer: Sarath Mohan
Production Designer: Rajat Poddar
Costume Designer: Abhilasha Sharma
Hair: Avan Contractor (BBlunt)
Make-up: Shrikant Desai
VFX Supervisor: Rajeev Rastogi

Not all those who wander are lost.

—J.R.R. Tolkien

Top: Atul Kulkarni brings gravitas to his cameo appearance in *Mere Pyare Prime Minister*. *Bottom*: Sonia Albizuri and Makarand Deshpande celebrate the much-awaited toilet in the slums.

Top Left: Anjali stakes a claim to happiness as Niteesh Wadhwa joins her in celebrating the colours of Holi.
Top Right: Inseparable—Kids express their love.
Bottom: Clueless but curious—Om Kanojiya tries out a western-style toilet.

Top: When a son creates a makeshift bathroom for his mother—Anjali Patil with Prasad, Om Kanojiya and Adarsh Bharti. Syna Anand (back to the camera) captures the poignant moment.
Bottom: Doing a whoopsie on water pipes—An everyday Mumbai scene.

Top: Anjali, Niteesh, Nachiket Purnapatre and Firdosh Mewawala react as I clean up for a welcome bijou appearance.
Bottom: A powerful cast of theatre artists—Rasika Agashe with Nachiket Purnapatre.

Top: Surrendering to a playful push by National Award-winning actor Anjali Patil.
Bottom: Small boys dress big and talk bigger as they travel to Delhi to confront the prime minister—Prasad, Om and Adarsh.

Top: Excremental inspiration! With Paweł Dyllus at a real slum in east Mumbai, where the film was shot.

Bottom: When music happens at the intersection of purpose and inspiration, how can friendship not follow?—With Loy, Shankar, Ehsaan and Gulzar.

Top: Seeking the attention of the kids as Syna, Om, Adarsh and Prasad seem buried in their smartphones.

Bottom: It takes a team to weave a dream—The cast and crew of *Mere Pyare Prime Minister* comes together.

Top: Sister-in-law Anupama, Bauji and Maa with Bhairavi.
Bottom: Bharathi's parents, Amruthakala and P.S. Anantha, played a huge role in raising Bhairavi.

Top: This papa doesn't preach—Losing myself in Bhairavi's cuddly being.
Bottom: The aunt's embrace—Mamta cuddles little Bhairavi.

Top: Peachy at the beach—Building castles she can reach. Bhairavi with Papa at Hamilton Islands, Australia.
Bottom: Bhairavi shows her flower power at a school play.

Top: Three water babies on a boat—With Bhairavi and Vedant on a diving holiday in Redang Island, Malaysia.

Bottom: Don't fear, daddy's here—Guiding Vedant through the water on his first underwater adventure.

Top: 3D frames, a boy and two dames—Bharathi, Vedant and Bhairavi at Disneyland, Hong Kong.
Bottom: Materfamilias—Bharathi with Vedant and Bhairavi during a zoo visit in Singapore.

Top: In cahoots wearing yellow boots—Vedant follows in his father's footsteps at Nubra Valley, Ladakh.
Bottom: Family vacation at the Thiksey monastery in Ladakh.

Top: All grown up and her own person—Bhairavi is a spitting image of me.

Bottom: An intriguing poster of Bhairavi's debut film as a writer made for the Bill and Melinda Gates Foundation.

The beauties and the beast at niece Tisha's wedding in Rajasthan.

The 4M's: Vedant, Bhairavi, Bharathi and I at our family home in Pali Hill, Bandra. In the foreground are Mocha and Gabach.

Epilogue
In a Lighter Vein
Reeta Ramamurthy Gupta

Thank you, dear reader, for staying the course through this bildungsroman. As we mulled over the closure of the book, plenty of titles, from sublime to mundane, came to our mind. The working title was 'Interval'. Our publisher put a full stop to it.

As the co-author, I was inspired to break a gender stereotype. Here was a director that never projected women as candy floss. The women in his cinema had a stellar place in the narrative. They evolved, forgave and matured with the story. Why not call his book 'A Proulxian Odyssey', inspired by Pulitzer-winning author, Annie Proulx? We would also be breaking new ground by using a female author's name as an adjective, a move beyond male author–based adjectives like Freudian and Kafkaesque. Proulx's writing itself symbolizes a seeker who takes inspiration from the world and uses it to create something stunningly new—very apt for Rakeysh Omprakash Mehra.

Our publisher was hysterical. How can you give us a sesquipedalian, bombastic title that the reader has to decode first! Can we get simpler please?

Then came another idea: here's a protagonist who enjoys learning. So why not title the book, 'The Sensitive Philomath'? Seemed like we could pull this off. But our very engaged publisher said, 'Ah!' and nodded sagely, which always means they didn't like it too much and I would have to do better.

Safer titles were 'Cinema's Lifetime Apprentice' and a derivative of the Ram Leela titled 'Deka Dekko: The Multifaceted Rakeysh Omprakash Mehra'. In the latter, we envisaged a Raavan theme, a director with Raavan's 10 heads, each with 10 varying expressions giving us a *dekko* (peek) into his artistic sensibilities—this was an input from ace photographer Amit Ashar.

Why Raavan, I asked? Why not Brahma, the creator with three heads? After all, Rakeysh is the creator of new cinema. The publishers nodded patiently. If I had ten heads, they would've merrily broken them all by now.

Teetering close to stretching their patience, finally the title that was meant to emerge—'Mirrors'—raised its head. Here was a man who had used a mirror metaphorically in just about every film of his. Aren't we all strangers when we look into the mirror, surprising ourselves with what we find?

Thus, we all agreed upon *The Stranger in the Mirror*.

I could hear a perceptible sigh. You know who let that out!

314

Afterword
Aamir Khan

The first time I met Mehra was in early 2003, when he came to my office to narrate to me the script of *RDB*. Before this, we had met briefly on a couple of occasions at public events.

The narration got over and I remember the first thing I said to him.

'Mehra,' I said, 'you realize you are setting out to make the fifth remake of Bhagat Singh and Azad.' (Just to remind you, the earlier four versions had all released in cinemas within 8 months to that day.)

Mehra stared at me in silence, pulling at a few strands of his beard, with a non-committal look on his face. At first, I thought he was about to say something, but then nothing came. In time, I would come to realize that this enigmatic silence was his response to most things.

But on that day, for some reason, this worrying reality—that we were embarking on the fifth remake of Bhagat Singh and Azad—seemed to deter neither Mehra, nor me. In that first meeting itself, I understood his take on these young, hot-blooded rebels—a very different and refreshing look at our real-life heroes. But what I did not understand on that day was how he was *seeing* the film and how he was *hearing* the film. That was something that took me by surprise when I saw the first cut.

One of Mehra's big strengths as a director is his ability to create stunning visuals. The scenes I read on paper suddenly came alive on screen in a manner that took my breath away. I am sure that Binod had a lot to do with this, but certainly, visual communication is one of Mehra's strengths.

Another is his sense of music. He always has the most amazing music in his films. Again, I am sure Rahman and Prasoon had a huge contribution in *RDB*, but I also think that some of Rahman's and Prasoon's best work is with Mehra.

With the stunning visuals by Binod of the car and bike chase at night, layered with Rahman's music and cut by Bharathi (while she was on acid), Mehra weaves a web of magic which transports the audience into another world. I was left wondering when we had shot this scene! In fact, this feeling came to me a number of times while watching the first cut of the film.

The thing I find most interesting about Mehra is that he is almost a polar opposite of me.

For example, I like to be clear in all my communications. No matter what I am conveying, or to whom, it is almost an obsession with me that the person should 'get' what I am trying to say. To achieve a high level of clarity, I use all the tools at my disposal: speech, gestures, pauses, intonations, emphasis, repetitions, etc. Mehra, on the other hand, uses as few tools as he possibly can. Perhaps speech... but, at times, not even that!

I am a control freak. Mehra, on the other hand, seems most comfortable allowing things to flow. It's almost as if he is quite prepared to explore where different energies take him.

Mehra is someone all of us love, he is someone all of us respect. We believe in him. We are charmed by him. He is intelligent. He is a great listener. All qualities of a great leader, but somehow, he does not appear to lead. Yet, I knew I was being led. I always wondered about this quality. I got the answer when I saw the complete film. He has learnt the unique art of leading from behind... just like DJ.

Let me clarify (old habit). Have you noticed how a shepherd strolls behind his sheep, playing a flute, nudging his herd in the right direction? He is usually behind the herd that he is leading.

The more I look back, the more I feel that the role I played—that of DJ in *RDB*—is uncannily like Mehra himself. All the qualities I mentioned above of Mehra are true for DJ too.

Some other qualities I haven't mentioned yet are: DJ's reluctance to grow up, take responsibility and face the real world. DJ has a very laid back attitude in life, almost poetic and philosophical.

Need I say more?

To the real life DJ,

Tune to college ke bahar bhi life ko nacha diya, kaakkey.

Tim-luck-luck-tim...

Love you, Mehra.

Acknowledgements

I would like to thank my producers, actors, music directors, production assistants, line producers, production managers, production coordinators, assistant directors, script supervisors, directors of photography, action directors, lyricists, editors, stuntmen, accountants, writers, location managers, camera operators, camera assistants, sound production teams, boom operators, key grips, lighting technicians, special effects supervisors, music supervisors, art directors, production designers, prop masters, stylists, make-up artists, hairdressers, costume designers, spot boys, caterers and every person who has been on my sets, contributing their great art to enhancing the stories I wanted to tell.

Index

321

323

This is not an allegation that can be sustained by reference to the Treaties.

The second allegation is of a different character. The attack on the Treaty of Locarno began with a demand for its denunciation; in other words, for the repudiation of the pledge contained in it. But those who engineered the attack have now discovered that the word repudiation does not sound well in English ears, and that a policy of repudiation will never be accepted by their countrymen.

So they have changed their ground, "The Treaty," they now say, "is already null and void for want of performance."

The object of the Treaty, they argue, was to procure the disarmament of France. France has not disarmed. Germany and Great Britain were deceived. The consideration in return for which the British guarantee was given has not been paid. "The Treaty of Locarno cannot be repudiated because it no longer exists."

Again the argument will not bear examination. The object of the Treaty was to preserve peace, not to secure disarmament, and, whether disarmament be secured or not, the preservation of peace is as much a British interest to-day as it was eight years ago.

Further, disarmament was not a condition of the Treaty, and no deception was practised on the Germans in this respect.

It is true that the representatives of the seven Powers who met at Locarno felt and expressed the firm conviction that the conclusion of the Treaties would hasten disarmament, as it would facilitate the realization of other German aspirations, notably, the evacuation of the occupied territory; and in fact the evacuation was completed in the first half of 1930, five years in advance of the Treaty date.

Disarmament has proved more difficult of achievement, but it is too early to assume that the attempt has failed. Indeed, the prospects of the Conference seemed more hopeful than ever before at the very moment which Germany chose for her withdrawal. But whatever the result, neither evacuation nor disarmament were conditions of Locarno, and the representatives of the Allies expressly refused to give any pledge about them, even going so far as to warn the Germans that they regarded the German claims to equality in armaments as unreasonable, just as they warned them that no German claim for the return of the colonies could be entertained.

The Treaty of Locarno remains, therefore, in full vigour, and the attack upon it has so far resulted only in the emphatic reaffirmation of the loyalty of this country to its pledged word. It is well that it is so, for Locarno is still the safety-curtain of Europe. To cast doubt upon its maintenance would be to encourage hopes and ambitions which can never be realized except by war; and if such a war breaks out in such a cause, those who think that we shall be able to remain idle spectators of the contest, indifferent to its issue, have either never read English history or never learned its plainest lesson.

One word in conclusion. The purpose of the Treaty of Locarno was to preserve peace and to promote reconciliation. It was not aimed at Germany any more than at France or Belgium. The guarantee given to France and Belgium was given in the same terms to Germany.

The enemy, if enemy there should arise, was not this country or that, but the aggressor—the nation which should break its pledges and make an unprovoked attack upon its neighbour.

There is in my mind no thought of hostility or ill will to Germany. There is, I admit, serious anxiety as to the trend of policy of the present German Government, and the effect of their daily propaganda on their people.

Against this we set Chancellor Hitler's repeated declaration that he earnestly desires peace. Can he not reassure the world by deeds as well as in words?

XI

GUSTAV STRESEMANN

WHEN the remains of Gustav Stresemann were laid to rest amidst the mourning of the people whom he had served so well, his patriotic labours were sincerely and rightly acclaimed. Even more remarkable was the universal recognition outside Germany that in him passed away the greatest German since Bismarck. Called to power at a moment of almost indescribable calamity for his country, his death found her restored to the comity of nations, one of the most influential and respected members of the League and with the date fixed when the last occupying forces would leave her territory. We may well pay our tribute of profound respect to the great qualities of foresight, insight, courage, loyalty and patience by which so much was achieved.

I was lunching on the yacht of a friend in Barcelona Harbour when Reuter's representative sent in his card with the request for my comment on Dr. Stresemann's death.[1] The news came upon me like a thunder-clap, for though no one who had seen him during the previous two years could fail to recognize that he was a very sick man, I had had no warning of any special danger. To the sense of the tragedy which had thus befallen his country and Europe there was added my personal sorrow at the death of a man for whom, in the converse of recent years, I had come to feel not only a profound admiration but a sincere personal affection.

[1] Oct. 3rd, 1929.

I first met Dr. Stresemann at the Conference of Locarno in October 1925. Nine months of slow, laborious and sometimes exasperating negotiations had at length made it possible for this meeting to take place between those of whom we still spoke as Allies and their former enemy. I was lunching with Asquith a little before my departure from London. "Do you know Dr. Stresemann?" he asked, and on my replying in the negative, he added, "you should go and see John's portrait of him—a proper *junker*! You will not have an easy time." This, too, was my own impression when I first met him face to face at the opening of the Conference on a Monday morning. It was only by degrees that I learned fully to know him and, in knowing, to appreciate him.

The circumstances of the Locarno Conference were peculiar and his position one of extraordinary difficulty. He had made his first tentative proposal for a pact of mutual guarantee in the previous January. A somewhat similar proposal had been suggested earlier by Chancellor Cuno to the American Government, who had communicated it to Monsieur Poincaré, then Prime Minister of France, but nothing had come of it. The new proposal at first raised some suspicion in Great Britain, and even more across the Channel. It was thought in some quarters to be merely a skilful diplomatic move intended to drive a wedge between our two countries. But the British Government felt at once that it demanded their most serious consideration, and represented to the French Government that it was on these lines, and on these only, that the guarantee of French territory originally offered in the non-ratified Anglo-American treaty could be renewed by this country after all that had occurred in the interval. The long months of negotiation—not too long for the important work which had to be done—had convinced us of Dr. Stresemann's sincerity, and had evolved from his first sketch a practical scheme (already communicated through their legal adviser to the German Government) which was probably more definite and more far-reaching than Dr. Stresemann had contemplated.

But German opinion was highly suspicious; the public had not yet grasped the meaning or possibilities of the new orientation which Stresemann desired to give to German policy, and, apart from all the bitter feelings remaining from the War and the quite-recent Ruhr occupation, was perhaps as much afraid of Western "entanglements" as any American has even been of becoming involved in European alliances. The Chancellor (Dr. Luther) and Dr. Stresemann left Berlin amidst extraordinary police precautions. They came to Locarno knowing that the successful issue of their Locarno negotiations would only be the beginning of a long and difficult domestic campaign.

In these circumstances it is not surprising that at the outset they were exceedingly susceptible and prone to suspicion. I had done my best to make it clear that on this occasion we met not as victors and vanquished but as equals. With the memory of the rather humiliating conditions of previous Conferences as fresh in my own mind as I knew it must be in theirs, I had sought to secure for our Conference room a round table where there should be neither top nor bottom. One of sufficient size was not available, but failing this a square table had been procured with no sign to differentiate one place from another.

Nevertheless, even before the Conference met difficulties arose. I reached Locarno about midday on the Sunday preceding the opening of the Conference. The French, Belgian and Italian delegations were established in the same hotel, and the Germans had already taken up their quarters in another. My first step was to leave cards upon them, a civility which I believe had not been paid at any of the previous Conferences. In the course of the afternoon Monsieur Briand called upon me to discuss the arrangements for the morrow and to ask me, at the desire of the Italians and the Belgians, as well as himself, to preside at the Conference. I accepted on the condition that the Germans joined in the invitation, but this, after some hesitation, they felt unable to do. In the state of German public opinion, they considered it impossible to accept a permanent President chosen from the Allies, and, whilst willing that I should preside on the first day at the request of the Allies, they demanded that the presidency should be held by each Power in turn. I refused this suggestion as unpractical and ridiculous, and not without some difficulty it was arranged that they should join in the invitation to me to preside on the first day, and that when we had settled our procedure I should declare that all was now so simple that in future we could dispense with a chairman!

Even to the last moment these difficulties persisted. The last differences had been settled, the initialling of the Treaties had been fixed for the morrow, when I received a message that the Chancellor and Dr. Stresemann wished to see me at six o'clock, and begged that I would summon Monsieur Briand to a meeting in my room at that hour. We met, and for four hours we travelled over again an oft-repeated discussion. We could advance no further, we had made our ultimate concessions. Reparations and evacuation were not on the programme of the Conference. These subjects must be left to time and the new spirit which we hoped that the Treaties of Locarno would create.

At ten o'clock we broke up, exhausted by the last-minute revival of painful and difficult discussions when we had supposed that final agreement had been reached. Only much later did Stresemann reveal the secret: the Chancellor had received a telegram from certain of their colleagues in Berlin forbidding the two Ministers to initial anything till they had discussed the draft with the German Cabinet. To have obeyed this injunction would have destroyed all chance of success; to part without agreement would have made agreement in future still more difficult. "When the Chancellor read the telegram," said Stresemann later, "he buried his face in his hands. For two minutes he sat silent; then suddenly raising his head, 'Tell them to go to Jericho!' he said. 'I initial all the same.'"

In pursuance of the arrangement we had reached, when the Conference met for the first time I seated myself beside the Syndic, and the other delegations found their places at the table naturally and without difficulty. Except for the speech of welcome by the Syndic and the brief answer which I made on behalf of the Conference, no speeches were made, and we proceeded at once to read a first time the draft upon which the British and Allied Governments had agreed as modified by our jurists in consultation with the legal adviser of the German Government during a visit which he had paid to London at our invitation.

The simplicity and business-like character of this opening, together with the long and careful preparation, laid the basis for the success of the Conference. Chancellor Luther, speaking fluent French, contributed not a little to our understanding of one another, but the brunt of the German case fell upon Dr. Stresemann. None of those who were present will ever forget the lofty character of the debates conducted between him and Monsieur Briand. The conversational tone which was carefully preserved in the discussions detracted nothing from the weight or power of their arguments. The courage, the resource, the tact, and the consideration shown by these two representatives of two powerful nations seeking to put an end to their secular animosities raised the discussion to the highest level of practical eloquence and moved the hearts of all who listened.

I cannot here trace the progress of the Conference from day to day or tell the story of Monsieur Briand's party of pleasure on the lake in the little steamer named *The Orange Blossom*, to celebrate my wife's birthday, during which we surmounted our greatest difficulties. But I must recall the final scene when the various treaties had been initialled and Stresemann made his last appeal. The German representatives, he said, had initialled with a full sense of their responsibility, intended to make this treaty their own, determined to stand or fall by it, and on their return to Germany to use their utmost endeavour to secure its acceptance by the German people. And then in tones of deep emotion which moved us all, he added that in so doing they acted in the confidence that from this treaty we should develop its natural and logical consequences in the political and economic spheres.

Not less moving was the response of Monsieur Briand. He said that he, too, had initialled with a full sense of his responsibility and, he could add, with the certainty that he spoke the mind of the French Government and the great mass of the French people; and then with a grateful acknowledgment of Dr. Stresemann's restraint, he added that now, his mandate exhausted, and speaking only for himself, but still confident that he represented the opinion of the great mass of the French people, if this were to be the end and no further consequences were to follow he would have thought it dishonest to embark on the negotiations at all, and he pledged himself to do his utmost to realize those unspoken aspirations which he was grateful to Dr. Stresemann for not expressing but which he knew lay nearest to his heart.

A few more moments and we had parted, but not before the Chancellor and Monsieur Briand had appeared at the window before the great crowd now assembled in front of the Court House and had shaken hands before the people in token of the new relations established between their countries.

To those of us who were Stresemann's associates in this first hour, it came as some consolation in our sorrow for his death that he lived long enough to gather the fruits of his far-sighted policy and to fix the date for the total evacuation of German territory. When the secret history of the conference at The Hague comes to be written, it will not be surprising if it be found that his was the hand which finally averted disaster. It is a comfort to us that he who took such risks and showed such courage lived to see his purpose accomplished, and was mourned by his own people as one whose immense services to the Fatherland were recognized, and who was respected by other nations as a great statesman, a loyal partner and a true friend of peace.

By his death a great German patriot passed to his rest.

XII

ARISTIDE BRIAND

SINCE the death of Gustav Stresemann the world has suffered
no loss comparable to the passing of Aristide Briand.[1] He
had witnessed the horrors of the War, and the cries of the
widowed and the fatherless had struck deep into his soul.
Peace had become with him a veritable passion; he was
indomitable in its pursuit, and his presence at the Quai
d'Orsay was a guarantee that the policy of France would
be peaceful. "There will be no war while I remain
Minister." That pledge he gave to the world; how faithfully he kept it all men can bear witness.

My first meeting with Briand after I became Secretary
of State for Foreign Affairs was at the Council of the
League of Nations held in Rome in December 1924. I
set myself at once to win his confidence, and through him
to regain for my country the confidence and sympathy of
France, for I was profoundly convinced then, as I still am,
that it is only by the maintenance of this mutual confidence
and by close co-operation between our two nations that the
rehabilitation of Germany and the restoration of Europe
can be achieved.

The occupation of the Ruhr had followed on our differences; the evacuation, first of Cologne, and then of the
whole Rhineland five years in advance of the Treaty date
were the fruits of our agreement. Briand shared my point
of view and was quick to respond to my advances.

Next year he became President of the Council of Ministers

[1] March 7th, 1932.

179

and Foreign Minister of France. Thereafter our co-operation was constant as long as I remained Foreign Secretary, and our friendship ripened into a close and affectionate intimacy. We had tried one another out in long and exhausting negotiations, and each had complete confidence in the good faith and loyalty of the other.

What manner of man was this who, amidst the rapid changes of French Governments, was not only twelve times Prime Minister, but held the portfolio of Foreign Affairs for seven consecutive years, until failing health forced him to resign; who won the confidence of Stresemann as completely as my own; who was throughout perhaps the most powerful single personality in the League of Nations, and became in some sort the living embodiment of its spirit?

Physically a man of medium height, with broad, stooping shoulders, deep chested, his head crowned with an untidy shock of greying hair. A heavy drooping moustache half hid a slightly crooked, full-lipped mouth, whose ugliness was redeemed by an enchanting smile that matched well the bright eyes dancing with an often slightly malicious wit. He was, indeed, incorrigibly witty; he could not help it. The good things sprang irresistibly to his lips in graver discussions no less than in his lighter moments. "Tell me Briand's latest," was the greeting with which Lord Balfour used to receive me on my return from my visits to Geneva, and we used to enjoy together the feast which Briand had provided.

The famous game of golf at Cannes which upset his Ministerial coach provided an example. Lord Riddell was at that time acting as a sort of super Press-agent for Mr. Lloyd George. Briand's first drive, as might be expected, had not sent the ball far. When Lord Riddell drove off with a skilled stroke: " *Tiens!* " exclaimed Briand, " *il lance sa balle comme une fausse nouvelle* " (" He sets his ball flying like a bit of false news ").

This is delightful chaff, but his thrust on occasion could be deadly. On his return to Paris he found that his colleagues had already decided his fall, and that the friend to whom he had especially entrusted his interests during his absence had joined his foes. Seizing the situation at a glance, he thrust his papers back into his portfolio and, rising from the Council table, announced that he was going to tender his resignation to the President of the Republic. Then, with his hand on the door, he turned to the friend who had failed him : " By the way, my dear X, can you tell me the value of thirty pieces of silver at the exchange to-day ? "

But Briand had not only wit; he had a sense of humour also, and this gift was richly shared by Stresemann. It did much to smooth over the difficulties of our first meetings at Locarno, and helped to turn many a dangerous corner in later discussions at Geneva. Both men could keep discussion on a quiet conversational level, even when treating of the gravest subjects, and both could enjoy a joke at their own expense as richly as a joke at another's.

One day in the lobby of the Assembly at Geneva the Press correspondents remarked the two men sitting apart engaged in a lively and apparently very merry conversation. " What were you two conspirators plotting behind my back ? " I later asked of Briand. It appeared that Stresemann had been anxious to explain the circumstances in which a high personage in Germany had made a rather provocative reference to war guilt and to invoke Briand's influence with the French Press to prevent them making heavy weather about it. Briand was able to say that Monsieur Poincaré and himself had already taken steps to this end, and then continued: " But why can't you let the question alone? As to the wisdom of putting this clause into the Treaty, I have my own opinion; but I can't alter it now. Why can't you leave it to the judgment of history? "

" But what," asked Stresemann, " will history say? "

" Ah," replied Briand, " I am no prophet, and will not anticipate her judgment. But there are three things which I think she will not say—she will not say that this time France was the aggressor; she will not say that Belgium invaded Germany; and she will not say, like Bethmann-Hollweg, that a treaty is only a scrap of paper." [1]

When people ask me what is meant by " the atmosphere of Geneva," I tell this story. It is no small thing that it should be possible for the representatives of France and Germany to be able to treat so grave an issue with so light a touch.

I recall another occasion at Geneva when a *bon mot* from him helped to quiet nerves and to restore good temper. The Council had been sitting morning and afternoon; the day was hot and sultry; the long room in which we met had been crowded with representatives of the Press and a public attracted by the dramatic quality of the debate which had been in progress; the atmosphere grew more and more oppressive as the afternoon wore on, and when at last the debate ended and the room was cleared in order that the Council, which had not felt able to accept the resolution drafted by its *Rapporteur*, might evolve another which should secure the assent of both parties, everyone was exhausted and nerves were on edge. There is no more

[1] This story has been printed in an incomplete form without the last phrase. I insert it here because it is certain that it was precisely that phrase to which Briand attached the greatest weight, as being most pertinent to our post-War problems.

Dr. Erich Salomon

Chamberlain with Stresemann and Briand

hopeless task than for fifteen or twenty men to try to draft a document. In a few moments the Council had as many drafts before it as it contained members. Whatever was accepted by one party to the dispute was rejected by the other, and the Council itself seemed as hopelessly divided as the parties themselves. I happened to have been the *Rapporteur* whose proposal had been rejected. I thought I had done my share and, leaving my colleagues to their task, I retired into the background to await the result of their united efforts. Presently I was joined by the representative of the Netherlands. " *Ouf!* " he exclaimed, " *c'est comme un accouchement dans une gare!* " and indeed the scene was one of not less embarrassment and confusion. Later we resumed our places at the table. The heat was oppressive. Only one member of the Council seemed insensible to it; he who never seemed warm enough had sat all day in a thick overcoat which at this moment he was wrapping more closely around him. " Look at our friend," said Briand; " I am sure that when he dies he will leave directions that he shall be cremated and, as they push the coffin into the furnace, you will hear his voice crying, ' For God's sake, shut that door. There's an awful draught ! ' "

We all laughed, the victim included—and reached agreement.

I cannot think of Briand without my mind reverting to Locarno. That was the culminating point of his career, and no lesser men than he and Stresemann could have made it a success. I have already described the closing scene of the Conference when Stresemann appealed to us all, but most of all to France, that this should be not the end but the beginning of a chapter in our relations and that we should draw from it the consequences, political and economic, which it logically implied.

None who heard them will ever forget the noble words of Briand's reply or the deep feeling with which he pledged himself henceforth to work unremittingly for peace. As I listened I felt my love for France justified, for in Briand's words I heard the voice of all that is noblest and most generous in the soul of the French nation. Is it permitted to me to add a note more personal to myself? As he left the room Briand found my wife waiting for me, and, taking her two hands in his, and deeply and visibly moved, he said again and again, " Ah, Madame, without your husband I would never have attempted it." I ask no other epitaph. Is it strange that I loved him? "

Other memories crowd upon me—the first meeting of the German and French statesmen in the Conference Room, the long and weighty discussions chiefly carried on between Stresemann and Briand, but often aided by the fluent French and softer speech of Luther; the more private conversations in my room, and, above all, the trip on the lake in the *Orange Blossom* to which Briand invited us, and at which we found the solution of one of our gravest difficulties.

In starting, we had evaded the vigilance of the Press, but when we finally returned to Locarno after nightfall the whole 150 correspondents present there were massed upon the quay. "What have you to tell us, Monsieur le Président?" they asked eagerly. But we had agreed that we could say nothing until we had reported to our colleagues and secured their consent. Briand was equal to the occasion. " Gentlemen," he said, " we have been studying ichthyology. In the shallows near the shore we found some little fish which we identified without difficulty. Further out we came upon bigger ones; they gave us more trouble, but we managed presently to classify them also. Then in the middle of the Lake were one or two really big fish. Ah! they offered a more difficult problem; we have not yet quite solved it, though we are on the way to putting them also in their proper place; but there was one quality possessed by all these fish which greatly impressed us—their silence"; and with a smiling "Good evening, gentlemen," he hurried off to the shelter of his hotel.

In this country we have ceased to cultivate oratory, but in France it is an art which is still studied, admired and practised. Briand was a great orator with a style all his own. He possessed a deep, melodious voice which could sink to a whisper or ring out like a deep-toned bell, but whether raised or lowered, whether you were seated beside him or at the farthest end of the hall, it was always audible and never noisy. I think that the adjective which best describes it is *caressing*, and this was the character of the speeches themselves.

Though he used no notes, he did in a way prepare for a speech, but the speech which he made was not the speech which he had prepared. He was singularly sensitive to the atmosphere of the moment and the mind of his audience, and the speech as delivered was in form and substance the result of his reaction to the feeling and mood of his listeners. I have heard a more perfect and sustained effort of oratory in the Assembly from Monsieur Paul-Boncour —one, indeed, which the skilled translators of the League confessed themselves quite unable to render into English —but I have never listened to a speaker so *persuasive* as Briand.

He was not a great reader; he hated writing. It was in talk that he expounded and, I think, not infrequently formed his ideas. These were large and generous, but seldom

worked-out and often in advance of the possibilites of the
moment. He consciously took Time for an ally and counted
on its aid in overcoming difficulties.

I remember an occasion when he was hurriedly recalled
from Geneva by a Cabinet crisis in Paris. He returned
after seventy-two hours, having formed his ninth Government. " Yes, my ninth," he told us, " and it's always the
same thing. So many portfolios to this section, and so
many to those others, but always I reserve one portfolio
to my own absolute discretion. That portfolio I allot to
Time. He is my most useful colleague." Patience was one
of his great instruments. If his hopes were disappointed,
then " Patience, and shuffle the cards."

He had a deep sympathy with the countryman and with
the sailors and fishermen of his native Brittany. He loved
the sea and the countryside—above all, the sea, and the sea
most of all when the waves ran high. " My barque," he
once wrote to me after a stormy debate in the Chamber,
" has not, I admit, been sailing on calm seas. It was pretty
well tossed about by the waves, and certain rocky points
on the surface were affording me matter for serious un-
easiness. . . . The deck is not yet too steady under my feet.
Happily, I do not suffer from sea-sickness. . . ."

Such was the man as I knew him—simple in his tastes,
warm in his friendships, a charming companion in a leisure
hour, a colleague of splendid loyalty in time of difficulty.
He loved France passionately, yet was ever in his own
phrase " a good European "; he served the cause of Peace
with all his might and in some measure it claimed him for
its victim. Only a few weeks before his death I sent him
the cartoon with which *Punch* saluted him on his retirement.
I cannot do better than close this article with his reply (the
original is, of course, in French) :

" COCHEREL,
" *February 6*, 1932.

" DEAR FRIEND,

" I have been greatly touched by your thought. You know what value I attach to our friendship.

" I shall keep this drawing from *Punch*, which goes straight to my heart. There is, in truth, in the art of the English humourists a feeling of delicacy and exquisite international courtesy of which ' *le vieux Punch* ' may be proud of maintaining, in our time, the tradition.

" In the attitude in which I am represented in the drawing one sees clearly that the English artist has felt how heavily a simple dove bearing an olive branch can weigh upon a man's wrist. You know something of this matter, dear friend, you to whom this bird is not less familiar. Believe me, the dove of Locarno will always symbolize for me, across all the difficulties of the present hour, the truth of a political thought to which you are as faithful as I am.

" I send you my best wishes for you and yours, and beg you to transmit to Lady Chamberlain my very respectful homage.

" I remain always very affectionately yours,

" ARI. BRIAND."

He could well be content to leave his cause to the judgment of history.

Thus I wrote on the morrow of Briand's death. The three years which have since passed have not provided a successor to the particular place which he held in world politics; still less have they dimmed the affection and esteem which I felt for him. Yet our friendship, measured in years, was a brief one. It was not its length but the character of the man which gave to it its value—his large sincerity of heart and mind, his courage, his patience under difficulties, his indifference to self, his far-sighted vision, his loyalty and truth, his honest striving for appeasement and reconciliation in a world bled white and scarred with suffering, yet still tossed and driven by the old hates and fears.

I am told that there is to-day in France some reaction against his fame; that passages selected from the Papers of Stresemann are used to represent him as the dupe of a Prussian Mephistopheles who trapped him with soft words while all the time plotting repudiation and revenge.

The charge is absurd to anyone who like myself collaborated with them both from day to day for the happiest years of their association. It is as unfair to Stresemann as it is unjust to Briand. There was neither knave nor dupe, but a great German and a great Frenchman who, from amidst the blood-soaked ruins of the past, sought to raise a new temple of peace. Each knew that the gulf which separated them and their two Nations could not be bridged in a day; for both of them Locarno was not a fulfilment but a beginning. It is perhaps because too much was expected from it that their fame has suffered a temporary eclipse; but their work stands and is the corner-stone of the arch of peace in Europe to-day.

XIII

RAYMOND POINCARÉ

MANY judgments were formed of Poincaré in the course of his career and found their echo at the moment of his death,[1] for strong characters like his, if they command the confidence of their followers, can scarcely escape becoming the objects of fierce attack by their opponents who may respect the man but cannot forgive the policy—least of all when it is successful. In the case of a man like Poincaré the last word was not spoken on the morrow of his death. The final judgment rests with history, for to history he belongs.

It is always rash to attempt to anticipate the verdict of history. "I sometimes think," my father once said in reference to Gladstone, "that great men are like great mountains : one cannot realize their greatness till one stands at some distance from them," and it may well be that history, when the time comes for it to be written, will find much to modify or change in the judgments which we form to-day.

Perhaps my only qualification for attempting an appreciation of the man and his work is that I stood at a little distance from him, in space if not in time, and that, though my life so nearly covered the same years and was so largely influenced by the same terrible events as his, I saw them from a different angle and in some measure from a position of greater detachment. My personal intercourse with him was slight and, after his illness, was confined to the receipt

[1] October 15th, 1934.

189

of messages of friendship and regard, which, from such a man, gave me the more pleasure because we had sometimes differed seriously on policy and they were therefore as unexpected as they were welcome.

In whatever society one had met him, the stranger would at once have recognized Poincaré for a Frenchman, and under his rather cold demeanour there burned a passionate love of France. It was something more fiery, perhaps more aggressive, than the common love of a man for the country of his birth. It was the love of one old enough to have realized all that was happening in 1870, who had seen his country invaded, his native province torn asunder and a large part of it transferred to an alien rule. Who shall blame him if this passion of love seemed sometimes to turn to hate? He could neither forget in defeat nor forgive in victory. Can one wonder that the youth of that generation grew to manhood with the hope that one day those wrongs would be redressed and the lost provinces restored and that their supreme purpose in life was to secure that, when that moment came, France should be prepared. It was in this faith that men like Poincaré and Clemenceau were bred; by it and for it they lived and toiled. It is to the lasting credit of Poincaré that at the most critical moment of the War, subordinating all personal feeling to the public interest, he called Clemenceau to the helm. It was a triumph all the greater that in one respect it was a triumph over himself, for to a man of his temperament the very restrictions which his position, as President of the Republic, imposed upon his actions and utterances, must have made more difficult co-operation with a man of such dominating and autocratic habit of mind as Clemenceau.

Surely these two men, bitterly as they were divided *ont bien mérité de la Patrie*—and not of France alone, but of all who cherish the freedom of the human soul, to whatever country they belong.

Poincaré brought to his task in those war years indomitable courage and a steadfastness of purpose that nothing could shake. He showed the same qualities in his last great ministry of National Union and perhaps it was at that moment that he rendered his greatest service to France. Such was the confidence which his name inspired that his mere presence " was worth an army corps." We do well to pay honour to men of such courage and integrity; they are not numerous in the world of politics but it is to them that in hours of crisis the people turn for guidance, and never turn in vain.

No portrait can be true to life which has no shadows. Men have the defects of their qualities and Poincaré was no exception to the rule. The force of his own convictions rendered him at times insensitive to the feelings of others and intolerant of all other points of view. I believe that he was a sincere friend to the *Entente*, yet his insistence on the occupation of the Ruhr in the face of repeated British objections caused a rift between the two nations which has perhaps even now not been completely mended. I met him in council at that time. So unyielding was his attitude, so sharp his language that I remember exclaiming to the Prime Minister: " But what Monsieur Poincaré proposes is not an ultimatum to Germany; it is an ultimatum to us ! " At such a moment, his firmness was not far removed from obstinacy, and the French lawyer seemed to have assumed the uniform of a Prussian corporal.

I said something of the kind to a French friend who was his staunch admirer. Poincaré was, I complained, so fixed in his own ideas, so rigid and uncompromising in his expression of them and so unwilling to make any concession even to an ally that co-operation became impossible. I have never forgotten my friend's reply which, indeed, once served me as a mirror in which to show a German in what light German policy appeared to the rest of the world: "*Il faut vous rappeller que Monsieur Poincaré est Lorrain, et qui dit Lorrain dit moitié Prussien.*"

But it is not on this note that I would close. During life he never rested. His work is done. France honours a great Frenchman who subordinated all else to the greatness of his country and we join France in her memory of one who, in helping to save France, helped also to save the liberties of mankind.

XIV

LORD MORLEY OF BLACKBURN

TURNING over the few letters from Lord Morley which I possess, all written in the later years of his life, I found this note penned when I had just been appointed Secretary of State for India:

" MY DEAR AUSTEN,

"You were, I believe, laying down the law on my hearthrug some thirty years ago. I was not yet in the H. of C. Who'd have thought that our humble roof sheltered two individuals destined to be Secretary of State for India. Somehow, I like to think of you sitting in my august chair. It is a grand and profoundly interesting office. . . ."

The letter is dated May 27th, 1917, but the incident to which it refers must have occurred nearer forty than thirty years before. Indeed, I think that I shall be right in saying that it took place in the summer of 1876, when I was not quite thirteen years of age. Morley had invited my father to spend two nights (it would be an anachronism to call it the week-end) with him at Brighton and Mrs. Morley had given my father permission to bring me with him. I was then at a private school at Hampstead, founded by a former assistant-master of University College School and carried on after his death by his widow. For convenience in educating her two youngest daughters and to provide companions for them, this lady had added some six or eight girls to the twenty or so boys who composed the bulk of the school.

I remember my feeling of shyness at thus going to a strange house which mingled with the joy of being with my father, but Mrs. Morley soon put me at my ease though I remained rather afraid of Morley himself. In any case I sat during dinner becomingly silent in the presence of my elders, who discussed amongst other things the subject of education. Morley declared himself in favour of the co-education of boys and girls. I felt that I could have put him right on a subject on which he was obviously very ill-informed, but I did not think my father would approve my intervention in the conversation; so, for the time, I stifled as best I could my indignation and remained silent; but Mrs. Morley confided to my father after I had gone to bed that when she had carried me off to the drawing-room, I had taken my stand on the hearth-rug and poured out my indignation at this monstrous heresy, declaring that it was all very well for theorists to declare that it would improve our manners, teach us chivalry and humanize school-life, but that I, who had practical experience of the system, knew that it did nothing of the kind. The girls were a nuisance at games, they worked harder than we did in class, and were constantly held up to us as an example; they wouldn't conform to our standards and so forth and so on. I picture myself as a kind of infant Winston Churchill, becoming an orator in the stress of my emotion and making up for my enforced silence in the earlier part of the evening by the violence of my denunciation of what I felt to be rank heresy born of ignorance. It must have been my first speech, delivered it is true to a small but kindly audience of one who enjoyed the humour of the spectacle of which I was quite unconscious at the time.

My elder sister, who liked long words (and never had any difficulty in spelling them), complained of me in my infancy that I had "no conversation"; but I must soon have made up for this early deficiency of speech, as this incident shows. I might have forgotten it had it not been so useful to my brother and sisters when it was told to them in later years, and there was added a later anecdote dating from my Rugby days. Charlie Howard, then my fag (and afterwards, as Lord Morpeth, M.P. for one of our Birmingham seats and later still Lord Carlisle) wrote to his mother a description of life at school which she was unkind enough to repeat to some member of the family. The account ended only when the lights were put out in the dormitory. . . . "Then," he wrote, "we discuss politics and things—at least when I say discuss, Chamberlain jaws us and tells us what we ought to think." Apparently a lifelong habit had already formed itself!

When one revives old memories one ceases to be master of one's thoughts. The mind wanders from incident to incident and one forgets the purpose with which one set out. Who shall say what fixes some unimportant trifle in one's memory and keeps it living, whilst much that is more important escapes remembrance? The Brighton hearth-rug has led me far from my theme. It was of Morley, not of myself, that I wanted to write.

Morley and my father met for the first time in 1873. It was that gallant sailor and eager, though luckless politician, the late Admiral Maxse, from whom George Meredith drew the hero of *Beauchamp's Career*, who made them known to one another, and the acquaintance thus begun ripened quickly into the closest friendship. It was well for my father that it did so, for two years later he was again a widower, his hearth was desolate and his whole world lay in ruins. What Morley's friendship had already come to mean to him may be guessed from a sentence in a letter from Morley to me soon after my father's death. He sent me, " for such use as you may desire," nearly four hundred letters written by my father to him: " Two or three of them, written when he was *in deep domestic sorrow*, are of a sacred sort and perhaps should hardly be seen by anybody but yourself and Beatrice " (my sister). And a year later in July 1876, the month in which, on his fortieth birthday, my father was first elected to Parliament, he wrote to Morley, " I value your friendship very much and it is the only bright spot in my new life."

Thereafter they met frequently. They visited Paris together or made longer tours on the Continent in their summer holidays, and Morley would visit my father first at Southbourne and afterwards at Highbury, his Birmingham homes. Notes passed between them frequently, making appointments for breakfast and a morning visit to the Royal Academy or for an early dinner and the theatre afterwards.

I remember one such occasion at a later time when my father accepted Irving's offer of a box at the Lyceum to see *Faust*, and between the acts discussed the consequences of Randolph Churchill's resignation and the possibilities of the reunion of the Liberal Party by a Round Table Conference; but by that time the differences had struck too deep a root and the Conference ended in failure. My father in thanking Irving for the box and telling him how much they had enjoyed the performance, ventured the criticism that Irving's *Mephistopheles* had rather too much of a French *petit-maître* about him to be a convincing German devil. Irving admitted the charge but asserted that a true representation of Goethe's *Mephistopheles* would be too coarse to please English taste.

When, in 1880, my father entered the Government and took the house in Prince's Gardens which thereafter remained his London home, I suppose that a week seldom passed in which Morley did not dine there at least once, and often more than once. When they first met, Morley was editor of the *Fortnightly Review*; by this time he was editor of the *Pall Mall Gazette* and in 1883 he entered the House of Commons as member for Newcastle-on-Tyne. When I came home during school holidays or university vacations it was one of my greatest pleasures to be present at these dinners where the talk ranged over art, literature and history, but dwelt above all on the political questions of the day. I wish I had tried to Boswellise some of these conversations, for the two men were among the few really good talkers whom I have known—and both could listen. When they held these symposia their talk was a liberal education for a youth like myself.

There is an echo of what my father thought of Morley's share in these talks in a letter written to me long afterwards (December 29th, 1914) by my great friend and Rugby Housemaster, Henry Lee Warner:

"I have been reading Burke's *Reflections* to my wife lately and we turned to Morley's remarks in the *Men of Letters* and came on his page on the political estrangement of Fox and Burke and Fox's generous words. It reminded me so of your father's remark that one evening with John Morley would do more for his son than many days' teaching at Rugby."

I sent this letter to Morley, who replied:

"I am delighted with that remark in L. W.'s letter. I am full at this moment of the old Tabagie Parliaments at Southbourne and Highbury. It is all very much alive in my memory."

The fact is that they had each opened a new world to the other. Morley, the university man, the disciple of Mill, the uncompromising author of the essay on " Compromise," the biographer of Voltaire, Rousseau and Diderot and the student of Burke, was a stimulating companion to a man who had left school at sixteen and, though he had afterwards read widely for himself, had no pretensions to be a scholar.

" I have always thought," I wrote to Morley after my father's death, " that the special attraction of your friendship to him was that while you were in general sympathy on the politics of the day, you opened many windows through which till then he had had no chance of looking."

And to Morley, the scholar and philosopher and publicist, the intensely practical life which my father led, immersed in the work of administration whether of city or country, was something equally new. Though in theory Morley gave the highest place to letters and declared that he would sooner have been the author of *The Decline and Fall* than Mr. Pitt, he had what almost amounted to a craving for a public life. He was equally ready to be either hero or martyr, to be crowned with laurels or to be burned at the stake, but the author's life did not satisfy him; he longed for the limelight and the perils and the triumphs of the platform.

After my marriage, I wanted my wife to know him and invited him to dine quietly with us as soon as we had settled in our new home. He accepted cordially and Sir William Anson completed our small party. In the course of dinner Morley, who was then Secretary of State for India, told us of his morning's work at the office. The Zakka Khel were giving trouble on the India frontier; was there to be a punitive expedition or not? Of course the soldiers wanted one; so did the Political Officer; so, too, the Government of India; so in fact did everyone. Jupiter-Morley was not convinced. "I called in Sir Richmond Ritchie, had a few final words with him and then decided finally against it. It had only taken a quarter of an hour, but I said to Ritchie, 'Do you remember Lord Justice Bowen's definition of hard work? It was answering yes or no on insufficient information. I'm tired!'"

Later, in the drawing-room, the conversation turned on the choice of careers. I suggested, not perhaps without a spice of malice, that to be a great writer would be the best gift a fairy godmother could bestow on an infant in its cradle. Morley vehemently repudiated my suggestion. The work of composition was the vilest drudgery and left one exhausted after an hour or two. "No, I'd rather be a great singer or a great actor."

"Or a great orator," Anson suggested. "He, too, is something of an actor."

"Yes," said Morley, "or a great orator. I'd sooner sway great audiences and sit down, as the reporters say, amidst prolonged applause than decide in my cabinet whether or not there is to be an expedition against the Zakka Khel."

Human nature is full of such contradictions. One night when I sat next Asquith at Grillons something led him to say to me: "What a book, Austen, you or I could write about the *real* men as we have known them, contrasted with the man the public thinks it knows."

"As for instance, so and so," I said, naming a man we had both known and who had been a colleague of Asquith's in Mr. Gladstone's Government.

"Yes," rejoined Asquith, "or John Morley!" for this

man of high purpose, with the lofty forehead, small deep-set eyes, strong mouth and commanding nose and face so deeply lined as to give in repose the stern and almost ascetic appearance which earned him the sobriquet of " Honest John," was not without his full share of human weaknesses. He had really beautiful hands and displayed them with as much coquetry as any fine lady. He was very sensitive, and cared curiously for the outward show and trappings of power. At this moment when he was going to the House of Lords and giving up the Secretaryship of State for India, he was insisting, greatly to Asquith's embarrass-ment, on receiving the Lord Presidency of the Council instead of the Privy Seal, since the former took precedence of the latter, and threatening to resign if his wish were not gratified. " I have a drawer full of his resignations ! " Asquith exclaimed impatiently.

But to return to Morley and my father. Morley himself has told us the story of that friendship in his *Recollections*,[1] and has sketched with the hand of a master both my father himself and the principal figures in the circle of friends whom he had gathered around him in his Birmingham home. As in one of Franz Hals' great Company pieces at Haarlem, you see the company gathered around the central figure, but each head stands out clearly from the crowded canvas and a few deft strokes give to each its special character and quality.

I had once said to Morley that I wished he would write some account of that remarkable circle and he had answered enigmatically, " Perhaps I have." Some years later he asked me whether I would be willing to read through the proofs of a fragment he had written about those early days, but on re-reading it himself, he wrote (December 4th, 1915) :

[1] Vol. I, Book II, Chap. 1.

"Since getting your pleasant assent to a bold proposal of mine, I have travelled over the ground of my draft of the fragment, and it will never do even for vision so friendly as yours. It needs much polish and reconstruction. So I will not do anything to make your Xmas other than a merry one."

A year later, on November 20th, 1916, he wrote:

"With some misgiving, I send you what I promised. It will read to you cold and meagre. The only excuse is that it is a part of my *Recollections*, and has no pretence to deal essentially and amply with him and his career.

"Please look at the episode on p. 116.

"Do not trouble to *write* me any remarks: you are too busy. I will come to you at I.O., if you should wish.

"Will you let Beatrice see it, if you please? Of course *sub sigillo*.

"Thank Mrs. Chamberlain for her most pleasant meal.

"Yr.

"M."

"Of course, I should be really grateful for any suggestions that may occur to you or your sister. There is no urgency."

I kept no copy of my reply, but he wrote again on November 23rd:

"A thousand thanks for your kind letter. But I feel no little remorse at the idea of throwing this load upon the hands of a man so intensely occupied as you are. I only beg of you not to let it get in your way. Remember it is not *his* biography and only in a very fragmentary and superficial way a piece of my own poor affair. I only want you to say, when you are ready, whether there is any blunder that strikes you, or any piece of an unfair implication.

"I hope Mrs. Chamberlain and you said 'How true,' of the lines of Mr. G. to Granville as to your father's merits as a talker of business. I thought it really good.

201

" The omissions were intentional. I was really afraid of sending more.

" Don't trouble to *write* when the time comes. It will be a delight to me to *attend* you, as the lawyers say.

" Yours always sincerely,

" M."

" You will know that I have not a shade of literary *amour-propre*, and *in one* sense the more faults you find, the more valuable for me."

In his *Life of Gladstone* he had quoted from a letter from Gladstone to Granville (October 8th, 1885) :

" Chamberlain has been here. He is a good man to talk to ; not only from his force and clearness, but because he speaks with reflection, does not misapprehend, or (I think) suspect, or make unnecessary difficulties, or endeavour to maintain pedantically the uniformity and consistency of his arguments," and Morley had added the comment, " No description could be more exact."

I was not entirely reassured by the statement that he had none of an author's *amour-propre*. No doubt he meant what he wrote, but would he in fact like it if I took him at his word and how would he receive my comments? I was not quite happy about the task I had undertaken. There was so much in what he had written that gave me pleasure and yet there were some things in which I thought his words were open to misconstruction, and two passages which showed a real misunderstanding of my father's attitude. However, I took him at his word and wrote fully and frankly.

Morley's reply was more than generous and showed how wrong I had been to doubt the spirit in which he would receive them. He wrote (January 3rd, 1917) :

" My dear Austen,

" Influenza has knocked me off my perch, and my recovery of strength is horribly slow. But I flew eagerly to the box when it was brought to me, and I have thoroughly digested both the letter and the spirit of all you say. To every one of your points I assent, and the result will be to lessen the chance of *jar*, and to make the whole picture richer, and more worthy of the best and truest sides of the original.

" This is the first letter written out my bed for a month, so forgive clumsiness and believe that I do most heartily appreciate your kindness, judgment, and honest candour. I may recast a good deal, in the light of your letter and an excellent one from your sister.

" The caucus oysters provided me with a good laugh, and several capital meals much approved by the medicos.

" All happiness to you and your house for the year.

" Yours always sincerely,

" M."

The " caucus oysters " need a word of explanation. In reading my father's letters to him I had been reminded that it was my father's custom for many years to send him a barrel of oysters every Christmas and the first gift of the kind had, I suppose, been recommended by my father as being of the " caucus brand." I thought it would be pleasant to revive this old custom and had sent them with the explanation that I must revive the old name for, writing from what he had called his " august chair " in the India Office, I dare not call them " natives."

When his book was published I wrote to him again and asked for a few words from him to paste on the fly-leaf of my copy. He replied :

" I am sorry you have had a ' sympathetic ' or other cough ; but it is at all events a comfort that when you were in Paris you were not infected with the desire to make a sympathetic *speech*. Don't you think so? . . . I enclose a word or two for your copy. There is nobody whose acceptance of the book gives me more contentment than yours. All possible good wishes to you and your household.

" Yours always,

" M."

The inscription enclosed was :

To

AUSTEN CHAMBERLAIN

———

From John Morley
with cordial regards
and a host of
cherished memories
November 1917.

The oysters reappear in other letters. They were the symbol of those cherished memories. With the gift of Christmas 1918 I must have recalled some of them, for he replies :

" I have not for many a day had a letter that gave me better pleasure than yours. It awakens a host of the most delightful memories that still linger in my mind, and your kind words move me to the core.

" I retain my lifelong attachment to the Bivalve, without fear of any disaster ; and we will drink the health of the giver of them with infinite cordiality, you may be sure."

My last letter from him was written on December 20th, 1920, when I had become Chancellor of the Exchequer for the second time :

" Thank you, with all my heart, Dear Austen, for your letter and the gift. They recall in these last days the earlier and the happiest days of all my long life. Warmly do I wish you and your household all the good you want.

"Irony is hard to keep out of our poor human affairs, and the same post that brings your letter, brings from my accountant an assessment for Income Tax, amounting to —— Thousands of pounds, and including the unholy item of Super Tax! All the same, I remain your grateful friend,

"MORLEY OF B."

Surely such friendships are rare. It was a cruel turn of fortune's wheel which parted the two friends in 1886 and made them protagonists in opposite camps. The strife was bitter for a time; hard words were spoken on both sides and for a time these rankled and kept the friends apart; but Time the Healer closed these wounds and the old feeling revived. When I wrote to Morley from Highbury at Christmas 1913, he answered:

"The happiest days of my life were passed in the house from which you write. If you think your father would care to hear it, I wish you would assure him that old memories are unabated with me and always will be."

In the same letter Morley wrote:

"Ah 1914! 'Oh that a man might know the end of this year's business ere it come!' I see not a patch of blue sky—not for the country, as you rightly put it."

He was thinking of Ireland, but his words, like the irony of a Greek tragedy, had a deeper meaning. In August war broke out. My father had died in the preceding month.[1] The last words exchanged between the two old friends were messages of peace.

[1] Lord Morley died September 1923.

XV

ARTHUR JAMES BALFOUR

I

"BALFOUR has the finest brain that has been applied to politics in our time." So Birkenhead, himself no mean judge, said to me as we walked away from a Cabinet meeting in which Balfour had taken a leading and decisive part, and such, I believe, would be the general verdict to-day. Yet in the obituary notices published on the morrow of his death,[1] his Prime Ministership was generally written down a failure; at best it was treated as the least satisfactory part of his public life.

This judgment needs revision. Balfour's premiership lasted less than three years in all; it began when the Unionist Party had already been in office for seven years and when the reaction from the "Khaki Election" and the South African War was already in full force; the Tariff Reform controversy broke out within a year and thereafter tended more and more to overshadow all other questions. Within six months it led to the resignations of the two most powerful figures in the Cabinet[2] and of three other Ministers at the head of first-class Departments of State.[3] Yet Balfour's courage never failed; he maintained consistently the line he had marked out for himself and he accomplished successfully and by his own force of will three great

[1] Died 1930.
[2] Joseph Chamberlain and the Duke of Devonshire.
[3] Lord Balfour of Burleigh, Mr. C. T. Ritchie and Lord George Hamilton.

reforms which, however criticized at the moment, have stood the test of time and still dominate the scene to-day. Simultaneously he carried through a revolution in our foreign policy. It is not easy to find a parallel to such an achievement accomplished in so short a time and amidst such difficulties.

Let me justify these words:

i. He established the Committee of Imperial Defence.

The conception was his; the form and manner of its constitution was his, and his was the direction given to its first steps, to be developed indeed later but never to be changed in any material respect. For the first time in its history our country was equipped with a body competent to examine the problems presented by the defence of the Empire as a whole and to work out schemes embracing in one common view the parts to be played by the army and navy acting on a common or co-ordinated plan prepared beforehand, instead of an imperfect co-operation hastily arranged when the crisis was already upon them. Nor did the change end there, for by the elastic constitution which he gave to the Committee, not only the fighting services but also the civil departments could be and were represented as required on the Committee and its sub-committees, and thus learned for the first time what would be required of them in war whilst they brought their special knowledge and experience into the common stock.

It is impossible to over-rate the service thus rendered by Balfour to the country and the Empire. Without this Committee and the work done by it under him and his successors, the outbreak of the Great War would have found us wholly unprepared for the problems with which it at once confronted the Government, and, humanly speaking, victory would have been impossible. It may be added that apart from the service which he rendered by creating such an organ, it would be difficult to overstate Balfour's personal contribution to its earliest inquiries. It may be sufficient on this head to say that when, more than twenty - five years later, the Government of the day appointed a committee with Birkenhead as chairman to review the problem of Indian defence, it was the unanimous view of all its members, including the chief military advisers of the Crown both in this country and India, that, though changed conditions naturally required some alterations in the tactical application of the strategical principles which Balfour had laid down, his statement of the strategic principles themselves could not be bettered.

ii. After a series of fruitless efforts by others to deal with the educational problems of the day, he devised and framed the Education Act of 1902 which, however disastrous its immediate effects on the fortunes of the party (and it nearly destroyed the Liberal-Unionist wing, driving masses of Nonconformists back into the Liberal fold), has held the field for thirty years. As Sir Charles Trevelyan confessed when Minister of Education in the late Labour Government, after the first revival of controversy had cleared away it was found to have removed the sectarian difficulties which had stood in the path of educational reform ever since Forster's Act of 1870, and the solution which Balfour provided has remained practically unaltered down to the present day. Without this measure every effort at the reform and development of primary education might still have been rendered abortive, as so many previous efforts had been, by the old religious controversies.

iii. He reformed the Licensing Law, making for the first time systematic provision for the reduction of redundant licences throughout the country. I believe that he found the basis for his Bill in a scheme which had worked for a time successfully in the City of Birmingham, but had then led to disagreement and been finally destroyed by a decision of Quarter Sessions. That the Bill was wholly his work I can testify, for I was a member of the Cabinet Committee which was appointed to draft a Bill and the draft which that committee produced bore no resemblance to Balfour's scheme which replaced it. This Act also has stood the test of time.

In each of these three matters the initiative, the conception and the execution of the new plan were wholly his own and so was the force of will which carried them through the Cabinet and Parliament. After the resignation of the five Ministers in the autumn of 1903 it may be said with truth that the Government existed only by and through him; yet it lasted another two years.

No Prime Minister ever took a closer interest or, except when also Foreign Secretary, as had been the case with Lord Salisbury and was again to be the case with Mr. Ramsay MacDonald in his first administration, a more active part in the conduct of foreign policy. At decisive moments when Salisbury was absent or unwell, Balfour had acted for him, and when he himself became Prime Minister it is safe to say that Lansdowne took no important step and sent no important despatch without first consulting him. It does not detract from Lansdowne's services as Foreign Secretary to say that his chief accomplishments would never have been achieved but for the constructive mind of Balfour and the constant support he gave him, not only in executing his foreign policy, but in conceiving and shaping it. To them, and to my father in the earlier stages, were due the Anglo-French *Entente* and the Anglo-Japanese Alliance—two events of the first order of magnitude which fixed the lines of our foreign policy for the next ten years and, conserved and developed by Lord Grey after the defeat of the Conservative Party at the close of 1905, were—I think it is not putting the case too high—decisive for our own fate and it may well be for the world's, when the day of Armageddon came.

It is true that, whilst all this was being accomplished, the Government was steadily declining in popular favour, and less and less able to rely even on its majority in the House of Commons until at last, as Lord Grey remarked, though he had known governments which had lost public favour without realizing it, and others which had realized it without admitting it, this was the first Government which openly avowed that it no longer possessed the confidence of the country but nevertheless asserted its determination to continue to govern as long as it retained the support of its parliamentary majority. Balfour himself openly justified this position as sound constitutional practice, but it is now no secret that his real reason and purpose were to conclude the Anglo-Japanese negotiations and to see the Treaty ratified before he surrendered power to Campbell-Bannerman, in whose policy he felt no trust. The result, when the elections at last came, is not likely to tempt any of his successors to carry on in similar circumstances.

To what was this debacle due? I have already called attention to the fact that when Balfour succeeded to the Premiership, the reaction against the Unionist Party, bred of seven years of office and the mistakes and losses of the South African War, had already begun. The Education Bill, great and enduring as has been its success when once in operation, deprived the Liberal-Unionist wing of the party outside Birmingham of the great bulk of middle- and working-class nonconformity, which had been its main source of strength in the towns and villages. Even in Birmingham itself the situation was only saved by my father's influence and the extraordinary exertions which he made to prevent a similar disaster befalling the party in that stronghold of Unionism. Thus the cohesion of the Government supporters was already badly shattered before ever my father's speech of May 1903 evoked that wide and immediate response which took him as much as others by surprise, and at once placed Tariff Reform in the front rank of the questions of the day.

This is not the place to write the history of these events which must be told by Mr. Garvin in his *Life of Joseph Chamberlain*. It is sufficient to say here that that history would have been very different if, during my father's absence in South Africa, the then Chancellor of the Exchequer [1] and those who acted with him, had not repudiated the decision to retain the Corn Duty and use it for the purposes of Imperial Preference, a decision taken by the Cabinet before my father left England in the previous autumn. It was from that repudiation that all our subsequent troubles sprang.

I do not pretend that I think Balfour's subsequent handling of the situation wise, but it was certainly not lacking in courage. He was not then or thereafter, so far as I know, a full-blooded Protectionist, but he was definitely a " fiscal reformer." The old Free Traders were consistent advocates of the principle of *laisser-faire* in fiscal and social questions alike. Balfour was neither a Protectionist nor a Socialist, but he did not believe that the old dogmas on which our

[1] Mr. (afterwards Lord) Ritchie.

Free Trade policy was founded were theoretically sound. He had always desired the power of retaliation or bargaining in negotiations with foreign countries, and believed that the time had now come definitely to break with the doctrine of *laisser-faire* in trade questions just as it had long been abandoned in industrial affairs. As regards Imperial Preference he clearly appreciated (as some of his colleagues did not) the vital importance of the problems which the development of colonial nationalism was creating. When the question was definitely raised by Laurier's pronouncements, he was, as usual with him, a little sceptical and very questioning, but never for one moment did he minimize its importance and he was quite determined not to bang, bar or bolt any new doors. His view on this matter was clearly stated in a letter to the Duke of Devonshire :

"If, as seems certain, Canada and other Colonies are prepared to employ their tariffs in order to further an Imperial ideal, and if, as seems probable, the rejection of their overtures will lead to their withdrawal and we become worse off as an Empire than if those overtures had never been made, I should be sorry to think that I belong to a Government or a Party which hastily rejected them." [1]

But—and this is vital to an understanding of his action then and throughout the controversy—the purpose which was dominant in his mind from the first moment that such a danger appeared was to prevent the break-up of the party. He thought Peel's action in 1846 inexcusable. Praise of Peel at any time drew from him the same sharp condemnation. "He committed the unforgivable sin ; he broke up his party." Balfour himself was determined not to repeat the fault. He felt that, on becoming leader, he

[1] See Bernard Holland's *Life of the Duke of Devonshire*, Vol. II, p. 328 (Longmans).

had accepted a trust and that his first duty was to maintain intact what had been committed to his charge. He understood and sympathized with the hopes and the anxieties of those who placed the Imperial problem first. He would go with them as far as he could without breaking up the party, but he would not go beyond the point at which he thought that party union could be maintained.

So he chose his position and refused to be driven from it. He made no effort to keep the colleagues who were not prepared to break definitely with the old hampering dogma; he accepted Chamberlain's resignation, not because he objected in principle to Imperial Preference, but because he did not believe it to be as yet within the range of practical politics. He made great efforts to retain the Duke of Devonshire, but his course was not shaken by his secession a few weeks later. No man ever faced greater difficulties with greater courage. He was not a successful party leader, but on a calm review of the obstacles which beset his path from the first and of his achievement, who shall deny his title to be named among our great Prime Ministers?

2

What, it has been asked was his real attitude to Politics? Was he merely a dilettante who had been seduced into the political arena by the accident of his relationship to Lord Salisbury, one who found pleasure in the dialectical duels for which the House of Commons afforded an opportunity, but at heart cared for none of these things? Was his real passion for philosophy, or natural science or some other study of his active and questioning mind? He cared for all these things; he cared for them intensely. It was said of Mr. Gladstone that he could talk on almost any subject so well, and with such wealth of knowledge that he appeared an expert on that subject to all except the experts in it. Balfour's knowledge was of another kind. It was the men of the profession, the experts themselves, who most delighted to discuss with him their own subject; and he himself loved to talk another man's "shop." "The man who talks shop," he once said, "never bores me, for he is talking of something that he knows. What I can't stand is the man who insists on talking about what he doesn't know." His intellectual interest was in fact almost as wide as the universe, but though other studies might have claimed him in his earliest years and were never completely abandoned, I am convinced that, at least from the time when he became Chief Secretary for Ireland, politics became his ruling passion to which, in the measure which their pursuit made necessary, he was prepared to, and in fact did, subordinate all the others.

As leader he had a very high sense of his duty to the party which had entrusted its fortunes to him, but he was very far from being a typical party man. I cannot do better than apply to him the description given by Sainte Beuve of the first Duc de Broglie: "He is one of the most original minds of his time; this is seen above all in the form, the method and the means of demonstration which he employs; even when he thinks what everyone else is thinking, when he reaches the same conclusions, he reaches them or convinces himself of them by reasons peculiar to himself. He has his own reasons for everything, perhaps true, sometimes subtle, always ingenious and never common."

Therein lay his weakness both as a leader and as a speaker. Things which seemed important to him often appeared of little consequence to his followers and to his opponents (as for instance in the Tariff controversy) a mere splitting of hairs, a quibble unworthy of the ingenuity with which he sustained it and of the serious issues at stake. He was not content to make a broad statement of his views without at the same time giving expression to all the qualifications which to his mind it required. In the course of the Tariff controversy after my father had left the Government, I once asked Balfour to put together in a single speech at the Albert Hall three simple statements of principle which were to be found separately in as many of his previous speeches. I assured him that if he would do this, he would make it much easier for my father to co-operate heartily with him. He readily agreed; indeed he drew from a drawer in his writing-table a couple of those long envelopes on which he was accustomed to make his notes and showed me that he had already jotted down two out of the three points which I had mentioned for incorporation in his speech. I reported to my father what had passed between us, who replied that if Balfour would do that, it would be very satisfactory and helpful.

The sequel is curious. My father rang me up on the telephone the morning after the Albert Hall meeting. "Well," he said, "Balfour has let us down. He hasn't said what he told you he would say."

"Oh yes he has," I answered and recited the three points, adding that he had made them all, and I proceeded to read them out from *The Times* which lay before me. "That's all right," said my father, but where do you find that?" Alas! there was the rub. The first statement came near the beginning, the second in the middle and the third near the end of the speech. The effect which I had hoped they would produce was wholly lost in the mass of intervening matter. In my despair I told Balfour of this conversation. I urged that it was useless to exhibit an easel-picture from the platform of a mass meeting; the details, instead of making it clearer, simply rendered its meaning indistinguishable. The speaker in such circumstances must work like the scene-painter; he could only get his effects by painting in the broadest outlines. Balfour sighed and confessed that that was doubtless true, but he could not change his ways. He was in fact always strongest in attack and weakest in exposition, much better in the House of Commons which had learned to know him, than in a mass meeting which was puzzled by his ways and often found it difficult to follow his argument and extract its meaning.

His power over the House was never more amazingly shown than in the months which followed his return to it as member for the City of London after his defeat at Manchester in the disastrous rout of the party in 1906. A mere remnant of his followers in the preceding Parliament had survived the debacle. The House was full of strange faces. The majority, flushed with victory after ten years of defeat, was intolerant and rude to him. It was not so much that they disliked him as that they despised him, and contempt is less easy to conquer than hatred. They openly jeered at him and constantly interrupted him when speaking. In the midst of it all he remained unmoved even when his friends were provoked to fierce indignation and remonstrance, and before the year was out, he had won the respect of every one of his opponents. However much they disagreed with him or smarted under his rapier thrusts, they felt that he gave distinction to the House and brought qualities to its service which no other of its members possessed in a like degree.

3

To the charm of his character and the pleasure of his converse, all who knew him bear witness. To me he was always the kindest of friends and the most helpful and encouraging of chiefs and colleagues. He gave freely and always of his best alike in council and in conversation, and his conversation had a peculiar charm for the men of a younger generation, for he was not only an admirable talker but a most encouraging listener. I have found many besides myself to confess that, after an evening spent in his company, one left with the feeling that one had been at the top of one's form and really had talked rather well. A night's reflection showed one that it was he who had worked the miracle, listening with such interest, drawing out one's thought and often transmuting it to more precious metal by his own alchemy. Only to pretension and conceit was he without mercy.

What was the real Balfour—the inner man whose secrets he guarded so jealously from prying eyes? Was he at bottom heartless and indifferent, as some have suggested, both for himself and others? I do not believe it. He was far more sensitive to any charge which touched his honour or pride than his contemptuous " I do not read the news-papers " would suggest, and I, who was at his right hand during the last two years of his Prime Ministership, know what it cost him to part with George Wyndham and Hayes-Fisher.[1] " Are you going to the Eton and Harrow match? " I asked him in one of his later years, and he answered almost with a shudder, " No; there are too many ghosts! " and I remember with what deep feeling he spoke

[1] Mr. George Wyndham, M.P., Chief Secretary for Ireland in Balfour's Government, resigned in May 1905. Mr William Hayes-Fisher, M.P. (afterwards Lord Downham) was Financial Secretary to the Treasury, but resigned in April 1903.

to me of George Wyndham and Alfred Lyttelton in the
early months of the War when his thoughts turned naturally
to the friends with whom he had worked in the past.
Whatever others may think, I at least am convinced that
he not only needed the sympathy and affection with which
he was surrounded but that he returned it.

Lord D'Abernon, in one of those brilliant "appreciations"
which he prefixed to his account of his Berlin Embassy,
asserts that Balfour "was hampered by no passionate
convictions." It may be a bold thing to differ from so
shrewd an observer, but in this instance I cannot follow
his judgment. Indeed to me the most remarkable thing
about Balfour is that with a mind so critical, so little inclined
to expect great results from any accomplishment within
the power of man, he yet did take so passionate an interest
in all mundane affairs. He was as keen as a boy about
the sports which interested him. Though he constantly
reminded us that Parliament could achieve little, and that
the best that could be hoped from legislation, even his
own, was that it would do no harm and might even do a
little good, he fought his battles with a passion that I have
seen elsewhere only in men of far more positive and
sanguine temperament. It is his distinction, to quote a
phrase of Lord D'Abernon's, to have "held towards life
an attitude attained only by the truly philosophic," to
have seen the littleness of man's life and his struggles and
yet never to have allowed his sense of this littleness to
paralyse his arm or to prevent him from doing with all
his might that which his hand found to do. He may have
cared little for much which other men thought important,
but he fought passionately and tenaciously for that which
he held to be true.

Lord D'Abernon poses many questions about the inner

man and concludes, " all these are problems which have remained insoluble during his life and will probably remain insoluble for posterity." Yet it is Lord D'Abernon who writes of him, " his general theory of life appeared to be that happiness is close to us, in freedom from bondage to imagined good, and in emancipation from the things of sense. No one less than he sought happiness in regions where happiness is not to be found."

To have combined the practice of so lofty a philosophy with so active and so combatant a life is given to few indeed.

XVI

ANDREW BONAR LAW

MR. BALDWIN, when unveiling a portrait of Bonar Law, said of him that he had a personality "lovable, elusive and wistful." No better words could have been chosen to describe him.

He was essentially a lovable man. It is the first word which springs to my mind when I think of him. It was not merely that in his own family he was surrounded, as so many of us are, with the most watchful and devoted affection; in a wider circle he won friends, as it seemed without seeking them, by the kindness of his heart, and perhaps not less by the rather pathetic solitude in which the inner man appeared to dwell, especially after the death of his wife, and by that air of wistful longing for it seemed he knew not what, of which Mr. Baldwin spoke. Again, as leader of the Conservative Party, he won the confidence and affection of his supporters in an unusual degree, and in difficult times, when other parties were breaking up under the stresses and strains of a revolutionary period, he retained their unbounded trust and kept them united.

How great was his influence with them may be illustrated by three cases in which his action was decisive. He precipitated the formation of the first Coalition Government under Asquith, and his action in allying himself with Lloyd George was a not less important factor in its fall. He it was who decided, I believe without any previous consultation with his Unionist colleagues and against the wish of some of them, to fight the " Coupon Election " after the Armistice on a Coalition basis; and, finally his attitude at the Carlton Club meeting of 1922 and his readiness to assume the Premiership, determined the attitude of the majority of the party towards the Coalition and brought it to an end. It is part of the irony of life that I should have wished to end the Coalition with the War, and that he should then have decided to continue it only to bring about its destruction when I had fallen heir to his inheritance and felt myself bound in honour by the ties which he had created. I saw him late in the afternoon of the day preceding the Carlton Club meeting. He was then still undecided as to his course, and spoke sadly and with much sympathy for me. It was a hateful position, he said. He thought he would plead the state of his health and keep away from the meeting altogether, but in that case he must leave Parliament and give up public life. If he came to the meeting, he must speak against me. I told him that his speech would be decisive; the vote would go in his favour, the Government would have to resign and he would have to form a new one. " Well," he said again, as I took my leave of him, " it's a hateful position; I expect that if I had remained in your place I should have acted like you."

Such apparent inconsistencies were not unusual with him and are not easily explained. His was indeed an elusive personality. Mr. Baldwin thought he had found the explanation in a childhood passed in very straitened circumstances in a lonely New Brunswick Manse, but he was at once taken to task by a Glasgow correspondent, who wrote that Bonar Law had left New Brunswick in early boyhood and had been brought up by relations in

Glasgow in ease and comfort, if not in luxury. Be that as it may, the picture of the New Brunswick home which Mr. Baldwin drew seemed the fitting background for his life and character. Whatever his creed in later days, his early Calvinistic training had left deep traces on his attitude to life. Of such things he and I never spoke. The nearest we came to them was one morning when we walked away together from the memorial service held at St. Margaret's for Alfred Lyttelton. We were silent for some moments and then, turning to me, he spoke: "If such things can so move you and me, Austen, who do not belong to that Church, what must not they mean to those who were brought up in its fold!"

Something of the bleakness and the solitude of the long winters of the land in which he was born seemed to cling to him through life. He did not care for society and, unless in a familiar circle, was shy and reserved. I have often seen him smile, but I cannot recall having ever heard him laugh outright. Mirth seemed a stranger to him. Even his pleasures were for the most part of the sedate and studious kind. I do not think he read much poetry or ever quoted it, but he would have found his kindred spirit in " Il Penseroso " rather than " L'Allegro."

> " Hence, vain deluding Joys,
>   The brood of Folly without father bred!
>   How little you bested,
>   Or fill the fixèd mind with all your toys!"

And he might well have ended with the same appeal:

·   ·   ·   ·

> " These pleasures, Melancholy, give;
>   And I with thee will choose to live."

Melancholy indeed seemed his chosen companion even when I first knew him before the happiness of his home had been laid low by his wife's early death. The air of sadness which was native to him seemed to call for sympathy and drew men's hearts to him; yet it was not easy with such a nature to give that sympathy except mutely. He did not wear his heart upon his sleeve or encourage others to do so. It was, perhaps, one of the ties which bound us to one another that we could understand and sympathize with each other without the need to put our feelings into words.

What was the secret of his hold upon the Party? He was a brilliant debater and a most effective platform speaker. He had a marvellous memory, a great and unequalled capacity for the lucid and logical presentation of his case. He had, in addition, a way of clinching his argument and driving it home to the mind of his audience which recalled to members of my family the speeches of my father. These qualities are sufficient to explain his parliamentary and platform successes; but they are not sufficient to explain the confidence which the party, and later the country, came to repose in him. That must be sought less in his gifts than in the character which he gradually and unconsciously revealed to them.

It was, indeed, the opening of a new chapter in the history of the Conservative Party when he became its leader. He had no connection with the great Tory families; he was unknown outside political circles; he had never held high office nor even sat in a Cabinet. To the ideas of the landed gentry, so influential and still so numerous in the Tory ranks, he was a stranger. He had singularly little regard for tradition and even less for the forms in which it was enshrined. Even to me, brought up in boyhood among advanced Radicals, he sometimes appeared an iconoclast, and in England at least he was a Nonconformist.

He once said to me, before the War had stirred deeper emotions, that he cared intensely for only two things: Tariff Reform and Ulster; all the rest was only part of the game. The success of such a man as leader of the Tory Party presents one of the paradoxes of our political life.

He was already forty-two when he was first elected to the House of Commons. Not very long afterwards he was sitting alone with me in the old smoking-room of the House of Commons, a prey to one of those moods of depression which beset him from time to time throughout his life. I tried to cheer him up. " No, Austen," he replied, " this is no place for me. It's all very well for men like you who came into it young; but if I had known then what I know now, I would never have stood for Parliament." So, many years before, when I had just become a candidate for the Border Burghs, W. H. Smith had said to me that I did well to begin young, for the House was no place for a man who, like himself, had come into it for the first time when he was already over forty. Yet W. H. Smith was then, as Bonar Law was later to become, the leader of the House and one of its most trusted and respected figures.

Bonar Law was endowed with far more brilliant parliamentary gifts than W. H. Smith, but the secret of success in both cases was the same; it lay in character—in their natural simplicity of life, in the absence of all pretension and affectation and in their single-minded devotion to duty.

This is not to say that Bonar Law was without ambition. Asquith once spoke of him as " mildly ambitious." This was entirely to mistake the man. He was not mildly but intensely ambitious—I sometimes think he was the most ambitious man whom I have known in politics. I once confessed to him that I had made many attempts to read Gibbon's *Decline and Fall*, but had never succeeded in persevering to the end. He was astonished and declared at once that he found that great procession of ambitious men, realizing their ambitions only to be cheated of their hopes, the most fascinating of all studies. He knew that he was ambitious and could not understand why others did not perceive it. "You make a great mistake about me," he once told the members of the Press Gallery at the House of Commons when they entertained him at luncheon. "You think I am a modest man with no ambition. I am really very ambitious." [1] And when he had to deliver his Rectorial Address at Glasgow University, he chose "Ambition" for his theme, and recalled how as he listened many years before to Mr. Gladstone's Rectorial Address, he had resolved that one day he too would be Lord Rector.

In another man, such ambition might have been his ruin. Bonar Law was saved by his strong sense of duty. When the first Coalition was formed, he would not permit his friends to press his claim to the Chancellorship of the Exchequer, and allowed Mr. McKenna to be appointed to it over his head. I know that he felt the slight to his position which Asquith's choice implied, but he would suffer no remonstrance to be made. Ambitious he was, but there was nothing mean or selfish about the ambitions which he entertained.

He and I had our differences; we did not always see eye to eye, and I confess it pained me when it was he who, emerging from his retirement, struck the blow which put an end to my leadership. But there was no bitterness in

[1] I had this story from the late Sir Alfred Robbins, who was among the hosts.

our divisions, no loss of mutual respect and affection, and I was glad indeed when his family put, as it were, the seal upon our friendship by choosing me to be one of the pall-bearers at his funeral in the Abbey.[1]

He was indeed a most lovable man.

[1] Mr. Bonar Law died October 1923.

XVII
FRENCH AND ENGLISH

No two nations have greater need to understand one another than England and France; and yet no two peoples find national understanding more difficult. " It is not," wrote Monsieur de Madariaga in days when he was still a member of the Secretariat of the League of Nations, "it is not that it is impossible to bring France and England to see eye to eye; only their eyes are so different." The clarity of the French mind which shines so brilliantly in its noble prose, is alien to the more slovenly habits of English thought. The stern logic which Frenchmen require is not only alien to the English character but repugnant to our experience. All our history is a compromise. The Thirty-nine Articles of the Church of England balance as delicately between conflicting dogmas, as the resolution which declared the throne of James II vacant and united in its support Whigs and Tories, High Churchmen and Independents, supporters of Passive Obedience and the right divine of kings and the sons of those who only a generation earlier had cut off the head of James's father. The men of the French Revolution proclaimed a new faith and sought to bring into existence a new order. It has been the claim of English reformers from our earliest days that they sought no innovation, but only the restoration of ancient liberties which had fallen into disuse. It was a wise saying that in Europe every man is born two thousand years old. We cannot escape from our past. Frenchmen and Englishmen alike are what history has made them. The French constitution has been made and remade. The British constitution has grown. The one is a structure carefully planned where every stress and strain has been calculated by the builders and provision made against it in advance—a classic building begun and finished in a single style. The other is a Gothic building bearing evidence, in the varying styles of nave and clerestory, of transepts and choir, of its slow development, and still resting on the rounded Norman arches of an earlier structure which themselves, not improbably, rise on Saxon foundations. There is much of history and character to be read in old buildings.

As in big things, so in small there is much which makes mutual comprehension difficult. The difference of manners, the different key in which the emotions are expressed are apt to lead the Englishman to think the Frenchman exaggerated and insincere, and to make the Frenchman judge the Englishman cold and unsympathetic even when he feels most deeply and most desires to show his friendliness; and more deadly still, the Englishman's absence of logic alike in thought and deed supplies the foundation for the charge of national hypocrisy to which he too often retorts against his critic, the charge of national cynicism.

It is easier to state these differences and to recognize the difficulties and misunderstandings to which they give rise, than to suggest a remedy. By contrast with the first approach of Englishman and Frenchman, generally uneasy and constrained, the first meeting of German and Englishman is usually easy and deceptively cordial. For one thing, the Englishman in general is no great linguist and knowledge of the English language is far more general among Germans than among Frenchmen. At first sight, too, their habits and modes of thought seem not very dissimilar; it is only as one goes deeper, that the profound differences appear. Our growth is rooted in a different soil and watered by different rivers. The deeper Englishmen and Frenchmen penetrate into each other's nature, the more they will find they have in common; the deeper Englishman and German go, the greater the divergence of faith and spirit which will be revealed between them. It is not without significance that it was precisely those Englishmen who knew Germany best, who had lived there or had formed German connections, who first foresaw and warned their countrymen of the coming peril. " What has been, may be." If the peril ever revives, the same deep forces will be at work, the same great issues at stake. England and France will need each other. Pray God they stand together or our common civilization will perish.

Our common civilization, yes, for we have a conception of the dignity of man and of the freedom of the human mind which is our common birthright. Alone, among the Great Powers of Europe, France and England still champion ideas deep rooted in their national character which elsewhere have lost their attraction. In the country of Goethe his lofty and inquiring intellect and his free spirit would find no home to-day; the passionate love of liberty which inspired Schiller would be silenced or driven to seek elsewhere the right to think its own thoughts and to express its soul. " According to plan " has become " According to pattern." Conform or perish! is the new law. Mr. Baldwin's words have a wider application and a deeper meaning than that which he gave them: " Our frontier is on the Rhine."

I am an Englishman. If ever, which God forbid! strife should break out again between France and England, I am with my country, right or wrong, and all the time. But

I hold, with deep conviction, that such a struggle between the two great democracies of western Europe would be not only fatal to them both, but a calamity for the world. I ask of Frenchmen nothing which I do not ask equally of my own countrymen. I plead with both for a closer study of their neighbour, for a willing recognition of the limits set by history and geography, by temperament and circumstance beyond which neither people can advance.

In such larger comprehension lies the beginning of wisdom and in the wise direction of our relations lies the safety of us all.

XVIII

ANGLO-AMERICAN FRIENDSHIP

BESIDE the Mall, near to the Admiralty Arch, there stands a monument erected by the officers and men of the Royal Marines in memory of their comrades who fell in the South African War and the Boxer troubles in China. It represents a private of the corps standing at bay with a fallen comrade at his feet.

On the pedestal are two bronze bas-reliefs. The one shows a party of marines working the big naval guns at the defence of Ladysmith; the other depicts an episode in the defence of the Peking Legations, and the moment chosen is one when, all the British officers being disabled by wounds or illness, the detachment was commanded by a United States officer, easily distinguishable by his uniform from the British troops in whose midst he stands. The scenes to be depicted were chosen by the marines themselves.

Is there in any other country a monument erected by soldiers to their fallen comrades where they have deliberately selected from a crowd of glorious memories that one moment which shows them fighting under the command of an officer of another country than their own? No words of mine could so well express the sense of comradeship and kinship which Britons feel for Americans.

Perhaps we sometimes exaggerate the kinship. No Englishman in common parlance would speak of an

American as a foreigner. It comes to us naturally to think of Americans as kinsmen from whom we have parted, with whom we have, alas, twice quarrelled and not infrequently disagreed, but still as kinsmen—men who shared all but a small fraction of our history, who speak the same language, who read the same Bible, who are co-heirs with us of the glories of English literature,

> " who speak the tongue
> That Shakespeare spake, the faith and morals hold
> That Milton held."

We are apt to forget how large a part of those who went even from our own islands went with bitterness in their hearts. Still more, perhaps, are we apt to forget how large a part of the population of the United States to-day is drawn from other sources with different habits, sympathies and traditions. But when all due allowance is made for the differences that do exist, we believe that we are nearer to Americans than to any other nation outside the British Commonwealth and that in fundamentals we stand for the same things.

It is a truism of British policy that the greatest British interest is peace, but a war between the United States and ourselves seems to us different in kind from any other war, so fratricidal, so unnatural that we refuse to contemplate it even as a possibility, and that for as long as I have known anything of British Governments it has never entered into their calculations of what was necessary for defence. The three-thousand-mile frontier between Canada and the United States is unfortified. It is policed rather than defended by such forces as either nation maintains in its neighbourhood. The British Islands from the Bermudas to the Caribbean tell the same tale of trust and confidence.

No European frontiers are so unguarded, nor do those who dwell on them live in such care-free security.

But, as I have said elsewhere, a mere negative statement of this kind would be a very inadequate description of our thoughts and policy. We desire not only to live at peace with the United States, but to cultivate the most cordial and the closest relations with them, and this desire has increasingly affected the course of British policy in recent years. In the Spanish-American War British sympathy was from the first entirely on the side of the United States. In China we stood with America in the early years of this century as supporters of the Open Door and as peaceful but determined opponents of the annexation of Chinese territory by particular Powers; at the Conference of Algeciras the objects of the British and American representatives were the same and they rendered one another reciprocal support, whilst more recently at the Conference of Versailles our delegations were habitually found in agreement on points on which both differed from the rest of the Allies.

These are cases in which common interests, common traditions and similar habits of thought caused our two nations to act in general agreement. A more direct instance of the influence of American opinion on British policy is seen in the termination of the Anglo-Japanese Alliance of 1905, or rather, in its conversion at the Washington Conference of 1921 into a quadruple treaty to which the United States and France as well as Great Britain and Japan are parties.

The case is an interesting one. The Anglo-Japanese Treaty had been for twenty years one of the sheet-anchors of British policy. Together with the conclusion of the *Entente* with France it marked the definite abandonment of the policy of "splendid isolation" which both English parties had followed towards the close of the last century. It was, moreover, considered as a particular guarantee of their security by the Commonwealth of Australia and the Dominion of New Zealand, and it was regarded by all of us as a bulwark of peace in the Pacific. Nevertheless, it was terminated because it gave rise to misunderstanding in America and was felt to be an obstacle to the friendship and confidence which we desired to see existing between us. It is not without significance that the strongest opposition to its renewal came from the Dominion of Canada, and that Canada, whose interests have not infrequently been the bone of contention between London and Washington, was on this occasion the connecting link between British and American opinion, just as Great Britain has at other times served as a bond of union between the United States and Europe.

This, I would claim, was conspicuously the rôle played by Great Britain in relation to the Pact of Paris, more commonly known among us as the Kellogg Pact. It is true that the idea of a treaty outlawing war was first broached by that great Frenchman and friend of peace, Aristide Briand, but it is not, I think, too much to say that the French were surprised and even alarmed when they saw their bantling presented to them in its American clothes. Mr. Kellogg's extended plan was warmly welcomed by all sections of opinion in Great Britain and the Dominions, but the first reaction in France was less favourable and the reply of the French Government seemed to English no less than to American ears less cordial than we should have expected. I believe that in the communications which followed, Great Britain played a useful and important part in interpreting the intentions and anxieties of either party to the other and, by the friendly explanations she invited and received, removed misunderstandings and secured agreement.

The very fact that the British Empire belongs to no continent but is represented on them all, gives to us a certain detachment which approximates our position in European affairs to that of the United States and fits us to be a connecting link between the Old World and the New. It is, indeed, my conviction that the wider American interests spread and the more the United States accept the consequences of their attainment to the position of a world power, the better shall we understand one another and the more shall we find ourselves driven by common interests and a common outlook to pursue a parallel policy.

It is, therefore, without jealousy that we have watched the phenomenal growth of the United States since the close of the Civil War, and we could give no greater proof of it than in accepting the doctrine of naval parity. To no other nation should we have made that sacrifice, to no other nation are we now prepared to make it. The sea has been our bulwark; it has been to us alike a defence and a highway : it is the sole means of communication between Great Britain and the rest of the Empire.

For historical reasons, a standing army has never held the place in the affections of the English people which it holds in most continental countries. On the other hand the navy has always been the popular idol and our naval supremacy has been the Ark of the Covenant, as sacred to all British parties as the Monroe Doctrine to the American people. Nevertheless we have accepted without hesitation the principle of parity with the United States, and the scale of our naval defence has in fact always been determined by other standards of comparison, whether the measure was, as at one time, equality with the fleets of the next two European Powers or, as in later times, a fixed superiority over the largest continental navy.

That the readiness and unanimity with which the principle of parity with the United States has been accepted in Great Britain is in part due to the sentiment of which I have already spoken is no doubt true, but sentiments may change and it is, therefore, well to note that in this case it has a solid basis of reasoning to support it.

The truth is that since the War of Independence there has only been one subject on which our respective views of public law have clashed, namely, the extent and limits of the rights enjoyed by a belligerent at sea against neutral commerce; and, at any rate at the point we have now reached in the world's development, the strength of the American Navy is not, paradoxical as it may seem, the decisive factor in determining how far in case of war we should press what we believe to be our rights against American opinion.

It is only in those wars in which all our resources are strained to the uttermost that the rigorous enforcement of our belligerent rights becomes a matter of high consequence to us. If in such a war the United States are engaged with us, as was the case in the later years of the Great War, no difference of interest or practice arises between us. If, on the other hand, they are neutral as in the early years of that struggle, it would be simple madness to drive them into the ranks of our enemies. The plain truth is, and we may as well frankly acknowledge it, that we could not afford to do so. It would not be necessary for them to send out a fleet or even to move a ship; it would suffice that they should place an embargo on supplies to us of money and munitions of war.

As Lord Grey of Fallodon says in his *Twenty-Five Years*:[1]

" The blockade of Germany was essential to the victory of the Allies, but the ill-will of the United States meant certain defeat. . . . The Allies soon became dependent for an adequate supply on the United States. If we quarrelled with the United States we could not get that supply. . . . The object of diplomacy, therefore, was to secure the maximum of blockade that could be enforced without a rupture with the United States."

We are, therefore, obliged by self-interest to refrain from pressing our rights beyond the point at which American acquiescence can be secured lest we should be deprived of the resources which are necessary to our defences.

Thus far I have spoken of the feelings of Britons toward America. What are the feelings of Americans toward Britain? It is a momentous question and on the answer much depends, both for our own peoples and for the world. America has become a world Power. She speaks as such and expects to be listened to as such; but no man and no nation can permanently maintain rights unless he or it accepts the responsibilities which flow from them. *Noblesse oblige;* in every privilege is inherent a corresponding duty. Unless the duty is accepted, the privilege cannot be sustained —good democratic doctrine, surely, which should appeal to the great republic.

The United States may still avoid entangling engagements in Europe. They may isolate themselves, but they cannot immunize themselves, as the course of the Great War shows. Their concern with Europe grows greater

[1] Hodder and Stoughton.

and their co-operation tends to increase as their commerce grows and their interests widen. Must not Americans sometimes ask themselves whether it would not be wiser—and safer—to try to guide events rather than merely to suffer their consequences?

I put the question only. I do not attempt to answer it. I venture only the prediction that if ever Americans are led by events to answer it in the affirmative, common interests and common habits of thought will make Great Britain and America the supporters of common ideas and associates in the cause of freedom and of peace.

Perhaps of more immediate interest to Americans than the dangers and difficulties of the Old World are the problems of the Pacific. New currents are stirring in the Far East; a new and, it may well be, a decisive era is opening. What is to be the attitude of the United States to these developments? American policy is obscure and perhaps not yet decided. Yet it is with America that the decision rests. It is by her that the lead must be given.

An Englishman can only say that the declared policy of the United States and Great Britain is the same—the maintenance of the integrity of China and of the Open Door for the trade and enterprise of all nations. Will this common purpose suffice to produce a common policy?

On the answer to that question peace may well depend, but the answer can be given only by America.

PART II
IDLE HOURS

XIX

OFF THE STAGE AT THE PEACE CONFERENCE

I

AN EVENING WITH LLOYD GEORGE

It must have been in March 1919, I think. I was Chancellor of the Exchequer and was summoned to Paris on some question of post-War finance, and travelled with Lloyd George. He had just paid his first visit to London since the reorganization of his Government after the general election of 1918. He had intended to employ that week in consultation with his colleagues as to their domestic policy, but he had found us in the midst of industrial troubles which threatened to involve us in a general strike throughout the South Wales coal-fields. He had to sacrifice everything to this emergency and had spent the week in continuous and harassing conferences with the warring representatives of masters and men. I expected to find him worn out. I myself who had taken but a small part in this business was tired and glad enough when, as the train started, Lloyd George settled down to read the morning's papers. At Dover I went to my cabin for a nap whilst Lloyd George, at the Captain's invitation, went up on the bridge and chatted with the Duke of Connaught and Sir Henry Wilson throughout the passage. In the train to Paris I joined the three at luncheon, and Lloyd George kept us all lively with his amusing talk, straying from the present to the past and back again, full of fun and good humour and wisdom, and apparently as free from care as a schoolboy on holiday. Then, with an apology to the Duke, he carried Wilson and me off " to talk business." As we approached Creil, he said, " And now I am going to have a nap." He was asleep almost before we left his compartment.

Arrived at Paris, I had just time to find the rooms assigned to me in the Hotel Majestic and to dress, before going to his apartment for dinner. There I found a party which included Balfour, such other Ministers as happened to be in Paris, and Sir Maurice Hankey. Lloyd George showed no sign of the anxieties and labours of the last few days and at the moment when I entered was assuring Balfour that there were at least six poets then writing in Welsh who, could the world but understand the language in which they wrote, would be recognized in all countries as poets of the highest order. Balfour observed dryly that it was a pity they did not give the world an opportunity to appreciate their merits!

We moved in to dinner and Lloyd George told admirably a moving story of the last Eisteddfod, how the seal of the envelope containing the name of the successful competitor had been broken and his name called that he might come forward and be crowned and installed in the Bardic chair. But no answer came. Silence succeeded to the burst of cheering which had greeted the announcement of the winner, a shepherd from the mountains. The name was called again, and in the breathless silence which followed came presently a piteous cry: " Killed on the Somme "; the chair was draped in black and crowned with the laurel wreath he should have worn, which was later carried to the lonely cottage where his mother dwelt in one of the mountain valleys.

Lloyd George finished, and turned rapidly to Balfour to ask what had been happening in the Peace Conference during his absence. Balfour could not report much progress. "After all, you have been away only seven days. I have been an exile from England since Christmas. Tell me what is happening there. What, for instance, is the new House of Commons like?"

"I'll tell you," said Lloyd George, his eyes sparkling with fun and a smile spreading rapidly over his face. "I made a speech to them. I addressed myself at first to the Opposition benches in front of me. They were very cold and hostile; I couldn't get a cheer. This, said I to myself, is not the House of Commons; it's the Trades Union Congress. So I turned as one does in such circumstances to the benches behind me, but neither was that the House of Commons; it was the Associated Chambers of Commerce."

2

MY LAST MEETING WITH BOTHA

The draft of the Treaty of Peace had been handed to the Germans and their reply had been received. We were again in Lloyd George's apartment—Lloyd George himself and Balfour, all the Dominion representatives and such British Ministers as were available. We had met in the morning, adjourned for lunch and met again in the afternoon. The question was should any concessions be granted, and if so, what; or should we insist that the treaty must be accepted as it stood. There had been much discussion as to what concessions could be proposed to the Allies with any chance of acceptance, but no difference as to the wisdom of conceding what we could. It must have been past six and I had to leave by the eight o'clock train for London, for my presence was needed in the house of Commons next day. "Well," I said, "I think we all seem agreed on the main question. You will not need me any more and I am content to leave further details to you."

"Wait a moment," said Lloyd George. "General Botha, you have not yet spoken?"

"Oh, I agree with the rest of you. It pays to be generous," and, laying his hand gently on Milner's shoulder, beside whom he was seated, he added with a friendly smile, "even a small country, driven to desperation, can give a great deal of trouble, as my good friend Milner knows."

That was the last time I saw Botha. He died[1] a few months later.

3

A DINNER WITH BALFOUR

The Peace Conference was in progress. We were a party of four dining in the Majestic, the headquarters of the British Delegation—Balfour and Ian Malcolm, then his Parliamentary Private Secretary, were the guests of Oliver Locker-Lampson, who served me in the same capacity, and myself.

In a momentary lull in the talk, Oliver suddenly asked, "Mr. Balfour, what do you think of the Prime Minister's brains?"

"Well," said Balfour after a moment's hesitation, "I'll tell you one thing about them. I've often been surprised when Lloyd George has come to what I thought the right decision on some complicated issue, to discover afterwards how little he appeared to have known about the essential

[1] August 1919.

facts. All I can say is that if I had known as little as he appeared to do, I should certainly have gone wrong."

This instinctive judgment, more like a woman's than a man's, accounts for some of his greatest successes—and no small part of his failures.

The talk turned to books. Again it was Oliver who spoke. " Mr. Balfour, if you were banished to an island and allowed to take with you the works of only one novelist, which would you choose? "

I suggested Thackeray.

" No, not Thackeray," said Balfour, waving aside my favourite novelist without discussion. " Dickens, perhaps, but certainly not Thackeray."

Other authors were discussed—Fielding, Scott, the Brontës. Then Balfour suggested Bulwer Lytton, whom he thought grossly underrated. I expressed my surprise, confessing that I found him unreadable. Balfour protested; " Look at *My Novel*, to take but a single instance—full of faults, no doubt, but what a bold conception and how great, even with all its faults, the measure of achievement! "

I was interested by the selection, for the last time I had been to stay with my father at Cannes, I had found him re-reading *My Novel*, and he, too, praised it for the same qualities, and declared Bulwer to be much underrated. Will Mr. Michael Sadleir bring him into vogue again?

I set up another of the authors whose fame Mr. Sadleir has revived—Anthony Trollope. I thought that not only the *Barchester Towers* series were perfect of their kind, but that the political novels—*Phineas Phin* and the rest— were equally good. They gave a perfect picture of political society at the close of the Palmerstonian period. Balfour seemed interested; he must look at them again. Finally he agreed with Oliver rather than stated for himself, that

as a Scotsman he could not do better than choose Walter
Scott, but he accepted the suggestion with less warmth of
approval than I should have expected.

Then I raised another and a more delicate question.
Recalling Andrew Lang's delightful Introduction to his
Old Friends, that entertaining volume of imaginary letters
from one character of fiction to another, I asked Balfour
who was his lady-love among the heroines of romance.

" Well," he said, " there's a girl in a book that you
fellows will never have heard of, called *The Initials*." [1]

" Arthur," I exclaimed, " not Hildegarde? "

" Hildegarde, Hildegarde—was her name Hildegarde?
Anyway the girl in *The Initials*."

It was so characteristic that though he knew he loved
her, he could not remember the name of the lady of his
affections.

Again I was interested. All my family were brought
up on this now wholly forgotten book, published sometime in the 'sixties of last century. My father also had
succumbed to the lady's charm. I remember an occasion
when we were driving from Innsbruck to Cortina and
had stopped to lunch in the hotel at the top of the Brenner.
There was no one but ourselves in the restaurant when
we arrived, but presently a train disgorged a crowd of
German tourists. Suddenly my father exclaimed," There's
Hildegarde! " I had my back to the new arrivals and
turned to see the lady. " Don't stare at her like that,"
said my father, almost angrily, " you'll make the girl
quite uncomfortable and she'll sit with her back to us! "

The story has a sequel. I told it on some occasion to
Sir Alfred Hopkinson. I happened to meet him some
time later. He reminded me of it. He had, he said,

---

[1] By Baroness Tautphœus, 1850.

with difficulty and only recently procured a copy "and I, an old man of eighty, have fallen head over ears in love."

I re-read the book after the conversation with Balfour but I could not share these transports. If, in my thoughts, I am ever unfaithful to Ethel Newcome, it is to Beatrix Esmond that they stray. Becky Sharp would have been a delightful companion at a dinner party, and if she cared to take the trouble, would have almost swept a man off his feet, but I couldn't marry Becky Sharp though, as Andrew Lang reminds us, her "kindness was so great that she even condescended to be amusing to her own husband."

XX

HOW GREAT SPEAKERS PREPARE
THEIR SPEECHES

A CORRESPONDENCE in a Sunday paper led me some years ago to write a note on the use made by my father in his public speeches of poetical quotations, and, if I may judge by the expressions of opinion which reached me, that glimpse into the methods of work of one of the great speakers and the greatest Parliamentary debater of his generation was not without interest. The newspaper itself remarked that " it is always fascinating to look into a prominent man's workshop," and this observation, spurring my own curiosity, has led me to try to carry the matter further.

How do great speakers prepare their speeches? Is there, or has there been, any uniformity of practice? Is there any golden rule which will lead the beginner to success? It is improbable, but, except among contemporaries, it is not very easy to collect the materials for an adequate answer. Notes of speeches are apt to be torn up as soon as they have served their purpose, or, if retained for a time, to be destroyed at the first overhaul of papers. Even if the notes themselves are by any chance preserved, they do not necessarily reveal the extent or the character of the preparation which went to their composition. Descriptions of the effect of historic speeches upon their listeners are common enough, but we more rarely get a glimpse of the craftsman at his bench sharpening his tools or shaping his work.

Yet the subject is surely a fascinating one. Nearly forty years ago I begged of John Bright the notes of the last great speech that he delivered in public, and I have often been tempted to make this the basis of a collection among my contemporaries. But the fear of being importunate, and the formidable frown with which Mr. Bright greeted that first request (though a couple of days later it was most kindly granted), have deterred me; and, apart from speeches of my father, I have but few examples.

There is another difficulty. Every successful Parliament man must be a debater, able to speak without preparation and without notes, or with only such notes as he may hastily jot down while listening to the opponent to whom he is about to reply. But some of our greatest speakers never use notes even for speeches that have been the subject of careful preparation; and in such cases, unless they themselves have disclosed their secret or some friend has observed and recorded it, we are thrown back upon speculation and guesswork. I suspect that in the more leisurely and rhetorical days of the late eighteenth century and of the early and middle part of the nineteenth century an ampler preparation than is usually practised to-day was in most cases both possible and necessary.

A good deal of information can, however, be gathered if one takes the trouble to search for it, though I do not think that anyone has yet sought to bring it together. Of Chatham's method I can find no account, and of his notes, if he used notes, none have survived. In the case of the younger Pitt we are more fortunate. His success in Parliament was immediate and decisive. Not even the memory of Chatham's lofty eloquence could lessen the fame at once acquired by his favourite son. "He is not a chip of the old block; he is the old block itself!" Burke exclaimed after listening to his maiden speech, and Lord Stanhope has preserved for us not only Pitt's own account of the training that he had undergone at his father's hands, but also a description of his method and examples of his notes. Chatham, he tells us, was not only accustomed to send the young Pitt specimens of oratory to study, but "bade him take up any book in some foreign language with which he was well acquainted, in Latin or Greek especially," and "to read out of this work a passage in English, stopping where he was not sure of the word to be used in English, until the right word came to his mind," [1] whilst "to train his son in sonorous elocution, Lord Chatham caused him to recite day by day in his presence passages from the best English poets, especially Shakespeare and Milton." When after this training in his boyhood he came to speak in the House of Commons, "he did not prepare the structure or the wording of his sentences, far less write them down beforehand. The statement of his friends upon this point," Lord Stanhope declares, "is much confirmed by his own notes, as scattered among his papers. These notes,[2] which are in his own handwriting, are all extremely brief, at most some figures for his finance, and some headings for his argument." And then Lord Stanhope gives as instances "his only written preparation for two of the most remarkable among his many great harangues."

[1] But then Pitt, as I would beg our schoolmasters to observe, had from first to last been encouraged to read the Classics for their inherent beauty and interest. "He had never, indeed, according to the fashion at Public Schools, applied himself to Greek or Latin composition. He had never mastered the *laborious inutilities of the ancient metres*." (My italics). Stanhope's *Life of Pitt*.

[2] These notes seem to have disappeared. The present Lord Stanhope tells me that nothing is now preserved at Chevening except a single sheet of notes, apparently scribbled by Pitt across his knee as he listened to a debate, and therefore useless for any elucidation of his practice on a set occasion.

Here are the notes as printed by Lord Stanhope for Pitt's speech on the renewal of the war in 1803 :

NOTES OF SPEECH (MAY 23, 1803)

Acts since the Preliminaries.
    Elba.
    Etruria.
    Louisiana.

Since definitive Treaty.
    Black Sea.
    Piedmont.
    Germany.
    Switzerland.

Cases which may arise.
    Encroachments on Austria or
        other parts of Continent.

On powers guaranteed by us   .   Portugal.
        Naples.
        Malta.
        Turkey.

On Maritime Interests   .   .   Spain or S. America.
        Portugal or Brazil.
        Holland or its Colonies.
        Egypt or Maritime Possessions
           of Turkey.
        N. America.

On objects immediately British   .   Shutting Ports of Europe.
        Sending forces to India, or
           advancing claims there.
        Press.
        French emigrants.

General state of Naval and Military
    preparation.

Finance system.

System of Foreign connection.

This is the speech of which Fox said that " if Demosthenes had been present he must have admired and might have envied," and which Lord Stanhope placed among the three best that Pitt ever made.

To me these seem the perfection of what notes should be, if (but what an *if*!) from such bare headlines, the speaker can make, I will not say a speech that Demosthenes might envy, but one which is at all adequate to the occasion. But for a set speech of immense consequence, both alike from the position of the speaker and the circumstances of the moment, the very baldness of these notes suggests to my mind careful preliminary thought and concentrated mental preparation.

Fox, on the other hand, appears to have given little thought to preparation and to have used no notes. The late Sir George Trevelyan describes him as " an extempore speaker," and attributes no small share of his facility to his early fondness for amateur theatricals. " The pains which he had bestowed on learning to speak the words of others, enabled him to concentrate his undivided attention upon the arduous task of improvizing his own. If only he could find the thing which required to be said he was sure to say it in the way that would produce the greatest possible effect." Thus his biographer; but then we have Fox's own confession that he acquired his pre-eminence in debate by speaking at least once every night for two sessions, an example which no possible victim of the practice would commend to aspirants to a like fame.

Of Sheridan's method I can find no trace; but Windham, whom Erskine May describes as his superior in education and attainments, and little inferior in wit, and to whom he assigns a higher place as a debater, is shown, by papers preserved in the Additional Manuscripts at the British Museum, not only to have made full notes, but, on some occasions at least, to have written out in full all that he intended to say. The manuscript of his speech on the

Rohilla charge against Hastings is preserved together with much material that went to its preparation.[1]

The Additional Manuscripts also contain similar drafts and notes of speeches by Charles Yorke and Huskisson,[2] and some of the first Lord Liverpool's speeches in the handwriting of his secretary. These, like the others, are written out in full even to the " Mr. Speaker " or " Sir " which opens the speech or introduces a paragraph. Lord Liverpool was certainly no orator, but it would be unkind and doubtless untrue to infer that his speeches were made by his secretary, though such things have been known to occur. I remember a Member of Parliament in my early days who made some very polished speeches, full of good things. " How do you hit on these things? " I once asked him. " Well," he said, " I have a very clever secretary, and I shut him up in one room, and myself in another, and we each write a speech. Then we compare notes and I take the best of both ! " *Sic vos non vobis*, oh ! private secretaries and Civil Servants ; but how you must suffer when your chief bungles your arguments and blunts your points !

In such cases as I have been describing, the preparation was evidently very careful and complete. But what is preparation?[3] My father once said to the late Sir E.

[1] Windham's Diary records on the occasion of this speech an experience which many a later Member must have shared :

June 1st, 1786.—Day of motion on the Rohilla War. . . . I have seldom found myself more clear than during my visit to him (Sir Philip Francis), and afterwards, *till I went to the House : but somehow, by the time I got there, my mind had got into some disorder, and my spirits into some agitation ; and by the time Burke had finished, I found myself in no good state to speak.*

[2] The Peel Papers, now in the British Museum, may show what Peel's practice was, but they fill, I think, nearly two hundred volumes and have not yet been catalogued.

[3] And what, it may be asked, is an impromptu? I have just come across the following entry in Anne Thackeray's Diary : *Wednesday (March 1st, 1854).* " I had an invitation from Mrs. Thomson Hankey, but Papa could not take me, having a public dinner to attend, at which he made the most beautiful impromptu speech, as I have good reason to know, as he delivered it to me from his bed the day before."—*Letters of Anne Thackeray Ritchie.*

Hamilton, then Mr. Gladstone's private secretary, that Mr. Gladstone told him that he did not prepare his speeches, unless it might be some peculiarly important and delicate announcement on foreign affairs. "I don't know what he means by preparation," retorted Sir Edward. "If he means that he doesn't sit down and write, I daresay it's true, but he lies on a sofa and *wombles* it in his inside. And I'll tell you this, Mr. Chamberlain, none of us like to go near him the day before he makes a great speech!" As a very wise parlourmaid once said of my father on a similar occasion: "No, Mum, it's not what he says, but what he looks!" What private secretary could not tell a like tale? I do not believe that any man ever made a good speech without feeling the strain beforehand *if he had time to think about it.*

No doubt in these busy days when the occasions for speech are so numerous and the opportunities for thought so few, much of the preparation is only semi-conscious or sub-conscious, the result of "wombling" at odd moments and amid other preoccupations, and much is left to the hazard of the moment. "Sir," said Dr. Johnson, "it concentrates a man's mind wonderfully to know that he is to be hanged in a fortnight," and a man's knowledge that in another moment he will be on his feet addressing three or four thousand people, or the fact that he is already doing so, is equally stimulating to his faculties. Under this pressure ideas that have been vaguely floating in the mind suddenly take shape and scattered thoughts fall as suddenly into place. "Why do you worry, Chamberlain?" Mr. Bright once said to my father who was lamenting the fate that compelled him to deliver three speeches "each with a beginning and a middle and an end" to three great mass meetings on one Saturday afternoon—"why do you

worry? there is always inspiration in a great crowd."
No doubt in such circumstances some things worth saying
will be forgotten and the *esprit de l'escalier* will torment
the speaker with the vision of lost opportunities as soon as
he sits down. But this matters little. Those are the happy
ones who, on such occasions, can resume their seats without
having said something that they would wish immediately
to recall.

Disraeli was as independent of notes as his great rival.
" He was," says Mr. Buckle, " gifted with a marvellously
retentive memory, which often, indeed, betrayed him into
plagiarisms of a sustained character in speech and writing,
but which, at any rate, enabled him altogether to dispense,
in his ordinary practice, with the use of notes." Disraeli
himself justified his practice by saying, " if I once used
notes, I should lean upon them; and that would never do."
" He depended," we are told, " in some degree on catching
inspiration from his hearers; he told Delane, he was ' much
influenced by my audience and the impromptu.' This
does not, of course, mean that there was not careful preparation before any great effort, or that, in particular, the biting
phrases by which he will always be remembered were not
deeply studied in his mind, and assiduously polished before
they were launched, apparently at random, upon the world.
In preparing the few speeches of importance which he
delivered outside Parliament he often made use of a highly
original method; he privately rehearsed them, either in
whole or in part, to an experienced reporter of *The Times*,
J. F. Neilson, in whom he placed especial trust."

In like manner Macaulay, when he spoke " had no notes
in his hand and no manuscript in his pocket," but his
speeches were most carefully prepared and were repeated
without the loss or omission of a single word. " If a debate

were in prospect he would turn the subject over while he paced his chamber or tramped along the streets. Each thought as it rose in his mind embodied itself in phrases and clothed itself in an appropriate drapery of images, instances and quotations; and when, in the course of his speech, the thought recurred, all the words which gave it point and beauty spontaneously recurred with it." [1] Macaulay's memory was, of course, phenomenal and has become proverbial. But it is curious to find how many men, who prepared their speeches carefully, yet used no notes.

The late Lord Salisbury and Mr. Bonar Law were of this number, and Lord Salisbury at least was not only a most effective but a most polished speaker. In answer to my inquiry, the present Lord Salisbury writes: " It is quite true that my father always spoke without notes. He had nothing in the shape of papers in his hands unless he was going to quote someone else. . . . He once told me that the epigrams (though he did not use the word, I am sure), or it may be the illustrations—for both of which his speeches were notable—occurred to him only as he was speaking. . . . I remember also that he was accustomed to use some *memoria technica* in place of notes." Towards the close of his last Administration Lord Salisbury told me that he regretted that he had not accustomed himself to the use of notes in his younger days, for by that time he had begun to feel the strain of being wholly dependent on his memory for the substance and arrangement of what he meant to say. It may be that neither he nor Mr. Bonar Law ever attempted verbal preparation unless of some passage of singular importance, but, even so, the strain of composing the whole speech without putting pen to paper, of marshalling the arguments, of arranging the order of presenta-

[1] Trevelyan's *Life of Macaulay*.

tion of the facts, or remembering that this thought or argument had been rejected and that other substituted in the course of preparation, must have been immense. Mr Bonar Law himself told me that two hours of such work left him as exhausted as a twenty-mile walk.

But if some men use no notes and some forgo preparation altogether, we can set against their example the practice of others not less illustrious. Of Canning's custom in his earlier years we have no certain knowledge, but it is not likely that he was less careful then than later, when he had long established his reputation as an orator and his position as a statesman. "Certainly during his last tenure of office when he was about to make an important speech, his whole mind was absorbed with it for two, or, perhaps, three days, beforehand. He spared no labour in obtaining and arranging his material. He always drew up a paper (which he used in the House) with the heads, in their order, of the several topics on which he meant to touch, and these heads were numbered, and the numbers sometimes extended to four or even five hundred. At these periods he was not easy of approach; interruption irritated him, except it related to the matter in hand." [1] Once again the private secretary reveals the strain of long preliminary labour which produced the smooth delivery and glowing rhetoric of the speech itself.

So, too, with Bright. Though he said that he had once written a speech and then found its delivery so great a strain that he had never attempted it again, he became, I think, by his slow and leisurely method of preparation almost word-perfect in what he intended to say, and could probably have repeated a speech the moment after its delivery with very little change of language. He was

[1] Stapleton's *Canning*.

accustomed, I have been told, to try in conversation the effect of his arguments and sometimes even of his phrases, but he had a fine ear for the cadences of language and an unfailing instinct for the right word which must have been a natural gift. " If my manner of speaking is good, it may have become so from reading what is good," he once wrote to a correspondent, and probably few could rival his knowledge of the Bible and of Milton and, rather surprisingly, of Byron. An aunt of mine, in whose house he was staying, once asked him to read some Browning on a Sunday afternoon towards the close of his life. He consented, but he did not care for Browning's poetry, and in a few moments had laid the volume aside and was reciting from memory long passages of Byron's poetry to which he was attracted, perhaps, as much by its rhetorical character as by its passion for liberty.

The mention of Byron and Browning recalls to my mind two stories of Bright that are worth telling. Bright and Browning dined one evening at my father's house in Prince's Gardens about the time of the publication of Donelly's *Cryptogram*. Half-way through dinner the lady who sat between them said, " It is time that you intervened, Mr. Chamberlain. Mr. Bright and Mr. Browning are coming to blows." It appeared that Mr. Bright, who enjoyed legal puzzles, and was said to know the evidence in the Tichborne trial better than any layman, had professed his belief that Donelly had succeeded in proving that Bacon wrote Shakespeare; and Mr. Browning's temper had not been proof against the strain. As, later, I held the door open for the guests to pass out of the dining-room, I caught the echo of the storm. " Stupid old man ! " growled Bright to my father; " I don't believe he understands his own poems." And a moment later, as Browning passed out, " Obstinate old fool! " he muttered, " I don't believe he ever read a play of Shakespeare in his life." And, indeed, I do not think that Bright ever showed any great appreciation of Shakespeare.

The second story I was told by my father. Bright was addressing the annual meeting of his Birmingham constituents in the Town Hall. He was speaking of the horrors of war (I do not know the occasion) and began quoting, " Lo! where the Giant on the mountain stands," throwing up his hands as he did so in anticipation of the coming image, when a look of agony crossed his face, and, turning to the chairman, he demanded fiercely, " What's the next line? " The chairman, poor man! was unequal to the occasion—how many of us would have done any better?—but the line was at once given by Mr. Sam Timmins (a well-known Birmingham figure of the time, whose name is recorded in the Free Library as one of its principal benefactors) and Mr. Bright sailed on:

" Lo! where the Giant on the mountain stands,
His blood-red tresses deep'ning in the sun,
With death-shot glowing in his fiery hands,
And eye that scorcheth all it glares upon."

But this is a digression. Mr. Bright's notes were very full. His biographer prints a facsimile page of the notes of a speech made in 1860. " Each idea in its order," says Mr. Trevelyan, " is represented by a few words or figures, while the ' key sentence ' or ' island,' as he used to call it, is written out at full." I possess the notes for two of his speeches, one as chairman of a Rochdale meeting in 1877, and the other the only speech he made on Mr. Gladstone's first Home Rule Bill. It was addressed to his constituents in the Birmingham Town Hall on July 1st, 1886, and was, I think, the last speech but one of his long public life.

The earlier speech must have occupied fifteen or twenty minutes in delivery, the later one more than an hour. The notes for the former cover three sides of small-sized letter paper; those of the latter, nine. Both are in small but very clear handwriting, and almost every word is underlined. Long sentences are written out in full, or nearly so. One page is here reproduced.

The first four lines conclude his examination of the Land Bill. Then he turns to the exclusion of the Irish members from Westminster and to the alternative suggestion that they should attend only for Imperial business. It will be seen how detailed all this is, even to the very characteristic aside " and rather commend them," which is followed up on the next page with the equally characteristic "Vote of censure —or two-pence income tax to pay for new Bombardment— or blunder on Afghan frontier." If these are "islands," Mr. Bright sailed amidst a veritable archipelago. The earlier notes are almost equally detailed, and hardly bear out Mr. Trevelyan's conclusion that he wrote out " only the heads of his argument with an occasional ' key sentence,' " and " ending up with the peroration transcribed in full."

The mention of a peroration reminds me of the advice of an old parliamentary hand—I think Lord Palmerston— to a beginner in the House. " You need not bother about the beginning of your speech because that will naturally arise out of the debate. Nor will the body of the speech give you much trouble, for that will be concerned with the subject under discussion, and unless you were fully conversant with the matter you would not speak; [1] but you must know your peroration or you will never be able to sit down."

---

[1] I suspect that Lord Palmerston—if Palmerston it was—was an optimist even for his own day.

where your security. Ask any Financier?
On what terms hold you safe in the monstrous
engaged
arranged & happened if support Gov.t Bill.
Speculation?
if not, no Concealment. Would frankly tell you
But Gov.t Bill. Irish members. "& Dublin Parl.t"
inevitable
only bright spot & compensation in Bill
Parl.t given. exclusion absolutely necessary
300. Irish members. Dublin. 100 in London
American Irish Contribution. perpetual Charitable
If League does not care about Foreign affairs,
fraud.
So rather commend them. Let them stay in Ireland?
But a new plan. occasional presence in London.
To have a sort of intermittent Irish fever
in House of Commons . so astonishing & so
ludicrous - how many? Commons & Lords too?
how come & when? Special Boat . & Train?
excursion & return Tickets. which & cheaper?
procession in Westminster Hall - invade House

In my early days of public speaking I studiously acted on this advice, so far, at least, as the peroration was concerned, but I found that the sentences so carefully committed to memory were not infrequently used half-way through the speech to fill a gulf suddenly yawning at my feet when all ideas had momentarily forsaken the earnest but very nervous orator.

"Get your transitions clearly in your mind," was the late Lord Goschen's advice to me, " the bridges which lead from one subject to the next; for the language you can trust to the moment." This is good advice, but Lord Goschen certainly wrote out much of his speeches beforehand and was able on occasion, like Disraeli, to go through them with a reporter before the meeting. I recall one such instance in the case of a speech that I heard him deliver one evening in my school-days at Rugby when he was closeted with the representative of *The Times* for an hour in the course of the afternoon. Lord Goschen was very short-sighted and wrote a minute and very illegible hand, and this must have added to his difficulties in using notes. More than once, the present Lord Goschen tells me, his father would appeal to him: "I know I have something good here, but I can't read it. Can you make it out?"

Mr. Winston Churchill has not found any of his father's notes preserved among his papers, but here Lord Salisbury again comes to my help. "Lord Randolph," he writes, " once lent me the notes of a speech he was going to deliver, or had been going to deliver, to help me for a speech when I was an undergraduate. The notes were most elaborate—headings, sub-headings and sub-sub-headings. He told me at the time that he had used every method —learning by heart, elaborate notes, and impromptu in debate." I daresay that most of us have done the same.

There was one of many delightful week-end parties at Taplow Court in the early years of this century when guests wandering about the grounds on Sunday morning reported that they had found the late Lord Percy reciting his Monday's speech in one alley, Lord Hugh Cecil preparing himself in another, and Mr. Churchill practising his peroration in a third.

Of Mr. Asquith's notes I possess one example—those for the speech which he delivered in August 1920, on the proposal to place my father's statue in the lobby of the House of Commons, and which I begged of him at the time as a memorial of the tribute paid to my father's memory by a political adversary who has ever been as generously appreciative of the qualities of his opponents as staunchly loyal to his friends. These notes are very full, but the occasion was exceptional. " They are, of course," wrote Mr. Asquith in a letter giving me permission to reproduce a page of them, " more elaborated (as to language, etc.) than what I should normally use at a public meeting, or for a speech in the House." And he added that his practice as to extent of preparation varied so much and his habit of consigning his notes to immediate destruction was so inveterate, that he could not give me a more typical example. The last sheet of these notes is given on page 265.

Here there is certainly evidence of careful and even of verbal preparation ; but Mr. Asquith's style was natural to him and differed little in his prepared and unprepared speeches. In both there are the same clean-cut and faultless sentences, the same wide command of dignified and sonorous language, and the same secure and easy progress, through whatever parentheses he allows himself, to a conclusion that is not only intelligible but grammatical.

Far different was the case of the late Lord Balfour. I have been told by my father that, when he first entered the House, Mr. Balfour was a bad speaker, and he never acquired the easy flow and smooth delivery which do so much for the comfort of the audience. His preparation was generally slight and never verbal. His notes were few and little consulted by him when speaking; and I think I have observed that even when he affected to consult them, it was often only a gesture securing a moment for reflection. The right word did not always occur to him at once, and he was far too fastidious to use, as most of us do, the first word which presented itself, when it was not the best one. Thus he hesitated, and paused, and sometimes recast the sentence, and so, as I have found, occasionally disappointed those who heard him for the first time. But his mastery of the House of Commons was complete. "He plays on you all like an old fiddle," a friend whom I had introduced to the gallery once said to me after hearing Mr. Balfour wind up a debate, and, whatever the imperfections of his manner, he dominated us all, almost as much, perhaps, by his personal charm as by his intellectual pre-eminence. He had, besides, a rare gift for rising above the party squabbles which sometimes disfigure debate and placing the discussion on a higher plane. I recall, though only vaguely after the lapse of so many years, one such occasion. The House was discussing some untoward incident which had occurred in one of our West African Colonies, and the debate had degenerated into a wrangle between that strange type of Englishman who takes for granted that his countryman overseas is always in the wrong and those others who will admit no criticism of a man of their own race bearing great responsibilities and facing great difficulties among an alien people. It was the old problem of Governor Eyre in a new garb,

But let me add

Here are accomplished

fed

stimulated

inspired

unselfish ideals.

dauntless courage

his several loy^ty to colleagues & friend

above all   fervent & obvious

Sense of public & personal duty

His example

treasured memories

& it is fitting that his effigy
take its place
among famous figures

Who in their long & honoured succession
impersonate & keep alive great
traditions of this House

MR. ASQUITH'S NOTES

and happily with far less serious issues. Balfour rose from the front Opposition bench in an angry House where nearly every speech was adding fuel to the flames. In a few sentences he expressed his judgment on the particular incident and turned to consider the principles which should govern the relations of white men and black in these tropical dependencies. The House was lifted out of itself into a serener atmosphere and was grateful to the man who had wrought the miracle.

I have preserved the notes of two of his House of Commons speeches. Of these, the more interesting are those for the speech which he made on Mr. Chaplin's amendment to the second reading of the Budget of 1903, on the occasion of the abolition of the shilling duty on corn, for in that debate not only were Mr. Balfour's followers sharply divided among themselves, but the Opposition had fiercely attacked his personal conduct and denounced what they were pleased to consider his breach of constitutional practice. The notes are written, as was Mr. Balfour's habit, on long envelopes headed respectively " Preface I," " Self II," " Finis." He spoke at the opening of the second day's debate, and the notes show every sign of having been jotted down as the debate of the previous day proceeded. The first two contain about half a dozen notes apiece. The third is much fuller, though the matter covered by it occupied about the same time in delivery. The second envelope concludes with

> " Here should end the case !—
> But large question.
> Ministerial responsibility " ;

and on this follows the final sheet which is here reproduced.

Finis

Shall we deal with it *gua*?
   Personal defence. No leader more
   wearisome than one

"Impossible; humiliating; unfair to
   party; to the Hon; to the country;
   to the civilized world; & the world;
   to the whole of things. —

I profoundly dissent. —

To judge fairly they must adopt
   my point of view.

I do not belong to the happy band
   who think everything perfect.

| Treaties coming to an end. Tariff.
| Colonial preference Prime Minister.

It cannot be denied New departures
Two courses open to a gov". possible.

   Silently make up your mind.
   Indicate doubts. Peel
                      Gladstone

Incomparably more difficult than
   either. Corn Laws or H. Rule.
      Foreign Countries. Colonies. H. population
As regards Home population — it depends on the

The report of this portion of the speech fills about a column of *The Times* and would, I suppose, take about twenty minutes in delivery. These are by far the fullest notes that I have ever seen Lord Balfour use, and anyone who takes the trouble to look at the report will find that all, or nearly all, the notes find expression and development in what he actually said. But this with him was unusual, I remember on one occasion, when we were in opposition, being left in charge for some time during a Friday afternoon's debate. After a time Mr. Balfour joined me, and, with one ear on the debate, chatted delightfully on many subjects as they crossed our thoughts. After a time he said, "Well, if I am to wind up, I suppose it's time that I began to think what I am to say," and, pulling out half a dozen long envelopes from the rack on the table of the House, he wrote without hesitation a headline at the top of the first and a second headline half-way down; then did the same with a second and, I think, a third envelope; then more slowly jotted in a very few sub-headings and the work was done. I watched as he wrote, and was fascinated not only by the quick working of his mind but by observing how the speech at once presented itself to him as a whole. The framework appeared the moment he put pen to paper. Some details were added almost at once; more appeared only in the speech itself, occuring to him as he developed his argument or as suggested by the interruptions with which he met. But the first idea of the speech sprang from his brain as a whole, consecutive and complete, though he had certainly done no conscious preparation beforehand. I once begged of him another set of notes, now, unfortunately, mislaid or lost, the interest of which lay in the fact that after opening in the manner indicated by the first headline, he never again approached the " signposts" that he had jotted down, but followed a new train of thought apparently suggested as he spoke, by his own opening words, and I suspect that, in the case of Lord Balfour, notes, even when most complete, were never more than headlines and certainly they were never allowed to hamper his freedom of movement in action.

This, indeed, suggests one of the difficulties of preparation. If a practised speaker knows exactly what he is going to say, and has it somehow firmly fixed in his mind, he can say it and yet preserve a large power of variation in reply to interruptions or in response to the inspiration of the moment. If, at the other extreme, he has only the broadest outline of the speech before him, he is quite likely to be equally successful, and sometimes more so, just because he knows himself to be dependent upon, and trusts entirely to, the inspiration of the moment. But there must be many who, like myself, have found careful but imperfect preparation a fatal snare, for the knowledge that you have not only something particular to say, but that there was a particular way in which you meant to say it, is paralysing unless that way jumps to your mind when the critical moment arrives. It was the realization of this fact that caused me after a time to act upon my father's advice: "Don't take so much trouble with your speeches as I have been accustomed to do. I don't mean that yours will be better because you take less, but, now that so many speeches are called for, the burden is too great."

My father, indeed, took immense pains with his prepared speeches. Such a speech as that with which he opened his Tariff Reform campaign at Glasgow in 1903, or those in which he developed his "Unauthorized Programme" in 1885 meant not only months of study beforehand but days of actual work upon his notes. When he first spoke as a young man in Birmingham he was not, I have been told by relations who were his contemporaries, a ready or even an easy speaker, and he himself said that in his early days he could only deliver one speech a month because it took him a fortnight to prepare it, and another fortnight to recover from it. Of course, in his later days he often made debating or impromptu speeches, and among them were some of the most effective. But if he had time—and especially for great meetings in the country or set occasions in Parliament—he thought no pains too great to get his argument into the best form and to secure that every passage conduced directly to the particular result that he desired to produce. For Parliamentary purposes the task would be simplified because the question put from the chair dictated both the subject and the scope of the speech, but of speeches at public meetings he would say: "The first great difficulty is to find your subject—to get your line. After that the main task is to exclude everything which, however good in itself, does not lead directly to the particular conclusion that you wish to enforce." Is not this exclusion of the irrelevant or the merely superfluous the secret of all great art?

Given plenty of time—and to get it undisturbed he habitually worked far into the night—his practice was to make a first draft of the speech in writing. This would cover four, or, more rarely, six or even eight, sides of notepaper in a very small hand. From this draft he made his speaking notes, and, in doing so, often discarded much of what he had originally written and introduced fresh matter. These notes, when finished, he would go over at least once, more often two or even three times, until, I think, they were clearly fixed in his mind. But even so, when speaking he used his notes freely and never sought to conceal them; but he could turn aside to demolish an interrupter or to answer an objection with no fear of losing the thread of his argument or forgetting the point which he had reached at the moment of the digression. This perfect ease and security on his part, coupled with his singularly clear voice, had much to do with the comfort and enjoyment of his audiences. And by the time I attended his meetings he seemed as easy a speaker, as free in his movements, and as completely master of his resources as any man could be, though even after that he still continued to develop his mastery of the technique of speaking until the last year or two of tremendous strain and lessening health. Few people, I think, who saw him just before a meeting when the work of preparation was done and he had resolutely banished all thoughts of speech and notes from his mind, or who listened to the delivery of the speech itself, so easy, so natural, apparently so spontaneous, without a sign of strain in voice or manner, could have guessed the immense and wearing labour that went to its preparation, but Mrs. Chamberlain, now Mrs. Carnegie, who could watch him at work in his library, has told me that few, if any, such set speeches in the country cost less than three days constant toil and that five was the more usual number. Again and again, I have known him shut himself up in his library from breakfast to lunch, from lunch to dinner, and again till the early hours of the morning, and emerge at last with nothing definite accomplished. " I cannot get my line," he would say, and he would admit at times that in despair he had taken refuge in a French novel. And then perhaps next evening he would say: " Well, whatever happens, I am going to make my speech before I go to bed to-night," and he would do it, though he had to work till three or four in the morning. When I think of the infinite trouble that he took, I am ashamed of such measure of facility as I have acquired by much practice and the all-too-ready acceptance of a lower standard.

But, although his preparation was so careful, my father would never do what some others of his day did habitually, that is, give to a representative of the Press the terms or even the substance of his speech before its delivery. To do this, he felt, would be to put himself under constraint to make the speech in that particular form and no other, and thus to subject himself to an intolerable strain at the moment of delivery. He used to relate that early in his parliamentary life—I think a couple of years or less after he entered the House—he took the chair at a public meeting in Birmingham at which Sir William Harcourt was the chief speaker. *The Times* reporter was closeted with Sir William for a couple of hours in the morning. Then he sought my father. "My editor," he said, "is prepared to place a column at your disposal if you will tell me what you are going to say." My father replied that he could not do it—he could not trust himself, the strain would be too great. "Then," said the reporter, "I am sorry, but there will be no report." "Well," rejoined my father, "I am much obliged for your offer, and I, too, am sorry that I cannot accept it, but I console myself with the thought that one of two things will happen. Either the public doesn't want to read me and then, though it is very kind of you to make the offer, it is useless to print my speeches, or they will want to know what I say, and in that case, sooner or later, you will have to report me."

But it is time to have done with both reminiscences and comment and to give an example of his notes. Here is a page of his notes for the Glasgow speech. (See next page.)

The speech was an unusually long one, occupying an hour

2. Realisation, ideal. Cement Union.
Consolidate race - meet clash, competition -
not only by isolated appeals - supported by force,
grow up of growing states that speak common tongue.

How attain? Claim if not heated in manner
worthy, dignity + magnitude - apart f.
personal bitterness + even party controversy

Disclaim imputation, unworthy motives
Claim equal consideration

Recognise changes only successful if National
policy - not forced by great majority accepted as
consent by overwhelming proportion

Glasgow one, most prosperous. Why not let alone?
Venice

Not predict equal catastrophe for B. industry
But signs, decay - cracks - foundations not
                                        broad enough

Am I wrong to warn? Strange that those who
indict for want, preparation, equally denounce
for preparing for greater struggle - if defensal
disappear - meet with antiquated weapons + old
                                        fashioned tactics

not well with B. industry.
Last years great expansion. 1900 a record
     total
Yet exports ~~~~~~~~~~~~ 1890   20 millions
          only increased   only
                                             in 10 y.
          in U.S.a under Protection   110
          Germany   56

In Free Trade Britain practically stagnant
Protected countries enormous progress

Character changed. Cobden's expectations
But Foreigners take less, our Manuf.
+ we take more, of theirs

MR. JOSEPH CHAMBERLAIN'S NOTES

S   273

and forty minutes in delivery. It not only presented the general case for Tariff Reform, but developed a detailed programme and contained a number of figures. I think it is not too much to say that in form, construction and language, in clearness of presentation and cogency of argument, it is an almost perfect model of what such a speech should be, and contemporary accounts speak of the sustained power and ease of its delivery. It had cost him immense labour and his notes were certainly longer, and, I think, fuller than usual, but, subject to this qualification, they are typical of all that he used for set speeches. They cover eight sides of notepaper, divided into paragraphs by lines drawn half across the page, but with scarcely any special marks to draw the eye to particular points. He made a second speech at Greenock the next day, and for this also he had prepared notes before leaving home. Indeed, in the course of that campaign most of his meetings went in couples, and he found the strain of having a second speech on his mind, when delivering the first, so great, that he presently resolved not to think about the second till the first was over—either making such notes as he could on the morning of the second day, or, as at Newport, on the day after he had spoken at Cardiff, abandoning notes altogether and trusting to his complete possession of the subject and the stimulus and inspiration of the moment— a trust which was in this case brilliantly justified not only by the immediate approval of the audience but also by the judgment of his readers. *The Times* wrote two days later of this unprepared speech: " Nothing bears more eloquent witness, not merely to his physical energy, but to the mastery of the subject and the abundance of the resources on which he draws, than the way in which he is thus able, time after time, to follow up one remarkable utterance with another, perfectly new in character, and not less impressive"; and it compared these speeches of his Tariff Reform campaign to his series of addresses in South Africa, "preaching the message of reconciliation and unity."

With this account of my father's methods I have carried my theme as far as my knowledge goes. No set rule emerges from the examination that I have made. Each speaker has his own method—often more than one. One man makes elaborate notes; another makes none. One man writes his speeches; another never puts pen to paper. We may choose what system we like or have no system at all, and we can still find some model to justify our practice. But one conclusion, I think, stands out clearly; those who say to public men, "Oh! speaking is no trouble to *you*," have not seen them in the hours of preparation. Their wives and their private secretaries tell a different tale.

XXI

FROM A FAMILY POST-BAG

My grandmother Chamberlain was one of the eighteen children of Harry Harben, Wholesale Cheesemonger of Mile End, and his wife Mary Woodgate. Several of the children died in infancy or early youth, as was the way with the prodigious families of those days, but two of my great aunts were familiar figures in my childhood. A third was known to me only by name, for she lived first in Scotland and later joined her sons who had settled in New Zealand.

The others formed a remarkable family group, closely united to one another by ties of strong affection, mainly occupied by the care of their families and households, but widely read, interested in all the pleasures of the mind in which their modest means enabled them to indulge, staunch Unitarians, regular attendants at Chapel, and shrewd critics of the long sermons which formed a main feature of the services, and withal endowed with a pleasant sense of humour and a ready wit which on occasion showed itself in their letters.

Most of their letters were destroyed by them or their children as being too intimate for other eyes than their own, but one or two have been preserved as possessing a wider interest for their descendants.

Of my grandmother's writing I have only a few lines. In my father's desk after his death I found a little cardboard box wherein was a battered silver thimble with these words barely legible in the faded ink of nearly one hundred years ago :

"Here rests from her labours a faithful servant after seventeen years and a half of constant devoted usefulness to one mistress. This thimble was given to Caroline Harben by her grandmother, Mrs. Woodgate, and had she continued Caroline Harben might still have been in her service. But her little son Joey (more ruthless than Time) stamped upon its worn frame and finished what the Old Destroyer might have spared much longer.

"It was here laid to repose January 17, 1840, by its grateful friend and mistress.

"CAROLINE CHAMBERLAIN.

"Camberwell."

Charlotte, the next sister who survived childhood and was through life my grandmother's dearest friend, married Edward Bailey, an ironmonger of Holborn where they lived over his warehouse. I remember her in her widowhood, a stately old lady always dressed in black silk with a widow's cap, but as ready to share my childish games and interests as she had been to share and encourage those of my father in his boyhood. It was in the Bailey warehouse that my father and his cousins indulged that taste for amateur theatricals to which Balfour attributed some at least, of the characteristic quality of his speaking. For the most part my great-aunt's life was a very quiet one. Her letters are filled with the little details of daily life, her household cares, the daily doings of herself, her family and friends. Their interest has faded with the ink in which they were written, but one great event stands out—her visit to Windsor in 1842. She tells the tale to her sister in the following lively letter :

" 272 HOLBORN,
" *February 9th*, 1842.

" MY DEAR EMILY,

" As I promised your good husband that I would write you full particulars of the important event to-day, I sit down to do it though I have very little time to do it in, as I am engaged to dine with Caroline at two o'clock and it is now twelve. I have not been able to begin before. Well, so as not to lose any more time apologizing, so, to begin with the beginning, you know I believe that Bab was vaccinated last Monday week. Well, last Monday afternoon Mr. Fincham called and said he had come on a strange errand, but would I have any objection to the Prince of Wales being vacci from my child. Guess my surprise! I acceded, of course, provided always my expenses were paid and every precaution taken that my child should not take cold. Mr. Fincham said he would mention all those conditions to Sir James Clark who had enquired of him for a case. Well, Monday morning I had a note from Finchy to say that Sir J. C. would call to inspect mother and child in an hour or two. About half an hour after that came Sir J. C. and Dr. Gregory. They gave me a good stare and soon satisfied themselves that I was not a poor thin scraggy creature. Then Master Edward was brought in and they both exclaimed what a beautiful boy (in regard to health and size they meant) examined the arm which they said was a most perfect specimen of vacci and felt all about his glands, and then pronounced him perfect in every way as to health, system and free from all tendency to humour or disease. It was something to get their opinion even had I not the pleasure I had afterwards. Sir James then said that he would fetch me in his carriage at one o'clock. He said you may take a nurse if you wish it. I said, drawing myself up sky high, Oh Sir James I cannot possibly go if I may not. Oh well take a nurse certainly. Well then there was such a getting up a stairs, such a ringing at the bell, the servants were all half mad,

Mrs. Edward Bailey (Charlotte Augusta)
From a painting made when Mrs. Bailey was about thirty-two, by Watkins

Rebecca ready to jump out of her skin, Edward so fussy, whilst I walked about in all the quiet dignity of nonchalance. I had never bought baby a hood, so he had nothing to wear. That added to the fuss having to send out for that. I chose a little black velvet hat in the shape of a beefeater cap with a chenille tassel, he has a very pretty crimson cloak trimmed all round with handsome swansdown so he looked very nice quite a little Henry the Eighth. I wore my fur tippet (which I have had altered and looks very handsome) and cuffs and my velvet bonnet, and my (word illegible) dress which you may remember.

"Well Sir J.'s carriage came at one and took us to the station where he met us and we went by the railroad to Slough where one of the Queen's carriages met us and conveyed us to Windsor Castle. We drew up at the Queen's private entrance and were shown into a very handsome bedroom, where I suckled baby and presently Sir James came in and said: Now Mrs. Bailey bring up the child, but I did not take his hint of bringing it up myself, but told Rebecca to follow and we went up and up and up when a nurse dressed in white opened a door and he said no not in that room, and opened another door and said to my great surprise Your Majesty, Mrs. Bailey—and sure enough there was her little Majesty standing at the end of a small room and Prince Albert (that Adonis) at her side perched on a nursery fender which was before the fire and in the middle of the little room was a nurse holding his Royal Highness the Prince of Wales with his shoulder bare. Tho' I was taken by surprise I had sense enough to make my obeisance to the Majesty of England (Majesty forsooth!! I towered over the little lady). I then with a mother's pride drew the handkerchief from my dear little boy's face and they exclaimed, Yes, he is a fine little fellow, so I suppose Sir James had been praising him. The operation was then performed and my baby behaved admirably and the Queen and the Prince admired him much and said he was a sweet-tempered creature. The Prince said 'See how sweetly he smiles.' The P. of W. roared lustily, but then they pierced him in three places on each arm. The Queen seemed very much struck with the size of my baby and at last asked what day he was born, and when I said the 29th of September, said, ' Oh! then he is five weeks older than His Royal Highness.' She expressed a hope that my baby would not take cold. She then took up his hat and shewed it to the Prince Albert and talked in German about it and then said ' It's a nice little hat '—Then Prince Albert came across the room and making the most graceful of bows and with the sweetest of smiles and softest of voices said, ' I thank you madam for allowing our child to be vaccinated from yours.' I murmured obligation—honour— my side—Royal Highness—put my hand on my heart and sank at his feet (almost not quite) overpowered by the magic brightness of his blue eyes—The queen asked me many questions as to when, how, where he was vacci, how it rose and all about it and by whom—We then backed out of the royal presence and then went downstairs again when Sir James said there was lunch preparing for me but I declined it, for which I am now rather sorry as I should liked to have seen what they would give me, but however he made me take a glass of sherry and a biscuit which was served on a beautiful silver salver with most elegant glass with the royal arms on them a decanter of sherry and one of water. Then Sir James said something about the queen and I was to follow him up stairs, so we went into a small waiting room of the Prince's hung with blue silk and the Portrait of George III, Queen Charlotte and all their family when children. Sir James then said that Her Majesty had long wished to be revaccinated whenever a favourable opportunity occurred and this being such a very fine specimen would if I had no objection be so now. Of course I had none, and accordingly she and the prince were both done. We could not see them but could hear the Prince laugh and the Queen say, ' take care of my skin its very thin! ' After that we went down again and then Sir James came and said : ' The Queen has directed me to give your nurse £5, you I shall see again, but I cannot stop now or you will lose the train,' and apologizing for not returning with me, he saw me into the carriage and we returned the same way as we went and I am happy to say baby is none the worse. Now what do you think of Fox of Bally o' Botherem!' Think of me, even me, having such good luck. But however I have seen no more of Sir James and if I do not hear of him to-day I shall write to-morrow and enquire after the young prince. The queen was dressed in French white watered silk made with a lace fichu and a gold chain with some large seals hanging on it at the waist a kind of gold cord suspended from the waist with some more gold seals and bracelets with more gold seals. I mean to ask Sir J. to explain, when I see him. The Prince had fawn-coloured Kerseymere trousers and Blk. Frock coat—the young prince a plainish handsome robe with long sleeves and a cap with blue ribbons and rosette lace and blue ribbons. He is a sweet little baby, more like the father than the mother. I have not time to say any more now but shall be happy to answer any questions you may honour me with. I am,

"Dear Emily,

"Yours affectionately,

"C. A. BAILEY."

This letter was intended only for her sister's eye. She drew up a more formal record for the baby, and had it attested by the nurse. To it she appended a note that, the baby having already been registered in the name of Edward after his father, she now had him christened Edward Albert in commemoration of this event. A few weeks later Sir James Clark wrote that he had " a little present from Her Majesty for Mrs. Bailey's little boy." It was a scarfpin with the Prince of Wales' feathers and motto in turquoises and rubies. The child died before its fourth birthday, and she could never bear to speak of the event again.

Another letter of hers gives a delightful glimpse of my grandparents' life at Highbury Place, Islington, whither they had moved from Camberwell when my father was about five years old. This letter was written to her daughter and describes the dinner given by my grandfather to welcome Dr. (then Mr.) Martineau, the great Unitarian divine, to London when he was called to the Essex Street Chapel.

" *Wednesday Morning, March* 30*th*, 1859,
" 271 HOLBORN, W.C.1.

" DEAR FANNY,

" While the remembrance of Caroline's elegant dinner and very pleasant evening, in fact entertainment altogether, are fresh in my mind, I will write of it, being alone, Emily having slept at Highbury, and having no urgent call on me this morning for any other duty.

" Well, I dressed myself in my Moiré and a fresh Widow's cap, and an enormous pair of plain net sleeves, by a quarter-past five, and presented myself before Emily, who pronounced the effect neat but not gaudy, then ordered a cab, in which I very soon found myself.

" I arrived at Highbury [1] about twenty-minutes to six, and was ushered into the drawing-room by a very quiet, pleasant-looking waiter. Caroline has had him several times, so doubtless Aunt Ellen knows him. There were Joseph, Caroline and Mary, all seated, looking rather stiff and uncomfortable and as if they were dreading an avalanche, but very nice ; Caroline, her pretty looks on, Joseph well, and Mary the very personification of a young lady and pretty withal ; she had on her black net, with a lace tucker, and with a black ribbon which was run through it, as is the fashion now—her shoulders looked beautifully white, and she had on her head an ornament made of beads, setting close on it all round like a wreath, and which was very becoming.

" The room also presented a large and pleasant aspect,

[1] Highbury Place, Islington.

the large round table was removed altogether, the mosaic one was in the bow, the vase in the corner by the door, and a card table with a cover on it in the centre, flowers in the centre of that. Then the garden looked so pleasant and fresh with the new grass and gravel.

" My going in relieved the stiffness a little, as we talked of indifferent matters and so took their thoughts off the fear of the overpowering intellect of the chief guest. Mr. Nettlefold presented himself next and then came Joseph's dreadful Incubus, and coming face to face with it in the broad daylight, all his imaginary fears vanished and ' Richard was himself again ' and the talk was cheerful and rather noisy for so small a party (young Joe [1] had joined us) till dinner was announced, which it very soon was. Mr. M. and Mrs. C., Mr. Blagdon and Mary, Mrs. N. and self, Joseph and Mrs. M. I sat next Mr. M. and Mrs. M. next Joseph of course. Two covers on the table. Asparagus soup—very good. Caroline thought it rather hot, I did not. That was helped all round and quickly removed— then the noble piece of salmon was displayed which Mr. M. would distribute, and helped it, as if to carve had been the study of his life, a little piece of thick, a little piece of thin and a smelt to everyone. There was a profusion of beautiful hot lobster sauce and cool cucumber—that was removed, and next to no time the table was covered again, boiled chickens at top, covered with white sauce and prettily ornamented with something green—a pretty little fore- quarter at bottom—tongue and stewed beef, asparagus, cauliflower, mushrooms and mashed brown potatoes. Mr. M. again displayed great skill in carving the chicks. Mr. Blagdon operated on the tongue. Champagne and Hock in course. Mr. M. enjoys a good dinner and never refuses the wine. Third course—Guinea Fowl, some kind of hot pudding, I daresay Caroline will tell you what, jellies, creams, and a peculiar dish—it looked like a sea or lake of custard surrounded by a range of snow-covered mountains, the peaks tinged by the rosy hues of the rising sun, some

[1] My father.

people might fancy it rather more crimson than rosy—
then cream and other cheese were handed round, then all
vanished, and the dessert made its appearance. Of course
there could not be much variety in that, this time of the
year. There were some noble-looking oranges. Everything that ought to have been so was smoking hot. I
never saw a dinner better served. Caroline determined
on a cook at last—but I daresay she will tell Ellen all about
her preparations and management.

" Mary was quite angry last night to think that I should
write before she would, but I told her that we should be
sure to tell of different parts of the affair. Even she and
Caroline were perfectly satisfied, but Caroline says she
suffered a martyrdom about it.

" As to the conversational parts of the entertainment, it
was very pleasant; there was not a single pause. The
two Josephs, Mr. Nettlefold and Mrs. Martineau were
busily engaged conversing together for some time. Mary
and Mr. Blagdon and Caroline and Mr. M. and self. I
took Mr. M. upon myself at the beginning of dinner for
I knew Caroline's mind would be a little preoccupied till
she saw how things were ' getting along,' and I plunged
boldly into Comte's philosophy, trusting to Mr. Martineau's
help for swimming safely ashore. Being discreet, and really
interested in it, I did not flounder. Very soon Caroline
was able to join in and Mr. Blagdon also and Mary turned
to Mr. M. and then I think we all talked—who listened
remains doubtful. We sat about half an hour when Caroline
bowed. Out we all went into the drawing-room; Dick
was the first evening guest. At about a quarter-past eight
the gentlemen made their appearance and we all had coffee,
then the evening company began to arrive in quick succession. Mr. and Mrs. Warren, Mr. and Mrs. Madge,
Mr. and Mrs. W. Sharpe—Sam ditto, Mr. Snider, Mrs.
Teschmaker, Mr. and Mrs. J. Preston, Charles and Emily,
Mr. and Mrs. Wainewright, and Annie Preston's hero and
comforter, Mr. Ireson.

" The dining-room had been cleared and thrown open

in a wonderfully short time and the rooms looked very pretty and well lighted. Everybody looked very nice. . . .

"Mrs. Warren had a magnificent black silk dress on, trimmed slightly with crepe. . . .

"I had a long conversation with old Sam Sharpe and made another plunge into dangerous regions but escaped again without slipping. I do not know how I should have escaped from *him* though, but Caroline thought I had had enough of him, so came to my relief. When I come to think of it, I had a good talk with everyone in the room, except that very unpleasant-looking man Mr Wainewright. Mrs. Madge and I sympathized in our feelings about him, and we agreed that a good rump steak and a jolly foaming pot of porter would do him a vast deal of good. As it is he is a cold, repulsive-looking man.

"Supper was served in the dining-room at a quarter-past ten. Towards the end of the evening Snider had an opportunity of delivering a little lecture to all who would listen, on his gun.[1] He had brought drawings with him. Mr. Cookson and Mr. and Mrs. Peter Martineau were there also. They were all gone by a quarter-past eleven; we—Charley, Snider and self—at twelve.

"There, my dear, is Maria with the lunch, and I have devoted nearly all my morning to you. Be grateful! It has turned cold and there is a sleety snow falling. 'Good Bording' I will re-commence my journal this evening.

"Wednesday evening. It has been raining all the afternoon and I have not been able to leave the house. The roofs of the houses and all high places are thickly covered with snow, and it looks like Christmas as depicted in the *Illustrated News*. It has been raining this evening, so I do not expect to see any remains of it in the morning. . . .

.   .   .   .   .   .

"Well, after they left I took up my book to divert my thoughts from diverging into painful channels—the second

---

[1] One of the earliest breech-loading rifles.

vol. of *Adam Bede*, a very prettily written book, hardly to
be called a novel. I finished the vol. and fear the third
cannot choose but be very sad; I almost dread to read it.

. . . . .

"Sunday to Carter Lane. Heard Mr. Ireson; found
his sermon quite refreshing after John Scot Porter's. An
awful small congregation, as all the world had gone to
hear Mr. Madge's farewell sermon, as the stipendiary of
Essex St. Chapel. . . .

"I see very little of Snider, he is so much absorbed by
this gun affair. It is fearful to think of the result to him
if it fails.

"This afternoon, if it continues fine, I shall call on Mr.
Ireson. I should have done so yesterday only for the snow.

"I shall get the third vol. of *Adam Bede* for my evening
entertainment, and shall live in the hope it will not be too
sad. There, I must leave off as I shall have Caroline here.

"Caroline has been and gone—no particular news. She
has nearly got over the fatigue of her party.

"I am going out directly, for, as the drawing-room is
still 'in dishabille' (after the sweeps and cleaning), and it
is five, some one is sure to call of our few visitors.

"Once more adieu, Your affectionate Mother,

"C. A. BAILEY."

I have said that my great-aunt was a staunch Unitarian.
A glimpse of this side of her—and of her kindness of heart—
is given in the following letter describing the gratitude of
a young protégé, the son of an old Irish woman who made
a precarious living by peddling combs and other nick-nacks
at the corner of the street:

"271 HIGH HOLBORN,
"September 23rd, 1856.

"My grand excitement has been my young priest in
embryo, young Gill. I enclose his letter. Please return it
as George wants to see it. About a fortnight or rather

286

more since, his mother called on me and sent up word that
she wished to speak to me, but not to beg. It did not
suit me to go down, so I did not see her, but the following
Sunday going to the School I met her, stopped and spoke
to her. She had called to say that her son had just returned
from Douai and was going to Rome and that he wished to
call and thank me for all my kindness to her and to him.

"I expressed my pleasure at hearing so pleasant an
account of her son. In consequence of my speaking, I the
next day or so received the accompanying letter which of
course I acknowledged saying that I should be very happy
to see him.

"He came on Saturday. I was pleased with him and
much interested in him, and invited him to tea on the
following Wednesday, not before as I thought that Em
would like to see him.

"On Monday he called to say that he found he had to
go into retreat at the Oratory at Brompton on Wednesday
to prepare himself for receiving minor orders called the
Tonsure on Saturday morning from the Cardinal, so I
fixed for him to come Tuesday. He brought me two
books to read—Cardinal Wiseman's Lectures on the
Catholic and Protestant Faiths, and a controversy between
a Protestant Society and Dr. Milner, a celebrated Catholic
divine. The last book, he informed me, had converted a
Mr. Bradshawe and, he hoped, would me. He should
pray for me morning and night.

"He (Gill) came on Tuesday. Em (Emily Bailey) was
pleased with him. Of course he has only two subjects of
conversation—Douai and the glory and advantages of the
Catholic Church. We were both very much struck at the
complete state of subjection in which his thoughts and
feelings—in fact all the powers of his mind—are. The
Cardinal knows what he is about in making a protégé of
him. He will have a most faithful, devoted working friend
in him. He is very enthusiastic and at present genuine and
would consider it a joy unspeakable to suffer martyrdom
for Mother Church.

"When he first called, I had expressed very plainly my religious views, which I found he repeated to the Cardinal, who sent an intimation through him that if I liked to call and discuss the point with him, he would be very happy to see me.

"Of course, I declined. He left about ten and I engaged him to dine here on Sunday. He came with a round collar on (he had a stuck-up one before), and Mr. Solly also dined here. He (young Gill) came bent on my conversion, for the moment the cloth was removed and Mary out of the room he said, 'Mrs. Bailey, will you pardon me, if it be a liberty, but will you tell me who were the great apostles of the Unitarian creed before the fifteenth century?

"I expect the Cardinal put him up to that question. Of course, I referred him to Mr. Solly, which I could do with great confidence and pleasure, knowing from his truly Christian temper that no ill-feeling would arise from the discussion. I would not have allowed it with everyone, of course.

"The young man was not equal to cope with Mr. Solly, but Mr. Solly dealt so gently with him that his self-love was not hurt in any way. But he says on his return he shall be better prepared and will overpower him with his proof of the fallacy of our pretensions.

"He says Mr. Solly is the first Protestant clergyman he has ever met. He remained till about half-past ten, and went away rather discomfited, I fear, at not having made some impression. I hope he will not consider it was his fault and so have to do penance. He entreated me again to go to the Cardinal and not to trust to books. 'Go with me to-morrow,' he said, 'and I am sure the light of the truth will burst upon you.'

"I declined, but comforted him by promising that if ever any doubts crossed my mind, I would apply to him (the Cardinal). I told him I had read seven of the Cardinal's lectures and felt even more than I did before that I never could enter the Roman Catholic Church, at which he was rather astonished.

" He asked me if I would die for my faith.

" I told him that I was not prepared to say ' yes ' to that without some consideration.

" Oh," he said, " then I have some hope."

" But," I returned, " I am quite prepared to say that I would sooner die any death you may choose than become a member of your Church.

" At which he raised his eyes, clasped his hands, but said never a word.

" When he left he said, ' Well, Mrs. Bailey, if I do not see you again before I leave, I will write you from Rome and send you proofs of the truth, and receive my best thanks for all your kindness. I shall never forget you and when I am in Rome the remembrance of these visits will be very pleasant to me.' He says as long as he can remember he had such a strong desire to be a Priest. When he was a little ragged boy, as he walked along the streets, he used to pray to God to make him a Priest. When he was thirteen, he might have been apprenticed to a French cook, which for a boy in his situation would have been a fine thing; but he reflected that if he bound himself to the cook, he should never be able to be a Priest, so in spite of his mother's tears and the entreaties of his friends, he went home to comparative starvation. He had been with the cook a year, having capital living, so it was something for a boy to give up.

" Soon after an opportunity offered for him to obtain a situation in Cardinal Wiseman's household if he could have some decent clothes. I supplied him with a suit and he got the situation and very soon obtained the Cardinal's notice and was allowed to serve his Mass for him and was with the Cardinal a year when the Cardinal was called to Rome. Then he broke up his establishment and the poor boy was in despair, so in a fit of despair he asked the Cardinal to send him to college and told him all his hopes. The Cardinal told him he had been thinking about it and, seeing him so very earnest, he would; and a fortnight from that time he was at Douai, and he said all the time he was there

T

he could hardly believe it was himself. He hopes to rise in the Church and do something to glorify her."

I conclude these extracts from a family post-bag with a letter from the youngest of my great-aunts, Mrs. Stanton Preston. It was written on the eve of my father's twenty-first birthday, but the opening sentences refer to another important event in the family, the cutting of her first tooth by her grand-niece, Penelope Lawrence, afterwards known to many generations of girls as the founder and first Principal of the famous Roedean School:

"DEAREST FAN,

"I write to congratulate you on Pen's first peg. I can fancy your inward rapture and the nurse's outward delight. How well I remember lecturing Sophy Lock on violent excitements—feeling myself every nerve quiver. What were the Pyramids to that enormous object of interest, which after all, by the by, was more felt than seen.

. . . . . .

"I have bought Fergusson's *Handbook of Architecture*, two vols., for Joe, and have sent it this evening to be ready for the morrow. I wonder how Caroline will get on. I mean by this in her feelings of worry or confidence about the dinner. It is sure to be all perfect, but she has reason to be uneasy with two strangers as *chefs de cuisine*. It seems hard to have to think of cooking when I know her heart will be too full for speech. But the longer I live the more convinced I am of the horrible unreal state in which our conventionalities place us—there will be Caroline anxious about eels and entrées, when behind all that her mother's heart is welling up with love and thoughts too deep for words, full of hopes and aspirations for her first-born, and full too of the recollection of the day when that young man, now nearly fulfilling all a mother's heart could wish, laid by her side as a baby. I can fancy your Uncle Joseph offering best cuts and passing the Madeira, while a more costly liquid glitters behind his dimmed glasses. Such is life, and I lose my time in moralizing over its defects until I have done the best I can with it as it is. Here endeth the first chapter of priggism. I saw your cook to-day. Favour is deceitful and beauty is vain—so I have no doubt she is true and useful. I have a new cook on the twenty-fourth. She promises well—but blessed are ye who expect nothing."

XXII

MY COTTAGE GARDEN

I

My own cottage and garden in Sussex are, alas! mine no longer, though I am glad to know that they have passed to the possession of another garden lover who cherishes the little garden as I used to do. The cottage stands where two lanes meet. Its framework, if you could see it, is exactly like that of the farmer's great barn opposite—huge oak timbers such as went to the building of the old wooden navy, some straight or bent with age, some curved by the natural growth of the tree, but all hewed and squared with the axe and adze; no saw or plane has spoiled their beauty. Between the balks of timber the walls are wattle and daub, but one side has been clapboarded against the south-westerly storms and the opposite one, facing the lane, is half brick half-tile. The old tile roof sags and wavers with the yielding of the beams. Just to the right of the cottage and shadowing the north-west corner is a magnificent old yew. As we pass in through the little wicket gate and up the short brick path, you will see, in spring, hyacinths or polyanthus in the narrow borders on either side, to be followed later by some bedding-out plants—almost the only ones I allow myself, for the garden is to need as little labour as possible—out of which will rise in turn two healthy groups of scarlet martagon lilies and another group of the new hybrid martagons which tempted me at one of the Royal Horticultural Society's shows. Over the front of the house Ampelopsis and Wistaria creep, a Pyracantha breaks the line and Cotoneaster horizontalis, beloved of the bees, half hides an ugly water-spout; but what I pride myself upon is the narrow border, scarcely a foot wide, which runs along the house. Snowdrops (Elwesii) and winter aconite give me my first flowers here; then comes a clump or two of narcissus; but the moment to see it is when it is one mass of Anemone apennina with Primula cashmiriana thrusting up its purple globes among their blue stars.

Under the yew tree, by adding some good soil and plenty of old mortar rubble, I have flourishing colonies of Cyclamen coum for spring and Cyclamen europæum for autumn, when its scent carries me in fancy to Italian woods about Bologna where I have picked great bunches of them to brighten up the old Brun's hotel. Hepaticas, our own wild wood anemones and crocuses, help out the seasons. But come round to the southerly side of the cottage. Here against the clapboarding grows Wistaria again, but the nurseryman sent one so pale in hue that it scarcely shows against the white paint and reminds me that flowering plants should be selected when they are in flower. A good Pyrus japonica gives on the other hand a blaze of colour, and a purple Clematis, which I cut down nearly to within a foot of the ground, is covered with blossom twice in the summer. The yellow jasmine, J. nudiflorum, flowers in January with Iris unguicularis (stylosa) at its feet, and a white jasmine scents the rooms in mid summer. Here too I find room for Carpenteria californica and Choisya and the Californian fuchsia (Zauschneria).

The flagged terrace is supported by a low wall of loose stone not more than two to three feet high. Amidst the flags grow thyme and pinks (D. deltoides and graniticus), Campanula pusilla, Hypericum Coris; grape hyacinths and other things have found their way along the cracks from the narrow ribbon border that tops the low wall.

The border at the top of the wall is kept for low and early flowering plants. Here you will find Iris pumila in four or five shades, I. histrioides and reticulata and Tulipa Clusiana and linifolia with mossy Saxifrages to follow. There are just two bushes of Daphne Mezereum to break the low line, and a fine specimen of D. Cneorum, which later loads the air with its scent of honey, and a little bush of Plumbago Larpentae carry on the interest later in the year. The wall itself is kept mainly for Saxifrages of the pyramidalis type which did extraordinary well, but the male fern has seeded itself in the crevices and threatens to become a nuisance.

I know nothing more lovely among tulips for the rock garden than the two species which I have mentioned. The scarlet linifolia increased with me and I grew it from seed, but T. Clusiana had a sad tendency to " dwindgle," as a farm-hand I once knew used to say of his young turkeys. I retain, however, a warm affection for it, which is partly a tribute to its own delicate beauty and partly to my own vanity.

When I first went to Geneva, in early March 1925, to represent Great Britain on the Council of the League of Nations, I visited Dr. Correvon's famous Alpine garden. It was too early for flowers but a gardener loves to see plants growing only one degree less than to see them blossoming. Whilst walking round I happened to remark upon a group of T. Clusiana whose leaves were pushing up, though the buds were not yet showing. Later the same day an English lady went to see the garden and Dr.

Correvon mentioned my visit. "Ah!" said the lady, "you have had the Minister for Foreign Affairs here? It is a great honour for your garden."

"Minister of Foreign Affairs, pooh!" exclaimed the Doctor. "There is a Minister of Foreign Affairs in every country, but there is only one who can identify Tulipa Clusiana by its leaves."

The story spread (shall I confess? I helped to spread it) and my reputation was made. There was one subject at least of which I knew more than my colleagues!

A second terrace, grassed this time and supported by a rather higher wall, finds room in the border at the top for half a dozen species of Cistus. These lasted through several winters, but it is wise to take cuttings every year or two and nurse them through the winter in a frame lest a spell of specially hard weather destroy the established plants. Here I had a bit of luck. I thought this would be a good place to put a plant of Hypericum (Hookeri, I think) in my first autumn and found when I dug my hole that I was among roots which in my inexperience I did not recognize. They turned out to be a darkish orange Alstrœmeria and grew up through and around the Hypericum, making a colour combination on which I received many compliments.

The wall below this terrace was kept mainly for Aubrietia, Alyssum, Helianthemums and Erodiums, but some white foxgloves seeded themselves between the stones towards one end.

I am not going to show you my rose-garden in front of the oast-house, for it was not very successful, nor my border of flowering shrubs and trees, for though I dug the whole of it (and it lay on a belt of stiff clay) three times over with my own hands in one year, I could never rid it of the squitch, bindweed, ground elder and all the other poisonous weeds with brittle ramping roots which had taken hold of it in war time. I have only one word of advice to give to anyone so situated. Clear the border, summon all your patience, disregard appearances and plant potatoes on the ground till you have got it clean; and do this before, not after, your Cherries, Pyrus, Crabs, Lilacs, Berberis and the like have begun to grow and make shapely bushes or trees. Once that has happened, you will never have the heart to disturb them. By the thorough policy you will eradicate the weeds. Nor need we linger at the herbaceous border. Let us go straight to my rock garden, or, as I would have you call it, my Alpine garden, for my purpose was to grow the Alpine flowers, not merely to repeat the Aubrietias and Alyssums of the wall.

2

It must be nearly forty-five years ago that, one Sunday morning, when my father and I were visiting Kew Gardens, under the auspices of the late Sir W. Thistleton-Dyer, he took us into one of the enclosures where, he said, he had something new to show us. The novelty was an unheated greenhouse filled with pans of Alpine plants. I remember saying to my father as we drove back that if I ever had a garden of my own, I should not attempt to grow orchids but that I must have an Alpine house. Thirty or more years passed before I owned a garden; by then much more was known of Alpine plants and their cultivation, and I determined to have a rock, or as I prefer to call it, an Alpine garden instead of the house. A house would require daily care and watering, and I could visit my cottage only at week-ends.

Thus when I obtained my cottage the first thing to decide was where to place the Alpine garden. Below the terrace, the lawn, whose earlier use as an orchard was recalled by two old apple trees still standing in its midst, sloped down to a hedge in which a stile gave access to a small field. But the hedge was not parallel to the house, and the shrubbery border on one side of the lawn was not parallel to the yew hedge which divided it from the kitchen garden on the other, so that the lawn formed an ugly rhomboid. This was corrected at the sides by the re-alignment of the shrubbery border, giving room for a herbaceous border in front of the flowering trees and shrubs, and at the bottom by planting a yew hedge parallel to the terraces, in front of which we placed a herbaceous border, broken in the centre by a wide grass walk leading to the stile. Between the two hedges there was now an elongated triangle. To the right of the grass-walk my wife made a small sunk garden filled with polyantha roses; the left and larger section I chose for the site of the Alpine garden which would thus be hidden from the house by the yew hedge as soon as it had grown about four feet high.

There, then, was the site, not perfect but not a bad one. The next thing was to make the garden. My first attempt was a failure, though I put up with it for two or three years. I did not know what I wanted beyond the fact that I wanted a rock garden. I did not know what was necessary except rocks. I called in a local man and said, " Make me a rock garden and let me have rocks, not pebbles." He fulfilled my requirements with good-sized blocks of the local sandstone, and at first I was very pleased with the effect. I visited spring shows, pored over catalogues and planted enthusiastically and optimistically, but my plants did not grow. I could repeat the easier successes of the terraces, but the things which I most wanted to see succeed dragged out a miserable existence or died upon my hands. Only two things do I recall as making really fine specimens; these were a Lithospermum prostratum, heavenly blue, for which I chanced upon just the right position at the top of a big rock with a cool root-run down the back of the stone into deep earth. In two years or so it had covered the top and hung three feet or more down the rock face. The other success was provided by two plants of Anemone sulphurea which will appear again in this story. But of drainage and soil and how to place the rocks I had thought little and knew less. It was all to begin again. The experiment had cost something, but it had taught me much. I wrote some articles, was fortunate in finding favour with a generous editor and accumulated a sufficient sum to start afresh. This time I knew what I wanted and I found the right man to understand my ideas and supply my deficiencies.

The rules for an Alpine garden are:

1. See that the drainage is good.
2. See that the soil is suitable and that in different places you have the various kinds which you will require.
3. The rocks should be large. Like icebergs, only the smaller part of them should appear above the surface.
4. Let the soil be well rammed down around and between them so that no holes are left in which the roots as they grow fail to find sustenance. The builder knew all this as well as I did, and it was a pleasure to see him and his fore-man handling and placing the great rocks. The largest weighed nearly 15 cwt.

I chose weather-worn limestone for the stone and I expressed my desiderata as follows:

1. I must have a cliff-face with northerly or cool exposure.
2. I wanted a peat-bog.

3. There must be a low Alpine meadow and
4. A high Alpine meadow.
5. There must be a moraine or scree.
6. The new garden must somehow be built around my beautiful Anemone sulphurea. They were doing too well to be disturbed.

I rejected the idea of a pool, for I felt there was not room for one, but I jumped at the suggestion of a Rhododendron forest. In the end the garden was all my fancy had painted; but here you must use your imagination. My Rhododendron forest consisted at first of two, later of three R. ferrugineum and three dwarf Himalayan hybrids. Daphne Blaygayana flourished among them. Give it a cool peaty root-run and throw a stone at it whenever you pass. It likes these rough love-makings and will reward you for them with its sweet waxy flowers in early spring. Androsace lanuginosa trailed over the rock in front.

I had not one but two cliffs, each some three feet high, and at the bottom a peat bed kept moist by drainage from the rocks and path. In the ledges and crannies of the cliffs I grew Primula marginata, Wilsonii, viscosa and some garden varieties, but Wilsonii never, I think, survived more than three winters. In the peat were P. rosea (this seeded itself freely and would grow in any damp shady spot in the path at the base of a rock), P. chionantha, involucrata and others, besides Orchis foliosa, Cypripedium calceolus and Pyrola rotundifolia, both collected by me in Switzerland, and Parochetus communis with a leaf like clover and a pea-shaped flower of the blue of G. verna. I name only enough flowers to give an idea of what I was striving for and the results obtained.

The low Alpine meadow, say twelve feet by eight, made a good place for Alpine crocuses and tulips and

Scilla autumnalis collected on the cliffs of Newquay and
Brittany. These were followed by Anemone fulgens,
and a marvellous magenta-coloured variety brought home
by Lady Chamberlain from Palestine. Later came A.
narcissiflora looking like apple blossom in bud, A. alpina
and sulphurea, and the yellow globe flower. The first
time I saw A. sulphurea it was a single plant in a pocket
of a great moss-grown limestone boulder beside a flooded
mountain stream in the Pyrenees and my heart leapt with
delight. The first time I saw A. alpina was when making
an excursion in the Jura with Dr. Correvon. It grew so
thick that in the distance I took it for a large patch of snow.
Then I added the great yellow gentian and other plants of
like size and similar habit. There was hardly one of these
which I had not collected myself, and the memory of the
places in which they were found added to one's delight in
seeing them grow and flourish.

The high Alpine meadows were on a smaller scale;
they were intended first and foremost for Gentiana verna,
but I always tried to get a succession of flowers if possible,
and I convinced myself by experience that except in the
case of those which live in some tight cranny of the rocks,
it is a mistake to plant one's precious things apart, as, in
his anxiety for their safety, the amateur is apt to do. Think
of the close short turf of the high Alpine meadow where
you find G. verna in masses. It is never alone; it has to
fight its way up and down through the turf itself and in
and out among Gentiana acaulis, Primula frondosa, Violas
and I know not what other small beauties. They grow
so thickly that you cannot put your foot down without
treading on several kinds, and they will be more likely to
succeed in your garden if you make them fight for existence
with plants of their own size as nature does. I planted

Narcissus minimus, Androsace carnea and Chamaejasme, Viola bicolor, Dianthus neglectus and such-like things with mine. But G. verna is notoriously contrariwise. After all, the best patch I ever saw in cultivation, two feet across each way and a sheet of blue like cloudless Italian sky on a summer day, grew within five miles of the centre of Birmingham. I asked the gardener how he managed it. "I grow them from seed," he said, "and prick them out." He did not appear to be aware that he had accomplished anything out of the ordinary. He had boxes of the seedlings in a frame. There is a variety of G. verna called angulata, which is a trifle larger in leaf, though otherwise indistinguishable to anyone but a botanist, which I found easier to grow.

There are few joys like a garden and in a small garden none which gives such constant interest and light occupation as an Alpine garden. In my own, every plant after the first twenty or so was planted and tended by me. It is the amateur's garden *par excellence*, for after this first making it requires no heavy spadework, whilst the plants have character and individuality and require constant attention and skilled treatment.

3

It is astonishing how much there is to say about a small Alpine garden. I have yet to deal with my screes, for in the end there were two of them, one less exposed to the full sunshine than the other. Both contained more chips than earth (indeed, I suppose the proportion was at least as ten to one) with limestone and granite mixed in varying proportions. Obviously the scree is the place for the Kabschia and Engleria saxifrages and many other treasures. Here, too, I grew Drabas, Hutchinsia alpina, Ranunculus

Seguieri, a lovely thing, Geranium Pylzowianum, to be watched closely lest it spread too far; its clear pink flowers prolong your flowering season. Papaver alpinum, orange and white, and Linaria alpina flourished in the scree and seeded regularly. Edrianthus pumilio with its grey leaves and lovely purple flowers sitting close down to the ground was another favourite, easily increased by cuttings. In the scree too I tried Omphalodes Luciliæ with its grey-blue leaves and feathery tufts of forget-me-not flowers of the palest porcelain blue shot with pink lights. The precise spot between two rocks had been specially made for it by an expert, but it slowly faded away. Then I found that admirable gardener, Mr. Hay of the Royal Parks, growing it as a bedding-out plant! He was kind enough to give me some plants and reveal the secret of his success—stiff loam and well-rotted cow-dung. Yet the plant comes from the hot limestone mountains of Greece and Asia Minor. To the four things which the compiler of the Book of Proverbs did not understand, he would, had he been a gardener, have added a fifth: the way of rock plants in cultivation. The best plant of Douglasia Vitaliana, a peat lover, which I ever had, grew into a fat cushion five or six inches across from a tiny slip which in ignorance or absent-mindedness I planted at the head of my limestone scree. Indeed I am disposed to say that whilst the scree is no place for any coarse thing, it is worth while to try in it any precious plant which has refused to do elsewhere.

It is a great advantage if you can water Alpines and especially the scree plants from below. In their native haunts, some sit in crevices on a steep rock-face where no rain lies and draw their moisture from the cool stones into which their roots penetrate deeply. Others sleep all winter under deep snow. They burst into life and blossom with amazing rapidity when the snows melt, but all through the hot summer their roots draw moisture from the water trickling just below the surface of the ground. In this country it is not possible to reproduce these conditions exactly; the raw damp days of February, when the air is cold and laden with moisture, are apt to be particularly deadly, especially to plants with hairy leaves. But something may be done to lessen their trials; a sheet of glass in winter is not a pretty object, but it is not at that time that you take your friends to admire your rock garden and the gardener in those months may well decide that safety first is his appropriate slogan whatever it may be for a political party. In any case let him try underground watering. If he has the conveniences or does not mind the cost, let him lay under his garden a leaden water-pipe with a few pin-prick holes in it. If, like me, he has not the convenience and is unwilling to face the expense, there is a simple alternative within everyone's means. Get a few two-inch agricultural drain-pipes; sink them vertically in the ground till their tops are only an inch or less above the surface, and hide them with a rock—the only one allowed to lie loose on the surface—or by a larger plant and, when watering, turn the hose or the spout of your watering-can down the pipe. A little care in the disposal of a few stones and some chips under the pipe will ensure the proper flow of the water and you can water at any time without danger of sunburn or of rotting out the crown of the plants. Incidentally, if you have not a convenient or sufficient rain-water tank and are dependent on the water company's mains, your water percolating through the soil will be more palatable to the plants.

Here you have the outstanding features of a rock garden

as I conceive it. It will of course need larger patches of colour to prevent it looking patchy. For these you can choose the dwarf Phloxes and Iris, the finer Aquilegias, the mossy Saxifrages, Anemones, Aubrietias, Helianthemums and the like. Once the garden is started, fill in gradually with other plants acquired from friends or growers (you need never pay more than a few pence except for special rarities) or, best of all, plants collected by yourself. In a short time you will be searching for space in which to bestow some newly acquired treasure and will be thinking which plant you will sacrifice to make room.

A word about collecting. In these days, if he can afford a trip to Switzerland, anyone can reach the Alpine plants, however poor a walker he is. I was past sixty before I saw the Alps in early summer and, coming straight from heavy office work, I was in no trim for climbing. Yet there were in my garden many plants which I had myself collected with Dr. Correvon or other friends in the week's holiday which I used to take after the sitting of the Council of the League of Nations in early June. Not an hour from Geneva I found a white Cyclamen europaeum which Dr. Correvon in all his rambles in the Alps and elsewhere had never lit upon. Another day he took me a drive along what is called the International Route (for it crosses the Franco-Swiss frontier more than once) and showed me a grassy slope where every outcrop of rock had its patches of Daphne cneorum. I had other glorious days with him in the Jura and yet others at Zermatt where the Professor of Botany at the University of Lausanne kindly made himself our guide. We went up to the top of the Görnergratch by train and before I could take my eyes from the glorious panorama of snow peaks and glaciers, he had found me a piece of Eritrichium nanum, the heart's desire of every Alpine grower. As we walked down, we passed through all the seasons from the places where the snow still lay in half-melted patches through which the earliest flowers were just peeping till we reached high summer in the meadows of the valley. That day I first saw Androsace glacialis and next day the Professor showed me a spot where the scarce Asplenium septentrionale was to be found.

Of course I had my disappointments. I lost my E. nanum by too much coddling when at home and neglect when I was absent. (I saw a capital piece only the other day growing in a stone trough in scree mixture in Sir Clive Wigram's garden at the foot of the Round Tower at Windsor Castle) but the Asplenium grew well in a crevice where it had Penstemon Davidsoni for neighbour, and the majority of my plants lived.

For collector's tools, a fern trowel with a long blade not more than one and a half inches wide, so firmly fixed *in* the handle that it will give you good leverage, and an Alpine ice-axe suffice. If any of the plants are short of fibrous root, plunge them in a bed of wet sand placed in the shade. It is amazing what root they will then make in a few weeks.

Reluctantly I end, for even to write of these bygone delights is itself a pleasure.

There are few joys like a garden and the Alpine garden is *par excellence* the garden for the amateur.

P.S. A cure for sleeplessness. If you find that after the worries and excitements of a busy day, say after winding up a debate in Parliament at midnight, you are too excited to sleep when you reach your bed, if then counting sheep passing through a gate proves, as with me, of no avail and you share my incapacity for thinking of nothing, visit your rock garden in imagination. I have put myself to sleep night after night in this way before my head had been five minutes on the pillow or I had covered six paces of my small garden.

XXIII

LIGHTENING OUR LABOURS

OFFICIAL files, tied up with the proverbial red tape, are usually forbidding-looking things. It takes a little time to know where to look and what to read among the mass of papers which accumulate about most subjects, and the minutes written upon them, able and instructive as they are, are generally strictly confined to a plain statement of the point involved and of the action recommended. But occasionally humour breaks out even in these discouraging surroundings. Mark Sykes once delighted his friends by illustrating the stock openings of Treasury letters: " My Lords are gratified to learn . . ." " My Lords are surprised to observe . . ." and so forth till the last " My Lords are at a loss to conceive . . ." represented by five little men in bed clasping their stomachs and obviously in great pain.

Fairfield at the Colonial Office occasionally illustrated his minutes in a like manner. He prepared a brief for my father's interview with the Bechuana Chiefs in the form of an imaginary conversation, " It was wholly admirable," said my father; " only the Chiefs did not give the answer he had expected, as, when, on my saying to Khama: ' You ask too much,' he replied: ' How can he ask too much to whom everything belongs?' Fairfield had not forseen that retort and had supplied no answer to it." The brief ended with instructions to the Chiefs as to their behaviour when presented to the Queen at Windsor. " This," added Fairfield, " is to prevent this kind of thing," and there followed a sketch of three little black men in the scantiest raiment turning back somersaults into the presence of a shocked and startled Sovereign. The Queen had indeed expressed a wish that they should appear in their native costume. My father had the task of explaining that it was unsuitable to the throne room.

Going in unannounced to see Lloyd George on one occasion when I lived next him in Downing Street, I found him chuckling over a file of papers. " What's the joke? " I asked. It was the first minute from Hilton Young, who had just become Financial Secretary of the Treasury, which had reached Lloyd George. An application had been made to the Prime Minister for a substantial grant for Antarctic exploration which the Exchequer was at that time in no position to afford. It had been referred in the ordinary course to the Financial Secretary who had minuted : " This may surely be refused. The South Pole is far away and, if Charity begins there, it will be a long time before she reaches home."

Lloyd George remarked that an amusing article might be written on official minutes and we began to recall some. There was Bright's famous minute written when he was President of the Board of Trade : " I have read Mr. Giffen's very able and interesting memorandum. I do not clearly apprehend whether he approves or disapproves the proposal which he discusses, but in any case I agree with him." Mr. Giffen, later Sir Robert Giffen, was, if I am not mistaken, at that time the principal statistical officer of the department and an acknowledged authority on his own subjects. It required a man as sure of himself and as grandly simple as John Bright thus to avow his own limitations while adopting the advice of one in whose judgment he placed trust.

Then there was the minute of a former Minister of Education, which is, I believe, still religiously guarded in the archives of that department. Marking some passage in a long memorandum with a pointing hand in the margin, the Minister had added, " This is the colonel of the whole question."

When I myself was made Secretary of the Treasury at the end of the year 1900, there was still in progress a correspondence with the Admiralty about the salary of one of the principal officers of a branch for which, as Civil Lord, I had been responsible. It was known at the Treasury that the Admiralty letters, though purporting to emanate from " My Lords " and signed by the Permanent Secretary, had in fact been written by me. So far they had been dealt with by my predecessor in my new post. In the natural course it would be to me that the last Admiralty letter would now come and it could not be separated from the file to which it belonged. It was an awkward dilemma; many marginal notes and minutes were written in that file which had never been intended for my eye. I have always thought that Sir Francis Mowatt, then Permanent Secretary of the Treasury, acted with equal skill and candour when he placed the whole file before me, and remarking that obviously many things would have been differently expressed if my arrival at the Treasury had been foreseen and reminding me that I was now in the position of the poacher turned gamekeeper, added that I should here find what was to be said on the other side and undertook that if I would give fair consideration to the Treasury case, he would accept my decision whatever it might be without carrying the matter to the Chancellor. The Treasury objections failed to convince me, as Sir Francis had of course foreseen; but I gained a respect for Treasury methods and for once I had the chance so rarely vouchsafed to us " to see ourselves as others see us." There was nothing in the marginal notes to feed my vanity. One of them ran simply: "This is silly." I think it fairly epitomized them all.

Of the men who have served with me in various offices, Sir George Murray, long since retired from office, but happily still with us, did most to lighten official labours. He was raciest in conversation as when, having failed to persuade me that something I proposed to do was in-expedient, he asked: "Well if you must do a silly thing like that, is it necessary that you should do it in such a d—— silly way?" and proceeded to indicate a much better method of carrying out my idea; or again, when he had at last wrung from me a confession that a Post Office appointment which I had suggested and he had opposed, was not wholly uninfluenced by parliamentary considerations, he cynically exclaimed: "Oh! if it's a job, why did you not say so at once? It's as good as done."

Asquith when Chancellor, told me that he had had before him a proposal for the construction of an under-ground passage from the War Office to the Horse Guards with cellars where papers might be stored and work carried on in case of aerial attack, upon which Murray had minuted: "This may be safely turned down. No sane enemy, acquainted with our institutions, would destroy the War Office."

Such flashes of humour in these dusty files are as rare as angels' visits, but my memory retains two other instances of Murray's caustic wit. When Postmaster General I had drawn up an elaborate brief for the use of Members of Parliament who were much troubled with Post Office " grievances " and did not know the answer. I had passed it to Murray with a request that he would examine it critically and make any alterations he thought desirable. He returned it to me with the following brief comment:

" Postmaster General.

" This is like the White Knight's story—very long, but very, *very* beautiful."

Later, when we were both at the Treasury, I asked Sir George to take the first opportunity of ascertaining verbally from Sir Anthony MacDonnell, then Under-Secretary in Ireland, what he meant by the " co-ordination " of the Irish Office, a subject on which both he and George Wyndham[1] were favouring us with a correspondence which was as obscure as it was voluminous. I had not long to wait for an answer: " I have seen Sir Anthony MacDonnell as you desired," Murray minuted to me. " As far as I can make out, what he means by co-ordination is the sub-ordination of everyone else to himself "—which is not a bad definition of what is usually meant by the blessed word co-ordination in the mouth of a masterful personality.

The Indian and Foreign Offices gave less scope for such sallies, though there was one Ambassador at least, whose dispatches were not only full of good sense and shrewd observation but were generally lit up by some flash of humour which made them doubly welcome, and memory dwells lovingly on a telegram reporting trouble at Mount Athos which, by an error in transmission, had been made to read, " The monks are violating their cows " instead of " their vows," on which Mr. Harold Nicolson had minuted: " This would seem to be a case for a papal bull." Dispatches from the Government of India and even the Viceroy's letters were uniformly grave and strictly confined to the

[1] Chief Secretary for Ireland.

business in hand, but one occasionally got a startling flash-light on happenings that seemed to belong to another age as they certainly belonged to another civilization.

I remember once asking Balfour during the Great War whether the papers I sent him about Afghanistan gave him the kind of information that he wanted. He replied that what he wanted to know was what the Amir was really thinking and doing. The attitude of Afghanistan was of course of great importance to us at that time when India's military resources, like our own, were strained to the utter-most. The Amir Habibullah was a strong ruler, and a really remarkable man, who steered his course with great skill and shrewdness through those difficult years, and kept the peace in spite of the incitements of German agents and the desires of the more restless and fanatical of his own people that he should declare " jehad " ; but we had then no Minister at the Afghan Court and were dependent for direct information on a weekly newsletter from an India agent, so I sent Balfour the last newsletter which we had received from him. The writer stated that he had accompanied the Amir to Candahar where His Majesty was greatly interested in laying out the palace gardens. " Often have I seen His Majesty," the letter continued, " surrounded by the high Officers of State, directing the laying out of the flower beds "—an idyllic scene amidst the war which was then raging in three continents. But there followed abruptly a passage de-scribing a scene of a different kind. It ran pretty much as follows : " Yesterday in the presence of a vast concourse of people on a hill outside the town, a woman, being the last of her clan and having refused blood-money in satis-faction for the murder of her husband, solemnly and in accordance with the Holy Law, cut the throat of the murderer."

But this is too grim a note to close upon. Let me end these random recollections with a lighter tale.

When I was at the Admiralty in the closing years of the last century, the name of a certain officer was put forward for a Good Service Pension. He had an unblemished record but for one incident which had occurred when he was a sub-lieutenant at Greenwich Naval College, when his papers showed that " My Lords' severe displeasure " had been expressed " for an improper answer returned to the examiners," and a footnote solemnly set out the offence as follows:

Question: " Describe a Daniell's Cell." [1]

Answer: " Not much is known about Daniel's cell. It was probably about thirty feet long by twenty feet wide and full of lions. But the lions are dead and so is Daniel. *Sic transit gloria mundi!* "

He got his pension.

[1] A type of electric battery.

INDEX

n